SCOTS LAW
INTO THE 21st CENTURY

Professor William Adam Wilson, M.A., LL.B, LL.D, FRSE 1928 - 1994

SCOTS LAW
INTO THE 21st CENTURY

Essays in Honour of W. A. Wilson

Edited by
Hector L. MacQueen, LLB, PhD, FRSE
Professor of Private Law, University of Edinburgh

W. GREEN/SWEET & MAXWELL
EDINBURGH
1996

First Published 1996

© 1996
W. Green & Son Ltd and contributors

ISBN 0 414 01140 6

A catalogue record for this book is available from the British
Library

Typeset by Wyvern Typesetting Ltd, Bristol
Printed and bound in Great Britain by Butler & Tanner Ltd, Somerset

In Memory of Bill Wilson

PREFACE

This collection of essays honours the memory of the late Professor W. A. Wilson. Each contribution is a consideration of an aspect of Scots law upon which Professor Wilson had commented or shown an interest during his long and distinguished career. Three broad themes link the essays together: first the current condition of Scots law, in particular in relation to the Roman or civilian part of its heritage, and the role of legal education and codification in protecting the law from what Wilson perceived as the danger of doctrinal drift; secondly, reading and interpreting statutes and the current condition of statute law; and thirdly, the present and future state of particular areas of Scots law, including European and international aspects. Contributors were given a limited number of words (in order to accommodate the very many who wished to take part in the project), and asked to deal with their several subjects in the light of Wilson's commentary upon it or his general views of law; but, as the contributions themselves will show, agreement with Wilson's view or approach was not made a necessary pre-condition. In fact, the contributors not only often disagree with Wilson's conclusions, but also with each other. This reflects the stimulus which Wilson's work provides in many different areas of law. It also makes this collection reflect the current debates about the future direction of Scots law as we contemplate both the possibility of a Scottish legislature and the continuing integration of the European Union.

Some contributions originally intended for this work will now appear elsewhere, the length constraints having proved too heavy; others who would have wished to contribute found themselves unable to do so in consequence of many other commitments.

The task of editing this collection has been made a pleasant one by the co-operation of the contributors and many others, amongst whom I would like to mention Miss Isabel Adam, Mr Ross Anderson, Professor T. St J. N. Bates, Mr T. Norman Biggart, Mr John Brims, Mr A. G. M. Duncan, Mr Nick Dyson, Mrs Norma MacArthur, Professor Victor Mackinnon, Sheriff Peter McNeill Q.C., Mr Dan McNicol, Professor John Murray Q.C., Mr Donald Robertson Q.C., Lord Justice-Clerk Ross, Mr W. David H. Sellar, Mr Alister Tulloch, and staff of Hillhead High School, and of the Special Collections Department of the University Library and the Archives of the University of Glasgow. Mr N. R. Whitty collaborated with me in the production of the Bibliography. It is also a pleasure to record the gratitude of all Bill Wilson's friends that his publishers agreed to the publication of a work in honour of one of their most distinguished authors.

H.L.M.
Old College
December 1995

FOREWORD
by
The Right Hon. Lord Ross

During the years from 1960 to 1993, Professor W. A. Wilson—known to all as Bill Wilson—had a very great influence not only on the many students he taught, but also on legal thinking generally and on the law of Scotland itself. This collection of essays gives well-deserved recognition to Bill Wilson's great contribution to legal education and scholarship.

I first met Bill Wilson over 40 years ago when he worked with Young and Cruickshank, W. S., who began to instruct me as a junior counsel. Our solicitor/advocate relationship continued in subsequent years when Bill was employed by Biggart Lumsden in Glasgow. He was a very competent solicitor who prepared cases for counsel with great care. But consultations with Bill were never dull for he was skilled too at letting counsel know the background to a case by describing a client's weaknesses and foibles in an amusing but never unkind way.

In 1960, after he had embarked on his academic career, he resolved to be admitted to the Faculty of Advocates, and I was delighted to accept him as a devil. It was never his intention to practise, and the Dean of Faculty of the time gave permission for Bill to devil part-time. He was a very good devil who prepared pleadings and draft opinions for me with great skill. At the last moment, after virtually completing his devilling, Bill decided not to be called. Why that was so I never discovered for Bill was never willing or able to tell me why he had changed his mind. I have no doubt that his decision represented a loss to the Faculty of Advocates.

After this, I continued to come across Bill from time to time, and I became aware of his growing reputation in the academic field. Apart from his many articles, his work on *Trusts, Trustees and Executors* with A. G. M. Duncan and his book on *The Law of Scotland Relating to Debt* are textbooks which have proved invaluable to members of the legal profession. It was with great sadness that I learned in 1993 that Bill had developed cancer, and his death in 1994 was widely mourned. His funeral, at which Matthew Clarke delivered such an eloquent tribute, was attended by numerous colleagues, students and friends.

I am delighted that his friends and colleagues have now prepared this collection of essays in Bill's honour. On behalf of all his other friends, I would like to express thanks to all the contributors to this volume, and particularly to Professor Hector MacQueen who is both a contributor and the volume's editor. As Hector MacQueen points out in the Preface, the essays cover many aspects of Scots law which all have some connection with Bill. The contributors recognise that Bill would not always have agreed with some of the views they express. Personally I have enjoyed reading the essays although I too would wish to sound a caveat that I do not necessarily agree with all that the contributors have said, just as I did not always share Bill's views on all legal matters. But the essays display penetrating analysis and sound scholarship in which Bill would have delighted; they are all well worth reading, and they represent a fitting tribute to Bill Wilson.

If Bill had been alive when this volume was being produced in his honour, I am sure that he would have greeted publication with a wry smile, some trenchant riposte, but also with well concealed delight. Those who now pick up this volume will have no cause to hide the pleasure they will experience in reading this admirable legal miscellany which honours the memory of one who in his lifetime made such a considerable and important contribution to the teaching and development of the law of Scotland.

As Bill Wilson's erstwhile devil-master I am happy to commend this collection of essays to all who admired him and who share his interest in and affection for the law of Scotland.

D.M.R.
Parliament House,
Edinburgh,
April, 1996.

CONTENTS

CONTRIBUTORS

Alan R. Barr is Director of the Legal Practice Unit, University of Edinburgh

John W. G. Blackie is Professor of Law, University of Strathclyde

Christine Boch is a lecturer in the Europa Institute, University of Edinburgh

Douglas Brodie is a senior lecturer in private law, University of Edinburgh

John W. Cairns is a reader in private law, University of Edinburgh

Eric Clive is a member of the Scottish Law Commission

Sandra Eden is a senior lecturer in private law, University of Edinburgh

David A. O. Edward is a Judge of the Court of Justice of the European Communities

Lilian Edwards is a lecturer in private law, University of Edinburgh

A. D. M. Forte is Professor of Commercial Law, University of Aberdeen

William C. Gilmore is Professor of Public International Law, University of Edinburgh

George L. Gretton is Lord President Reid Professor of Law, University of Edinburgh

Anne Griffiths is a senior lecturer in private law, University of Edinburgh

C. M. G. Himsworth is a reader in public law, University of Edinburgh

Robert Lane is a senior lecturer in the Europa Institute, University of Edinburgh

R. D. Leslie is a senior lecturer in private law, University of Edinburgh

William W. McBryde is Professor of Law, University of Dundee

R. A. A. McCall Smith is Professor of Medical Law, University of Edinburgh

Ewan McKendrick is Professor of English Law, University College London.

Hector L. MacQueen is Professor of Private Law, University of Edinburgh

Gerry Maher is Professor of Law, University of Strathclyde

Colin Munro is Professor of Constitutional Law, University of Edinburgh

Stephen C. Neff is a senior lecturer in public international law, University of Edinburgh

Kenneth G. C. Reid is Professor of Property Law, University of Edinburgh and a member of the Scottish Law Commission

Joe Thomson is Regius Professor of Law, University of Glasgow

Neil C. Walker is Professor of Legal and Constitutional Theory, University of Aberdeen

Niall R. Whitty is a member of the Scottish Law Commission

Stephen Woolman is a member of the Faculty of Advocates

MEMOIR OF PROFESSOR WILLIAM ADAM WILSON, M.A., LL.B, LL.D, FRSE.

Lord President Reid Professor of Law in the University of Edinburgh
July 28, 1928–March 14, 1994

HECTOR L. MACQUEEN

One year after Bill Wilson's death, during the debate before the First Division in the great case of *Sharp v. Thomson*,[1] counsel referred the court to an article published in 1962 in which Wilson discussed the introduction of the floating charge into Scots law under the Companies (Floating Charges) (Scotland) Act 1961, and anticipated the very problem which now confronted the court.[2] The recollection of those present when this citation was made is of an electric and perhaps decisive moment of recognition and silent tribute to the insight of a great lawyer and teacher. One judge and three counsel had been taught by Wilson at Edinburgh, and another judge had once been a colleague there. When the decision of the court was issued in May 1995, the judges all followed the view expressed by Wilson in 1962, and the article was expressly cited in the opinion of Lord President Hope.[3]

The affection and respect in which the legal community held Bill Wilson was demonstrated by the huge numbers from Scotland and beyond who turned out, not only for his funeral service at Greyfriars Kirk in Edinburgh on March 18, 1994, but also for the first of what are to be the annual W. A. Wilson Memorial Lectures, which was given by the Lord Advocate, Lord Rodger of Earlsferry, on May 17, 1995.[4] The Lectures are the first fruit of the appeal fund set up in Wilson's memory, the many donations to which were further eloquent testimony to his reputation. Numerous obituaries sought to do justice to his achievements and personal standing.[5] At least three books have been dedicated to his memory.[6] Now this collection of essays by some former pupils and colleagues also honours one of the great Scottish academic lawyers. Each essay relates in some way to an aspect of

[1] 1995 S.L.T. 837; 1995 S.C.L.R. 683.
[2] "Floating Charges", 1962 S.L.T. (News) 53 at p. 55. See also "The Companies (Floating Charges) (Scotland) Act 1961", (1962) 25 M.L.R. 445.
[3] 1995 S.L.T. 837 at p. 843E–F.
[4] The lecture, entitled "Thinking About Scots Law", will appear in the first issue of the *Edinburgh Law Review*, to be published in September 1996.
[5] See *The Scotsman*, March 18, 1994 (Robert Black); *The Herald*, March 18, 1994 (Joe Thomson); *The Times*, March 22, 1994 (Kenneth Reid); *The Guardian*, March 24, 1994 (C. M. G. Himsworth); *The Independent*, April 6, 1994 (Hector MacQueen); *Edinburgh University Bulletin*, April 21, 1994 (Robert Leslie); 1994 S.L.T. (News) 130 (M. G. Clarke); Special Minute, University of Edinburgh Senatus, July 6, 1994 (C. R. Munro); (1994) 15 S.L.R. (T. St J. N. Bates); (1994) 9 SPTL Reporter 29 (W. D. H. Sellar).
[6] J. M. Thomson, *Delictual Liability* (1994); H. L. MacQueen, *Copyright, Competition and Industrial Design*, (2nd ed. 1995); *Gloag & Henderson The Law of Scotland* (10th ed. 1995).

his contribution to the law, whether as teacher, textbook expositor, or sharp-witted commentator in print and speech. It is impossible for words to recapture for those who did not know him the essence of a remarkable personality; but the variety of approach and opinion in these essays may reflect something of his intellectual range.

This introductory memoir sketches Bill Wilson's life and career. Although intensely sociable, he was also in some ways an intensely private man; in particular, his characteristically elliptical comments about and allusions to his career before he entered university life in 1960 revealed rather less than seemed to be the case at the time. This account is based on what can be obtained from various records, and the recollections of various family members and other friends, whose assistance, freely given, is gratefully acknowledged.

Bill Wilson was born at 1.50 p.m. on July 28, 1928 at 338 Crow Road in the Broomhill district of Glasgow.[7] It was just a month before Mrs May Donoghue made a fateful day trip to Paisley from 49 Kent Road in the Barras, and had an alleged encounter with the decomposed remains of a snail which set in train developments in the law of delict which would be one of Wilson's major interests in later life.[8] He was the only child of Hugh Wilson and Anne Craig Adam, who had married on August 2, 1927.[9] Wilson was brought up in Glasgow, and from 1933 attended Hillhead High School ("almost within the shadow of the tower of [Glasgow] University"),[10] where his father taught in the primary department.[11] Wilson had the school's highest marks in the Qualifying Exam at the end of his primary schooling. The bombing raids of the Second World War were to affect the continuity of his school education, however; the whole school was evacuated to the south-west of Scotland for a spell late in 1939 until air-raid shelters could be built in Glasgow,[12] while on April 1, 1941 Wilson and some others were again evacuated, this time to Callander, where he attended McLaren High School until the end of June that year.[13] He was a prefect in his final year at Hillhead.

In 1945 Wilson went up to Glasgow University and commenced three years of study leading to graduation in 1948 with an ordinary M.A.[14] It was an extraordinary period in universities, with classes swollen in size by a huge influx of those who had been in the armed

[7] Register of Births, Deaths and Marriages, ref. 644/22–1928.671.
[8] See *Donoghue v. Stevenson*, 1932 S.C. (H.L.) 31. For Mrs Donoghue's trip on August 26, 1928 see A. F. Rodger, "Mrs Donoghue and Alfenus Varus", (1988) 41 Current Legal Problems 1, and W. W. McBryde, "Donoghue v. Stevenson: The Story of the 'Snail in the Bottle' Case", in A. J. Gamble (ed.), *Obligations in Context: Essays in Honour of D. M. Walker* (1990).
[9] Register of Births, Deaths and Marriages, ref. 644/12–1927.192.
[10] W. A. Wilson, "Studying Statutes", 1992 J.R. 213.
[11] On the school from 1933–1945, see A.D.C., *Hillhead High School 1885–1961* (1962) at pp. 40–54. Hugh Wilson is mentioned at p. 52, and there is a line drawing of him in the centrepiece (see key at p. 45).
[12] A.D.C., *Hillhead High School* at p. 47–50. Wilson was accommodated in Kirkbean.
[13] I am grateful to John Brims of Central Regional Council Archives Services for assistance on Wilson's time at McLaren High School.
[14] Information on Wilson's academic record was obtained from Glasgow University Archives.

services during the War; the presence of these much older and infinitely more worldly-wise people affected the whole character of the
university in a way which could sometimes be intimidating for those
who had only just left school. Wilson's university subjects included
Latin (ordinary), history (ordinary), social economics (ordinary),
moral philosophy (ordinary), and political economy (ordinary and
higher); at ordinary level in the last-named subject he was ninth-equal
in the class and gained a first-class merit certificate. The intellectual
influence of these early studies can be detected in his later work on
law. But it is evident that all along his intention was to be a lawyer.
In this period, the LL.B was exclusively a second degree, but some
law subjects could be taken during the preceding M. A.. Wilson
passed civil law in 1945–46, but apparently retook it in 1947–48, perhaps because otherwise his first year performance would not have
counted towards his LL.B.[15] Political economy was also a recognised
subject for the LL.B, and the Adam Smith Chair of Political Economy
was in both the Faculties of Arts and Law. In Wilson's time, the Civil
Law Chair was held by the gentlemanly figure of John Spencer Muirhead, whose course was the foundation of his textbook *Outline of
Roman Law*, the second edition of which appeared in 1947. Alec
Macfie, "who looked on Political Economy in the older fashion as
social philosophy and not as a kind of applied mathematics",[16] occupied the Adam Smith chair.

In 1948 Wilson commenced three years of study for the LL.B at
Glasgow University, combining lectures in the early morning and the
late afternoon with his solicitor's apprenticeship in the firm of
Mackenzie Roberton & Co. at 176 St Vincent Street for the remainder
of each day. University study at Gilmorehill and apprenticeship in
central Glasgow involved difficulties of transport and timekeeping,
only partially alleviated by some of the classes (jurisprudence and
mercantile law) being held in the Accountants' Institute at the foot of
St Vincent Street.[17]

Nonetheless Wilson had a brilliant record as an LL.B student.[18] In
his first year he won first prize in the Scots law class of Andrew Dewar
Gibb, a first-class merit certificate in public international law, and a
second class merit certificate in forensic medicine. Only in constitutional law did his record show a mere pass. In second year, Wilson
went on to win a certificate of merit in conveyancing, for which he
was also joint winner of the Robert McFarlane Bursary and the Robert
Ross Prize. He gained second equal prize in mercantile law, and a
certificate of distinction in the evidence and procedure class. Perhaps

---

[15] The *Glasgow University Calendars* of the period indicate that higher standards were
required of LL.B students taking civil law than for Arts ones. The latter passed at 50
per cent, the former at 70 per cent. However, the records do not show that Wilson
sat the civil law exam in 1947–48.

[16] D. M. Walker, *A History of the School of Law, University of Glasgow* (1990) at p. 62.

[17] Walker, *History* at pp. 69–70.

[18] Nine volumes of Wilson's student lecture notes, covering Scots law (5 volumes), mer-
cantile law (3) and evidence & procedure (1) were presented to Glasgow University
Library in 1995, and are preserved in its Special Collections Department as M.S.S.
Gen. 859–867.

surprisingly, however, he only passed in jurisprudence. Finally, in his
third year, Wilson received the University Prize (fourth equal) in international private law, and obtained a pass in accountancy.

Professor David Walker, who took his LL.B at Glasgow between
1945 and 1948, has given us not always flattering vignettes of the Glasgow Faculty at this time.[19] It is of interest to speculate about the possible influence, positive and negative, of Wilson's teachers on his later
career. He himself said that his lecturing style was influenced by that
of Dewar Gibb, the Regius Professor of Law, and "a good lecturer,
who frequently enlivened his discourse with asides, frequently digs
at English law and the House of Lords . . .".[20] John Glaister, the Professor of Forensic Medicine, "always perfectly groomed and precise,
was a riveting lecturer who enlivened lectures with showing slides,
handing round specimens and plaster casts, weapons and other materials".[21] But Gibb and Glaister were apparently exceptional amongst
the Glasgow Faculty of the time in their teaching abilities. Most of the
rest were mediocre or bad teachers, some mere dictators of other
men's published prose; and there were of course no tutorials. In the
light of the teaching and intellectual standards to which Wilson was
subjected, it would seem that he was an excellent illustration of Walker's comment that those students who became very competent lawyers
"succeeded by innate ability and private study as much as, or possibly
more than, by reason of the instruction they received".[22]

After graduation as an LL.B and the conclusion of his apprenticeship in 1951,[23] Wilson commenced his National Service. From November 1951 to November 1953 he served in the Royal Army Service
Corps at Aldershot. He did not glory in his military career; his work
was mainly clerical, and he learned how to type. He spent free weekends reading law in Reading Public Library. But his wry humour
found things to relish: on his call-up form he listed his sporting interests as playing cards and riding bicycles, and he later recalled a kit
inspection in which the inspecting officer noticed two crumbs on his
fork and said, "I'm surprised at you, Wilson; a man with your background, living like an animal!" Others have told how during this
period Wilson bought a watch, the strap of which broke, but which
continued in use for many years, kept in its owner's pocket with the
strap unmended.

Wilson embarked upon practice as a solicitor in Scotland late in
1953, working mainly in the field of reparation in an era which he
was later to term "the glorious years" of the subject.[24] He began with
Young & Cruickshank, W.S. at 23 York Place in Edinburgh before

---

[19] Walker, *History*, at pp. 52–72.
[20] Walker, *History*, at p. 58. Some of the flavour of Gibb's discourse may be found in
his *Law from Over the Border* (1950). Gibb's Scottish Nationalist politics, which had a
distinctly racist slant in relation to the Irish (see his *Scotland in Eclipse* [1930]), do not
seem to have influenced Wilson, unless in the negative.
[21] Walker, *History*, at p. 61.
[22] Walker, *History*, at p. 72.
[23] Wilson's certificate of enrolment as a member of the Law Society of Scotland is preserved in Glasgow University Library Special Collections as MS. Gen. 522/4.
[24] "The Progress of the Law, 1888–1988", 1988 JR 207 at p. 214.

moving to Black, Cameron & Campbell of 55 West Regent Street, Glasgow. His first published articles—all on reparation—appeared at this time. In March 1957 he was employed in the firm of Biggart Lumsden at 105 West George Street in Glasgow, where he was to remain until his entry into university life at the beginning of the academic year 1960–61. In this firm he continued as a reparation practitioner, a notable client being the Iron Trades Employers Insurance Association, at the time insurers of most of the heavy industry in west and central Scotland.[25] He was offered a partnership but preferred an academic career, having decided to leave practice after defeat for Biggart's client in *Harvey v. Singer Manufacturing Company*.[26] He gave up his practising certificate in November 1960, although he remained on the solicitors' roll until his death.[27] Wilson had decided against going to the Bar but, following his appointment as a lecturer at Edinburgh University in 1960, he nonetheless devilled to Donald Ross (later Lord Justice-Clerk), whom he had instructed while in practice as a solicitor.[28] This was apparently because the then professor of Scots law told his new lecturer that he should become an advocate so that he could be on equal terms with the course tutors. Certainly Wilson was permitted to devil part-time while also giving his lectures and tutorials, and never intended to practise. He had all but completed his devilling when in 1961, for reasons which remain mysterious, he decided not to be called.

Wilson's appointment as a lecturer in the Department of Scots Law at Edinburgh University occurred at a time of momentous change in Scottish legal education. Since at latest the mid-1950s there had been vociferous and growing pressure for the reconstitution of the LL.B as a full-time and first degree.[29] This was finally accomplished in 1960, after the Law Society of Scotland agreed to a degree and an apprenticeship which were both full-time. This development necessitated more full-time teachers of law in the universities, and provides the context in which Wilson's appointment must be placed. Attention has rightly been drawn to his love of the ideal of the university, and the anger he felt in his later years when he perceived real threats to that ideal[30]; it was possibly pursuit of this ideal which drew him to and kept him in academe.

The 1950s had also seen the development in the Aberdeen law faculty of a neo-civilian crusade, led by Professor T. B. Smith with the encouragement, while he lived, of the influential Lord President

---

[25] MS. Gen. 522/4 (above, n. 23) is endorsed with his enrolments between October 1957 and July 1959 on the lists of solicitors practising before the sheriff courts of Lanarkshire, Stirling, Dumbarton, Clackmannan, Ayr and Bute, and Renfrew and Argyll.

[26] 1960 S.C. 155. The defenders were found liable although they could not have foreseen the precise circumstances of the pursuer's accident. In later university tutorials, Wilson used models of the "cut out" table tops and the dead table which feature in *Harvey*: as Joe Thomson, my informant here, comments, surely one of the earliest examples of the use of visual aids in teaching.

[27] Information from the Law Society of Scotland.

[28] I am grateful to Lord Ross for information on Wilson's period as his devil.

[29] See D. M. Walker, "Legal education in Scotland, 1889–1988", 1988 J.R. 184; also Walker, *History*, at pp. 72–8.

[30] Clarke, 1994 S.L.T. (News) 132 at p. 132; Sellar, (1994) 9 SPTL Reporter 30.

Cooper. They sought to save Scots law from extinction through unthinking and uncritical acceptance of the processes of Anglicisation. Smith and his followers emphasised the civilian roots of Scots law, which made it essentially distinct from the English common law and more akin to the systems of other European countries. Given the extent to which Scots law had been influenced by English law since the Union of 1707, it was no longer a "pure" civilian system; rather it was a "mixed" system like others, such as South Africa, Louisiana and Québec, where a civilian base had been subject to common law influence. The best future for Scots law lay in emphasising its civilian aspects and looking for models to the other mixed systems.

In 1958 Smith had taken up the Chair of Civil Law at Edinburgh, and was thus the most prominent of Wilson's new colleagues. Their relationship was not an easy one. At least some of Wilson's early publications can be read as signals of his dissent from the neo-civilian position. He emphasised the study of modern statutes, not the common law[31]; and he argued that there was little distinctively Scottish about commercial law.[32] In 1967, a little before Smith was appointed to the Chair of Scots Law, the two men had a rather sharp exchange in the correspondence columns of *The Scotsman* about the patronage enjoyed by the Faculty of Advocates in connection with some of the Edinburgh law chairs.[33] By 1988, however, he could write that those "who have been cynical about, or opposed to [Smith's] views, have been forced to move some way towards them".[34] It became apparent that he was of their number when he later criticised law teachers, "the present writer included", for departing from the civilian paths prescribed by Smith and thereby undermining the doctrinal foundations of Scots law.[35] Some of the reasons for Wilson's apparent change of view are explored elsewhere in these essays, as well as the question of whether that change was right and, if so, what should be done about it.[36]

This lay ahead, however, when Wilson began what may be termed the public part of his career in 1960. His progress up the academic ladder was relatively rapid: Senior Lecturer in 1965,[37] Associate Dean of the Faculty 1966–69,[38] and Lord President Reid Professor of Law (the first holder of that chair) in 1972.[39] He was Dean of the Faculty

---

[31] See Bibliography.

[32] "Scottish Commercial Law", 1966 J.B.L. 320.

[33] See *The Scotsman*, August 11, 18 and 28, 1967.

[34] "The Progress of the Law 1888–1988", 1988 J.R. 207 at p. 213.

[35] "The Importance of Analysis", in D. L. Carey Miller and D. W. Meyers (eds.), *Comparative and Historical Essays in Scots Law: a Tribute to Professor Sir Thomas Smith Q.C.* (1992), p. 171. A more civilian approach was also evident in his last years of teaching. It should however be noted that he played an active role in ensuring that the Edinburgh Chair of Civil Law remained unfilled after it fell vacant in 1987.

[36] See J. M. Thomson, "When Homer Nodded"; J. W. Cairns, "Roman Law and the Scottish Legal Curriculum", both *infra*, pp. 19 and 28.

[37] It is said that he was offered a chair in the new Law School in Strathclyde when it was founded in 1965.

[38] In this office he wrote the first edition of the guide for Directors of Studies in the Edinburgh Law Faculty which has since become known as *Wilson's Practicks*.

[39] One of Wilson's best (and best-performed) stories against himself concerned this appointment: see Clarke, 1994 S.L.T. (News) 130 at p. 131.

of Law for the first time from 1976 to 1979, and was re-elected for a second term of office in the critical period 1988–1991. The esteem in which he was held in the University beyond the Faculty of Law was shown by his election as a senatus assessor on the University Court in 1992. He undertook many external commitments which were not merely honorific: Chairman of the Joint Standing Committee on Legal Education, Director of the Scottish Universities Law Institute, Deputy Chairman of the Consumer Protection Advisory Committee, Scottish representative on the Commission for European Contract Law, and membership of the Law Reform Committee of the Law Society of Scotland. Honours did come his way as well: Fellowship of the Royal Society of Edinburgh in 1991 and, in a gesture which afforded him great pleasure in the last weeks of his life, an honorary LL.D from the University of Glasgow.[40]

Wilson read law constantly, and no member of the Edinburgh Faculty spent more time than he in its law library. His early published output was principally in the form of journal articles on a wide variety of topics, and it was only following his elevation to a chair that books (all published by W. Green & Son Ltd.) began to appear, although the flow of articles never ceased.[41] The first, written jointly with Gordon Duncan, was *Trusts, Trustees and Executors* (1975); a second edition was underway by the time he died. The most idiosyncratic of Wilson's books, and in some ways the most revealing of his whole approach to legal study, was his *Introductory Essays on Scots Law*, which first appeared in 1978 and had a second edition in 1984. He became one of the joint editors of that Scottish legal bible, *Gloag & Henderson's Introduction to the Law of Scotland*, in its 1980 edition; another appeared in 1987, and he left his work on yet another complete at the time of his death.[42] Perhaps his most influential book, and certainly the one which embodied the areas of substantive law in which he took the greatest interest, was *The Law of Scotland Relating to Debt*, which had two editions (1982 and 1991). He saw debt at the heart of the law: "In the eyes of the law, a person goes through life with a swarm of creditors buzzing round his head and each of his acts and each event which happens must be considered in the light of its effects on creditors."[43] Wilson wrote of his book as cutting a new swathe through the law, and in his concise economical fashion certainly succeeded in re-ordering a very wide range of material. Conciseness and economy were indeed the hallmark of all his writing, which was well-suited to the composition of texts, but which, as many of his articles and the *Introductory Essays* show, could be a vehicle of pointed humour as well. He also took enormous pleasure in the byways of the law: the extension of Scots law to the Isle of Rockall, the measurement of territorial waters off the west coast of Scotland, and the location of the

---

[40] The degree was awarded posthumously on June 15, 1994.

[41] There was an early work on conveyancing, the manuscript of which Wilson lent to a student who returned it minus one, never recovered, chapter.

[42] The edition appeared in October 1995. *Gloag & Henderson* was the Scots law text in Glasgow University when Wilson was a law student, Dewar Gibb then being one of the editors.

[43] *Introductory Essays on Scots Law*, (2nd ed. 1984), p. 4.

lost port of Morison's Haven were three well-known examples with a maritime flavour.[44] He left unfinished at his death a work on statutory interpretation, which had been the subject of many of his articles. These manifested a quite original approach to the topic, which is discussed elsewhere in this collection of essays.[45] It should also be noted that he was amongst the first to see the possibilities for computer applications in law, and produced an expert system entitled "Can John and Mary Marry?"; this concluded with the tune of "Here Comes the Bride" if the answer turned out to be yes.[46]

But it was not for all these achievements and honours that so many people turned out at Bill Wilson's funeral and made donations to the Appeal Fund in his memory. It was for his teaching, its style, and the way in which he dealt with students in and out of the University. For many, a Bill Wilson lecture in the "crash course" which opened the teaching of Scottish legal system was their first exposure to the joys of Scots law. A unique style of delivery, combining his characteristic economy of words with rising and falling cadences of speech, a relish for Latin maxims and Scots technical terms, long pauses with eyes half-closed while he rocked gently to and fro on the balls of his feet, and a final devastating punchline, was to lead to innumerable attempts at affectionate imitation which could never quite capture the amazing original. The stories are legion: opening the last lecture of term with an emphatic "Goodbye, bastards!" just after the statute removing the last legal disabilities flowing from birth out of wedlock came into force; gravely considering a student's question on vesting subject to defeasance at the end of a tutorial before leaving the room with the words, "I have been waiting for 25 years for someone to ask me that question"; and referring to a work of Professor Diamond, and saying "Spelt thus" while drawing the figure of a diamond on the blackboard, are only a few of the many well-attested examples. He covered nearly all the subjects on the Scots law curriculum, but was perhaps most associated with Scottish legal system and mercantile law. The influence of such teaching is hard to measure, save that no-one who experienced it ever forgot the manner of it; the substance may not always have stuck in quite the same way. He never taught a full honours course, although he put in guest appearances at those of others when invited. At one such seminar, Wilson concluded his discourse, and silence fell, to be ended after a minute or two by the professor's ironic comment, "I thought intellectual discussion took place in honours classes."

There was also Wilson's sociability. He was an essential figure at faculty and other parties in Edinburgh, and his own, whether in his office or his sparsely furnished flat, were justly famous. Invitations to these parties were in an increasingly spidery and indecipherable holograph which straggled across unpretentious printed forms, while

[44] *ibid*; pp. 31, 33 and 78.
[45] See H. L. MacQueen, "The Contribution of W. A. Wilson to Scots Law", and G. Maher, "Statutory Interpretation: the Wilsonian Analysis", both *infra*, pp. 10 and 103.
[46] See further L. Edwards, "What Studying Statutes can do for Artificial Intelligence and Law", *infra*, p. 113.

his preparatory but extraordinarily generous purchases of drink and nibbles were carried out with the aid of ancient shopping bags. At parties and elsewhere he sought to speak to all, especially students, while a mischievous sense of humour delighted in the pricking of pomposity or finding feet of clay in the great. Morning coffee and lunchtimes found him at the Edinburgh Staff Club, the daily centre of a circle of colleagues, often joined by friends dropping in from Parliament House or other business in town. Late on sunny afternoons he could sometimes be found leaning on the balustrade of the terracing in the Old College quadrangle where he would embark upon conversation with anyone who happened to pass by. He kept up his school and university circle of friends, and loyally returned to visit his parents in Glasgow at weekends until their deaths. Few Scots were more faithful attenders at the annual conference of the Society of Public Teachers of Law.

A key part of Wilson's legend was a liking for alcoholic refreshment, although this was generally indulged only at the end of the day, and sometimes solemnly restricted to weekends only (although such self-imposed constraints might be joyously broken). Another of his rules was never to cross Princes Street before 11 p.m. on his way home to the New Town from Old College. He did not marry, but enjoyed teasing on the subject of his relationships with women. For example, on being asked why a man of so few material possessions had two dressing gowns, he replied that one was for cooking and the other for adultery; but there was no other evidence that he engaged in either activity. Just weeks before his death, he gave a memorably witty speech at a faculty dinner in his honour in a performance which epitomised the man; but in all ways this was a very special occasion, for he disliked being centre stage at formal events. He never participated in graduations, for example, even when Dean, and never gave a professor's inaugural lecture.[47]

The first warnings of the cancer that was to kill Bill Wilson came during the Christmas/New Year vacation of 1992–93, when he was hospitalised for the removal of a melanoma on an arm. In November 1993 it became known that he was suffering from another, inoperable cancer. He resigned his chair at Christmas 1993 and took a short holiday in Paris before returning to Edinburgh for the last time. Although visibly weakening, he continued to come to the University and receive friends in his home until very near the end. He was finally admitted to the Marie Curie Cancer Care Centre in the Fairmilehead district of Edinburgh where, watched over by his cousin Miss Isabel Adam, he died on March 14, 1994.[48]

---

[47] Two junior colleagues did however attend in academic dress the first of Wilson's mercantile law lectures following his professorial appointment, regarding this as some sort of substitute for the inaugural that never was.

[48] Register of Births, Deaths and Marriages, ref. 746–1994–201.

THE CONTRIBUTION OF W. A. WILSON TO SCOTS LAW

Hector L. MacQueen

Bill Wilson was not usually a man to court the limelight on the public stage. In 1990, however, he took to the columns of *The Scotsman* to launch a thunderbolt against the reforms of the legal profession then being made under what became the Law Reform (Miscellaneous Provisions) (Scotland) Act 1990.[1] The Act's breaking of the legal profession's "monopolies" in conveyancing and court representation would "lead to more business, more profits and more power going to the banks, the building societies, the large legal firms and the large accountancy firms, many of them controlled south of the Border. This cannot be good for Scots law, it cannot be good for Scotland, and it cannot be good for the ordinary Scotsman using legal services". In uninhibited rhetorical vein, he launched an attack on the "robotic barmen" of the Scottish Office, "dispensing a recipe ... dictated by the competition theorists in the bowels of the Department of Trade ... [which] has always evinced a hostility towards a separate Scottish legal system".

In his later career Wilson was deeply concerned about the future of the Scots law and legal system in the face of an increasing threat from Westminster.[2] He thought a key moment to have been the election of the Labour Government in 1964:

> "1964 marks a change in the attitude of Westminster to Scots law; previously there had been an attitude of ignorant neglect towards Scots law on the part of U.K. departments which had some responsibilities in Scotland; this turned to a sort of active hostility."[3]

The Department of Trade took over commercial law for the whole of the United Kingdom; U.K. law, U.K. courts and tribunals and U.K. administrative bodies (mostly in the area of "social law") began to develop in a way which paid little heed to Scots law. The Lord Advocate's Department retained some responsibility for Scots private law but the remainder, "in so far as it has not been surrendered to United Kingdom Departments", lay with the Scottish Office, within which "the responsibility rests on civil servants, often chemists or philosophers by training, who have no particular knowledge of, or feeling for, the system".[4] Pressure groups such as the business community

---

[1] *The Scotsman*, January 24, 1990. See also the reply by the then Solicitor-General for Scotland, Alan Rodger Q.C., in *The Scotsman*, January 31, 1990.
[2] The fullest account of these threats is in "The Progress of the Law, 1888–1988", 1988 J.R. 207.
[3] *ibid.*, at p. 215.
[4] *ibid.*, at p. 231.

and the consumer lobby were also responsible for changes not in the best interests of Scots law as a distinctive system.[5] And finally "populist Conservatism" under Mrs Thatcher, upholding a competitive market economy and the reduction of public expenditure, had also had an adverse impact upon the separateness of the Scottish legal system.[6]

There were also threats from within the system. The judges had made no significant contribution to the protection of Scots law: "the best that can be said for the judges is that they have kept the system going; that is perhaps their function".[7] Wilson was concerned by judgments of the Court of Session which seemed unaware of the consequence that business properly related to Scotland might otherwise go off to England.[8] Inadequate judicial analysis and a tendency to pragmatism at the expense of logic and principle also offended.[9]

Latterly Wilson saw another threat in the failure of university teaching of Scots law to follow the paths prescribed by T. B. Smith, namely to search for the law's civilian roots and to seek solutions for its problems in comparisons with other mixed jurisdictions. "A legal system which has no doctrinal foundation must drift . . . The law teachers are to blame, the present writer included".[10] Elsewhere he wrote:

> "What Professor I. D. Willock has called the 'Cooper-Smith ideology' has had a tremendous impact in and furth of Scotland. It has produced a reaction from a younger generation of academic lawyers. In crude terms, while the earlier school went about the world crying 'Scots law is Best', the later school take as their slogan 'Scots law is Worst'. Reaction of one generation to another will no doubt continue but perhaps the time has come for the debate to descend to a more concrete plane. Can there be a profitable analysis of the circumstances surrounding, and justification for, such rhetoric as 'It is ridiculous that the law on X should be different on each side of the border?' Are the rules which prevail in England suitable for a country with a somewhat different economic and social structure? Professor Willock asserts that employment and social security law—both UK based—are the central areas of the system now. Are rules which change with each government law of the same order as principles which have stood for a thousand years?"[11]

---

[5] *ibid.*, at pp. 216–219. Note also "the usual hysteria of the consumer movement" mentioned in "The Importance of Analysis", in D. L. Carey Miller and D. W. Meyers (eds.), *Comparative and Historical Essays in Scots Law* (1992), p. 170.

[6] This was the background to the 1990 attack on the reforms of the legal profession, mentioned at the beginning of this essay, and to Wilson's rather cynical interest in the Child Support Agency, for which see "The Bairns of Falkirk: The Child Support Act 1991", 1991 S.L.T. (News) 417, and "Studying Statutes", 1992 J.R. 213 at pp. 220–221.

[7] "The Progress of the Law, 1888–1988", 1988 J.R. 207 at p. 231.

[8] *ibid.*, at p. 231. Another example is *Bank of Scotland v. IMRO*, 1989 S.L.T. 432.

[9] For example, in the legislation on floating charges: see his criticisms of *Lord Advocate v. Royal Bank*, 1977 S.C. 155 at 1978 J.R. 253, and "The Progress of the Law, 1888–1988", 1988 J.R. 207 at p. 220.

[10] "Importance of Analysis", *supra*, at p. 171.

[11] "Knowing the Law and Other Things", 1982 JR. 259 at p. 271.

Wilson identified six features of varying importance in the role of academic lawyers[12]:

1. *Knowing the law*—"the first task of the academic lawyer, and the one which students, the legal profession and the public at large most strongly expect of him".[13]

2. *Propagation of knowledge of Scots law as a distinctive system*, achieved through teaching and writing.

3. *Commentary* upon decided cases, for use on appeal or in later cases: he described this as providing pabulum[14] for the courts, and was critical of the attitude of the Scottish judiciary towards the use of academic writings, which he encapsulated with the words "Better Read When Dead"—a rule "of the same order of rationality as trial by ordeal".[15]

4. *Law reform*. "Law reform is conventionally regarded as one of the most important interests of the academic lawyer. It is doubtful, however, whether the setting up of the Law Commissions has left the academic lawyer, as such, any substantial role to play in the reform of private law."[16]

5. *Empirical research*. "Ten years ago, when sociology of law became fashionable it seemed that we would shortly learn much more about how the civil law actually worked. We have been disappointed. The sociologists have chosen to sit by the fire honing their concepts and hardly any work has been done in the field ... This is unfortunate because the interface of law and social sciences is where the most important developments in academic law will take place in the rest of this century. In ten years it will be impossible to become an academic lawyer without a preliminary qualification in the social sciences."[17]

6. *Analysis*. "It can be argued that a jurist's opinion as to what the law is, is of much less importance than his analysis of the setting in which the decision as to what the law is has to be made. Perhaps, indeed, analysis is the characteristic activity of the academic lawyer."[18]

This list shows that Wilson placed knowledge and analysis of the law ahead of commentary and law reform as the main concerns of the academic. Knowledge was not simply what the legal sources tell us, however; it was legitimate to approach law in other ways, in particular from the perspectives of social science.

Wilson's understanding of the activity "characteristic" of the academic lawyer, "analysis", is most clearly stated in an article entitled "The Importance of Analysis", at the outset of which he briefly outlines what he means by the word:

---

[12] See "Knowing the Law and Other Things", *passim*.

[13] *ibid.*, at p. 260.

[14] "Anything taken in by an animal or plant to maintain life and growth; food, nutriment" (*Oxford English Dictionary*).

[15] "Knowing the Law and Other Things", *supra*, at p. 267. See further K. G. C. Reid, "The Third Profession: the Rise of the Academic Lawyer in Scotland", *infra*, p. 39.

[16] "Knowing the Law and Other Things", 1982 J. R. 259 at p. 270.

[17] *ibid.*, at pp. 271–272. This comment, written in 1982, shows that Wilson was no prophet on these matters.

[18] *ibid.*, at p. 269.

"for those of an academic or theoretical turn of mind it is important to establish what the logical possibilities are before determining the rules which are to apply to them. Analysis of the factual
situation is the first stage and evaluation of the possible rules and
selection from them of what is to be the law is the second stage."[19]

The key word in this passage is "logical". Philosophy was central
to Wilson's legal scholarship. This was not merely a matter of once
writing a note on the Hohfeld analysis.[20] Wilson was interested in
logic, "the study of inference ... concerned with the rules of *valid*
inference ... by which those inferences whose premises really entail
their conclusions ... may be distinguished from those whose premises
do not."[21] In particular logic informed his many studies of statutes,
which he treated as linguistic phenomena to which the disciplines of
logic, particularly deontic logic,[22] semantics[23] and syntax,[24] should be
applied for the resolution of the difficulties of statutory interpretation.
"[M]ost of the time the lawyer is dealing with language; he is a word-
monger. It is therefore worth considering some of the inherent features of language which create difficulties for the law."[25]

Wilson's first major article was an analysis of the problems of the
fact/law distinction "in so far as these arise in the application of statutes".[26] A statute was a declaration that if a certain state of affairs (the
"particular proposition") existed, a legal consequence would follow.
The particular proposition might be broken down into a number of
sub-propositions.

"To induce the court to affirm the particular proposition, the
party invoking the statute will present, in one form or another,
a number of statements from which, in his contention, the particular proposition can be inferred. It is not essential that each of these
statements should yield the inference that the particular proposition is true; they may each only contribute to the inference that
a sub-proposition is true and the truth of the particular proposition will then follow when all the sub-propositions are established. The task of the court is to decide whether the assertion of
the statements justifies the assertion of the particular
proposition."[27]

[19] "Importance of Analysis", *supra*, at p. 162.
[20] "A Note on the Hohfeld Analysis", 1972 J.R. 162.
[21] A. Bullock and S. Trombley (eds.) *Fontana Dictionary of Modern Thought*, (1988) at p.
485.
[22] "The branch of logic in which a systematic study of the relations between propositions expressing *obligation* and permission are studied" (*ibid.*, p. 215).
[23] "(1) The branch of LINGUISTICS that studies MEANING in language (and sometimes in other symbolic forms of communication) ... (2) In PHILOSOPHY and
LOGIC, (a) the study of the RELATIONS between linguistic expressions and the
objects in the world to which they refer ..." (*ibid.*, p. 768).
[24] "In LINGUISTICS, a traditional term for the study of the rules governing the way
words are combined to form sentences in a language" (*ibid.*, p. 840).
[25] *Introductory Essays on Scots Law* (2nd ed. 1984), p. 10.
[26] "A Note on Fact and Law" (1963) 26 M.L.R. 609.
[27] *ibid.*, pp. 609–610.

The article then goes on to analyse the different types of statement with which a court may be presented, and the different types of inference which may be drawn from them, tying them in with the theory of appellate jurisdiction in British courts, *viz* that appeals are generally on questions of law, not fact.[28]

In 1974 he began a sequence of articles which were intended to be the basis of a book on statutory interpretation. The first of these considered the way in which each sentence of a statute contributed to the legal change the statute was intended to achieve, producing a classification of different types of sentence—operative, substitutional, factorial, additional and others—as well as analysing the linkages between them.[29] This led to the conclusion that "one method of simplifying legislation would be to reduce each provision to a set of separate conditions which must be fulfilled for a certain legal consequence to follow. The process can be carried further by reducing the conditions to 'unit facts'"[30], an echo of the earlier article on fact and law. The ideas were developed further in a 1987 paper which divided questions of statutory interpretation into two categories: first, proposition questions, *viz*, the questions which arise when formulating the statute as a proposition that if a set of factual conditions is satisfied a legal consequence follows; and secondly, semantic questions, *viz*, those which arise in applying the proposition to particular facts.[31] At the end of his career he was beginning to formulate a procedure for the interpretation of statutes.[32]

Wilson's work shows a fascination with the effort to be precise in law, the attempt to make language achieve particular goals despite its essentially open texture.[33] In one of his lecture handouts he quoted Wittgenstein: "Alles, was sich aussprechen, lässt aussprechen" (everything that can be expressed can be expressed clearly).[34] This belief informed comments such as that which he made on a particular problem in the law of evidence: "It is felt that judicial discretion is not a satisfactory solution and by consideration of an analysis . . . rules could be developed".[35] The article on fact and law discusses how far a statement may be analysed to make it more exact, concluding that "it is not necessary to decide whether there are any 'basic' statements which cannot be analysed further in this way. It may be that the process must stop when everything has been reduced to centimetres, ang-

---

[28] See also on this issue "Questions of Degree" (1969) 32 M.L.R. 361, and "The Theory of the Case Stated", 1969 B.T.R. 231.

[29] "The Complexity of Statutes" (1974) 37 M.L.R. 497.

[30] *ibid.*, at p. 508.

[31] "Questions of Interpretation" (1987) 8 S.L.R. 142.

[32] See G. Maher, "Statutory Interpretation: the Wilsonian Analysis", below, pp. 103–112; also W. A. Wilson, "Trials and Try-ons: Modes of Interpretation", (1992) 13 S.L.R. 1. Much of Wilson's thinking on the subject appears in simplified form in *Introductory Essays, supra*, at pp. 87–105.

[33] For reference to the "open texture" of language see *Introductory Essays, supra*, at p.10.

[34] I am indebted to George Gretton for the information about the lecture handout and the identification of the source as Wittgenstein's *Tractatus Logico-Philosophicus* (1921), para 4.116. Professor Gretton advises me that Wittgenstein later changed his mind: see his *Philosophische Untersuchungen* (1953).

[35] "The Importance of Analysis", *op. cit.*, at p. 167.

stroms and decibels. It may be that this is what a judge had in mind
when he said that figures are probably the only things that do represent facts".[36] The vagueness of words "can in some cases be
removed by a definition in terms of a measurement—a 'small lobster'
can be defined as 'a lobster 9 inches long measured from the tip of
the beak to the end of the shell of the centre flap of the tail when the
lobster is spread as far as possible flat'; but in most cases this is not
possible".[37] He went on: "A definition limits a concept in some directions but except for mathematical concepts, it is not possible for the
definition to set limits to the concept in all directions."[38]

Such considerations inform two essays on "Measures and Standards" and "Legal Geography". The first of these shows the variety of
measurements used in law, and how they are defined and calculated.
Significantly it begins with a quotation from Holmes to the effect that
law should be reduced to exactness and quantitative determinations
wherever possible.[39] "Legal Geography" is essentially concerned with
the division and definition of territory for various legal purposes,
much of which again necessarily involves measurement and definition
as far as possible of something which might naturally be rather impre-
cise. A particular example was the definition of territorial waters by
Orders in Council and the way in which the problem of bays, gulfs
and estuaries was tackled by the legislation.[40]

Wilson's passion for precision and clarity in legislation was
offended by what he saw as "the crumbling of the massive pillars of
principle of statutory interpretation",[41] and the "blurring of the distinction between what is law and what is not law".[42] Some law which
is not case law may not be in the statute book, and there are rules
governing society which are not law at all. Subordinate legislation
may be of wide effect but inaccessible. A plethora of other material
may be needed to interpret legislation properly. Statutes may not be
in force, may not be the law or only precariously so, or may be
amended by statutory instrument. Amongst other things, this made
the academic lawyer's primary task of knowing the law "much more
difficult".[43]

Wilson also applied his analytical techniques to the common law.[44]
The most striking example is an article on economic loss in delict,

---

[36] "A Note on Fact and Law", *op. cit.*, at p. 611. The quoted judge was Lord Johnston
    in *J & M Craig Ltd. v. C. I. R.*, 1914 S.C. 338 at p. 347.
[37] *Introductory Essays on Scots Law* at p. 10.
[38] *ibid.*, at p. 10. Note also the keen if somewhat cynical pleasure in the "higher algebra"
    deployed to calculate child support rates under Sched. 1 of the Child Support Act
    1991: "The Bairns of Falkirk: The Child Support Act 1991", 1991 S. L. T. (News) 417.
[39] *Introductory Essays on Scots Law* at p. 21. The quotation from Holmes is in an article:
    "The Theory of Legal Interpretation", (1899) 12 Harv. L. R. 443 at p. 456.
[40] *Introductory Essays on Scots Law*, at p. 33.
[41] "Studying Statutes", 1992 J. R. 213 at p. 213. Since the lecture was given the decision
    in *Pepper v. Hart* [1993] A.C. 593 has removed another of the "pillars". See further
    N. C. Walker, 'The Crumbling Pillars of Statutory Interpretation", *infra* pp. 126–137.
[42] "Studying Statutes", *supra*, at p. 219.
[43] "Knowing the Law and Other Things", *op. cit* at pp. 260–266.
[44] See *e.g.* "*In Modum Probationis*" 1968 J. R. 193. In "Importance of Analysis", there
    are discussions of error in contract, anticipatory breach and criminal evidence.

where the cases are analysed in terms of primary and secondary trans-actions upon which the negligent act impinges at different points.[45] The relationships and claims which arise are illustrated by a line dia-gram and a parallelogram. By this analysis of the varying facts of the cases he was able to categorise those where (as the law then stood) there would be liability and those where there would not. A simpler illustration of what Wilson meant by analysis of the different possibil-ities inherent in a situation can be seen in his discussion of the four kinds of bastard.[46] Heinous bastards were the product of a union between ascendant and descendant; incestuous bastards were the product of other incestuous relationships; adulterine bastards were the product of intercourse with another man's wife; and simple bas-tards were the products of any other relationship.[47]

Wilson's fascination with the use of logic in law, in the sense of determining the validity of inferences made from a statement, is also apparent in his discussions of evidence and procedure.

> "The facts are much more important than the law. In the aca-demic study of law facts tend to be ignored; in practice the courts devote much more time to disputes about fact than to debates about law and practitioners spend most of their time ascertaining facts and putting facts into order ... So universities should pay more attention than they do to the processes by which facts are investigated and ascertained."[48]

An essay on "Truth Finding" starts with the precognition of wit-nesses—"an exercise in the problems of communication".[49] Leading questions are defined through the terminology of linguistics—"Ques-tions in examination must be what linguists call 'wh-questions' and not 'yes-no' questions or 'tag' questions—'What did you see when you entered the room?', not 'Did you see a man in the room?' nor 'There was a man in the room, wasn't there?' ".[50] Again, "it is import-ant to observe the nature of the inference involved in the use of cir-cumstantial evidence. If facts A, B and C are held to establish fact D it does not mean that D has been proved by logical deduction or neces-sary inference. As a matter of logic it is *possible* for A, B and C to be true and D to be untrue; but the basis of the finding is that it is in the nature of things highly *improbable* that, if A, B and C are true, D is not".[51] It was in this context that he explored the use of new forms

---

[45] "Mapping Economic Loss", in A. J. Gamble (ed), *Obligations in Context: Essays in Honour of D M Walker* (1990), at pp. 146–147.
[46] The reasons for the classification were the ability of the bastard (i) to be legitimated and (ii) to claim aliment. Wilson pointed out that the classification thus failed to cover certain provisions of the French Civil Code on the rights of illegitimate children upon intestacy.
[47] Wilson's explanation in lectures that all other bastards were simple bastards usually reduced his class to helpless mirth. See further on this subject A. R. Barr, "Old Bas-tards and Other Children", *infra*, at pp. 160–169.
[48] *Introductory Essays on Scots Law*, at p. 5.
[49] *ibid.*, at p. 53.
[50] *ibid.*, at p. 55.
[51] *ibid.*, at pp. 57–58.

of proof, coming from both science and social science.[52] He also touched on the statistical techniques of surveys and sampling. "It can be established by mathematical proof that a sample drawn from a much larger population can provide good evidence of the characteristics of the whole population."[53]

The whole structure of civil procedure is itself an exercise in applied logic by which contending parties define precisely the matter disputed between them, whether of fact, law or both. Wilson highlighted an American classification of defences into three types—"There is 'No, I didn't'—a denial of the facts; then there is 'Yes, but'—the facts are admitted but the action cannot succeed because of some other facts— the condonation of adultery, for example; thirdly there is 'So what?'— even if the facts are true they do not afford the remedy sought—that is exactly the idea of relevancy".[54] He concludes with the observation that this system "is an excellent instrument for getting at the truth".[55] Finally, an essay on "Appeals" opens with discussion of the extent to which an appellate court can reconsider matters of fact as well as law—for example, the inference from circumstantial evidence discussed above is as open to the appellate court as to the judge of first instance, and similarly with the evaluation of primary facts, e.g. does conduct amount to negligence or not?[56]

This general emphasis on logic and analysis was not merely an arid philosophical exercise without practical application. So far as legislation was concerned, it was an attempt to make both drafting and interpretation more exact and precise, and thus to render the law more accessible and predictable. In evidence and procedure, the purpose and function of the rules were clarified by the understanding of their roots in logic.[57] Logical analysis also lent itself to the application of computers in law, and Wilson pursued with some success the creation of expert systems on marriage, succession and civil procedure.[58]

All this, however, renders even more poignant some sentences of Wilson's final tribute to T. B. Smith: "But analysis is not everything. The choice of the right legal rule may be more important."[59] In some sense he was conceding that a legal system is not value-free, and that choices had to be made. But his comment should not be seen as a denunciation or renunciation of his own approach and achievement. The article in which it was made is entitled "The Importance of Analysis", and he carried on applying his analytical approach until the end. It is an approach difficult for others to understand or appreciate, and

---

[52] For a further illustration see "Photograph and Photofit", 1989 S. L. T. (News) 1.

[53] *Introductory Essays on Scots Law*, at p. 60.

[54] *ibid.*, at p. 66.

[55] *ibid.*, at p. 69. See further S. Woolman, "Pleadings", *infra*, pp. 277–283.

[56] See *ibid.*, at pp. 71–74. Compare on this "Questions of Degree", and "Theory of the Case Stated", both cited above, n. 28.

[57] Wilson's student lecture notes, now preserved in the Special Collections of Glasgow University Library, show that his teacher, Robert Macdonald, started by emphasising that the basis of the law of evidence was general principles of logic (M.S. Gen. 867, f.2r).

[58] See further L. Edwards, "What Studying Statutes can do for Artificial Intelligence and Law." *infra*, pp. 113–125.

[59] "Importance of Analysis", *op. cit.*, p. 171.

few did so in its author's lifetime. This essay will have served its purpose if it has succeeded in showing the intellectual coherence and
power of what surely may be properly termed the Wilsonian argument, coming through in nearly all his published work, that the life
of the law does indeed lie in logic as well as, or perhaps rather than,
in experience.[60]

---

[60] cf. O. W. Holmes, *The Common Law* (1881), p 1: "The life of the law has not been
logic; it has been experience".

WHEN HOMER NODDED?

Joe Thomson

Introduction

In one of his last essays, Bill Wilson made a famous recantation: "But analysis is not everything. The choice of the right legal rule may be more important".[1] After eulogising Sir Thomas Smith's attempt to resurrect the civilian tradition of Scots law, Wilson then bemoaned the fact that T.B.'s academic successors had departed from the paths he had prescribed:

> "The teaching of Roman law in universities has declined. The Chair of Civil Law in the University of Edinburgh is vacant and will probably remain vacant. Academic discussion of law makes little reference to Civilian principles. This sad decline causes surprise both to Scottish practitioners and to foreign lawyers. A legal system which has no doctrinal foundation must drift. It may be under the delusion that it is proceeding in the light of pure reason. The law teachers are to blame, the present writer included."[2]

This passage is quite remarkable given that Wilson had spent much of his academic life denying—and, at times, deriding—the relevance of civilian principles for contemporary Scots law. Of course, the context of Wilson's paper cannot be ignored—it was, after all, an essay in honour of the late Professor T. B. Smith. And, remembering Wilson's sense of mischief, the recantation might well have been tongue in cheek; a white lie rather than a white sheet.[3] But if it was intended to be taken seriously, then it is the present writer's contention that Wilson was wrong and, indeed, wrong for many of the reasons that he himself espoused.

The Nature of Contemporary Scots Law

One of the most remarkable features of Scots private law has been its ability to adopt rules and principles from a wide range of sources. While the civilian tradition undoubtedly was influential, from the

---

[1] "The Importance of Analysis", in D. L. Carey Miller and D. W. Meyers, *Comparative and Historical Essays in Scots Law* (1992), p 171.
[2] *ibid.*
[3] Wilson's essay ends: "Having begun this essay in cap and bells, having continued it in what some may regard as a straitjacket, he concludes it in a white sheet" (p. 171).

nineteenth century onwards its influence diminished.[4] But it is important to remember that there are areas of Scots common law which were
largely unaffected by civilian concepts: for example, land law, succession and criminal law. That said, even today the civilian tradition
may occasionally influence the development of Scots law. In *Morgan
Guaranty Trust Company of New York v. Lothian Regional Council*,[5] consideration was given to civilian sources in deciding that, in an action
for repetition under the *condictio indebiti*, the error of law rule had no
sound foundation in principle in Scots law. The case also reminds us
that a principle of Roman law would not be transplanted into Scots
law unless it was consonant with "the most solid grounds of natural
equity and justice; that the Roman law is not with us authoritative,
that it has influence no further, than it is able from its equity and
expediency to perswade".[6]

The modern Scots law on delict is greatly influenced by developments south of the border. Scots lawyers who regard *Donoghue v.
Stevenson*[7] as the paradigm of the rational superiority of Scots law over
Anglo-American jurisprudence, would do well to remind themselves
that the pursuer lost in the Court of Session.[8] *Junior Books v. The Veitchi
Company*[9] apart, the current debate on delictual/tortious liability for
pure economic loss has been fired by English decisions which Scots
lawyers ignore at their peril.[10] Indeed, the potential rationalisation of
this difficult area of the law in *Henderson v. Merrett Syndicates*[11] should
be adopted in Scots as well as English law, regardless of the prov-
enance of Lord Goff's analysis.[12]

In the field of contract, Scots law has remained untrammelled by
English doctrines such as consideration. However, the influence of the
civilian tradition on the modern Scots law of contract remains elusive.
One example must suffice. Scots law accepted the civilian doctrine of
pollicitatio.[13] But while the obligation arose immediately on the promisor's declaration of his/her will, the obligation could not be enforced
by the obligee unless the promise could be proved by the promisor's
writ or oath. As a result of the Requirements of Writing (Scotland)
Act 1995,[14] a gratuitous unilateral obligation (except an obligation
undertaken in the course of business) is not *constituted* unless there is a
written document subscribed by the granter.[15] Thus, the fundamental

---

[4] The reasons why are discussed in Lord Rodger of Earlsferry, "Thinking about Scots
law", *Edinburgh Law Review*, forthcoming (the first Wilson Memorial Lecture).
[5] 1995 S.L.T. 299.
[6] Petition and answers in *Stirling v. Earl of Lauderdale* (1733) Mor. 2930, cited in *Morgan
Guaranty, ibid.*, at p. 314.
[7] 1932 S.C. (H.L.) 31.
[8] A similar fate awaited Master Hughes: *Hughes v. Lord Advocate*, 1963 S.C. (H.L.) 31.
[9] 1982 S.C. (H.L.) 244.
[10] On these decisions and their Scottish counterparts see J. M. Thomson, "Delictual
Liability for Pure Economic Loss: Recent Developments", 1995 SLT (News) 139.
[11] [1995] 2 A.C. 145.
[12] *cf.* D. Brodie, "Assumption of Responsibility", *infra*, pp. 204–213.
[13] On *pollicitatio* see generally T. B. Smith, *A Short Commentary on the Law of Scotland*
(1962), ch. 32.
[14] s. 1 (2) (a) (ii).
[15] ss. 1 (2) and 2.

civilian principle underpinning the theoretical basis of unilateral, gratuitous obligations in Scots law has been removed by a statutory side wind.[16]

Wilson's insight was to appreciate the importance of analysis in the search for underlying principle. Given that Scottish judges have gone awhoring after false gods in Anglo-American jurisprudence, the task of giving intellectual coherence to the modern Scots law of obligations is difficult; resort to civilian principles will not suffice.[17] This was Wilson's true intellectual legacy which he passed on to his pupils, some of whom are, of course, the law teachers whom he chastised in his recantation.

For better or worse, social policy in the nineteenth and twentieth centuries has been implemented by legislation. Much of this legislation is regulatory, dealing with such matters as planning, housing, the environment, licensing, education, child maintenance and taxation. Clearly, such legislation purports to implement a wide range of policies, some of which are inevitably conflicting. Yet these vast tracts of law must be accommodated into the Scotish legal system. Moreover, significant areas of private law are essentially the creatures of statute, for example, the sale of goods, partnership, companies, individual and collective labour law, sex and racial discrimination, and consumer credit. One of Wilson's major achievements was to place statutes at the centre of the academic legal curriculum. Again, he saw the need to construct refined intellectual tools to interpret this deluge of legislation; careful analysis was required before a semblance of order could be achieved. In this task, the civilian tradition had little, if any, role to play. And the difficulties remain formidable.

Legislation is also the means by which the recommendations of the Scottish Law Commission for the reform of Scots law are implemented. In reforming the law, the Commission, while carefully considering the solutions in other jurisdictions, endeavours to find the best rule for the perceived social and economic problems the law is attempting to solve. The existing Scots or civilian principle will be jettisoned if that is necessary to provide a better solution. Scots family law has, for example, been radically overhauled and bears little, if any, resemblance to the "system" of rules and principles which regulated family relationships in Scotland for hundreds of years.

The problems raised by statute and well-intentioned law reform can be illustrated by considering sections 4 and 5 of the Law Reform (Miscellaneous Provisions) (Scotland) Act 1985, which implemented the Commission's recommendations on reform of the law on irritancies. By section 4, a landlord cannot irritate a lease for non-payment of rent unless he has give notice to the tenant in accordance with section 4(2). In *C.I.N. Properties Ltd v. Dollar Land (Cumbernauld) Ltd*[18] the landlords irritated a sub-lease for non-timeous payment of rent,

---

[16] One would like to be an angel on the wall to eavesdrop on the Elysian debate between Smith and Wilson on this particular point!

[17] See, *e.g.*, Wilson's analysis of negligence in *Introductory Essays on Scots Law*, (2nd ed. 1984).

[18] 1992 S.L.T. 669.

after having given the requisite notice under section 4(2). As a result, the tenant not only lost its investment of £2.2 million, but the landlords gained possession of the site for 120 years at a rent of £1 per annum. The House of Lords refused to allow the defenders to purge the irritancy. As Lord Keith of Kinkel observed:

> "in the light of the decision in *Dorchester Studios (Glasgow) Ltd. v. Stone*[19] and of the limited reform of the law relating to irritancy clauses concerned with non-payment of monetary obligations in leases which Parliament enacted in s. 4 of the Law Reform (Miscellaneous Provisions) (Scotland) Act 1985, following consideration of the matter by the Scottish Law Commission, it is not open to this House to bring about any more far reaching development of the law in this field than was thought appropriate by Parliament. . . . I am bound to say, however, that I do not regard the result in this case as satisfactory".[20]

While attracted to the possibility of attaching conditions to granting a decree of irritancy under which compensation would be paid to the tenant, if the landlord would receive a substantial benefit from improvements to the subjects brought about by the tenant or his predecessors in title, Lord Keith refused to do so: "Had it not been for Parliament's intervention by s. 4 of the Act of 1985, I should have considered favourably a submission that the law might appropriately be developed on those lines".[21]

This is a remarkable example of judicial inactivism, even where the injustice of the result is readily apparent. Reforming legislation is used as an excuse for failing to reform the law by judicial creativity. In the present writer's view, additional protection for the tenant through the development of common law doctrines would not necessarily have been inconsistent with the statutory protection provided by section 4(2). The need for a theoretical model of the legitimate interaction of the common law and statute is obvious; and this should be a concern of today's Scots academic lawyer.

Section 5 of the Law Reform (Miscellaneous Provisions) (Scotland) Act 1985 raises more conventional issues of statutory interpretation. In short, section 5 provides that a landlord cannot rely on an irritancy clause in respect of a breach, other than a failure to pay rent, "if in all the circumstances a fair and reasonable landlord would not seek so to rely". This provision fell to be construed in *Blythswood Investments (Scotland) Ltd v. Clydesdale Electrical Stores Ltd (in receivership)*.[22] The Lord Ordinary (Cullen) held that the court had to consider what a fair and reasonable landlord would do in the circumstances of the actual landlord in the case. Accordingly, the advantages the landlord would obtain if the irritancy was exercised was a factor to be taken into account:

---

[19] 1975 S.C. (H.L.) 56.
[20] 1992 S.L.T. 669 at p. 671.
[21] *ibid.*, at p. 672.
[22] 1995 S.L.T. 150.

"On any view the object of the language [of section 5] is to import the standard of behaviour which would be expected of a fair and reasonable landlord; and in my view, the provision was correctly interpreted by counsel for the pursuers when he submitted that it involved considering what a fair and reasonable landlord in the position of the actual landlord would have done; and accordingly in what he described as the 'factual matrix' of the particular case. This seems to me to be in accordance with the sense of the section and also is consistent with the tenor of the report by the Scottish Law Commission".[23]

However, while Lord Cullen recognised that this was the inevitable result of the width of the language used in section 5(1), he recognised that there were practical difficulties in dealing with the weight to be attached to such evidence. The court would have the unenviable task of balancing the advantages to the landlord from exercising the irritancy against the losses sustained by the tenant if it were exercised. He was "not wholly confident that it is a result which the Scottish Law Commission had in contemplation".[24]

Not only does this decision illustrate the difficulties of statutory construction faced by the courts, it also serves as an example of well-intentioned law reform changing well-established—if harsh—rules, with unfortunate and unforeseen results. Again there is the need to analyse such developments and attempt to integrate them into the existing law. New over-arching fundamental principles must be found from analysis of the current rules in order to create a coherent, systematic exposition of contemporary Scots law. It is difficult to see the significance of the civilian—or any other—tradition in this process.

Blythswood Investments (Scotland) Ltd is indicative of another trend in modern Scots law, *viz*, the increase in judicial intervention to assess the fairness of contractual terms and the exercise of contractually stipulated remedies. Wilson was sceptical of the consumer lobby. He dismissed the amendment of the Unfair Contract Terms Act 1977 to extend its provisions to non-contractual notices as "an unnecessary concession to the usual hysteria of the consumer movement".[25] For better or worse, it has been decided that the assessment of the fairness of an exemption clause, for example, is a justiciable issue, and if there is to be any certainty in the law, analysis of the relevant weight given by the courts to particular factors in particular contracts is required. In *Knight Machinery Holdings Ltd v. Rennie*,[26] the court was called upon to adjudicate whether a clause which provided that a buyer was deemed to have accepted defective goods unless he had given notice of the defect to the seller within seven days of receipt of the goods, was fair and reasonable for the purposes of the Unfair Contract Terms Act 1977. Since teething problems were common with the machinery

---

[23] 1995 S.L.T. 150 at p. 155.
[24] *ibid.*
[25] "The Importance of Analysis", *op. cit.*, p. 170. See Law Reform (Miscellaneous Provisions) (Scotland) Act 1990, s. 68.
[26] 1995 S.L.T. 167.

bought in this case, an Extra Division of the Court of Session held that it was not reasonable at the time of the contract to expect that it would be practicable for the buyer to give the requisite notice in relation to this type of machine. In rejecting the seller's contention that the clause only demanded that the buyer should inform the seller that he was having problems with the machine, the court held that before it could pass the reasonableness test, the least that could be expected of a term conceived wholly in the interests of its author at the expense of the other party's rights was that its meaning should be clear and unambiguous. But how far can this view be taken? Can an ambiguous clause ever be fair and reasonable? These issues are far removed from traditional civilian jurisprudence, but they are real issues facing Scots lawyers today.

There is, of course, a further dimension to contemporary Scots law, namely European Community law.[27] Wilson was in the vanguard of those who realised the significant impact that E.C. law would eventually have on Scots private law.[28] While recognising that E.C. law can be seen as a distinct normative system, it is increasingly a source of Scots private law. There is therefore the need for Scots lawyers to integrate the E.C.-derived rules and regulations into the existing legal structure.

Two examples must suffice. In the field of product liability, much of the common law, where negligence has to be established before there is delictual liability, has been overtaken by the strict liability regime laid down in Part 1 of the Consumer Protection Act 1987, which purports to implement Product Liability Directive (85/374/E.E.C.). It is expressly enacted in section 1(1) of the 1987 Act that its provisions should be interpreted to comply with the Directive. In spite of the fact that the statute is hideously complex,[29] there is, to the present writer's knowledge, no reported Scottish decision on its interpretation.[30] Given the amount of ink spilt by commentators in analysing the Directive and the 1987 Act, this is surely problematic. Is the reason the practitioner's ignorance of the statute's potential ambit, or the distaste of traditional lawyers in pursuing the interests of the consumer, or the fact that, until recently, E.C. law was not a compulsory part of the legal curriculum?

The Unfair Contract Terms in Consumer Contracts Regulations 1994[31] are intended to implement Directive No. 93/13/E.E.C. on Unfair Terms in Consumer Contracts. The essence of the scheme is to subject terms in consumer contracts—other than terms which constitute the "gist" of the contract, for example, the price of goods or services—to a fairness test, i.e., when "contrary to the requirement of good faith" any term "causes a significant imbalance in the parties' rights and obligations to the detriment of the consumer". Not only will exemption clauses come under judicial scrutiny, but also other

---

[27] See further C. Boch and R. Lane, "European Community Law au Pays du Tartan", *infra*, 254–264.
[28] His first article on the subject appeared in 1962.
[29] For an outline see J. M. Thomson, *Delictual Liability* (1994) at p. 138.
[30] However, it is believed that some cases relying upon the 1987 Act have been settled.
[31] S.I. 1994 No. 3159.

terms such as forfeiture clauses, accelerated payments clauses, and penalty clauses.[32]

The scope of the Regulations is problematic but there is a view that they apply to consumer contracts relating to the sale or lease of heritage.[33] If this were so, then, for example, irritancy clauses would be subject to the fairness criterion. What is clear is that consumer contracts for the provision of financial services are covered by the Regulations, with the consequence that the terms in standard securities can be subject to judicial scrutiny. Thus even in that most indigenous area of Scots law, conveyancing, the winds of E.C. law are blowing: not only must contract lawyers attempt to integrate the Regulations into their exposition of the law of contract, but property lawyers have also to grasp the E.C. nettle.

It has been argued that Scots law has always been adept at accommodating rules and principles transplanted from other legal systems. Today, however, Scots law consists of a vast range of rules derived from a plethora of sources. Traditional Scots legal principles of private law have been overlaid—or undermined—by rules generating from Anglo-American jurisprudence. Legal regimes which govern important socio-economic areas of contemporary life are almost entirely statutory—labour law, company law, even family law. Law reform gathers apace, implemented by statute, earnestly seeking the best rule regardless of its doctrinal genesis. E.C. law has an ever increasing impact—for better or worse—on traditional areas of private law. While Bill Wilson may have been right that, "[a] legal system which has no doctrinal foundation must drift",[34] in the present writer's view the civil law tradition cannot provide such a foundation for contemporary Scots law.

Conclusions

What then is to be done? Before suggesting some possible lines of approach, we must ask ourselves whether "drift" matters. There is no direct link between the *substantive* content of the rules of private law and the Scots sense of national identity. What is important is the continuation of a separate Scottish legal system with its own court structure, procedure and judges. The genesis of the rules applied in the legal system is unimportant—be the rule civilian, English or E.C. in its origins. Scots law can then simply be defined as the law which applies to the geographical area of Scotland and which is enforced in the Scottish courts.[35]

However, this is to be simplistic. The systematisation of legal rules into a coherent, rational structure has for centuries in Western civilisation been a hall-mark of a mature culture. Because of the complexity

---

[32] For an indicative list of potentially unfair clauses see Sched. 3 to the 1994 Regulations.

[33] See J. M. Thomson, "Unfair Contracts: Builders' Missives and Plain Terms", (1995) 40 J.L.S.S. 275.

[34] "Importance of Analysis", *op. cit.*, p. 171.

[35] See J. M. Thomson, "Scots Law, National Identity and the European Union", 1995 Scottish Affairs 25.

of the law in modern societies—often as a result of attempting to implement social and economic policies through legislation which can be an unsuitable tool for social and economic engineering—traditional forms of legal exegesis break down. In the present writer's view, it was Bill Wilson's greatest academic achievement to realise that this was so; hence the kaleidoscopic nature of his interests.[36] When we look at his oeuvre, these interests may appear almost random and unconnected: indeed, he might be considered, at times, a miniaturist. That, of course, is precisely to miss the point. Modern Scots law cannot be systematically expounded as a set of interlocking, internally consistent principles.[37]

Insofar as the general areas of private law are concerned, the law of persons, obligations, property and succession, scholars must accept that the developments in the nineteenth and twentieth centuries constitute contemporary Scots law—warts and all! Attempts must be made to analyse the law as it is, search for new unifying principles and reformulate the law in a new, rational and coherent way. Crucially, the relevant legislation must be taken on board and given the centrality in the exegesis which it deserves. Inevitably, this will result in specialist monographs and articles.[38] The trend towards contextualising areas of the law must continue. Labour law, for example, can be given internal coherence if it is treated in the context of the relationship between capital and labour. Similarly, company law should be expounded in the context of the needs of a modern capitalist economy, environmental law in the context of the elimination of pollution, medical law in the context of medical ethics. These non-legal criteria operate not only to define the limits of the subject being treated but also to provide a basis for informed criticism of the law. In any modern exposition of the law, full account has to be taken of the E.U. and other international dimensions, which must be integrated into the discussion of the substantive law. As hinted above, given the central importance of legislation in modern Scots law, it is essential that more sophisticated—and lucid—work on statutory interpretation, including constitutional law dimensions, is undertaken.

There is, of course, a price to be paid. If Scots law is expounded in this way, there is a danger of failing to see the wood for the trees— how one area of law interlinks with another—and of being unable to appreciate the overall intellectual achievement which is a sophisticated legal system. To some extent, this may be avoided by a more imaginative view of the legal curriculum. Given the recent developments in the law of delict and restitution, it is surely no longer intellectually desirable to teach law students contract, delict and restitution as separate subjects rather than as the constituents of a general course on obligations. If this is done, in one important area of private law,

---

[36] See the range of topics in his Bibliography (*infra*, pp. 284–285) and in *Introductory Essays on Scots Law*.

[37] From this viewpoint D. M. Walker's *Principles of Scottish Private Law*, (4th ed. 1988), must be regarded as a failure, albeit magisterial.

[38] The high quality of many of the volumes published under the auspices of the Scottish Universities Law Institute and some of the major articles in *The Laws of Scotland: Stair Memorial Encyclopedia* is evidence that this process is well under way.

at least, the student will see how the principles and rules "fit" together to form a rational and coherent whole. Nevertheless the problem remains—and it is a real one. The solution is as old as law teaching itself: a course on Roman private law not so much from the point of view of its historical significance for Scots law but rather as providing an overview of a relatively simple legal system which can be seen in the round.[39] In this context, Bill Wilson's recantation was correct. But insofar as he believed that the study of the civilian tradition could still provide the rational foundations of contemporary Scots law, it is hoped that this essay in his honour has shown he was wrong. On that day, Homer did indeed nod.

[39] See further, J. W. Cairns, "Roman Law and the Scottish Legal Curriculum", *infra*, pp. 28–38.

ROMAN LAW AND THE SCOTTISH LEGAL CURRICULUM

John W. Cairns

Professor Wilson remarked in his contribution to the memorial volume for Sir Thomas Smith that:

> "Sir Thomas Smith's great contribution to Scots law was to remind his countrymen of the civilian roots of the Scottish system and of the connections between Scots law and the laws of the other "mixed jurisdictions". It was in these fields that Scots law should seek solutions. However, after Sir Thomas left university teaching, his successors departed from the paths he prescribed. The teaching of Roman law in universities has declined. The Chair of Civil Law in the University of Edinburgh is vacant and will probably remain vacant. Academic discussion of law makes little reference to Civilian principles. . . . This sad decline causes surprises both to Scottish practitioners and foreign lawyers. A legal system which has no doctrinal foundation must drift. It may be under the delusion that it is proceeding in the light of pure reason. The law teachers are to blame, the present writer included."[1]

Those who knew Bill Wilson will recognise many ironies in this oblique and somewhat obscure statement. As Dean, he had in fact had a major hand in ensuring the Chair of Civil Law was left vacant. In a typical spirit of mischief he would occasionally at faculty meetings suddenly attack the teaching of civil law and at least once moved to cut the course in half. The reasons for Wilson's hostility to Roman law are not evident: perhaps having to take the course twice in Glasgow had had an inoculating effect, and the inoculation was only starting to wear off at the end of his life. A man of very warm likes and (more importantly) dislikes, the personalities of some of those involved in teaching civil law may have originally influenced his attitude. The white sheet of repentance seems, however, to have been sincerely worn. In his final years of teaching the class on Scottish legal system, Wilson emphasised to the students the importance of Roman law in the Scottish legal tradition.

In the quotation above, Wilson described Sir Thomas Smith's successors as having departed from the paths he prescribed. There are two ways of interpreting this. He could be referring to those who succeeded Smith as teachers of Scots law, or to those who succeeded Smith as teachers of Roman law. In fact, it is quite evident from the context that Wilson is alluding to the former. The whole point of the

---

[1] W. A. Wilson, "The Importance of Analysis", in D. L. Carey Miller and D. W. Meyers (eds.), *Comparative and Historical Essays in Scots Law* (1992) at p. 171.

repentance and the emphasis of the passage is upon the failure (as he now saw it) of those, including himself, who had rejected and denigrated the civil law tradition in their teaching of Scots law. This is worth stressing because, while occupying the Chair of Civil Law, Sir Thomas Smith had departed from the traditional curriculum for teaching Roman law. Smith frequently restructured the course of civil law during his occupation of the Chair. Rather than Roman law proper, he nonetheless always emphasised study of the modern civilian legal systems, which he considered held important lessons for Scots lawyers. As an obituarist put it, "Smith . . . made a courageous but belated attempt to move the teaching of [civil law] at Scottish universities from the abstract study of ancient Roman rules to the developed principles of the Civil Law, which had entered Scottish Private Law".[2] The success of Smith's approach has been doubted,[3] and it is widely recognised that the professor largely adopted this method because of the nature of the contemporary teaching of Scots law in Edinburgh. It is, however, only fair to say that, as an approach to the teaching of civil law, it undoubtedly exercises a strong attraction for those lawyers who see the traditional teaching of actual Roman law as a somewhat pointless exercise, and who always tend to refer to the teaching of the law of slavery (though actually crucial in understanding Roman law— especially the law of property and obligations) as demonstrating their point.[4] Some go farther and see the traditional Roman law course as positively dangerous. Smith's obituarist thus said that "[i]n retrospect, it is difficult not to share Tom Smith's view that the return to the teaching of undiluted Roman Law has proved even in the short term disastrous, and that the damage done to Scottish legal education is likely to be lasting".[5] The reasons for this are not spelled out, but they must be that teaching civil law in the traditional type of course has promoted the doctrinal drifting that so worried Wilson.

These views seem to raise two issues: first, whether under the term "civil law" one should teach the ancient Roman law or medieval Roman law or the Roman law of the *ius commune*[6]; and secondly, whether one should only teach areas of Roman law that are relevant to modern law. In resolving these issues, discussions over the meaning to be ascribed to the term civil law for the typical first-year course have exercised a strange interpretative fascination for some, who have seen the term as demonstrating that the course on civil law must encompass more than Roman law. This is surely beside the point,

---

[2] Lord Hunter, "Thomas Broun Smith, 1915–88", (1993) 82 Proceedings of the British Academy at p. 461.

[3] See J. O. M. [Lord] Hunter, "Professor Emeritus Sir Thomas Smith, Q.C.—A Personal Appreciation", 1982 JR 5 at p. 10.

[4] See, *e.g.*, *ibid.*, For Smith's own account of what he considered to be important, see T.B. Smith, "Strange Gods: The Crisis of Scots Law as a Civilian System", in T. B. Smith, *Studies Critical and Comparative* (1962), at pp. 87–88. On the importance of the study of slavery for understanding Roman law, see M. I. Finlay, *Ancient Slavery and Modern Ideology* (1980). On the reception of the Roman law of slavery in the modern world, see, *e.g.*, A. Watson, *Slave Law in the Americas* (1989).

[5] Hunter, "Thomas Broun Smith" *op. cit*, p. 461.

[6] In this paper, I shall generally use the term "ancient Roman law" in the sense of the law of Justinian and earlier.

since the usage in Scotland is simply a historical survival. The fact that since 1968 admission to the Faculty of Advocates has required a pass only in the civil law of property and obligations has also been taken to suggest that what ought to be taught is not the ancient Roman law—or at least not all of it—but rather, either civil law in the special-ised sense of the Roman law as received in medieval and early-modern Europe as it has influenced Scots law, or merely those parts of ancient Roman law that were the background to the modern law in those two areas. Thus, the quotation from Wilson's essay honouring Smith's memory introduces us to a debate not only over the import-ance of the teaching of Roman law, but also over what should be taught under that title.

The proper way to teach civil (or Roman) law has recently become a contested issue in Europe generally, especially in Germany and the Netherlands, provoking a heated discussion of the teaching of Roman law in continental Europe. This has taken place in the context of a debate that it is necessary to develop a new European *ius commune*.[7] This new debate has crossed the North Sea, and been interpreted in terms of the earlier controversy over Smith's approach to the teaching of civil law. It has been similarly linked to ideas of the need to develop a new civilian legal culture and a European *ius commune*, although given a somewhat curious local twist because of the position of Scot-land within the United Kingdom.[8] The reasons behind this are com-plex, and require a brief historical and comparative exposition.

From at least the Renaissance, there have been two strains of schol-arship in Roman law. The first emphasised the use of Roman law in everyday practice and developed what was described as the *usus modernus*; the second emphasised the need to have a historical under-standing of Roman law. These two approaches cannot be looked upon as necessarily opposed. If the first was Bartolist and the second Humanist, both regarded Roman law as a living system. The dis-tinction lies in modes of interpretation. Scholars who were more humanistically oriented, such as Gerard Noodt, were by no means unconcerned with legal practice, but rather thought that the historical and textual criticism of legal humanism was necessary to reach the true meaning of the applicable Roman texts. This was important, not only in itself, but also as demonstrating the *ratio juris* underlying the law. The Roman texts were still regarded as authoritative.[9] In the period of the Enlightenment, theories of natural law strongly influ-enced all legal study, including that of Roman law. The nineteenth century saw a number of developments that are not yet entirely understood. On the one hand, the German historical school presided over a revival of historical study of the Roman law, while on the other,

---

[7] See further J. W. G. Blackie and N. R. Whitty, "Scots Law and the New Ius Com-mune", *infra*, pp. 65–81.

[8] A. Rodger, "Roman Law in Practice in Britain", (1993) 12 Rechtshistorisches Journal 261; R. Evans–Jones, "Roman Law in Britain (sic) Scotland", (1994) 13 Rechtshistor-isches Journal 494; R. Evans–Jones, "Civil Law in the Scottish Legal Tradition" in R. Evans–Jones (ed.), *The Civil Law Tradition in Scotland* (1995) at p. 3.

[9] G. C. J. J. van den Bergh, *The Life and Work of Gerard Noodt (1647–1725): Dutch Legal Scholarship Between Humanism and Enlightenment* (1988), at pp. 108–135.

many continental European countries codified their laws, cutting off the direct theoretical relevance of the civil law. In Germany the *usus modernus* inevitably continued, since Roman law was in theory still in force in much of the German lands, but it reached new heights of doctrinal sophistication with the development of the analytical, systematic *Pandektenrecht*. While the *Pandektenrecht* focused on modern use of the *Corpus iuris civilis*, it should not be thought that it was in some form of opposition to a more historical approach to the texts; rather, each reinforced the other, especially since the Pandectist scholars privileged the classical Roman law over the Justinianic and the medieval as being a purer expression of an essentially universal law.[10]

After codification in Germany, the study of Roman law there, as already elsewhere, became primarily a historical exercise, focusing on the ancient law. Very recently this has come to be criticised. The argument has been presented, with varying degrees of forcefulness, that the study of Roman law should focus not on the ancient law, but rather on the Roman law of the pre-codification *ius commune*. This has been given a political twist, by arguing that such study would help foster the scholarly development of a European private law, to which such historical study ought to be directed. The obvious analogy with nineteenth-century Germany makes it no surprise that the most convinced—and convincing—proponents of this approach have been German, although not all have been advocating an essentially historical method to achieve this aim.[11] A review devoted to promoting this end has also recently started publication in that country.[12] So strong has been the model of nineteenth-century Germany, that, in the fashion of Savigny, the (somewhat surprising) call by the European Parliament for a code of European private law has been queried on the grounds that the juristic science required to create such a code has not yet developed adequately.[13] While there have been many

---

[10] See, *e.g.*, K. Zweigert and H. Kötz, *Introduction to Comparative Law* (2nd ed) translated by T. Weir (1992) at pp. 145–146.

[11] See, *e.g.*, H. Coing, "Europäisierung der Rechtswissenschaft", (1990) 43 Neue Juristische Wochenschrift 937; P. Ulmer, "Vom Deutschen zum Europäischen Privatrecht?", (1992) 47 *Juristenzeitung* 1; R. Zimmermann, "Das römisch-kanonische ius commune als Grundlage europäischer Rechtseinheit", (1992) 47 Juristenzeitung, 8; H. Kötz, "Was erwatet die Rechtsvergleichung von der Rechtsgeschichte?", (1992) 47 Juristenzeitung 20. In English, see R. Schulze, "European Legal History—A New Field of Research in Germany", (1992) 13 Journal of Legal History 270; R. Zimmermann, "Roman Law and Comparative Law: The European Perspective", (1995) 16 Journal of Legal History 21.

[12] See "Editorial" (1993) 1 Zeitschrift für Europäisches Privatrecht 1.

[13] *Official Journal of the European Communities 1989*, No. C 158/400; F. Sturm, "Bemühungen um ein einheitliches europäisches Vertragsrecht", (1991) 46 Juristenzeitung 555; W. Tilmann, "Entschließung des Europäischen Parlaments über die Angliechung des Privatrechts der Mitgliedstaaten vom 26.05.1989", (1993) 1 Zeitschrift für Europäisches Privatrecht 613. See R. Zimmermann, "Civil Code or Civil Law? Towards a New European Private Law", (1994) 20 Syracuse Law Journal 217. The Lando Commission has been trying to set out a set of common principles of European contract law which has been seen as a more viable proposition: R. Zimmermann, "Konturen eines Europäischen Vertragsrechts", (1995) 50 Juristenzeitung 477. By a resolution of May 6 1994 the Parliament has again called on the Commission to act towards the preparation of a code: *Official Journal of the European Communities 1994*, No. C 205/518.

programmatic statements about the need to create such a new European *ius commune*,[14] the single most sustained contribution to develop such a literature is Reinhard Zimmermann's magisterial work *The Law of Obligations: Roman Foundations of the Civilian Tradition*, first published in 1990.

It is no surprise that the proponents of such an approach have met considerable opposition on a variety of grounds. The publication of Zimmermann's book brought forth some hostile reviews. Thus, Joachim Rückert has suggested that the book is misconceived as history essentially because it has an anachronistic approach.[15] Another critic has described the work as one of comparative law that potentially threatens the discipline of legal history.[16] More recently Tomasz Giaro has argued that legal history should be an autonomous discipline and that this type of approach threatens the distinction between legal science and legal dogmatics.[17] These remarks seem to derive from an overly prescriptive and narrow view of what is legal history and what is not. That underlying Zimmermann's book there is a programme for modern law surely does not in any way invalidate it. Yet the reaction of critics is none the less instructive. That they feel the book is a threat is important.

What is the problem, and why is it important in considering the role of Roman law in the Scottish legal curriculum? There are obviously two different though related issues—one of research, the other of teaching.

Turning to the first of these, the danger clearly does not lie in this type of research project being objectionable in itself: it clearly is not. Rather, the danger lies in the claims becoming that this is the way legal history *ought* to be studied, and that any other mode of studying it is a waste of time. The argument easily shifts to one that legal history *should* be used to illuminate the modern law. If this position is adopted, then it is obvious that what is being argued for is not legal history, other than in the most old-fashioned "Whig" sense. This kind of argument is very attractive to those modern lawyers who have always been sceptical of the value of the historical study of law other than for unhistorical purely utilitarian purposes. Now one must stress that the most sophisticated proponents of the use of history to help create a modern *ius commune* do not in fact argue against the field of legal history as a study in itself, but their arguments, by suggesting a change of focus, give ammunition to others who are not so well disposed to legal history.

In this context, it is useful to examine Zimmermann's elegant response to the recent dispute over the teaching of Roman law in the

---

[14] *supra*, note 11.
[15] J. Ruckert, "Privatrechtsgeschichte und Traditionsbildung", (1992) 11 Rechtshistorisches Journal 122.
[16] D. Simon, "Zwillingsschwestern und Stammesbrüder oder What is What?", (1992) 11 *Rechtshistorisches Journal* 574.
[17] T. Giaro, "Europäische Privatrechtsgeschichte: Werkzeug der Rechtsvereinheitlichung und Produkt der Kategorienvermengung", (1994) 21 Ius Commune at p. 4. See also T. Giaro, "Zivilistik als Geschichte und Theorie", (1995) 14 Rechtshistorisches Journal 345.

Netherlands mentioned above, here focusing on the remarks he made about research. He points out that, in the past century, the study of Roman law in the ancient world up to the time of Justinian has become a science of great sophistication, which he claims has allowed "Max Kaser to present us with what appears, for the time being, to be an authoritative picture of classical and post-classical Roman law".[18] After Kaser's work, Zimmermann considers study of the ancient Roman law has become much less pressing, although he does concede "that there is, and . . . there has to be classical Roman scholarship after Kaser".[19] What he thinks is much more important is study of Roman law—and also canon law and local laws—in the period from the start of the Reception to the modern era. That we are very ignorant of this is undeniable. That legal history has to be studied comparatively is likewise undeniable. One cannot quarrel with the programme of needed research as set out by Zimmermann.[20] One point, however, has to be made. If such research is to be geared solely towards an anachronistic understanding of the origins and development of our modern law, it becomes of doubtful worth as legal history, and will thus defeat even utilitarian aims, as it will prevent us from understanding the law in context and the influences on it. It must also be stressed that, excellent though Kaser's works may be, the discipline of ancient Roman law continues to develop, change, and progress: it must continue to do so.

In turning to the issue of teaching Roman law, it is helpful to sketch out the dispute over this in the Netherlands. Willem Zwalve argued that "Roman law [was] doomed if it continue[d] to be taught as a purely historical subject". Rather, it should be taught to equip students with a better understanding of the living law. A response by Hans Ankum argued that it was necessary to teach Roman law as an object in itself, and not with the aim of helping illuminate modern law.[21] This debate seems to me to raise very different considerations from that over the priority of different fields of research. Both Ankum and Zwalve relied on Zimmermann's *Law of Obligations* in support of their position. Zimmermann's response, as is obvious from the above, emphasises the necessity for an historical and comparative approach to law, not only to further the development of a new *ius commune*, but, especially in the German context, to allow law students a better understanding of their own law. He nonetheless suggests that teachers should follow their own inclinations in this matter.[22]

The initial university legal curriculum in Scotland consisted of Roman (civil) law and canon law. Canon law dropped away at the Reformation, and shortly thereafter Roman law itself ceased to be

---

[18] R. Zimmermann, "Roman and Comparative Law" *op. cit.*, at p. 27. The reference is to M. Kaser, *Das römische Privatrecht, Erster Abschnitt* (2nd ed. 1971), and *Das römische Privatrecht, Zweiter Abschnitt* (2nd ed. 1975).

[19] R. Zimmermann, "Roman and Comparative Law" *op. cit.*, at p. 27.

[20] *ibid*; at p. 26.

[21] I have drawn on the account in *ibid.*, p. 21. The articles by W. J. Zwalve ("De toekomst van het Romeinse recht", (1993) Ars Aequi 455) and J. A. Ankum ("Stenen voor brood", (1993) Ars Aequi 459) were unavailable to me.

[22] R. Zimmermann, "Roman Law and Comparative Law" *op. cit.*, at p. 27.

taught in any Scottish university, except for a somewhat unclear and attenuated existence in King's College, Aberdeen. The Faculty of Advocates, however, placed a tremendous emphasis on learning in civil law, and, as is well known, intending members of the Faculty commonly studied Roman law abroad.[23] This led the Faculty to press for the creation of effective chairs in civil law in Edinburgh. In 1710 the Chair of Civil Law was established in the University of Edinburgh, to be quickly followed by the creation of one in Glasgow.[24]

In the course of the eighteenth century, the focus of training for admission to the Faculty of Advocates changed. While civil law retained its place, the study of Scots law became more important.[25] In the nineteenth century, after the reforms of the Scottish universities following the Universities (Scotland) Act 1858, with the consequent creation of the new degree of LL.B., the Faculty of Advocates accepted possession of this degree for admission, and modelled the examinations for those not possessing it on those for the degree. Civil law was a required subject for this degree and for admission to the Faculty. In 1968 the Faculty of Advocates spelled out in greater detail its requirements for admission specifying that what was necessary for admission was a pass in the civil law of property and obligations.[26] Of the Scottish universities offering the degree of LL.B., only Aberdeen retains a compulsory course in civil law (though cut to the length of a half course concentrating on property and obligations), while Strathclyde does not teach the subject at all (seemingly a matter of pride to one of its first teachers).[27] From the appointment of James Muirhead to the Chair of Civil Law in Edinburgh in 1862, the civil law course has tended to focus on the ancient Roman law to the time of Justinian in its historical development.[28]

The strongest arguments against this traditional teaching of Roman law in Scotland have been put by Robin Evans-Jones in two closely related papers. Evans-Jones argues that "civilian culture" in Scotland is weak although the Scottish universities have recently had a distinguished history of teaching Roman law. He claims:

---

[23] See, e.g., J. W. Cairns, "The Law, the Advocates and the Universities in Late Sixteenth-Century Scotland", (1994) 73 Scottish Historical Review 171.

[24] See J. W. Cairns, "The Origins of the Glasgow Law School: The Professors of Civil Law, 1714–61", in P. Birks (ed.), The Life of the Law: Proceedings of the Tenth British Legal History Conference Oxford 1991 (1993) at pp. 152–154.

[25] J. W. Cairns, "The Formation of the Scottish Legal Mind in the Eighteenth Century: Themes of Humanism and Enlightenment in the Admission of Advocates", in N. MacCormick and P. Birks (eds.), The Legal Mind: Essays for Tony Honoré (1986) at p. 253.

[26] The Laws of Scotland: Stair Memorial Encyclopaedia, vol 13, paras. 1278–1283 and 1301.

[27] I. P. Miller, "Teaching Law in Britain's First Technological University", 1969 S.L.T. (News) 83 at p. 84 (I owe this reference to Mr Niall R. Whitty).

[28] It is worth pointing out in any case that, even before this, what was taught was an exposition of the law in the Institutes and the Digest: it was not taught as a kind of T. B. Smithian ius commune. Muirhead's importance was in emphasising the historical content of Roman law.

"Many teachers have adopted an exclusively archaeological approach in order to unearth that product of genius, classical Roman law, from the miasmatic *Corpus Iuris Civilis*. In comparison with classical Roman law, Scots law derived from the *ius commune* has often been treated as unworthy of serious attention. Teaching of civil law in the Scottish universities for the last thirty years has been an antiquarian science concerned with the study of a legal system which, albeit unsuited to the modern legal system in many respects, is nevertheless seen by its proponents as intrinsically superior to Scots law."[29].

Elsewhere he has further found the explanation in the fact that "professors of civil law have in the main been English ... [who] have shown only occasional interest in Scots law", a lack of interest which is reinforced by the way "most of the professors adopt the David Daube approach". The result, according to Evans-Jones, is that since these individuals see "classical Roman law as the apogee of achievement ... Scots law derived from the *ius commune* ... has never been seen as anything other than nine pence in the dozen". Evans-Jones goes on thereafter in both papers to present a complex and interesting argument that teaching ancient Roman law has had detrimental effects on Scots law, causing it either to follow English law or inappropriately adopt ancient Roman law, rather than follow the principles of the *ius commune*.

Evans-Jones's arguments that the attitudes and "cultural perceptions"[30] of the teachers of Roman law have led to a devaluing of modern Scots law are unconvincing and certainly exaggerated. First, it is notable how he uses the loaded terms "antiquarian" and "archaeological approach" to describe the traditional mode of teaching Roman law in the Scottish universities, while deploying sarcastically terms such as "apogee" and "product of genius" to describe the classical law of Rome. Secondly, if one in fact reviews the professors of civil law in Scotland from the last war onwards, there is little evidence that they have regarded Roman law as superior to Scots law or denigrated Scots law in any way. All of the three notable Scots who have held chairs of civil law (T. B. Smith, Alan Watson, W. M. Gordon) have researched in Scottish legal history and Scots law rather widely, even though two of them taught Roman law according to the "David Daube approach". Of the three English holders of chairs of civil law in Scotland (about whom such dark hints are made) (J. A. C. Thomas, Peter Stein, Peter Birks), only one (Thomas) devoted no scholarly attention to Scots law, and one (Stein) in fact has made major contributions to Scottish legal history. The other holders of such chairs were, of course, Daube and the Australian Geoffrey MacCormack, who has also written on Scottish legal history. Thirdly, despite Evans-Jones's remarks about the last 30 years, in fact, from 1862 onwards, professors

[29] R. Evans-Jones, "Civil Law in the Scottish Legal Tradition", *op. cit.*, at p. 8 (paragraph break omitted).
[30] R. Evans-Jones, "Civil Law in the Scottish Legal Tradition", *op. cit.*, at p. 8; R. Evans-Jones, "Roman Law in Britain (sic) Scotland", *op. cit.*, at p. 500.

of civil law, at least in Edinburgh, have primarily taught civil law as an "antiquarian science", even if in this century adding some account of Scots law at the end. It is telling that the main student textbook in Scotland was for many years Muirhead's edition of Gaius's *Institutes*.[31] The main difference one can see in the recent past is that in Daube, Stein, Thomas, Watson, Gordon, MacCormack, and Birks the Scottish universities had for the first time scholars of Roman law of the highest quality and international reputation.

Of course, Evans-Jones could claim that his opinion still stands that the teaching of ancient (as distinct from medieval) Roman law has not been a good thing, even if we discard the role of the professors as fifth columnists. Two issues arise from this. What evidence is there that the teaching of Roman Law according to the "David Daube approach" has resulted in the disasters claimed? Secondly, what would Evans-Jones put in its place?

The first of these is easily dealt with. While Evans-Jones has argued elsewhere about the detrimental effect of teaching ancient Roman law, the problem he has identified is surely one with attitudes to Scots law, rather than the fault of the teaching of Roman law.[32] Moreover, the recent strong doctrinal revival in Scots law has happened alongside the continued traditional teaching of ancient Roman law. Obvious examples of this are Kenneth Reid's reconceptualisation of the law of property,[33] and the recent writing on unjust enrichment.[34] Indeed, the very criticisms that Evans-Jones makes identify the problem in the past to have been, not so much the teaching of Roman law, but rather the failure of judges and others to understand Roman law properly and to appreciate the doctrinal history of their own legal system.[35] This undoubtedly reflects the poor and essentially unintellectual nature of legal education this century in Scotland until the reforms creating the modern full-time degree of LL.B. with honours. As legal education has improved, so has doctrinal writing on Scots law.[36] It is also worth recalling the personal importance of the individual professors of civil law in the advance of legal education in Scotland.

Turning to the second question, Evans-Jones is not specific about what he would substitute for the traditional course, although the evident influence of Sir Thomas Smith's approach is instructive.[37] Given

---

[31] J. Muirhead, *The Institutes of Gaius and Rules of Ulpian* (1880, repr. 1895).

[32] See, *e.g.*, R. Evans-Jones, "Unjust Enrichment, Contract and the Third Reception of Roman Law in Scotland" (1993) 109 L.Q.R. 663.

[33] *Stair Memorial Encyclopaedia*, Vol 18 (1993), paras. 1–800.

[34] See, *e.g.*, H. L. MacQueen and W. D. H. Sellar, "Unjust Enrichment in Scots Law", in E. J. H. Schrage (ed.), *Unjust Enrichment: The Comparative Legal History of the Law of Restitution* (1995) at p. 289.

[35] R. Evans-Jones, "Unjust Enrichment, Contract and the Third Reception of Roman Law in Scotland", *supra*; R. Evans-Jones, "The History of the *Actio Quanti Minoris* in Scotland", 1991 J.R. 190.

[36] See K. G. C. Reid, "The Third Profession: The Rise of the Academic Lawyer in Scotland", *infra*, pp. 39–49. See also R. Zimmermann and J. A. Dieckmann, "Das schottische Privatrecht im Spiegel seiner Literatur" (1995) 3 Zeitschrift für Europäisches Privatrecht 898.

[37] On his views of the teaching of Roman law, see Smith, "Strange Gods" *op. cit.*, at pp. 87–88.

timetable constraints, the logic of his argument suggests that he would favour the replacement of the traditional one year (or half-year) course on Roman law with an account of the Roman law of the *ius commune* in Scotland as it potentially affects the development of modern Scots law in the context of a progressively integrating Europe. That such a course would have a value is undeniable. It is arguable whether it would be legal history, but that does not necessarily matter. What must first be addressed is the question of whether or not it is practicable. It is a fair assumption that such a course would have to replace the existing courses in civil law—whether half-year or full-year in extent, whether optional or compulsory—normally taught in the first year of a student's legal education. We would therefore see the effective end of the teaching of Roman law in Scotland, other than as a subject taught as an option in later years. The course would have to cover some background in Roman law and European history to make sense (I am inclined to question whether indeed it could make any sense unless the students had already studied Roman law). There would be a major problem in finding materials from which to teach: one could hardly require the students to read the *Glossa Ordinaria*. One suspects the course would have to be taught from secondary material almost exclusively. Such a course for novice students seems a rather tricky proposition indeed.

It is useful here to enumerate the advantages of the traditional course lasting an entire year on Roman law to the time of Justinian. Students gain a sense of a system of law as a whole (thereby helping counteract the fragmenting effect of the curriculum). They gain a sense of law as an organic and developing discipline. They gain a sense of the influence of politics and economics on law. They gain access to a body of rigorous legal argument which will serve them in good stead for the rest of their studies—it is a course with a high juridical content. They can grasp the development of a legal system from primitive beginnings to high sophistication. The study of Roman law prepares the students for further legal-historical studies and for the study of comparative law. The work of the glossators and commentators is incomprehensible without a knowledge of the ancient Roman law.[38] Furthermore, it has excellent primary sources accessible to students in the *Institutes* of Gaius and Justinian: they can deal with and read the historic material. Moreover, that the course lasts a year allows treatment of the reception in outline, so that students can go on well prepared to deal with the history of Scots law and other historical courses at a more advanced level. Finally, although the regulations of the Faculty of Advocates require a pass only in property and obligations, it is obviously necessary for students to acquire a decent knowledge of the law of persons and actions, as the status of an individual radically affects legal practice, while the law of actions is so central to Roman law that it must be studied. Indeed, simply to teach those aspects of Roman law which are found in the modern legal

---

[38] On the importance of a knowledge of ancient Roman Law in its entirety for the study of legal history and comparative law, see A. Watson, *Roman Law and Comparative Law* (1991).

systems of Europe is a distinctly odd way to approach the subject and one likely to lead to misunderstandings. For example, Zimmermann has shown that to understand the modern rule on redhibition in German law it is necessary to appreciate that the Roman rule arose out of the sale of slaves, while the development of the *ius commune* in this area has to be explained in terms of the existence of pre-Justinianic remedies of both the *ius honorarium* and the *ius civile.*[39]

These advantages are inherent in the traditional type of course on Roman law. It is difficult to see how a course focusing on the law of the *ius commune* could compete. There would be an inevitable tendency for it to focus on "schools" and movements—the topic is too vast otherwise—and the juridical content would inevitably be lost or reduced. Such a course would be useful, however, in advanced classes, when students had mastered Roman law and come to grips with areas of Scots law, so the treatment could be partial. Moreover, the necessity to focus exclusively on secondary sources for teaching could be offset by requirements of research and paper writing. But even in advanced classes problems arise because of the intractable nature of the material, especially when students have no knowledge of Roman law.

It is very easy to identify the project of those in favour of a new *ius commune* with that propounded by Sir Thomas Smith. It has its obvious virtues. But that there should be a return to Smith's approach for the teaching of civil law is far from clear, especially given the history of its doubtful success. It is in this instructive to recall that it was the teachers of Scots law whom Bill Wilson saw as having to don the white sheet, while Reinhard Zimmermann in this respect has also stressed the importance of the teaching in Germany of private law rather than of Roman law.[40] This must be correct. Accepting the premises of the argument not only about the need to develop a new *ius commune*, but also those about the need to prevent doctrinal drifting, what is needed must be to alter the teaching of modern private law. What would then be needed is the traditional course on Roman law to support such teaching and the teaching of legal history. A persuasive case for departing from the traditional course of Roman law based around Justinian's *Institutes* and emphasising an historical understanding of the development of Roman law has yet to be made.[41]

---

[39] R. Zimmermann, *Law of Obligations*, at pp. 322–328.
[40] R. Zimmermann, "Roman and Comparative Law", *op. cit.*, at p 27.
[41] I am grateful to H. L. MacQueen, G. McLeod, K. G. C. Reid, and A. Watson for their comments on earlier drafts.

THE THIRD BRANCH OF THE PROFESSION

The Rise of the Academic Lawyer in Scotland

KENNETH G. C. REID

We live in a golden age. Scots law, as it marches towards the beginning of a new century, moves with head erect and with confident step. The patient, until recently sickly and in rapid decline, has risen up from its bed and is dancing a jig.

Needless to say Bill Wilson would not have put matters quite like that. Wilson's taste in metaphor tended towards the caustic rather than the uplifting. But he would not, I think, have disputed the essential facts. All of a sudden Scots law[1] has become interesting, fashionable, exciting even. Books and articles pour off the printing presses. Our universities flourish. Our students study law intensively and full-time. Quite frequently they take courses at a university in France or Germany or elsewhere in continental Europe under the ERASMUS programme.[2] Foreign scholars visit our shores in large numbers and return home to tell of what they have found. The Court of Session bench, stronger perhaps than at any other time this century, wrestles almost daily with interesting and important issues both in our private and in our public law. To the business of law reform the Scottish Law Commission brings formidable scholarship and a proper conceptual rigour. In the courts and elsewhere legal debate is conducted at a high level of sophistication and refinement.

Of course much still needs to be done. Some serious gaps remain in our literature. We have lost the art of the book review. The casenote, which in England has been such an influential source of dialogue between jurist and judge, is almost unknown in Scotland.[3] We need to know very much more of our past, through a sustained study of doctrinal history, before we are able confidently to chart our future. Insufficient attention is paid to comparative law. In short our initial metaphor may mislead. Perhaps this is only a silver age, and one with occasional lapses in the direction of bronze. But at least it is not the

---

[1] My comments are restricted to Scots law as a body of rules. I am not here concerned with the legal profession or with the mechanics of the legal system.

[2] The ERASMUS programme allows students to obtain credit at their home universities in respect of study at universities in other member states of the E.U.

[3] Wilson regarded the provision of case notes as one of the key duties of the academic lawyer (1982 J.R. 259 at p. 266). But although Wilson produced some outstanding examples of the *genre*, Lord Rodger of Earlsferry is justified in complaining of "the almost complete absence in Scotland of the kind of contemporary detailed analytical case note which is the hallmark of many modern legal journals" (Lord Rodger of Earlsferry, *Savigny in the Strand*, being the inaugural John Maurice Kelly Memorial Lecture, published by University College Dublin (1995), p.14.)

stone age. Viewed from our present lofty position, 1960, the year in which Bill Wilson first entered academic life as a lecturer at Edinburgh University, seems firmly set in the stone age.

A study of the legal press in and around 1960 reveals numerous complaints and anxieties about the then state of Scots law. In the first place, it was said, there were no books. In the second place there was no law, for relatively few cases of legal importance reached the courts and most advocates subsisted on an unwholesome diet of divorce and reparation.[4] And in the third place there were no lawyers. Few students were being attracted to study law and fewer still could then be persuaded to enter practice, particularly in the solicitors' branch of the profession where many legal offices were "old, cramped, dirty and very inadequately supplied with books and modern office equipment".[5] There were fewer solicitors in 1960 than there had been half a century earlier.[6] David Walker in Glasgow and T. B. Smith in Edinburgh thundered in the legal press, warning, in the manner of Old Testament prophets, that only repentance and reform could save Scots law from extinction as a distinctive system. Not everyone cared. An unintended consequence of their rhetoric was a vigorous correspondence in the pages of the *Scots Law Times* on the question of whether Scots law should not, after all, seek assimilation with the law of England. "It seems to me", wrote one correspondent, "that this small country cannot afford in the middle of the twentieth century to have its own legal system."[7]

This bout of introspection and self-criticism proved unexpectedly productive. Two initiatives taken in 1960 have been of enduring importance for the future development of Scots law. These were the introduction of full-time study for the degree of LL.B, and the establishment in February 1960 of the Scottish Universities Law Institute (SULI) for the publication of textbooks on the law of Scotland. The two events were of course connected, and it may be doubted whether the SULI initiative could have succeeded without the expansion of the universities brought about by the full-time degree.

Expansion of the Universities

In Scotland, unlike in England, the tradition was for lawyers to learn their law in the universities. But until 1960 the LL.B was a part-time degree, with classes first thing in the morning and last thing in the

---

[4] C. K. Davidson, "The Scottish Law Commission 1965–95" (1995) 1 S.L.P.Q. 18 at pp. 18–19. A similar picture emerges from Lord Stott, *Lord Advocate's Diary 1961–1966* (1991), and also from the *Faculty Digest* for the period.

[5] D. M. Walker, "The Prospects of the Profession in Scotland", 1960 S.L.T. (News) 97 at p. 98.

[6] 3,259 solicitors took out practising certificates in 1960 compared with 3,412 in 1910. One of the reasons for the recommendation of the Reid Committee in 1963 that registration of title to land be introduced was that there were too few solicitors to handle the existing, labour-intensive system. See Registration of Title to Land in Scotland (1963 Cmnd. 2032), para. 63.

[7] 1960 S.L.T. (News) 28 (H. R. Aylmer). Other letters along similar lines were published at 1960 S.L.T. (News) 35 and 55.

afternoon.[8] In between classes most students worked in law offices as apprentices. The LL.B could be taken only after a preliminary degree in Arts, and students proceeding directly to legal study took the B.L., which was considered to be an inferior qualification. In 1960 the four Scottish universities then teaching law[9] abolished the B.L. degree and prescribed full-time study for the LL.B. The requirement of a prior Arts degree was discontinued. The aim of the reform was ambitious. Under the old system law had been seen largely as a vocational subject, taught to part-time students by staff who were themselves often part-time. Examinations concentrated on rote-learning at the expense of understanding or of evidence of ability to apply the law.[10] The new system, by contrast, insisted that law was an academic discipline and worthy of serious study in its own right. Naturally a serious academic subject required full-time attention from its students. As David Walker explained in 1959:

> "[F]ull-time study is not being introduced so as to give students more time to loaf about the Union. It is being demanded to give them sufficient time, as they have never had hitherto, to read books and articles and cases, to think about them, to discuss them, and it is anticipated that different teaching techniques will be used, demanding more active participation by the students in place of the merely passive attitude many are content to adopt at the present."[11]

It may be taken for granted that this vision of the scholar-student was not realised at once. More than a change in degree regulations was required to effect a fundamental change in academic culture. The old guard, who had taught under the old system, remained at their posts, in some cases for many years to come, and no doubt the new LL.B was of a variable standard. But in the longer term Walker has been amply vindicated.

The introduction of full-time study had an immediate effect on student numbers. In the last year of the part-time LL.B the University of Glasgow admitted 40 undergraduates to study law. In the first year of full-time study it admitted 114. Table 1 shows the total number of undergraduates studying law at Scottish universities in selected years during the period from 1938 to 1991. It will be seen that the figures remained more or less constant until around 1960. There was then a rapid expansion, so that by 1980 there were more than three undergraduates for every one undergraduate 15 years earlier. Since 1980

---

[8] Useful accounts will be found in D. M. Walker, "Legal Education in Scotland", 1988 J.R. 184, and in the same author's *A History of the School of Law: The University of Glasgow* (1990).

[9] Aberdeen, Edinburgh, Glasgow and St Andrews (later Dundee).

[10] For example, writing in 1922 Lord Cooper commented that: "A perusal of the questions set over a period of years discloses a marked tendency to a stereotyped and periodically recurring form of inquiry calculated to elicit as an answer a short extract from the lectures on the subject in question. The more faithful the reproduction, the higher are the marks awarded" (*Selected Papers 1922–1954* (1957), p.7).

[11] D. M. Walker, "The New Glasgow Law Degree", 1959 S.L.T. (News) 121 at p.132.

Table 1

Numbers of undergraduates studying law in Scotland

1938–39	490
1953–54	556
1965–66	1034
1974–75	1588
1980–81	1850
1990–91	2218

Source. Third Survey of University Legal Education in the U.K. by Professor John Wilson, published in (1993) 13 *Legal Studies* 143. The figures are confined to the Universities of Aberdeen, Dundee (formerly St Andrews), Edinburgh, Glasgow, and Strathclyde.

the increases in numbers have been modest. To some extent, of course, these figures parallel what was happening in other academic disciplines, with a rapid growth of universities in the 1960s being followed by a levelling out in the 1980s. By the early 1990s the effect of this long period of expansion, when coupled with the economic recession, meant that the legal profession in Scotland could no longer absorb all the law graduates being produced by its universities.

More students meant more teachers. Table 2 shows the growth in the number of law teachers in Scottish universities between 1938 and 1994. Only full-time academics are included, although in the early period especially many of the teachers were part-time.

The figures cannot be taken entirely at face value. Not every member of a law faculty was (or is) engaged in teaching the law of Scotland, and a small number did not teach positive law at all. Nonetheless the figures are startling. In the mid-1950s, in the last years of the part-time LL.B., there were 40 full-time members of staff in the Scottish law faculties. In 1960–61, the first year of the new degree, there were 57. Twenty years later that number had more than

Table 2

Numbers of full-time law teachers in Scottish universities

1938–39	26
1953–54	40
1960–61	57
1965–66	79
1974–75	108
1980–81	149
1990–91	135
1994–95	190

Sources. University calendars and direct approaches to the universities concerned. The 1994–95 figures include for the first time the University of Abertay, Dundee and Glasgow Caledonian, Heriot-Watt, Napier, Paisley, Robert Gordon's and Stirling Universities.

doubled. A contributory factor was the opening during this period of a new law school at the University of Strathclyde. After about 1980 numbers remained fairly stable. The sudden increase recorded between 1991 and 1994 is due to the conferral of university status on the University of Abertay, Dundee and on Glasgow Caledonian, Napier, Paisley and Robert Gordon's Universities. These institutions all taught some law already, but the change in status led to an expansion of law-teaching and, in some cases, to the introduction of a law degree.

In 1994–95 there were 190 full-time teachers of law in Scotland. But the bare figures do not tell the whole story. Rapid growth in numbers was accompanied by a professionalisation of the law teacher. Put crudely, the part-timer whose energies were expended chiefly in the law office was replaced by the career academic whose life was given up to the academic study of law. Of course that is not to say that career academics did not exist before 1960—or indeed before 1920—or that there are no part-time law teachers today. (There are, some of them very distinguished).[12] But it is the scale of the change which is important; and Wilson's appointment to a full-time university post in 1960 is a convenient symbol of that change. For Wilson was one of the first of the new breed of legal academic, as well as one of the most distinguished. After 1960 Wilson devoted the 34 years which remained to him to the systematic study of the law of Scotland. In his early years he read Stair's *Institutions* on Friday afternoons, because "there didn't seem anything better to do". Rapidly he acquired a mastery of the law which few could approach and none, I think, could better. And through his teaching and his writing he exerted a powerful influence on the development of a number of different areas of Scots law. In this Wilson was typical of the best among his peers, for it is by teaching, and especially by writing, that the new legal academic has made his (or her) mark.

Growth of a Legal Literature

In an important article published in 1960 David Walker surveyed the recent history of legal scholarship in Scotland.[13] Walker pointed to the large number of books written between 1880 and 1918. Since 1918, however, "only half a dozen works of any consequence" had appeared. The legal system was now dying for lack of an up-to-date literature:

> "In 1960 the student or practitioner is worse off than his father in 1914 and in too many cases has still to rely on the same editions of the same book, while on many subjects which are new since

[12] Of course legal practitioners (whether or not associated on a part-time basis with universities) can and do make important contributions to the literature of the law. The *Stair Memorial Encyclopaedia* is a remarkable example of what can be achieved by lawyers who are engaged full-time in practice.

[13] D. M. Walker, "Legal Scholarship in Scotland", 1960 S.L.T. (News) 10.

1880 and even since 1914 there is little or nothing at all. Thus Rankine's *Landownership* of 1909, his *Leases* of 1916, Gloag on *Contract* of 1929, Fraser on *Parent and Child* of 1906, and Dickson on *Evidence* of 1887 have still to be used ... It is clear that unless a great deal of work is done in the next decade on the production of modern Scottish books, students and practitioners of Scots law will be working with hopelessly antiquated and inadequate tools and will inevitably be swamped by English law."[14]

Two obstacles were acknowledged as standing in the way of the revitalisation of legal scholarship. In the first place, no one would write law books; and in the second place no one would buy them once written. Failure to buy (a contributory factor in the failure to write) was felt to be particularly unpardonable:

"It is difficult to resist the conclusion that many practitioners are too ignorant to appreciate the need for books or to know how to use them; or too mean and short-sighted to buy them."[15]

T. B. Smith was (for once) more succinct, observing tartly that "it is easier to buy law books than to write them"[16].

The immediate response to this crisis was the launch in February 1960 of the Scottish Universities Law Institute (SULI) to publish major texts on Scots law. In the first few months 10 books were commissioned: on constitutional law, private international law, parent and child, guardianship and ward, wills and succession, landownership, delict, moveable property, and contract. Initial success was rather mixed. While some of the commissioned books were published relatively quickly (Anton's *Private International Law*, Mitchell's *Constitutional Law*, Walker's *Delict*, and Gordon's *Criminal Law*), others did not appear for very many years by which time the nominated author had sometimes been relieved of his burden (not always willingly). Thus *Contract* (McBryde) did not appear until 1987, *Scottish Land Law* (Gordon) until 1989, *Corporeal Moveables* (Carey Miller) until 1991, and *Parent and Child* (Wilkinson and Norrie) until 1993. We still await a book on succession.

The problem of finding suitable authors remained a serious one, at least in the early years. Practitioners were too busy to write long books[17] and there were insufficient academics with the requisite ability and enthusiasm.[18] But, overall, progress was very rapid indeed. Table 3, which is derived from a search of the computerised library catalogue at Edinburgh University, shows the number of books on Scots

---

[14] 1960 S.L.T. (News) 10 at pp. 12–14.

[15] 1960 S.L.T. (News) 10 at p.14.

[16] T. B. Smith, "The Scottish Universities Law Institute: The First Year", 1961 S.L.T. (News) 97 at p.98. See also (1960) 74 S.L.R. 10.

[17] At least until, like Jack Halliday, they retired. In retirement Halliday wrote his four-volume SULI work on *Conveyancing Law and Practice*.

[18] Even as late on as 1971 T. B. Smith was still complaining that "we are desperately short of experienced authors free to write". See "Authors and Authority", (1972) 12 Journal of the Society of Public Teachers of Law 3 at p. 19.

Table 3

Numbers of books published on Scots Law

1961–65	14
1966–70	10
1971–75	7
1976–80	18
1981–85	22
1986–90	46
1991–95	43

Source. The computerised catalogue at Edinburgh University Library. Two search criteria were used: the word "law" in the title of the book, and any derivation of the root word "Scot" in the subject categorisation. The results of this search were then edited to remove inappropiate books, and also periodicals, pamphlets and government and Scottish Law Commission publications. Second editions were not counted.

For the period before 1961 the best source is L. F. Maxwell and W. H. Maxwell *A Legal Bibliography of the British Commonwealth of Nations* (1957), vol. 5, pp. 1–128.

law published since 1960. Output in the 1960s and 1970s, while a great improvement on the immediately previous decades, was modest enough—24 or 25 books a decade. But in the 1980s 68 books were published, and the trend shows no sign of slowing down in the 1990s. In the last 10 years alone some 87 books have been published.

Of course more does not necessarily mean better. The two great publishing projects of the period, the SULI series and, from 1981 onwards, the *Stair Memorial Encyclopaedia* have not led to work of a uniformly high standard although the best texts, particularly in the SULI series, have been of outstanding quality. Other books have also been of a variable standard. Some are deliberately modest in aim, for example student texts or practitioners' manuals. Others contain little in the way of analysis or speculation and merely summarise the relevant cases and statutes. In more ambitious works an author's enthusiasm and industry have sometimes exceeded his ability and experience.[19] Nonetheless, the transformation since 1960 has been truly astonishing, and amidst the ephemera there is a large and growing body of excellent texts. If Scots law is in good shape today this is largely because there now exists, for the first time for many years, a legal literature sufficient to service the legal system.

The reasons for the change are not hard to find. In the first place, the legal profession today is very much larger than it was in 1960, and the reluctance to buy books (if indeed it ever existed) has been overcome. Secondly, there are now several very active law publishers

[19] As T. B. Smith has observed ("Authors and Authority", *supra* at pp. 20–21), "[I]t is perhaps unfortunate that academic promotion has come to depend so much on evidence of publication—often the fruit of a first research degree or deliberately to accumulate academic 'poundage' . . . In an ideal world one might encourage the jurist to produce ripe fruit in the autumn of his days rather than cull blossom in the spring."

in competition with one another. Commissioning editors are frequently to be found in the legal undergrowth, usually clutching *pro forma* contracts. Finally, there is the contemporaneous expansion of the universities. In the period since 1960 the third branch of the profession has come of age. Legal academics are not only much more numerous than in the past but also more specialised. A university professor may now spend a lifetime researching the law of X, and although specialisation can have disadvantages, it is unavoidable if major treatises are to be produced. Specialisation is particularly important in a legal system where the majority of practitioners remain generalists.

Not Read Till Dead

To be useful books must be read as well as bought. Practitioners, especially those involved in litigation, have always read law books, at least to some extent. But until very recently the Scottish courts adhered to the traditional common law practice of "not read till dead"—that is to say, of not listening to citations of books written by living authors.

Of course it was not always so. For example, George Joseph Bell, who held the chair of Scots law at Edinburgh University, was cited frequently by the courts during his lifetime.[20] The move away from living authors seems to have occurred during the second half of the nineteenth century.[21] However, even in modern times the not read till dead rule was not applied rigidly. Candlish Henderson, who retired from the chair of Scots law at Edinburgh University in 1947, but who did not die until 1964 aged 90, was the author of a distinguished book on *Vesting* (2nd ed; 1938) which was very regularly cited by the courts during his long lifetime.[22] More generally, the rule seems to have been relaxed during the interwar years, only to be revived in the 1950s.[23] Even then, living authors might sometimes be cited where the purpose was to deliver a judicial rebuke.[24] The not read till dead rule was applied with greater vigour in the Division than in the Outer House, and with greater vigour in the Outer House than in the sheriff court. Unexpectedly, perhaps, it had been abandoned altogether in the House of Lords by about 1970.[25]

---

[20] For citations of Bell, see D. M. Walker, *Scottish Jurists* at p. 343.

[21] T. B. Smith "Authors and Authority" *supra* at pp. 10–11.

[22] A Lexis search discloses 45 citations between 1950 and Henderson's death in 1964. Of course it is possible that the courts took his death for granted.

[23] G. W. Wilton, "George Joseph Bell", (1928) 44 S.L.R. 277 at p. 281; H. L. MacQueen, "On 'Gloag on Contract' ", (1986) 54 S.L.G. 6. T. B. Smith "Authors and Authority", p. 6 writes of Lord Cooper that he "held that, if appeal lay from the House of Lords, it was to the editor of the Law Quarterly Review. Citing of living authors and periodic literature was not discouraged in his court. Some present here [in 1972] may live to see a like attitude accepted generally in the future."

[24] As in *MacLeod v. Kerr*, 1965 S.C 253 (T. B. Smith). In reply Smith produced one of his most vigorous and telling articles: see "Error and Transfer of Title", (1967) 12 J.L.S.S. 206.

[25] The House of Lords had turned a "blind eye" to the rule: see Lord Reid, "The Judge as Law Maker", (1972) 12 Journal of the Society of Public Teachers of Law 22.

It is interesting to explore the explanations given for the rule. In an article published in the *Scots Law Times* in 1950 a member of the bar explained that:

> "One may, or rather one must, without intending any disrepect to professors, point out that an expression of opinion in a textbook, unless it is a paraphrase of a leading case, is of far less weight and value than the words of a judge. The gradations in intellectual ability are infinite, and no one in his sober senses would say that a professor of law has the ability of a Master of the Rolls, or a Lord Chief Justice."[26]

Those professors who were not stupid (if indeed any such existed) were too clever by half, and lived in some kind of intellectualised dream-world far removed from the needs and concerns of the rugged practitioner.[27] A different approach was to regard academics as professional—or even as social[28]—inferiors. The hirsute academic with dirty shoes was, more likely than not, a failed practitioner or, worse still, a youth not even professionally qualified to plead before the courts.[29]

The single most common explanation for the rule was that a living author might alter his opinion. Thus a court should not risk attaching weight to what might only be preliminary thoughts, to be superseded later by mature reflection. I have always found this idea difficult to understand. After all, an ill-considered opinion does not become more persuasive merely because its author dies without having had time to see sense and recant, while the second thoughts of an elderly professor are not necessarily better than his first thoughts as a youthful lecturer. It seems obvious that each book, and each part of each book, should be judged only on its merits.

Wilson described the not read till dead rule as being "of the same order of rationality as trial by ordeal",[30] and it seems likely that its true foundations are cultural rather than rational. Scots law is a "mixed" legal system only in its doctrine. From its English neighbour it has acquired a passion for case law, so that the mixed system has come to be powered by a common law engine. For much of its recent history Scots law has complied with the comparatist's cliche which opposes the professors' law of the civil law systems to the judges' law

---

[26] 1950 S.L.T. 1 at p. 2. The writer was C. de B. Murray, who was himself the author of a modest book on *The Law of Wills* (1945). The reference to the *English* judiciary is particularly odd.

[27] The present writer and a colleague were once referred to by a Lord Ordinary as "two individuals whom I understand to be academic lawyers" (*Deutz Engines Ltd v. Terex Ltd*, 1984 S.L.T. 273 at p. 275). As T. B. Smith has noted, on such occasions the word "academic" is being used pejoratively. See Smith, "Authors as Authority", in J. van der Westhuizen *et al* (eds.) *Huldigingsbundel Paul van Warmelo* (1984) at p. 186.

[28] T. B. Smith, "Authors and Authority" at p. 7.

[29] In *Mercantile Credit Co. Ltd v. Townsley*, 1971 S.L.T. (Sh. Ct.) 37 at p. 39 an article written by a member of the current Court of Session bench was described as something "which many may consider to be written in arrogant vein, coming as it does from one who is not (at least yet) qualified to represent another in a Scots court".

[30] W. A. Wilson, "Knowing the Law and Other Things", 1982 J.R. 259 at p. 267.

of the common law systems. Traditionally English law has paid little heed to the professor, and nor, from about 1850 onwards, did the law of Scotland.

In the last few years the not read till dead rule has been quietly dismantled in Scotland. The change was a gradual one and cannot be dated precisely. The beginnings of change may go back as far as the 1970s, when some of the early SULI books first began to be used, in a tentative way, by the courts. However, citation of living authors remained unusual, especially in the Division, until around 1990, but has now become fairly common. A search using the Lexis database shows the overall pattern.[31] Two of the first SULI books were Walker's *Delict* and Anton's *Private International Law*, published in 1966 and 1967 respectively. Although both were cited relatively early on by the Outer House,[32] neither book was cited by the Division until the late 1980s, more than 20 years after first publication.[33] In fact *Delict* was cited by the House of Lords almost 10 years before it was cited by the Division.[34] Much the same pattern can be found in books published during the 1970s. For example, Clive's *Husband and Wife* of 1974 was not cited by the Division until 1993, although it had been used in the Outer House within a year or two of first publication.[35] However, by the second half of the 1980s the position had apparently been transformed. Both McBryde's *Contract* (1987) and Gordon's *Scottish Land Law* (1989) were cited by the Division within months of publication,[36] and for the first time for many years the courts seemed eager to welcome the latest work from the law schools. Of course citation figures say nothing about the use actually made of the works in question, and further research in this area would be instructive. I suspect it would show that, while courts will sometimes give weight to the views of an author and use these views as an aid to reaching the decision,[37] the majority of citations are decorative in character. The typical example is the use of a textbook as a convenient expression of a rule which is in any event well established by the existing authorities.

Interestingly, the change in citation policy has not—or not yet—been at the expense of the older writers. Since its publication in 1987, McBryde's book on *Contract* has been cited on 50 occasions, which is

---

[31] The search was carried out by using the formula "Walker w/6 Delict". No doubt this will not pick up absolutely all citations of the book in question, and a small number of the citations which were picked up turned out to be irrelevant.

[32] Walker in *Travers v. Neilson*, 1967 S.C. 155, and Anton in *Hoy v. Hoy*, 1968 S.L.T. 413.

[33] Walker in *B v. F*, 1987 S.L.T. 681, and Anton in *Armour v. Thyssen Edelstahlwerke A. G.*, 1989 S.L.T. 182.

[34] *Dick v. Burgh of Falkirk*, 1976 S.C.(H.L.) 1.

[35] *Blance v. Blance*, 1978 S.L.T. 74 (Outer House); *Perrin v. Perrin*, 1995 S.L.T. 81 (Inner House).

[36] *Grosvenor Developments (Scotland) p.l.c. v. Argyll Stores Ltd*, 1987 S.L.T. 738 (McBryde); *Upper Crathes Fishings Ltd v. Bailey's Exrs.*, 1991 S.L.T. 747 (Gordon).

[37] e.g., *Morgan Guaranty Trust Co. of New York v. Lothian Regional Council*, 1995 S.L.T. 299; *Sharp v. Thomson*, 1995 S.L.T. 837. *Morgan Guaranty* contains (at p. 311A) the following generous acknowledgement by the Lord President of the work of academic lawyers in the field of unjustified enrichment both in Scotland and in other jurisdictions: "The discussion has been greatly assisted in recent years by the work of academic lawyers, whose detailed research and vigorous criticism has already had a marked influence on debate among the judiciary".

a creditable total; but in the same period Gloag's work on *Contract* (2nd ed; 1929) was cited almost four times as frequently. Similarly Rankine's *Landownership* (4th ed; 1909) is currently being cited more than twice as often as Gordon's *Scottish Land Law*.

The change in the treatment of the work of living authors signals an important change in our legal culture. Here the connection with the rise of the legal academic is obvious. The jurists—finally—wrote the books whereupon the judges read them. In the end the literature was probably too rich to ignore. A parallel development took place in England at much the same time and no doubt influenced the position in Scotland.[38] The change is a welcome one, and not just for professors of law. In a small jurisdiction each branch of the legal profession must play its part to the full, and the jurists—the third branch of the profession—have much to offer to the other branches. The legal academic has the time and the resources to make an exhaustive study of his subject. He is the specialist in a world largely composed of generalists. The best academic work displays a mastery of the source material, both native and foreign, which illumines the law in the chosen field and suggests a framework for its orderly development in the future. In an uncodified system it is the textbooks which must provide the map of the law.

One thing only remains to be explained. Although the first modern textbooks appeared as long ago as the 1960s regular citation by the courts had to wait for a further 20 years. As an explanation for the delay it is surely not fanciful to point out that many of the judges of the 1990s are the law students of the 1960s. Almost one half of today's Court of Session bench obtained law degrees after the watershed year of 1960.[39] Indeed four judges[40] served at one time or another as full-time academics, while others have taught part-time at a university or have also made significant contributions to legal literature. This is perhaps one final legacy of the great changes wrought in 1960.[41]

---

[38] For the position in England, see P. Birks, "Adjudication and Interpretation in the Common Law: a Century of Change", (1994) 14 Legal Studies 156 at pp. 61–71; B. S. Markesinis, "A Matter of Style", (1994) 110 L.Q.R. 607 at pp. 621–623. In a lecture given in 1987 Alan Rodger referred to the "recent tendency" among higher judges in England "to be nice to academics ... which is not shared by their brethren in Scotland and which is probably to be deplored as much as the former tendency to be rude" ("Mrs Donoghue and Alfenus Varus", (1988) 41 Current Legal Problems 1 at p. 16).

[39] However, usually law was a second degree and involved only two years of full-time study. In 15 years' time the bench will be largely composed of judges who took the four-year honours degree, a fact which is likely to strengthen further the bonds between judge and jurist.

[40] Lords Coulsfield, Gill, Dawson, and Rodger of Earlsferry.

[41] The three tables were largely the work of Martin Richardson. I am grateful to him for his care and skill in assembling the information from a variety of different sources. I am also indebted to my colleagues George Gretton and Niall Whitty for commenting on an earlier draft of this paper.

SCOTTISH LEGAL EDUCATION AND THE LEGAL PROFESSION

DAVID EDWARD

Many members of the Scottish legal profession were surprised, opening their *Scotsman* on January 24, 1990, to find a centre-page article by Professor William Wilson entitled *The Death Sentence for Scots Law*. It began:

> "The Law Reform (Miscellaneous Provisions) (Scotland) Bill, presently before parliament, should be titled the Scots Law (Abolition) Bill because that indicates its object and probable effect. Like all such bills, it is a cocktail: on top float a few cherries and bubbles—easier divorce, control of charities, licensing reform—which will no doubt attract most of parliaments's attention.
>
> "Under the surface, however, fulminates a toxic brew which may well prove fatal to the Scottish legal system and to the law of Scotland—the provisions which will alter the structure of the legal profession."

Up to that time, Bill Wilson had not generally been seen as the doughtiest champion of the Scottish profession nor, in particular, of the Faculty of Advocates which, after completing his period of devilling, he decided at the last moment not to join. But there could be no doubt as to the authorship of this scathing philippic. No-one else could have written:

> "It seems surprising that we give an expensive education lasting several years to intending solicitors and advocates to equip them to appear in court, but, apparently, any Tom, Dick or Harry is to be able to come in off the street and give the judges the patter. It is a striking feature of the bill that it pays hardly any attention to legal education or, for that matter, to any other kind of education."

or this:

> "No doubt we would be left with the criminal law intact, as the English would not want to go to Glasgow and if they went would not understand what the witnesses were saying."

Wilson's article received a characteristically robust counterblast in *The Scotsman* a week later from the Solicitor General, Alan Rodger,

Q.C.[1] Perhaps, at the end of the day, honours were even between the two friends and Glasgow LL.Ds-to-be. At any rate, it is happily characteristic of the Scottish legal scene that it was Lord Advocate Rodger who was invited to deliver the first W. A. Wilson Memorial Lecture, beginning with a warm tribute to those special qualities which so endeared Bill Wilson to his students and contemporaries.

The Wilson/Rodger exchange in *The Scotsman* about the future of Scots law reminded the present writer of an earlier exchange between Walter Scott and some of his Whig contemporaries who were enthusiastic for reform. It would not have displeased Wilson to be cast in the role of Scott. Lockhart tells us[2] that Scott was

> "earnest and serious in his belief that the new rulers of the country were disposed to abolish many of its most valuable institutions; and he regarded with special jealousy certain schemes of innovation with respect to the courts of law and the administration of justice, which were set on foot by the Crown Officers for Scotland. At a debate of the Faculty of Advocates on some of these propositions, he made a speech much longer than any he had ever before delivered in that assembly; and several who heard it have assured me that it had a flow and energy of eloquence for which those who knew him best had been quite unprepared.
>
> "When the meeting broke up, he walked across the Mound, on his way to Castle Street, between Mr Jeffrey and another of his reforming friends, who complimented him on the rhetorical powers he had been displaying, and would willingly have treated the subject-matter of the discussion playfully. But his feelings had been moved to an extent far beyond their apprehension: he exclaimed, 'No, no—'tis no laughing matter; little by little, whatever your wishes may be, you will destroy and undermine, until nothing of what makes Scotland Scotland shall remain.' And so saying, he turned round to conceal his agitation—but not until Mr Jeffrey saw tears gushing down his cheek—resting his head until he recovered himself on the wall of the Mound."

Underlying Wilson's *Scotsman* article was the belief that the Scottishness of the legal system lay, not in any special intellectual attributes, but in its availability to the ordinary man who had only to step off the street of any Scottish town to have access to the independent professional help and advice of a solicitor and, if need be, of an advocate. His argument was that continuity of the best traditions of the Scottish profession required the continued protection of monopoly rights—for solicitors in the field of conveyancing,[3] for advocates in rights of audience. Competition theorists and the consumer movement

---

[1] Now Lord Rodger of Earlsferry.
[2] J. G. Lockhart, *Life of Sir Walter Scott* (first published 1837–38), Chap. XV, end.
[3] A monopoly imported from England in the Law Agents and Notaries Public (Scotland) Act 1891; *cf. Aitken v. Kirk* (1876) 3 R. 595, where Lord President Inglis declared himself against such a monopoly, while Lord Deas was in favour of it.

might find this politically incorrect but it was part of "what makes Scotland Scotland".

This point of view was typical of those whose training for the law consisted in an ordinary M.A. completed by the age of 18 or 19, followed by the part-time LL.B. with a concurrent apprenticeship. Like most of his contemporaries, Wilson learned his law mainly by doing it. His pride in the "ordinariness" of the Scottish legal system is illustrated by his choice of an unpretentious monosyllable to describe the subject matter of his lucid restatement of many of its basic principles.[4]

The system of legal education which produced Wilson and many Scots practitioners of the same stamp was in tune with the Scottish legal profession, and with the legal system generally, at the same period. In 1960 they were, in essentials, what they had been since well before the Second World War.

Compared with the law of other countries, Scots substantive law remained static and uncomplicated. *Gloag & Henderson* was more than an "introduction" to the law of Scotland: it contained most of what the average practitioner needed to know. Its first edition of 1927 had been written to replace the 1911 edition of a book of *Principles* first published in 1754. Although the standard textbooks were wildly out of date (the second, 1929, edition of *Gloag on Contract* being amongst the more modern), they were still serviceable because the law had not changed much since they were written.

The conveyancing forms in current use were essentially shorthand versions of those that delighted Jonathan Oldbuck. The law of succession was the old law of most of continental Europe, and was not reformed until 1964 and then only through the determination of Lord Advocate Shearer.[5] Irregular marriage had been abolished[6] but recently enough for the present writer to have called the "blacksmith" from Gretna as a witness of marriage by declaration *de praesenti*.

Carse v. Coppen[7] put paid in 1951 to any harebrained enthusiasm for new forms of security. Trusts could not be varied and trustees' powers of investment, in the absence of express authority in the trust deed, were limited to the "funds" of which Lady Bracknell so greatly approved but which, by 1960, had joined land as something that gives one position and prevents one from keeping it up.[8]

Constitutional law consisted in a theory of the Constitution which was last seen in operation in the aftermath of Crichel Down. Administrative law was the law of local government. *Ridge v. Baldwin*[9] was still to come and rediscovery of the supervisory jurisdiction of the Court of Session lay more than 20 years ahead.

---

[4] *The Law of Scotland Relating to Debt* (1st ed. 1982); (2nd ed. 1991).
[5] The late Lord Avonside.
[6] Marriage (Scotland) Act 1939, brought into force by the Marriage (Scotland) Act 1939 (Commencement) Order 1940.
[7] 1951 S.C. 233.
[8] Oscar Wilde. *The Importance of Being Earnest*, Acts I and IV. As to the "funds" see J. Donohue and R. Berggren (eds.), *Oscar Wilde's The Importance of Being Earnest* (1995), p. 319.
[9] [1964] A.C. 40.

Even in the growth area of personal injury litigation, contributory negligence as a total defence had only disappeared in 1945[10] and the defence of common employment in 1948.[11] The Occupiers Liability (Scotland) Act did not come until 1960.

The structure and procedures of the courts had changed relatively little since well before the turn of the century, and there were few statutory tribunals. The *average* age of both Divisions of the Inner House was over 70 and several judges were over 80. Nonetheless, the Second Division under Lord Justice-Clerk Thomson, with Lord Patrick beside him, was the most impressive court the present writer can remember, not excluding the House of Lords under Lord Reid.

The practising Bar was extremely small—considerably smaller than it had been at the beginning of the nineteenth century. Between 80 and 90 advocates practised almost exclusively in Parliament House, making occasional sorties to public inquiries and, in the case of juniors, to the sheriff court and the High Court circuits. (Two judges sat in Glasgow for one week per month.) There was no legal aid in criminal cases and most accused were represented by junior juniors who were paid travel and living expenses by the Crown.

The Court of Session sat every day except Monday with undefended divorces on Saturday morning. Most cases (appeals, reclaiming motions, proofs or jury trials) took two days, starting on Tuesday or Thursday. Dates for proofs and jury trials were fixed once a month by the Parliament House solicitors playing happy families with counsel's diaries in the Principal Clerk's little kingdom opposite the door to the bench of the High Court. Appeals, reclaiming motions and debates were listed, without prior consultation, in Friday's rolls for the following Tuesday, and in Monday's for the following Thursday.

Instructions frequently had to be passed to other counsel and the rawest junior could be called upon, at less than three days notice, to open an appeal before the Division or a debate in the Outer House. After quite a short time, most of the juniors had appeared with most of the seniors, and before most of the judges.

When defences were lodged, one automatic continuation of 14 days was allowed for adjustment of the pleadings. Thereafter any continuation had to be justified by personal appearance of counsel at the adjustment roll. Leave to amend after closing of the record was granted very grudgingly, if at all.[12] Until the House of Lords insisted on a laxer approach, the rules of pleading were strictly applied and much linguistic ingenuity was devoted, for the pursuer, to guarding against the uncertainties of precognition[13] and, for the defender, to

---

[10] Law Reform (Contributory Negligence) Act 1945.

[11] Law Reform (Personal Injuries) Act 1948.

[12] See, *e.g.*, *Dryburgh v. N.C.B.*, 1962 S.C. 485; *Strachan v. Caledonian Fishselling and Marine Stores Co.*, 1963 S.C. 157.

[13] 'See Lord Justice-Clerk Thomson in *Kerr v. H.M. Advocate*, 1958 J.C. 14 at p. 19. G. G. Stott Q.C. (Lord Stott) was particularly skilled in the art of deceptively simple pleading, being responsible, *e.g.* for the formula "The pursuer lost his footing" to cover all possible variants of "tripped", "slipped" or "stumbled".

taking nice pleas to the relevancy, objections to evidence and motions to withdraw.[14]

Under this dispensation, cases moved fast. In *Strachan*,[15] where the action began in March, a minute of amendment lodged on 27 November was refused because a jury trial had already been fixed for 18 December, all in the same year. The *Harris Tweed* case[16]—apparently the longest Scottish civil proof then on record—was completed, including speeches, in just over 50 court days. Undefended divorces were frequently completed within eight weeks from precognition to decree.

Speed of dispatch was assisted by the absence of photocopiers. Until the appearance, in about 1961, of the Minnesota Minifax, which produced barely legible copies on self-destructing pink paper, productions had to be copied in a darkroom or by a typist who, if lucky, might have an electric typewriter.[17]

The infrastructure of an advocate's practice was minimal. The four advocates' clerks operated from a room about 15 feet square where they shared one coin-operated telephone. Their main function was to fix consultations and arrange for the typing of opinions and, if one was lucky, notes.

Advocates were expected to have "chambers" in the square mile north of Princes Street ("the area"), to which papers could be delivered and where consultations could be held.[18] The majority lived in the area and held consultations in their study. Those who lived outside the area shared consulting rooms, principally at 9 India Street and 25 Heriot Row where the street doors were covered with brass plates. Manuel Kissen, Q.C., was unique in having his own private consulting room in Randolph Cliff.

Few fees were negotiated. For decades, the Faculty had worked on a scale of fees per item of work actually done (summons, defences, adjustment, unopposed motion, opposed motion, debate, proof, jury trial, *etc.*). The scale applied to almost all cases and even opinions, although it was said that, before the War, a really busy senior could command more. During the War, no-one charged more than the scale and this convention continued after the War. In about 1960 junior's fee for drafting a summons or defences was raised to six guineas,

---

[14] J. O. M. Hunter Q.C. (Lord Hunter) and G. C. Emslie Q.C. (Lord President Emslie) were the masters here.

[15] See above, n. 12.

[16] *Argyllshire Weavers Ltd v. A. Macaulay (Tweeds) Ltd*, 1965 S.L.T. 21.

[17] The volume of paperwork at that time can be illustrated by the fact that the writer had two long pockets made in the tails of his advocate's tail-coat: one for papers for the day's motions and the other for the papers for the day's trial, proof or debate.

[18] Parliament House was bolted and barred by 5 p.m. and was thereafter accessible only at the price of being as 'umble as Uriah Heep to Mr Dewar, the resident superintendent. There were in any event only four consulting rooms in the Advocates' Library and none in the Juridical Library in Charlotte Square, which was the only library open after 5 p.m. It was not until the mid-1970s that the empty "Drill Hall" and bookstacks in the basement of the Advocates' Library were refurbished to make it possible for advocates to practice entirely from Parliament House. There were those who opposed that project as extravagant expenditure on facilities which would never be fully used. At least one solicitor threatened not to instruct any counsel who had "chambers" at Parliament House. The threat was not carried out.

senior's fee for the first day of a proof to 45 guineas and junior's to 30 guineas. Brief fees or fees for preparation were almost unknown except in the House of Lords where taxation followed English practice, the brief fee being 150 guineas.

The level of fees did not keep pace with inflation. The old rule had been that the fee was payable with instructions except in "spec." cases[19] where the instructing letter was marked "Fee after taxation". Payment with instructions was impossible under the civil legal aid scheme introduced in 1949 and, for reasons which are not now very clear, the Faculty agreed to accept the words "Fee noted: x guineas", typed at the foot of the letter of instructions, as the equivalent of payment with instructions.[20]

The consequence was that an advocate had virtually no control over the amount of his fee or the time of payment. Indeed, it was rumoured that the cashier of Dundas & Wilson, C. S., had a drawer in which he kept the cheques for counsel, already signed by a partner, until such time as he felt that counsel deserved to be paid.

This arrangement continued until 1971 when Faculty Services Ltd. was established in the teeth of opposition from solicitors and advocates' clerks as well as some influential advocates.[21] The best available information suggested that, at that time, the *total* annual income of the practising Bar (by then about 120 strong) was between £350,000 and £400,000.

Apart from a small portfolio of investments, the Faculty of Advocates, as such, had no regular income except the fees payable by intrants. Until 1966, entry money and associated fees of more than £400 had to be paid in a lump sum on presentation of the petition for admission. As will be seen from the figures quoted above, that was a serious barrier to entry.

A further barrier to entry was that the Faculty required intrants to pass examinations in general scholarship and law. Exemption from the law examinations was given, then as now, on a subject-by-subject basis to those who had passed university degree examinations at LL.B. standard.[22] Exemption from the examination in general scholarship was granted to those who had a Scottish M.A. or an Oxbridge B.A.[23] and, after 1966, to those who had attained first or second class honours in the full-time Scottish LL.B.

The normal preparation for the Scots Bar was the combined M.A., LL.B. degree, which could be achieved in five years[24]. Those who had

---

[19] See X *Insurance Co. v. A and B*, 1936 S.C. 225.
[20] The writer has the impression that this happened when civil legal aid was introduced, but the *Stair Memorial Encyclopaedia*, Vol 13, para. 1293, dates it to 1957.
[21] "Edinburgh people, when they are getting something for nothing, are immensely grateful": Jimmy Maxton speaking at the committee stage of the National Library of Scotland Bill (July 30, 1925).
[22] For an explanation of the difference between the LL.B and B.L. degrees, see D. M. Walker, "Legal Education in Scotland, 1889–1988", 1988 J.R. 184. The examination papers were the same for both degrees, which were differentiated by the pass mark. The writer's impression is that the "LL.B. standard" was 66 per cent and the "B.L. standard" 50 per cent.
[23] An Oxbridge B.A. in law counted as an "arts" degree.
[24] At least one Scottish solicitor still in practice was fully qualified by the age of 21, having gone to university at 16.

taken the B.L. degree had to sit the examination in general scholarship.[25] This requirement was thought to have reached a pitch of absurdity when H.D.B. Morton,[26] who, as litigation partner of Biggart Lumsden[27] had instructed most of the busiest members of the Bar, was subjected to an examination in logic and metaphysics.

The Faculty did not require any form of apprenticeship or practical training. "Devilling" (pupillage) with a practising advocate was a *de facto* requirement only because an intending advocate had to give up full-time paid employment for a year before admission ("the idle year"). Those who did the part-time LL.B. spent their first two years as "Bar apprentices" in solicitors' offices for which they were paid about £70 a year,[28] and devilled during their final year.

It was not until 1968 that the Faculty's Regulations as to intrants were comprehensively revised, abolishing the examination in general scholarship and making compulsory a period of training in a solicitor's office and a period of devilling.[29]

The formal structure of the solicitors' branch of the profession had been substantially changed in 1949 with the creation of the Law Society of Scotland modelled on its much older English counterpart. Previously, the structure of the Scottish profession had been more akin to that of the profession on the continent, albeit with English overlays. The Faculties of Procurators, each with its own Dean, were the equivalent of the local bars of France or Belgium; and the Faculty of Advocates that of the *Ordre des Avocats aux Conseils* in France or the *Ordre des Avocats à la Cour de Cassation* in Belgium.

The Law Society of Scotland was given responsibility for administration of the civil legal aid scheme, the Accounts Rules and the Guarantee Fund, but it was some time before it was recognised, even by solicitors, as speaking for the profession as a whole.[30] Indeed, the idea that either branch of the profession needed to be "represented" by a professional body, whether internally or externally, was altogether novel. Except for those who listened to J. D. B. Mitchell,[31] "Europe" was not relevant, and neither the Faculty nor the Law Society had even heard of the CCBE, or the possibility of cross-frontier practice, until 1970.[32]

---

[25] Special exemptions were given to B.L.s who had served in the war.

[26] Lord Morton of Shuna.

[27] The Glasgow firm where he and Wilson worked together as reparation lawyers during the 1950s. They were close friends.

[28] Bar apprentices with Messrs Simpson & Marwick, W.S., of whom the writer counts himself fortunate to have been one, were not paid but were given a set of *Session Cases*.

[29] See D. A. O. Edward, "Faculty of Advocates: Regulations as to Intrants", 1968 S.L.T. (News) 181.

[30] When the writer was elected Clerk of Faculty in July 1967, he paid a courtesy call on the Secretary of the Law Society, R. B. Lawrie, who later said he had been greatly surprised by this visit since he had had no previous contact with the Clerk of Faculty. When the new system for payment of counsel's fees was being set up in 1970–71, some solicitors claimed that the Law Society, with which the Faculty had negotiated, had no power to commit them.

[31] Not, at that time, including the writer.

[32] Scotland's introduction to the CCBE, on which England had enjoyed observer status for several years, was (like so much else) due to Lord Cameron who put the Clerk of Faculty in touch with Ercole Graziadei, the first President of the CCBE.

Very few solicitors' firms had more than four partners, and there were many sole practitioners. A great many solicitors lived out their lives as qualified assistants since many—perhaps most—partnerships required a capital contribution except from the partners' own sons.

Insofar as there was specialisation outside the four big cities, the choice was essentially between court work (*i.e.* civil litigation, since nearly all criminal work was unpaid and undertaken by court solicitors on the Poors Roll) and conveyancing, wills, executries and the day-to-day work of the law agent and man of business.

The image of the solicitor as law agent ("doer") and man of business corresponded to what most solicitors actually did. One Charlotte Square firm which handled the affairs of a duke was said to be responsible for buying his toothbrushes, and one duke—perhaps the same duke—resigned from the New Club when it amalgamated with the University Club on the ground that "I'm damn'd if I'll dine with my agent".

Some advocates and solicitors worked as legal advisers for central or local government, for nationalised industries or for those few quangos that existed. But most of these bodies instructed solicitors in private practice.[33] The really influential lawyers in the public sector were not legal advisers employed as such, but the county clerks, town clerks and secretaries (*i.e.* chief executives) who were almost invariably solicitors.

In today's terms, the Scottish legal system was unimaginably primitive. But, by and large, it worked and the ordinary Scots man and woman got a reasonably good service. In many respects, lawyers had a greater influence than they do now, not least in ensuring respect for the law on the part of public authorities.

As far as legal education was concerned, if academic folklore is to be believed, it was "utterly unsatisfactory":

> "The timetables were designed to enable students to serve their professional apprenticeships concurrently with their studies, but while this had the slight benefit that students while studying had seen the inside of offices, met clients, handled bundles of titles, drafted pleadings, attended at court offices, stamp office and the like, gone to prisons to take precognitions and so on, their time and attention were divided. The system militated against thorough study, reading cases and periodicals, discussion and thought about their subjects. Study consisted in attending, noting and learning lectures.
>
> "It was unbalanced; even given the existence of a course in Mercantile Law (which overlapped with that on Scots Law) the time devoted to Private Law and Criminal Law was totally inadequate. Three weeks for all contract, three hours for sale, five or six hours for delict, three hours for criminal law; no wonder there were whole tracts of law neglected and important topics never mentioned.... There was far too much reliance on part-time teaching by practitioners.

---

[33] "Contracting out" is nothing new!

"Much of the instruction was mediocre, consisting of little better than dictation of what was in standard books. In most courses one quickly spotted what textbook the lecturer had based his lectures on. It was all geared to producing competent clerks, not to opening students' eyes to what Law was and did, or failed to do, in society, domestically and internationally."[34]

It is true that Professor George Montgomery read to his students each morning at 9 o'clock from a transcript of *Gloag & Henderson*, not forgetting the chapter headings ("Agreements defective in form province of writing"[35] was solemnly announced—without punctuation—as one of the topics for consideration). His warnings against reliance on that invaluable work were greeted with rapture by his class. Many things might have been different if, in 1947, the Faculty of Advocates had elected Hector McKechnie to the Edinburgh Chair of Scots Law. But it should also be recorded that George Montgomery was a kind man who tried to know all his students by name and, in the most unobtrusive way, gave practical help to a number of them.

Intellectually, the pre-1960 system was far from being wholly rotten. In the decade before 1960, David Daube, Peter Stein and J. A. C. Thomas were teaching civil law in Scottish universities, Dewar Gibb and T. B. Smith were teaching Scots law, A. H. Campbell and A. E. Anton, jurisprudence and J. D. B. Mitchell, constitutional law. They and—practitioners though they were—the four professors of conveyancing (Farquhar MacRitchie, A. J. McDonald, G. L. F. Henry and J. M. Halliday) offered more than the reheated porridge of past years. On the bench in that same decade, Lord Reid, Lord President Cooper and Lord Justice-Clerk Thomson, to name but three, were products of what, in all essentials, was the same system. Without practitioners, the Stair Society would not have got off the ground.[36]

There was much good—even inspired—law teaching in Scotland before 1960. Those who want to know what it was like at its best need have gone no further than Bill Wilson's ordinary class, for his teaching belonged, in content and method, far more to the pre-1960 than the post-1960 tradition.

The combination of lectures and apprenticeship was not wholly unsatisfactory either. It is not only in the classroom that students can "have their eyes opened to what law is and does, or fails to do, in society", and it is more than a "slight benefit" for the law student to have experience of the realities of legal practice. Indeed, several of Wilson's *Introductory Essays on Scots Law* were designed to tell the full-time student what he would probably have learned in his first month in a law office.

The reforms of 1960, in the form they took, were possible only at a time when the universities were expanding and money was available

---

[34] D. M. Walker, "Legal Education in Scotland, 1889–1988", 1988 J.R. 184 at pp. 188–189.

[35] Chap. 8 in the 10th ed. (1995).

[36] Leaving aside the considerable contribution of practitioner-scholars like Sheriff P. G. B. McNeill, it is interesting to note that the volume for 1951 (Vol. 14), *Acta Dominorum Concilii et Sessionis, 1532–1533*, was edited by Ian H. Shearer (Lord Avonside).

to recruit full-time staff and provide well-stocked libraries. They would not have been possible now. A particularly unhappy consequence of the way they were carried out was a divorce between the law schools and the practising profession, especially between the University of Edinburgh and Parliament House. Devoted part-time teachers like R. R. Taylor, Q.C.,[37] from whom the writer learned almost all he knows about private international law, were discarded as worthless. The profession, for its part, behaved no better towards the new full-time teachers.

The prevailing atmosphere of mutual suspicion and distrust wasted valuable time and energy during a period of rapid change. It was almost 10 years before the Joint Standing Committee on Legal Education was set up in 1968, following the law teachers' conference at The Burn at Edzell to which the writer, as Clerk of Faculty, was invited to explain the proposed reform of the Faculty's entry regulations.

Succeeding years have had rocky patches, but they have shown what can be achieved: vigorous law schools attracting students from all over the world, a wealth of new law books, the *Stair Memorial Encyclopaedia* almost complete, and a profession incomparably better prepared for practice in a modern world. In spite of the "Scots Law (Abolition) Bill", the Scottish legal system is still operational and is still distinctively Scottish.

But experience also shows that the Scottish is no different from any other legal system in its liability to become stagnant—resistant to change rather than willing and able to meet it. Only the danger is greater in Scotland. John Buchan said in his speech at a dinner for Ramsay Macdonald in November 1931:

"We Scots are a strange folk. We despise incompetence, but we do not greatly admire success. Our sentimental allegiance has usually been given to heroic failures."[38]

In 1996, the Scottish profession is subject to competitive pressures, and the law schools to financial and other constraints, which were unimaginable in 1960. The problem then was how to break out of a circle in which Scotland had no higher ambition for its law schools than that of preparing students for practice in the undeveloped legal system of a branch economy. Today's problem seems rather to be that of reconciling greatly enhanced academic and professional expectations with unprecedented financial and competitive pressures. If the waste of time, talent and energy that characterised the 1960s is to be avoided, it would be as well that the profession and the law schools face this problem together.

Even by continental standards, the Scottish system of legal education and training is now a long one. Students who have been allowed to embark on it feel, not unnaturally, that success in the degree should ensure them a place for the Diploma, that success in

---

[37] Later Sheriff Principal of Tayside, Central and Fife.
[38] Quoted in Andrew Lownie, *John Buchan, the Presbyterian Cavalier* (1995), pp 297–8.

the Diploma should ensure a place as a trainee, and that successful completion of traineeship should ensure a place in the profession. Legitimate or not, these are expectations which neither the law schools nor the profession are any longer in a position to meet, and the system as a whole is perilously dependent on government funding of the four-year degree and the Diploma.

It is true that the law schools now offer a range of options which ought, in theory at least, to prepare the law graduate for a wide variety of possible careers. It is neither necessary nor desirable to provide a place in the Scottish profession for every law graduate. But for the student who wants, as most do, to keep open the option of practice in Scotland, the choice of subjects for study at university is predetermined to a substantial extent by the professional requirements of the Faculty and the Law Society.

Professional bodies have to ensure that intrants to the profession are equipped with the minimum knowledge and competence to be let loose on the public. It does not follow that teaching in the law schools must cover all the detailed legal rules that the intrant is liable to meet with in practice. For one thing, there are too many rules in too many potential areas of practice for any course to cover them all. For another, the rules are quite likely to change, so that today's knowledge may be useless in five years' time. Some degree of selection in the scope of legal education and training is inevitable. This was recognised in 1960 and, broadly speaking, has been accepted ever since.

What has changed is the extent to which acceptance of a selective approach is now possible, not only for the law schools, but also for the profession. It has become an accepted part of the professional scene that practitioners should be able to specialise and to "advertise" their specialist skills. Post-qualifying legal education and distance-learning using modern technology are available to update and fill gaps in knowledge and to introduce the practitioner (and the law teacher) to new fields of law and practice.

Less obvious as yet, but potentially of greater importance, is the consequence of abolishing the "monopoly" rights of the two branches of the profession. So long as members of the public were compelled to address themselves to a solicitor or an advocate for the provision of particular services, the professional bodies were under a corresponding obligation to ensure that their intrants were competent to provide those services. The corollary of the public's right to choose other providers is that the profession is no longer responsible for ensuring universal provision. The theory, at any rate, is that the market will provide.

The professional bodies must, of course, continue to ensure (so far as it has ever been possible to do so) that the public is protected against incompetence and dishonesty on the part of their members. But that should concern the conditions under which lawyers are permitted to practise rather than the qualifications they must have in order to enter the profession at all.

The very length of time taken to qualify in Scotland, combined with difficulties of funding, has now become a deterrent to some who might have chosen the law as a career—particularly those late intrants who might, with encouragement, have contributed wider knowledge or experience to the Scottish legal system.[39] The cynic may say that any deterrent helps to reduce the problem of over-supply of law graduates. But financial barriers to entry are not the less objectionable because they are indirect, and squandering available talent is hardly the best way to ensure the survival of a legal system which, whatever its merits, remains small and vulnerable.

England offers a fast track to the late entrant which Scotland does not. It would be absurd if the requirements of mutual recognition were to produce a situation in which it would be quicker to qualify in England, and thereafter transfer to Scotland, than to qualify in Scotland in the first place.

There are those who say that short courses like the English one-year Common Professional Course are academically disreputable. That is as may be, but the late intrant can be fully qualified in England after three years (as a barrister) or four years (as a solicitor). In Scotland, the late intrant can qualify in less than five years only by foregoing that more intensive, and therefore presumably more formative, study at honours level which the reforms of 1960 were designed to promote. From the point of view of a history, philosophy or chemistry graduate, or of an engineer, surveyor or accountant, is it self-evident that two years' study at ordinary level, taken at a pace suitable for students straight from school, are qualitatively superior to a one-year intensive course designed for the late intrant?

Study at master's level (more intensive than anything contemplated in 1960) and study abroad (almost unimaginable then, except in America) are becoming the norm for young lawyers of talent. We might almost be getting back to the situation in the nineteenth century when Scots lawyers regularly went to study in Germany.[40] But how many "lads o' pairts" without parental support will be able to take advantage of these opportunities in future? Will late intrants be able to contemplate them at all? If they can, will they come back to practise or teach in Scotland?

The progress from ordinary to honours level followed by the Diploma and traineeship or devilling has its own logic. Just as the Scottish approach to teenage education has been to promote a broad range of study at school before specialisation at university, so the approach of the Scottish law schools has been to introduce the student to a broad range of topics before going on to consider any of them in detail. It is sensible, and ultimately more rewarding, to learn some Latin grammar and basic vocabulary before trying to read Latin poetry.

But the question that needs to be considered now is not whether, as a matter of principle, the curricula offered by the law schools progress from the general to the particular, but whether everyone must proceed through the same curriculum at the same speed, especially at the price for late intrants of never reaching the most challenging

[39] The writer can say from personal knowledge that a number of such people are deterred.
[40] See Lord Rodger of Earlsferry, "Scottish Advocates in the Nineteenth Century: the German Connection" (1994) 110 L.Q.R. 563.

part of it. The answer to this question seems to depend on what one expects the curriculum as a whole to achieve.

Leaving aside the view that law should be taught as a social phenomenon, it is conventional to draw the battle-lines between the proponents of "black-letter law" or "rules" and the proponents of "principles". All would probably agree with the late Professor A. H. Campbell that their aim is to teach the student to "think in a lawyer-like way". But some maintain that this should be done by concentrating on legal principles, leaving black-letter law for the Diploma or other courses for practitioners, while others insist that the essence of law teaching consists in the study of legal rules and how they are applied.

In truth, neither approach has ever been wholly valid. There are few, if any, fields of law which have been entirely based on principle or from which principle has been entirely absent. The division of moveable estate between widow's part, bairns' part and dead's part was in one sense a rule and in another a principle. From a social point of view, it said something about the Scots' view of the family and the rights of women which the English did not share. It would all depend on how the student was invited to look at it.

Wilson's suggestion that a greater part of the curriculum should be devoted to statutory interpretation might, at first sight, be thought to argue in favour of the "black letter" or "rule-based" approach. Like most of his suggestions, it was more subtle than that.

It might, it is true, be inferred from the huge volume of treaty texts, legislative texts, regulations and guidelines with which the lawyer is now faced that the law has become more rule-based than it used to be. But it has become so in a highly sophisticated and diverse way. We are in the era of *Pepper v. Hart*[41] and other developments beyond imagining in 1960.

The Scottish Law Commission has just proposed the abolition of "Three Bad Rules in Contract Law",[42] one at least of which—the rule against oral evidence to supplement a written contract—used to be as sacrosanct as any principle of the Ten Commandments. "Good faith" now has a statutory meaning operating alongside whatever meaning it may have had in the common law.[43] Which is the rule and which the principle?

Even in quintessentially "rule-based" fields of law like social security, employment, V.A.T. and company law, which affect widely different sectors of society and of the profession, the conscientious practitioner must now be familiar with quite new techniques of interpretation. They presuppose an understanding of, and a capacity to apply, "principles" of European Community law derived from a variety of legal traditions as well as an awareness of other languages.[44]

---

[41] [1993] A.C. 593.

[42] *Three Bad Rules in Contract Law*, Scot Law. Com. No. 152 (1996).

[43] See reg. 4 of the Unfair Terms in Consumer Contracts Regulations 1994, implementing Art. 3 of Council Directive 93/13/EEC of April 5 1993 on unfair terms in consumer contracts (O.J. 1993 No. L 95/29), and *The Laws of Scotland, Stair Memorial Encyclopaedia*, Vol 11, para. 1129.

[44] See, *e.g.* Case C-449/93 *Rockfon A/S v. Specialarbejderforbundet in Danmark*, judgment of December 7 1995, not yet reported; and, in the House of Lords, *Commissioners of*

If the law is changing fast, so is legal method. It used to be said (perhaps it is still being said) that Scots lawyers argue from principle while English lawyers argue from precedent. Comparison of the weekly parts of the *Scots Law Times* and the *Weekly Law Reports* suggest that the boast is an empty one, the ultimate proof of its emptiness being the speeches in the *Woolwich* case.[45]

What is significant now is not whether we argue from principle or precedent since courts on either side of the Border do both, but a thorough-going change in attitudes to the sources of law and the process of reasoning from them. In 1960 the House of Lords was bound by its own previous decisions. When this changed in 1966,[46] could any teacher or practitioner have foreseen, not simply the result of *Woolwich*, but the authorities that would be cited and the reasoning that would be adopted by the majority?

On an even more fundamental level, there seems to be a growing divergence between those who think the judge should limit his ambitions to applying law made by others (essentially the attitude of the French revolutionaries) and those who believe that the judge is and ought to be a "law-giver" (a vision embodied in the statue of Forbes of Culloden in Parliament House). This has taken on political overtones in relation to the European Courts and, latterly, to judicial review and some of the radical judgments of the House of Lords.

The law student cannot be expected fully to understand this dispute without some sense of history and political science.[47] The practitioner cannot ignore it since it is part of his job to predict for his client how the courts will interpret and apply the law.

It will be in the ability to deploy sophisticated skills in a rapidly changing legal environment that the lawyer of the future will have the edge on the bank, the building society or the accountant. At the very least, the elements of these skills must be available to the client in the high street, in the sheriff court and in statutory tribunals since it is there, far more than in Parliament House, that the new and unexpected problems are going to arise, usually at short notice. They will not be spotted, far less solved, by lawyers whose horizon is limited to yesterday's law.

For the law teacher especially, it is an ever-present dread that he is teaching yesterday's law. He may be doing so because practitioners or their professional bodies have urged him to concentrate on teaching what they regard as "relevant" skills. He may be doing so because people in power insist that the function of the modern university is to produce competent technicians. He may even be doing so in the belief that he is keeping alive "what makes Scotland Scotland".

Bill Wilson saw farther than that. In his own idiosyncratic way he

---

Customs and Excise v. Robert Gordon's College, 1996 S.L.T. 98. For a fuller discussion of this aspect of the problem, see the article in this book by R. C. Lane and C. Boch.

[45] *Woolwich Equitable Building Society v. Inland Revenue Commissioners* [1993] AC 70.

[46] Practice Statement (Judicial Precedent) [1966] 1 W.L.R. 1234.

[47] In the writer's experience of talking to a wide range of student groups, the most penetrating questions are often asked by those who are studying "mixed" degrees involving disciplines other than law, including some of those from the "new" universities.

deployed the philosophical techniques he had learned on Gilmorehill to explore the effect of modern developments on the teaching and practice of law. His insistence on "the importance of analysis" goes to the heart of the problems which this essay has tried, in a rather impressionistic way, to identify.

It is useless, in 1996, to discuss legal education in the simple terms of a conflict between black-letter law or rules on the one hand and principles on the other, or between principle and precedent. The debate cannot be limited to whether particular skills should be taught in the ordinary class, the honours class, the Diploma or not at all. As a framework of discussion, these categories are no longer adequate. They need to be more carefully defined and new avenues explored.

To the question "What solution do you propose?", the writer can only take his cue from Bill Wilson and reply "Let us first, together, analyse what the problem is".

SCOTS LAW AND THE NEW *IUS COMMUNE*

John Blackie and Niall Whitty

Introduction

One late autumn the eye of anyone passing the door to Bill Wilson's room in the Scots Law Department in the Old College at Edinburgh University would have been caught by a notice in his own hand-writing. It stated simply "In S iberia". This was the nearest thing to a sabbatical that he ever took. To those in the know it meant that he was away in Madrid taking part in the work of the Com-mission on European Contract Law, a body whose work took him yearly for some 12 of the last years of his life to a variety of European cities and towns. The placename could be taken either as indicating enthusiasm (South Iberia) or alarm (Siberia). Doubtless both were true. A new *ius commune*[1] presented itself as both Jekyll and Hyde. The two pillars on which the idea stands were, however, overtly recognised by him. It is European/civilian in its origin. It is analytical in its approach. Or as it was put by him the other way round: "But analysis is not everything. The choice of the right legal rule may be more important".[2]

The concept of a new *Ius Commune*

As we point out below, certain practical and political developments have assisted the growth of the idea of a new *ius commune*.[3] How-ever, its strength and importance for us lies not in these things but in its intellectual basis. The term, *ius commune*, when used with reference to the "old" *ius commune*, can have several different mean-ings. All relate to the fact that from the middle ages to the late eighteenth century there developed a legal literature which was

---

[1] The literature on this idea and movement is very extensive indeed, now, and too extensive to be done full justice in an essay of this length. We have concentrated on the most recent work, much of which is in German, and some in other European languages. One of us (Blackie) is alone responsible for the research in and deployment of the German sources.

[2] W. A. Wilson, "The Importance of Analysis", in D. L. Carey Miller and D. W. Meyers (eds), *Comparative and Historical Essays in Scots Law: A Tribute to Professor Sir Thomas Smith QC* (1992) 162 at p. 171. In this essay at least the author made it clear that the "right legal rule" would be (presumptively) a civilian one.

[3] To focus too narrowly on such developments may in fact lead to a use of the phrase *ius commune* in a limited sense as being primarily concerned with creating and apply-ing law to activities that are in their nature "transboundary", important problems as these most certainly are. See *e.g.* the title of an editorial: M. Faure, "*Ius Commune* and Transboundary Environmental Pollution" (1995) 2 Maastricht Journal of Euro-pean and Comparative Law 217.

used by lawyers giving advice, by judges and by legislators which constituted a common core of ideas and attitudes for the whole of Europe: "a juridical 'grammar' so to speak[4] ... ways of thinking about law"[5] So the meaning of the term that is echoed in the idea of a "new" *ius commune* is not that, *e.g.*, which describes the process of filling in gaps in the law when the local system has no rule. Nor is meant a concern with rediscovering and then applying particular rules of Roman law.

The phrase, *ius commune*, may to some suggest (wrongly) that what is being promoted is an antiquarian view of law or a hankering after a golden age when law could be hidden in the decent, and to most people impenetrable, clothing of a classical language. There is, however, no better phrase. It is at one and the same time a convenient shorthand for a reference to a general core of ideas as being relevant to any system of private law and a reminder of a common inheritance in a tradition of thought.

What then is meant by a "core of ideas ... relevant to any system of private law"? It has been put in different ways. In one succinct but quite comprehensive formulation, it is a "common foundation of concepts, principles, traditions of thinking and rules".[6] The essence is, as it was for the "old" *ius commune*, a shared "legal grammar"[7] What is at issue is, therefore, a way of structuring and focusing discourse when considering the elaboration, classification and inter-relation of legal rules within private law. It concentrates on underlying unities, and differences, as a method of throwing light on what the approach of the law really is, or alternatively, should be, whether it be to the structure of a discrete area within private law, or to some specific law reform or to the correct decision by a court in a particular case. It can use the more traditional approach often favoured by comparative lawyers, that of garnering "solutions" to narrow and specific "problems". But it goes wider and deeper than that. There is a close analogy with grammar and language which change and develop over time—even producing different languages—but nonetheless maintain a common core which itself is capable of development.

In private law,[8] as far as Europe is concerned, that common core

---

[4] F. Wieacker, *A History of Private Law in Europe.* (trans. Tony Weir, 1995) at p. 55.
[5] *ibid.* at p. 57.
[6] H. Kötz, "Europäische Juristenausbildung", (1993) 1 Zeitschrift für Europäisches Privatrecht (Z.Eu.P.) 268 at p. 270: "Einheitliches Fundament von Begriffen, Prinzipien, Denktraditionen und Regeln".
[7] A widely used phrase as in R. Zimmermann, "Roman Law and European Legal Unity", in A. S. Hartkamp, M. W. Hesselink, E. H. Hondius, C. E. du Perron and J. B. M. Vranken (eds.), *Towards a European Civil Code* (1994) 65 at p. 69.
[8] This may also be perhaps said of the rules in mercantile law. The relationship between the law merchant and private law remains problematic in Europe. See *e.g.* E. H. Hondius, "Towards a European civil code: General Introduction", *ibid.*, 1 at p. 7. It has on occasion been considered problematic in Scotland: *Pall Mall Trust v. Wilson*, 1948 S.C. 241 *per* Lord President Cooper at p. 243: "A tract of cases ... in which the Courts ... embarked upon the perilous enterprise of mitigating the supposed rigour of the feudal theory by engrafting upon it equitable rules borrowed from the law merchant."

lies in the civilian tradition. As with the relationship of Latin to the Romance languages, it is not the original civil law but the civilian tradition which constitutes the common core. For that common core has continued to exist and evolve even after the period of codification, which, indeed, has been suggested to have been only an "episode"[9] in an ongoing development. Law is, and always has been a developing thing, and it always will be so. To comprehend this properly one looks backwards (legal history), sideways (comparative law) and forwards (legal development and law reform). The doctrinal reason for focusing on the civilian tradition is that it enables one to do these things particularly fruitfully.

The Relationship of the New *Ius Commune* Movement to the English Legal Tradition

Some writing on the idea of a new *ius commune* has sought to link the development of English law historically with the "old" *ius commune*. Part of this has been work to try and show that certain famously distinctive doctrines of English law are, viewed in this way, not really so different, *e.g.* "consideration" in contract law and the idea of *causa* in *ius commune* writings on contract.[10] There is also now a considerable body of evidence for the influence of European ideas in the past on English (and Anglo-American) law.[11] Further, it has not escaped the notice of writers in Europe in this century that American law has influenced European jurisdictions, as a matter both of law reform and of textbook writing.[12] Examples exist, too, of direct influence of English legal ideas.[13] This has prompted the view that "No longer can scholars trying to understand the western legal tradition pretend that it is divided in two hermetically sealed sub traditions; the common law and the civil law."[14] Moreover, the recent occasional references by English judges

---

[9] R. Zimmermann, "Civil Code and Civil Law: The 'Europeanization' of Private Law Within the European Community and the Re-emergence of a European Legal Science", (1994/95) Columbia Journal of European Law 64 at p. 89, noting (at n. 139) that the expression was also used earlier in Th. Mayer-Maly, "Die Wiederkehr von Rechtsfiguren" (1971) Juristenzeitung (JZ) 3. For continuity of the French Civil Code with its past, see J. Gordley, "Myths of the French Civil Code", (1994) 42 Am. J. of Comp. L. 459.

[10] See *e.g.* in particular, R. Zimmermann, "Der europäische Charakter des englischen Rechts. Historische Verbindungen zwischen civil law und common law" (1993) 1 Z.Eu.P. 4.

[11] In particular, M. Reimann (ed.), *The Reception of Continental Ideas in the Common Law World 1820–1920* (1993).

[12] M. Reimann, "Patterns of Reception", *ibid.*, at p. 7.

[13] *e.g.* E. Deutsch, *Haftungsrecht, Allgemeine Lehren* (1976). pp. 7ff; "Die Untersuchung soll dem Vorbild des englischen Rechts folgend nach der Subtraktionsmethode erfolgen" (considering the relationship of the terms "damage" and "interest" to each other). By the "Subtraktionsmethode" is meant the standard analysis as found in Salmond and Heuston, *Law of Torts* (20th ed., 1992) Chap. 2, §2.2.

[14] U. Mattei, "Why the Wind Changed: Intellectual Leadership in Western Law" (1994) 42 Am. J. of Comp. L. 195 at p. 198; J. Gordley, "Common Law and Civil Law: eine überholte Unterscheidung" (1993) 1 Z.Eu.P. 498.

to French and German law[15] have a counterpart in at least one instance where 13 years ago the Bundesgerichtshof in Germany cited American and English decisions in connection with the question of damages for "wrongful life"[16]

There are, however, important differences of style,[17] of angle of approach to problems, and of the use of sources, which the new *ius commune* movement will overlook only at its peril.[18] Its significance for Scotland we consider would rather be diminished than increased by trying to smooth out and water down the differences between civilian legal systems and English law. It is true that historically there was more interaction between the old *ius commune* and English law than has sometimes been stated. But interaction with, and interest in, another legal tradition does not inevitably result in adopting its distinctive styles and ways of thought.[19]

While, thus, it is important to be aware of these distinctions, that does not exclude in certain contexts a proper use of Anglo-American material. One should not cut oneself off from creative and helpful thinking from that source. What is important is to have a coherent and structured understanding as to when that source of material will be helpful. Too often in Scottish decisions where English material has been exploited in the last two centuries, such an understanding has been absent.[20] It is not just our law that requires this structured understanding. Part of that understanding will relate for each legal system

---

[15] Especially *per* Lord Goff of Chieveley in *Maloco v. Littlewoods Organisation*, 1987 S.C. (H.L.) 37 at pp. 76 and 84; *Henderson v. Merrett Syndicates Ltd* [1995] 2 A.C. 145 at p. 184; *White v. Jones* [1995] 2 A.C. 207 at p. 255.

[16] BGHZ 86, 240, 250–251, referred to in Ch. von Bar, "Vereinheitlichung und Angleichung von Deliktsrecht in der EU", (1994) Zeitschrift für Rechtsvergleichung (ZfRV) 221 at p. 231. For an English translation of this case (by K. Lipstein) see B. S. Markesinis, *A Comparative Introduction to the German Law of Torts* (3rd ed., 1994) at p. 124.

[17] See in particular, P. S. Atiyah and R. S. Summers, *Form and Substance in Anglo-American Law* (1987) at pp. 1–2; B. S. Markesinis, "A Question of Style" (1994) 110 L.Q.R. 607; J. E. Levitsky, "The Europeanization of the British Legal Style" (1994) 42 Am. J. of Comp. L. 347 at pp. 379–380.

[18] This is clear even if one is not committed to the view that the different *mentalités* are so far apart that the approach of English lawyers differs "irreducibly" from that of lawyers from other traditions, the view propounded in P. Legrand, "Comparative Legal Studies and Commitment to Theory" (1995) 58 M.L.R. 262 at p. 271 and P. Legrand, "European Legal Systems Are Not Converging" (1996) 45 I.C.L.Q. 52; compare B. S. Markesinis, "Learning from Europe and Learning in Europe", in B. S. Markesinis (ed.), *The Gradual Convergence* (1994) 1 at pp. 30–33.

[19] A. F. Rodger, "Scottish Advocates in the Nineteenth Century—the German Connection" (1994) 110 L.Q.R. 563. Such a result might only be temporary: M. Reimann, *Historische Schule und Common Law. Die deutsche Rechtswissenschaft des 19 Jahrhunderts im amerikanischen Rechtsdenken* (1993) and review of the same by F. Ranieri (1985) 14 Rechtshistorisches Journal (R.J.) 153.

[20] This problem may have its origin in the rather vague principle used in the eighteenth century to justify use of English case law, the idea of all well-governed realms having principles in common. See (in the context of criminal law) J. W. Cairns, "Hamesucken and the Major Premiss in the Libel, 1672–1770; Criminal Law in the Age of Enlightenment", in R. F. Hunter (ed.), *Justice and Crime: Essays in Honour of the Right Honourable The Lord Emslie* (1993) at p. 138. For further factors see J. W. G. Blackie, "The Use of English Case Law by the Court of Session in the Eighteenth Century" (forthcoming).

to the historical background to the establishment and development of its rules.[21] There may also be certain "big" questions, such as increasingly arise in areas where a dominant view exists in the legal culture of Europe.[22] That should be seen then as part of a process of seeking the dominant view or views in the legal culture of the western world, or even the whole world.

At the same time in working out detailed legal rules, there is a need to take account of political and cultural differences, a need which is more apparent in some areas of law than others. It is particularly apparent perhaps in family law,[23] and also to some extent in delict. Awareness of differences, however, should prompt exploration in detail of rules and concepts, especially where they are superficially similar but in fact differ.[24]

The Aims of the New *Ius Commune* Movement

What, then, does this movement aim to achieve? It has in fact several aims, namely:
1. to enable lawyers of each European country to understand their own law better;
2. to ensure coherence and logic;
3. to enable legislators and judges to draw on another accessible source of ideas;
4. to enable practitioners, especially in transnational practice,[25] to advise on a coherent law over a wide range of issues;
5. to avoid the limitations in the work of lawyers and, in particular, law teachers[26] and scholars that have arisen from being confined to the national law; and
6. to educate students to understand the private laws of some of the countries of the European Union.

---

[21] In appropriate contexts Greek and Portuguese decisions make reference to German (and sometimes other continental) material because of the influences in the shaping of some provisions of their codes. (Ch. von Bar (above at n. 16) at p. 230.)

[22] Ch. von Bar, *ibid.*, at p. 231: "herrschende europäische Rechtsansicht".

[23] Although see the movement towards a unified set of family law provisions: D Martiny, "Europäisches Familienrecht—Utopie oder Notwendigkeit?", (1995) Rabels Zeitschrift (RabelsZ) 419.

[24] For criticism of a failure by the European Commission to explore fundamental concepts in delict such as these when formulating directives, see Ch. von Bar (above at n. 16) at pp. 229–230 and for a similar failure to address consistently the meaning of "consumer" see R. Zimmermann, (above at n. 9) at p. 79.

[25] An activity which itself may foster a new *ius commune*. See R. Bakker, "Europeanization v. Provincialism in Legal Education", in B. S. Jackson and D. McGoldrick (eds.), *Legal Visions of the New Europe* (1993) 325 at pp. 339–340.

[26] For a detailed discussion of the issues that arise for the practice of legal education see in particular, G. R. de Groot, "European Education in the 21st Century", in B de Witte and C. Forder (eds.), *The common law of Europe and the future of legal education/ Le droit commun de L'Europe et l'avenir de l'enseignement juridique* (1992) 7; H. Kötz, "A Common Private Law for Europe: Perspectives for the Reform of European Legal Education", *ibid.*, at p. 31; O. Lando, "Teaching a European Code of Contracts", *ibid.*, at p. 223.

The Role of the European Union

The European Union can be a convenient heading under which to focus the question of the europeanisation of private law.[27] Further, the European Union does have certain institutions which can act as a focus for work in this area. The European Parliament in 1989,[28] and again in 1994,[29] has passed resolutions favouring europeanisation including the establishment of a commission to work out priorities. The institutions of the European Union can achieve harmonisation in particular areas.[30] Since Maastricht[31] the cooperation of the different national justice systems in cross-border matters is promoted, a development of at least some significance.[32] Moreover the fundamental freedoms (movement of goods, services and people)[33] could partially justify the creation of a European private law through the case law of the Court of Justice, although its present approach makes this uncertain.[34]

On the other hand there is a danger in focusing on the existence of the European Union as justifying the creation of a new *ius commune*.[35] It limits the concept in a geographically artificial way. It may tie the concept inappropriately to a political programme or programmes.[36] It disregards some wider European groupings.[37] Moreover, the European Union is associated with unwelcome piecemeal legislative harmonisation, and also might paradoxically be tempted to swing to the opposite extreme and engage in inappropriate grandiose attempts at comprehensive codification.[38]

It is difficult to assess how far political developments within the European Union, *e.g.* towards subsidiarity or further integration, will

---

[27] As in the title to R. Zimmermann's article, "Civil Code and Civil Law: the 'Europeanization' of Private Law within the European Community and the Re-emergence of a European Legal Science" (above at n. 9).

[28] Resolution on action to bring into line the private law of the member states (O.J. 1989 C 158/400).

[29] Resolution on the harmonisation of certain sections of the private law of the member states (O.J. 1994 C205/518).

[30] O. Remien, "Denationalisierung des Privatrechts in der Europäischen Union?" (1995) ZfRV at pp. 116–133.

[31] Treaty on European Union, Art. K. 1 (6).

[32] O. Remien (above at n. 30) at pp. 126–127.

[33] See von Wulf-Henning, "Die Freiheiten des EG-Vertrages und das nationale Privatrecht", (1994) 2 Z.Eu.P. 5. For a positive view see W. von Gerven, "The Case-law of the European Court of Justice and National Courts as a contribution to the Europeanisation of Private Law" (1995) 3 European Review of Private Law (Eur. Rev. of Priv. L.) 367.

[34] *Keck*, 24.11.93 discussed in O. Remien (above at n. 30) at pp. 130–132 reported now *sub nom Keck and Mithourd* [1995] 1 C.M.L.R. 101.

[35] The possibility that the European Union may in fact lack the legal competence for this has sometimes, therefore, been seen as desirable, since it avoids the danger of the rigidities that might otherwise emerge and undermine the flexible developments that should occur.

[36] Although there is a strand of thinking in Europe that sees such a programme as desirable because it fosters economic development through free trade etc. (*e.g.* M. Bangemann, "Privatsrechtvergleichung in der EU", (1994) 2 Z.Eu.P. 379).

[37] Taupitz, *Europäische Privatrechtsvereinheitlichung heute und morgen* (1993) at pp. 32 ff; Häberle, *Europäische Rechtskultur* (1994) at pp. 13f.

[38] Although this seems less likely now given the current political climate.

affect the new *ius commune* movement. The literature in Germany reveals both optimistic[39] and pessimistic[40] views.[41]

Is German Law too Dominant?

Probably German literature has been the predominant force in promoting the new *ius commune* movement. It might well be asked, therefore, whether this is not some German movement masquerading under the veil of rational solutions for all. This question does have to be taken seriously. But the answer to it is, No. Certainly aspects of German academic legal culture have played a part in pushing the main German protagonists of a new *ius commune* towards that path. There is in some quarters a background of dissatisfaction with the tendency towards scholastic hair-splitting found in modern German academic literature associated with the elaborating of theories on the basis of the wording of articles in the civil code.[42] Occasionally there is now to be found an article on a point of modern law referring to material in the wider European tradition from before 1900.[43] However, the vast majority of German academic writing continues happily, and doubtless quite fruitfully, without calling on this wider tradition.

In fact other European countries also have a literature seeking to promote a new *ius commune*. There is a whole book[44] and a periodical literature in Dutch.[45] There has been particular interest on the part of some French academics in developments in respect of contract law.[46] There is work in Italian[47] going back many years.[48] There could well

---

[39] M. Bangemann (above at n. 36).

[40] I. E. Schwartz, "Perspektiven der Angleichung des Privatrechts in der Europäischen Gemeinschaft" (1994) 2 Z.Eu.P. 569.

[41] A passage in the current introduction to the paperback edition of the German Civil Code bought by a very large number of first year German law students typically for such a work sits on the fence and expresses the view that one day uniformity ("Vereinheitlichung") in the private law of the European Union will come although only in the "further future" ("ferner Zukunft"). Against that background the recommendation is that one should pursue work "now on a European level, and now on a national level": see H. Köhler, *Einführung zum Beck-Texte im dtv Auflage, BGB* (37th ed., 1995).

[42] *e.g.* R. Zimmermann and J. du Plessis, "Basic Features of the German Law of Unjustified Enrichment", [1994] R.L.R. 14 at p. 43.

[43] G. Dolezalek, "Plädoyer für Einschränkung des §950 BGB", (1995) 195 Archiv für die civilistische Praxis (AcP) 392.

[44] E. H. Hondius, *Naar een Europees Burgelijk Recht* (1993).

[45] For references see E. H. Hondius, *Preadviezen, uitgebracht voor de Vereniging voor Europees Recht* (1993), cited in O. Remien (n. 30 above) at p. 116, n. 7.

[46] *e.g.* G. Gandolfi, "Pour une code européen des contrats", (1992) Revue trimestrielle de droit civil 707; D. Tallon, "Vers un droit européen du contrat?", in B. Teyssié (ed.), *Mélanges offerts à André Colemer* (1993) at pp. 485–494. Bill Wilson's interests in European languages did not stop at Germany. On one occasion he related, having returned from a meeting discussing European contract law, that he had unfortunately failed to grasp the significance of the words "votre chardon" barked at him by a French professor when discussing the question of implied terms in contracts.

[47] *e.g.* G. Gandolfi, "L'Unificazione del diritto dei contratti in Europa: mediante o sense lei legge?", (1993) 39 Riv. dir. civ. II at p. 149 cited by O. Remien (above at n. 30).

[48] *e.g.* Natalino Irti, "L'età della decodifcazione" (1978) 4 *Diritto e società* 613.

be literature elsewhere which we have not identified.[49] It may be that French legal literature, which is in turn generally more influential than the work of smaller countries, is less influential than German at present. It may be, too, that the influence of American law in Europe is about to decline at least somewhat. These trends may have a link with politics and power but also with the degree to which German legal writing has become outward-looking.[50]

Apart from such considerations, however, there are a number of reasons why German work has been the dominant force in promoting the new *ius commune* movement. First, Germany has for long been the dominant centre outside the United States for the study of comparative law.[51] Secondly, Germany has financially and physically the largest system of higher education outside the United States. Thirdly, many German writers write also in English to give their ideas wider currency.[52] Fourthly, the influence of German lawyers on work in the United States has been very considerable in this century, especially through refugees from Hitler's Germany.[53] There has recently in academic literature been a considerable regorging[54] back across the Atlantic of that river of ideas which arose on the austere German hillside, and which in the meantime has been augmented by Anglo-American tributaries.[55] Some German refugee scholars engaged in the task of seeking to identify common principles and rules which should be valid in every rational legal system. It has recently been argued that "consciously or unconsciously" the new *ius commune* movement is an outgrowth of that work.[56] In fact the new *ius commune* movement actually rejects such grand designs. It seeks rather to recognise the distinc-

---

[49] We have identified much literature that we have not been able to cite in this essay.
[50] See for a stimulating discussion and a useful citation of literature on this type of issue more generally in the development of law in modern times, U. Mattei, "Why the Wind Changed: Intellectual Leadership in Western Law", (1994) 42 Am. J. of Comp. L. 195.
[51] K. Zweigert and H. Kötz (trans. T. Weir), *Introduction to Comparative Law*, (2nd ed. 1992). The first edition appeared in German in 1971 and from its publication in English (trans. T. Weir) in 1977 has been *the* book for any one in the United Kingdom interested in comparative law. Professor Kötz was one of the first to raise the idea of a new *ius commune* and has continued to write frequently on the topic (see *e.g.* n. 6 above).
[52] As in the examples cited in this essay: R. Zimmermann (above and below at nn. 7, 8, 42, 69 and 98), H. Kötz (above at n. 26), P. C. Müller-Graf (below at n. 59) and M. Reimann (below at n. 71).
[53] See in general M. Lutter, E. C. Stiefel and M. H. Höflich (eds.), *Der Einfluß Deutscher Emigranten auf die Rechtsentwicklungen in den USA und in Deutschland* (1993).
[54] Helped along by academic enthusiasm for "legal transplants" (the important concept first developed in A. Watson, *Legal Transplants* (1974; 2nd ed., 1993), and now "legal formants" (the consideration of the particular forces that result in transplants) (R. Sacco, *Introduzzione al diritto comparato* (5th ed., 1992), discussed in U. Mattei (above at nn. 14 and 50); A Watson, "From Legal Transplants to Legal Formants", (1995) 43 Am. J. of Comp. L. 469 and W. Ewald, "Comparative Jurisprudence (II): The Logic of Legal Transplants" (1995) 43 Am. J. of Comp. L. 489.
[55] R. Buxbaum, "Rudolph B Schlesinger—A Tribute" (1995) 43 Am. J. of Comp. L. 317.
[56] R. Buxbaum's description of the new *ius commune* movement as being one "to find and develop a unitary European private law" suggests, however, wrongly, that the idea of a new *ius commune* is about developing fixed rules to be held in common.

tive traditions of legal systems within a common (European) inheritance.

Methods

The further development of the new *ius commune* movement hinges on what are the priorities amongst its aims and, consequentially, on what are the best tools for achieving those priorities. Such words as "harmonisation" or "unification" used in the literature are, we consider, dangerous. They may give the wrong impression that in the longer term the method to be adopted is codification on a European basis.[57] For us the aim that takes first priority is that of promoting a better understanding and development of our law. This suggests that the first essential is the creation of a legal literature drawing on European materials, which would work on the larger corpus of case law and legislative material from Europe as its prime source.[58] Codification, because of its tendency to delay and distort legal evolution, does not fit well with the idea of a new *ius commune*. A developing literature would better serve evolutionary development of law, while at the same time allowing for variety. Any formulation of rules will, then, best be in the form of "Restatements".[59]

Criticisms of the new *Ius Commune* Movement

Some criticisms are quickly answered. Some concern the effect of the idea of a new *ius commune* on the study of legal history, which is not our concern here.[60] Some proceed on incorrect assumptions, such as that the movement means by *ius commune* a total unity of specific legal rules[61] or that it proposes to look at everything always through the

---

[57] It is unfortunate that the title of one of the few collections of writing in English on the idea of a new *ius commune* is *Towards a European Civil Code* (above at n. 7), although many of the contributors consider codification undesirable and some consider it not feasible, even if they think it theoretically desirable.

[58] See in particular W. von Gerven, "Court decisions, general principles and legal concepts: ingredients of a common law of Europe", in B. de Witte and C. Forder (eds.), *The common law of Europe and the future of legal education/Le droit commun de L'Europe et l'avenir de l'enseignement juridique* (1992) at p. 339.

[59] For a discussion of the matter in English, see P. C. Müller-Graf, "Private Law Unification by Means other than of Codification", in A. S. Hartkamp, M. W. Hesselink, E. H. Hondius, C. E. du Perron and J. B. M. Vranken (eds.), *Towards a European Civil Code* (1994), Chap. 2.

[60] A group of critics centred in Germany argue that the idea of a new *ius commune* distorts the study of legal history in Europe. See in particular: D. Simon, "Römisches Europarecht" (1993) 12 R.J. 315; R. M. Kiesow, "Würzelmänner" (1993) 12 R.J. 637; K. Moriya, "A und B, Über den Berner Rechtshistorikertag", (1995) 14 R.J. at pp. 413–419.

[61] *e.g.* W. Brauneder, "Europäisches Privatrecht—aber was ist es?" (1993) 15 Zeitschrift für neuere Rechtsgeschichte (Z.N.R.) p. 225.

same spectacles.[62] A further criticism is that we are too tied up with
the economy of England.[63] But so are we tied up with the economies
of Europe and the world. Yet another is that continental material is
too logical for us.[64]

But there are more challenging criticisms, too. The most challenging
is that it cannot help us where help is really most needed, that is in
working out the details of law.[65] Any lawyer must recognise the truth
that whatever other problems there may be, undoubtedly "the devil
is in the detail".[66] Yet it does not follow that a movement that so far
has been dominated by a focus on rather broad ideas cannot move
on to concern itself with detail.[67] To a significant extent this has
already begun.[68] While in Scotland the movement's currently most
typical manifestation is in work on a core area of private law where
even the broadest classifications are not yet fixed, that is the law of
unjustified enrichment, that does not mean that in such an area, and
in others, it will not in the future have much to offer at the level of
"fine tuning".[69] Those with an interest in investigating other legal systems have generally started to become much more aware of the limitations that arise from disregarding detail.[70] Supporters of the new *ius
commune* are aware of the need to avoid this trap.[71]

There remain, though, two further practical challenges to be faced.
The first is the language problem.[72] In today's law, development at a
detailed level will often be effected through our case law. It is, it must

---

[62] P. Caroni, "Der Schiffbruch der Geschichtlichkeit Anmerkungen zum Neo-
    Pandektismus" (1994) 16 Z.N.R. 85 at p. 93.
[63] A. D. M Forte, "A Great Future Behind it? Scottish Commercial Law and the Mil-
    lenium", (1994) 2 Eur. Rev. of Priv. L. 375.
[64] *i.e.* the idea that a legal idea developed in Europe is too logical for us as pragmatic
    people; *e.g.* Sir Frederick Lawton, changes to the courts-martial system should be
    "based on the experience of those who have to work it, not on the reasoning of
    continental lawyers" (letter to *The Times*, December 28, 1995, referred to in a letter
    in response by Professor P. Rowe, *The Times*, January 1, 1996, supporting the conti-
    nental ideas by reference to a Canadian case, *R. v. Généraux* (1993) 88 D.L.R. (4th)
    110.
[65] Lord Rodger of Earlsferry, "Savigny in the Strand", (1993–5) 28–30 Irish Jurist 1 at
    p. 19.
[66] *ibid.*, at p. 16.
[67] A visit to any of the less frequently visited parts of *Morison's Dictionary* will immedi-
    ately show that the old *ius commune* was used for detailed questions, even procedural
    ones. See *e.g. Blackwood v. Earl of Sutherland* (1701–1703) Mor. 1793–arrestment of sums
    due when common debtor furth of the jurisdiction.
[68] As a result some writers who were initially very sceptical of the new *ius commune*
    movement have become to some extent supporters. Compare Ch. von Bar, *Internation-
    ales Privatrecht 1, Allgemeine Lehren* (1987), §2,83 and §2,92 with Ch. von Bar (above
    at n. 16).
[69] A phrase used on occasion *e.g.* by Lord Denning.
[70] This awareness is not confined to those interested only in private law. See *e.g.*
    R. Dehousse, "Comparing National and EC Law: The Problem of Level of Analysis"
    (1994) 42 Am. J. of Comp. L. 761 at pp. 762–767.
[71] M. Reimann, "Patterns of Reception", in M Reimann (ed.) (above at n. 11) at p. 17.
[72] It is notable, *e.g.*, that no British book on products liability seems to exploit the case
    law that has emerged in other E.U. countries on products liability, in all of which
    the law is based on the same E.C. Directive as Pt I of the Consumer Protection Act
    1987, on which there are no cases reported whatsover. (See M. v. Delft-Baas, "Is the
    producer of children's tea under a duty to warn?", (1995) 3 Eur. Rev. of Priv. L. 95).

be admitted, quite unrealistic to expect lawyers to cite, and judges to digest, decisions from other jurisdictions in foreign languages.[73] This will be so even when computerised databases sit on every lawyer's desk. The second practical problem is finding the materials. Full text computerised materials, whether by way of the Internet or C.D. Roms, may in the future go a significant way to easing this difficulty. However, for the present there is an acute problem. Quite a lot of German and French material can be found in Scotland, but not much else. There is no library in England, either, that contains for example, up-to-the-minute material on Spanish or Portuguese private law. Even in very well-resourced Germany it may be speculated that not much current Scottish or, for example, Greek case law is accessible to many.[74] These are real pragmatic problems.

Even if more material becomes available in English, at best that would be only a partial solution. As such, too, it would not in fact always be welcome. Variety is riches in a legal culture.[75] From it comes creativity within the wider framework of common traditions of thinking. Much of the richness of European legal material arises precisely because there are different languages. Would one be able to focus the debate about the relationship between contract and delict so well if it were not that one jurisdiction had come up with a phrase for one approach, the French phrase "non cumul",[76] or be able to focus the issue of the property consequences of invalid contracts so well without the help of the German, "Abstraktionsprinzip"[77] or the law of remoteness and legal causation without the English "commonsense"?[78] All three are untranslatable into anything shorter than a full sentence in the other languages.

The solution to the practical problems depends on the deployment of resources, and in the Scottish context, that means resources to help

---

[73] One has to go back some way to find a Scottish judge actually asking to have contemporary foreign language sources cited to him (*Ross v. Governors of George Heriot's Hospital*, June 6, 1815 F.C. *per* Lord Meadowbank at pp. 409–410 (discussed in J. W. G. Blackie, "Stair's Later Reputation as a Jurist", in D. M. Walker (ed.), *Stair Tercentenary Studies* (1981) 207 at p. 209)). For the self-asserted modern language skills, non-skills and pretended skills of House of Lords and English Court of Appeal judges in more recent times see *James Buchanan and Co. Ltd v. Babco Forwarding and Shipping (U.K.) Ltd* [1978] A.C. 141 (skill in the case of one apparently not faltering at Dutch (*per* Lord Wilberforce at p. 154: 22 dan van vervoerkosten") and *Fothergill v. Monarch Airlines Ltd* [1981] A.C. 251 (for a modest but not overcautious assessment by a Scot (*per* Lord Fraser at p. 286)).

[74] "Wer ausserhalb Schottlands liest die Scots Law Times, welcher Nichtgrieche Nomikon Vima?" (O. Remien (above at n. 30) at p. 125). But even some who are not regular visitors to Scotland do (at least Ch. von Bar at p. 223 (n. 22) reference to C. Boch and R. Lane, "A New Remedy in Scots Law", 1992 S.L.T. (News) 145).

[75] This is recognised on the continent, too. *e.g.* "Die Pluralität der nationalen Rechte ist ein Teil der Identität der europäischen Rechtskultur", P Haeberle, *Europäische Rechtskultur. Versuch einer Annäherung in zwölf Schritten* (1994) at p. 27.

[76] Focusing the debate of course is not the same thing as coming to a conclusion: see *Henderson v. Merrett Syndicates Ltd* [1995] 2 A.C. 145 *per* Lord Goff of Chieveley at p. 184.

[77] *The Laws of Scotland: Stair Memorial Encyclopaedia*, Vol 18 (1993) paras. 606–618 (K. G. C. Reid).

[78] *Admiralty Commissioners v. Owners of SS Volute* [1922] 1 A.C. 129 *per* Lord Birkenhead L.C. at 144.

lawyers and the courts. Two organs suggest themselves, namely: bodies directly funded by the government[79] and university law faculties. The manpower is already stretched. But it may be that over the next twenty years academics will mediate the detailed case law in continental jurisdictions to Scottish lawyers more generally.[80] Likewise, law reform in Scotland may approach European continental legal materials on a more detailed level than hitherto.[81]

It is not generally appreciated in Scotland just how many steps have already been taken to make detailed material available. The development of a general periodical literature is only one aspect.[82] At least one journal, specialising in a particular area of private law on a Europe-wide basis, is about to appear,[83] and collections of decisions are in preparation.[84] It takes hardly longer to get from Scotland by plane to Hamburg, where the best library of European and British material on the continent relating to private law is, than to London, and the accommodation is cheaper. All the legal academic needs is money to pay for language training, air fares, subsistence and photocopies.

Another criticism that relates to a pragmatic difficulty could be raised, namely the sheer volume of available material. It is a problem, however, that will emerge throughout the Western world, and already exists in the United States.[85] For a small legal system like ours, it will increasingly present difficulties. Moreover these do not just concern manpower and time, but whether it is sensible for a legal system to go about its business using such elaborate tools. As far as litigation is concerned, legal arguments have to be paid for by litigants. The more material is cited, the longer the time of lawyers and the courts devoted to the case will be, and time costs money. If there were confidence in the academic literature, then that could act as a sieve to relieve the courts of the need for all the background material to be

---

[79] See Lord Rodger of Earlsferry, (above at n. 65) at p. 16.

[80] As in the work of B. S. Markesinis, which is by no means undetailed or limited in scope (above at n. 18).

[81] *e.g.* the recent work of the Scottish Law Commission with a view to reform of aspects of our law relating to people incapacitated or partially incapacitated through mental illness *etc.* briefly considered on one point a French provision, Loi no 85–1138 of December 20 1988 relative à la protection des personnes qui se prêtent à des recherches biomédicales, as am. by Loi No 90–86 of January 23 1990 (Scot Law Com. Discussion Paper No. 94, *Mentally Disabled Adults, Legal Arrangements for Managing their Welfare and Finances,* 1991 para. 3.47) and more extensively other aspects of the German Betreungsgesetz of 1990 (BGB§ 1905; also Gesetz über die Angelegenheiten der freiwilligen Gerichtsbarkeit, Art. 67) (*ibid.*, paras 1.9, 3.24–25, 3.33 and 3.55). There was input, too, from a conference in Spain (see *Report on Incapable Adults,* Scot Law. Com. No. 151, 1995, para. 1.5) but no German or other commentary on that material is referred to.

[82] Three new journals are well-known in the United Kingdom, the *European Review of Private Law, Zeitschrift für Europäisches Privatrecht,* the *Maastricht Journal of European and Comparative Law.*

[83] On delict, from the Centre for Liability Law at Tilburg (referred to in Ch. von Bar (above at n. 16) at p. 231).

[84] *e.g.* a case book on European contract law by W. von Gerven (Belgium) referred to in Ch. von Bar (above at n. 16). Note also B. S. Markesinis (above at n. 18).

[85] Much American academic writing is not of direct relevance to the development and application of substantive law rules.

looked at. In the long run this latter approach may be essential anyway. No legal system can go on simply using an ever bigger pile of material. All the same, especially in a small legal system like ours, at present it is often extension of the pile that is looked for.

A more challenging criticism is that in using material from another system a judge cannot have confidence that he understands it, because the material may depend on an unidentified doctrine of that other system which is foreign to existing analysis in ours. A judge, too, might reasonably feel that he could not be confident in using the material which, even if apparently on the face of it not based on such a doctrine, he feared might be so based.[86] Similarly a decision in another system may depend on detailed analysis of a provision in one of its codes.[87] These difficulties are greatly exacerbated by language difficulties. Difficulties of understanding, however, arising from *e.g.* the common law/equity dualism, can occur with English[88] or Commonwealth[89] material. This problem as it relates to European (and other) material will remain in some areas. But looked at generally it can be exaggerated. Some concepts developed against a doctrinal background foreign to one's own may be perfectly understandable. So, recently, in an English case[90] it has been suggested from the bench in the Court of Appeal[91] that the non-existence of a concept of a contract in favour of a third party could be challenged in the House of Lords. Reference was made *inter alia* to a periodical article[92] that discusses German material[93] together with American case law and writing.[94] It may be that the new *ius commune* movement will be especially valuable for us in the big questions of frontier jurisprudence, as for example in medical law. But also, with sufficient resources, legal academics may be able to follow the detailed working out of an idea

---

[86] Lord Rodger of Earlsferry (above at n. 65) at p. 25. Although one might point out that there is nothing really abstruse about the German doctrine of *Drittenschadensliquidation*, which would have been capable of covering the idea of "transferred loss" as developed earlier in *Leigh and Sillavan Ltd v. Aliakmon Shipping Co. Ltd* [1985] Q.B. 350 *per* Goff, L.J. at 399, an idea not used by the House of Lords in the appeal [1986] A.C. 785.

[87] See especially, Lord Rodger of Earlsferry *ibid.*, at p. 25 noting that despite Lord Goff's invocation in *Merrett v. Henderson* [1995] 2 A.C. 145 at p. 184 and *White v. Jones* [1995] 2 A.C. 207 at p. 255 of German, Dutch and French law, he falls back in the end on *Hedley Byrne v. Heller.*

[88] For *e.g.* the case of the law of nuisance see N. R. Whitty, *Stair Memorial Encyclopaedia*, Vol. 14, s.v, "Nuisance", especially para. 2095.

[89] Did the Court of Session really understand the doctrinal background to the Australian material cited to it in *Nordic Travel Ltd v. Scotprint Ltd*, 1980 S.C. 1 and referred to *per* Lord President Emslie at p. 20 (though material disregarded by the other two judges, Lords Cameron and Stott)—cited for consideration of the detailed application of our native law of "fraudulent [now unfair] preferences"?

[90] *Darlington Borough Council v. Wiltshier Northern Ltd* [1995] 1 W.L.R. 68.

[91] Although Steyn, L.J. at p. 78 notes that counsel stated that he would not, if the case went to the House of Lords, seek to challenge the privity rule as such. (Leave to appeal to the House of Lords was refused by the Court of Appeal but granted by the House of Lords Appeal Committee (see at p. 81)).

[92] B. Markesinis, "An Expanding Tort Law—The Price of a Rigid Contract Law" (1987) 103 L.Q.R. 354.

[93] *ibid.*, at pp. 356–371.

[94] *ibid.*, at pp. 371–384.

within the European systems and mediate it to the profession and the courts.

The Special Relevance of the New *Ius Commune* for Scots Law

The intrinsic intellectual worth of the new *ius commune* movement is such that it is essential for Scots law to engage with it. There are, however, features of our system that make it especially significant for us. These can be summarised under three broad headings. First, we are a small legal system. Secondly, some of the methods we use to develop our law are similar to the methods used by the new *ius commune* movement. Thirdly, we have a civilian heritage. This is not the place to deal in detail with these three matters. However, they are of great significance.

The role of small legal systems in the new ius commune
Small legal systems differ from big legal systems in many ways. For our purposes in this context the most important difference is that in a small system there is often not sufficient case law to carry out the necessary fine-tuning and adjustment of rules and doctrines. Other small systems find this to be so as well. The Scandinavian ones deal with the difficulty by forming a distinctive group and reference is made to material emerging from all of the systems in the group. Greece and Portugal make significant use of decisions in Germany, as occasionally does Austria.[95] For Scots law South Africa with its similar history and non-codified law has the potential to be particularly useful.[96] It has in recent times occasionally been used in the Court of Session and the High Court of Justiciary. But the most potentially useful does not logically exclude the useful or even the fairly useful.[97] Further, on a particular topic there may be material which because of its coherence and intellectual penetration is simply better on that topic than anything else yet produced.[98] An advantage of Scotland is not only that such material may actually fit better (than English law) with the general underlying structures of our law in a particular area, but also that as a small legal system we are not so likely to be prevented from borrowing it by a large mass of wrong-headed case law.[99]

The new *ius commune* is an empire which draws sustenance from

[95] For examples from the case law of these countries see Ch. von Bar (above at n. 16) at p. 230.
[96] *Morgan Guaranty Trust Company of New York v. Lothian Regional Council*, 1995 S.L.T. 299. This is the view of Lord Rodger of Earlsferry (above at n. 65) at p. 25.
[97] South African writers on the law themselves at least in recent years have been heavily influenced by aspects of private law in some modern European Systems.
[98] The general approach of the law in Germany to the question of unjustified enrichment may well be one such. See most recently R. Zimmermann and J. du Plessis (above at n. 42) and R. Zimmermann, "Unjustified Enrichment: The Modern Civilian Approach" (1995) 15 O.J.L.S. 403.
[99] See *e.g.* W. J. Swadling, "Restitution and Unjust Enrichment", in A. S. Hartkamp *et al* (eds.) (above at n. 7) 267 at p. 282: "But even were the English law sufficiently developed to be susceptible of codification it is doubtful whether any assimilation of the common law and civil law in this area could be made."

all places where interest in it is taken and relevant work is done. It seeks the widest gene pool of ideas. It recognises that in the on-going process of legal evolution, important developments may take place in apparently minor species on the rim of its world.[1]

Methods used to develop our law

The factors just considered would be of less significance if the Scots method of developing private law, *i.e.* primarily through case law,[2] were fundamentally different from methods in mainland Europe. No one now thinks that case law is not significant in those systems, although they are all codified. It has even been asserted that English judges are just like continental European judges in the way they go about analysing and deciding issues of law.[3] Much work remains to be done on analysing judicial technique, and the ways in which judges deploy the *instrumentarium* acceptable in their system. It is not likely that following such an examination the differences would be seen to be unimportant. Such an examination would be likely to show significant differences even today between Scotland and England.[4] Recently some English judges have been using academic literature, and it has been thought that this bodes well for the new *ius commune* idea making headway in England.

However, in noticing this sporadic, although apparently enthusiastic, use in England of academic periodical articles, something important that distinguishes Scots judicial technique has been overlooked. This is the much more significant role of the textbook in Scotland.

In this century textbooks have generally been cited more frequently than in England[5] Simply counting the number of cases in which reference is made to this source does not, however, reveal the full picture.[6] Moreover, in this context particular care must be taken with general

---

[1] It has been suggested that the most interesting law reform usually seems to be accomplished in small jurisdictions: F. M. B. Reynolds, "Drawing the Strands Together?", P. B. H. Birks (ed.), *The Frontiers of Liability*, Vol. 2 (1994) 156 at p. 160. For dissemination in Germany of ideas from small systems in Europe see Ch. von Bar (ed.), *Deliktsrecht in Europa* (1994).

[2] Although in some areas, family law for example, the role of modern legislation is such, that judicial development is largely at the level of fine tuning.

[3] R. Goode,"The European Law School" (1993) 13 Leg. Stud. 1 at p. 3.

[4] It follows that it is not correct to look on the ways in which case law forms our law as identical to the ways in which English case law forms English law. Compare D. A. O. Edward, "The Scottish Reactions—An Epilogue", in B. S. Markesinis (ed.), *The Gradual Convergence* (1994) 263 at p. 264.

[5] In 1936, *e.g.*, textbooks were cited by the court and/or counsel in 41 per cent of Scottish civil (including Lands Valuation Court) cases as reported in *Session Cases* (excluding House of Lords cases). In England in that year in the equivalent cases reported in the *Law Reports* the figure is 11.66 per cent.

[6] *e.g.* in the 178 civil cases reported in Vols. 1 and 2 of the *All England Reports* of 1990 from courts below the level of the House of Lords, textbooks were cited in 31 cases. Taking the first 178 cases reported in the *Scots Law Times* in that year from the Court of Session and the Lands Valuation Appeal Court the figure is 32. This was the year in which the *Scots Law Times* first started to list "textbooks referred to" in its reports. This is still not done in the *All England Law Reports* or other general series of English reports.

statistics.[7] It is the nature of the role of the textbook in judgments that generally differs between the two systems. In the Scots cases the texts are repeatedly cited for major points of law.[8] They are even, indeed, heavily relied on on points of law where the law is identical in England, where by contrast in England typically textbooks would not be cited, or at best would be merely referred to in passing.[9] In Scots cases textbooks are referred to as "authorities,"[10] and sometimes authorities which a judge will not be willing to depart from.[11] They may be associated with the high authority of "institutional writers" (and preferred to them, if appropriate).[12] In the English cases textbooks are generally[13] not referred to as "authorities" but separately classified as another sort of material.[14] They are rarely cited at length on important points.

[7] The figure of 31 for England in the above sample is not directly comparable with the 32 for Scotland. Just over 25 per cent of the English figure is made up of cases concerning international private law. There is a distinct tradition of embracing textbooks as a source of authority in this branch of the law in England, especially in the use of Dicey and Morris. *Conflict of Laws*, treating its "rules" as a quasi-code (see *e.g.* in this sample *Arab Monetary Fund v. Hashim (No 3)* [1990] 2 All E.R. 769 *per* Lord Donaldson of Lymington, M.R. at p. 775 and Bingham, L.J. at p. 782. A further 16 per cent of the English sample is accounted for by not directly comparable material: 2 cases in ecclesiastical courts and 3 cases where the reference is to an official compendium of procedural rules (*The Supreme Court Practice* and *The County Court Practice*).

[8] This can occur on occasion in England, too, as in this sample in the important case on "consideration", *Williams v. Roffey Bros & Nicholls (Contractors) Ltd* [1990] 1 All E.R. 512—though this is in the very English framework of a discussion of a rule named after a case—"the rule in *Stilk v. Myrick*" (*per* Purchas, L.J. at p. 525). It is the frequency of instances that marks the difference between the systems and shows the tendency of ways of thinking within them.

[9] Compare in this sample cases on the rule that a "qualified acceptance" does not give rise to a contract, but itself constitutes an offer from the person purporting to accept, *Rutterford Ltd v. Allied Breweries Ltd*, 1990 S.L.T. 249 at p. 251 (J. Craigie, *Conveyancing*, (3rd ed., 1899), W. M. Gloag, *Contract* (2nd ed., 1929) W. W. McBryde, *Contract*, (1987); *Findlater v. Maan*, 1990 S.L.T. 465 at p. 468 (W. M. Gloag, *Contract*, 2nd ed.)) with the leading English case *Butler Machine Tool Co. v. Ex-Cell-O Corporation (England) Ltd* [1979] 1 All E.R. 965—no texts cited by Lawton, L.J. and Bridge, L.J.; Lord Denning, M.R. at p. 968: [after quoting a passage from Lord Cairns, L.C. in *Brogden v. Metropolitan Railway Co.* (1877) 2 App. Cas 666 at p. 672] "that is well observed in Benjamin on Sale"; "Such was *British Road Services Ltd v. Arthur V. Crutchley & Co Ltd, per* Lord Pearson; and the illustration given by Professor Guest in Anson's Law of Contract".

[10] *e.g. Colquhouns' Trs v. Marchioness of Lorne's Trs*, 1990 S.L.T. 34 at p. 37 *per* Lord Sutherland.

[11] *e.g.* "Professor Rankine's work. The rejection of such an authority is not a step which I am prepared to take" (*Upper Crathes Fishings Ltd v. Bailey's Exrs*, 1990 S.L.T. 46 at p. 49 *per* Lord Clyde; "a number of authorities for the proposition that rent was one of the cardinal or essential terms of a lease (Erskine, II, vi. 20; Bell Prin., §. 1197; Baron Hume's Lectures (in Vol. II of the Stair Society publications) at pp. 56–57; Rankine on *Leases* (3rd ed.) p. 1 [followed by three cases]." (*Shetland Islands Council v. B.P. Petroleum Development*, 1990 S.L.T. 85 *per* Lord Cullen at p. 86).

[12] *Bank of Scotland v. Seitz*, 1990 SLT 584 *per* Lord Prosser at p. 593: preferring Gloag's ("high authority") view to the apparent view of Stair on the question of the place at which payment is to be made when the contract does not specify it.

[13] For the only use of the word in connection with textbooks in England in this sample, *Williams v. Roffey* (above) *per* Purchas, L.J. at p. 525: "current textbooks of authority: See *Chitty On Contracts* (25th edn, 1983) vol. 1, para. 185 and *Cheshire Fifoot and Furnston's* [sic] *Law of Contract* (11th edn, 1986)".

[14] See typically *Sen v. Headley* [1990] 1 All E.R. 898 (considering whether there can be such a thing as a *donatio mortis causa* of real property) *per* Mummery, J. at pp. 904–906: "The English authorities . . . The overseas authorities . . . The textbooks". Tanta-

They are typically treated as subsidiary supporting material.[15] In another essay in this book it is pointed out that in the 1950s and 1960s Scottish judges were often reluctant to cite living writers.[16] But even in that period the dead continued to be frequently cited. The way that the courts use writings is a distinctive feature of our case law. It is not a surprising one in a small legal system.[17] It provides a good background tradition for a judge to approach material from a new *ius commune*.[18]

The Scottish civilian heritage

Views differ as to the extent to which Scots law is a civilian system. We consider that the soul of Scots law is civilian. The new *ius commune* movement can greatly assist the resurgence of the civilian tradition so that it becomes a stronger creative force in the development of our law.

---

lisingly for a Scot this part of the judgment ends with the words "References to textbooks on Scots law and South African law . . . have not shed light on the problem". But neither this report nor that of the argument of counsel in [1990] Ch. 728 at p. 731 reveal what books these were.

[15] *e.g. Bristol Airport p.l.c. v. Powdrill* [1990] 2 All E.R. 493 *per* Sir Nicholas Browne-Wilkinson, V.C. at p. 502 (reference to "28 Halsbury's Laws (4th edn) para 503").

[16] K. G. C. Reid, "The Third Branch of the Profession: The Rise of the Academic Lawyer in Scotland" *supra*, pp. 46–49.

[17] Lack of a large flow of reported decisions may encourage lawyers and judges to look to textbooks for fine-tuning as well as for formulations of basic principles and concepts.

[18] British commentators often assume that courts in Europe are always citing academics. In fact many rarely do—the Cour de Cassation in France for example—although some do—the Bundesgerichtshof in Germany, for example. (See for a particularly wide range of such material a recent banking law case BGHZ 1995 127, 129.) However, what is common to the various European systems' ways of thinking is that law as set out in academic writing (along, of course with code provisions where relevant) provides the main point of departure for their lawyers.

A SCOTTISH CIVIL CODE

Eric Clive

Introduction

In 1992 Bill Wilson observed that "a legal system which has no doc-trinal foundation must drift."[1] This contribution in his memory will argue that the enactment of a Scottish civil code would be the best way of providing the necessary doctrinal foundation for Scottish pri-vate law.

What is a Doctrinal Foundation?

"Doctrine" has several shades of meaning. It can mean "a thing taught".[2] For there to be a doctrinal foundation, using this sense of the word, it is clear that there must be something, whether a text or a principle, which all competent teachers accept as the starting point. There must be one "thing taught" and not as many things taught as there are teachers teaching. Before there can be a foundation in teach-ing there must be a foundation for teaching. "Doctrine" can also mean "a body or system of principles".[3] In this chapter the term "a doctrinal foundation" will be used in a sense which reflects something of both of these meanings—namely a systematic conceptual foundation for teaching.

Is a Firm Doctrinal Foundation Necessary?

It would be possible for a primitive legal system to get by without a firm doctrinal foundation. It might have, say, nothing more than forms of action and a rule that precedents were to be followed, or it might have a series of legislative provisions dealing with specific problems in an uncoordinated way. But it would seem to be necessary for an advanced legal system, worthy of the word "system", to have a firm doctrinal foundation, not only to prevent drift but also to be reason-ably predictable in its results, and capable of orderly explanation and development.[4]

---

[1] "The Importance of Analysis", in D. L. Carey Miller and D. W. Meyers (eds.), *Comparative and Historical Essays in Scots Law* (1992), p. 171.
[2] *Chambers 20th Century Dictionary*, which also gives "a principle of belief".
[3] One of the meanings given in the *Shorter Oxford Dictionary*.
[4] On the need for "a map of the law" see P. Birks, "The Need for the Institutes in England" (1991) 108 Zeitschrift der Savigny-Stiftung für Rechtsgeschichte-Romanistische Abteilung 708.

Does Scottish Private Law Have a Firm Doctrinal Foundation?

In some areas Scottish private law does have a firm doctrinal foundation, but in many others it does not. It seems doubtful, for example, whether it has a firm doctrinal foundation on such matters as: the concept of a juridical act; the effect of error; the meaning and effect of rescission; the meaning and effect of legal incapacity; the general theory of unjustified enrichment; the role of good faith; the requirements for the creation of an irrevocable *ius quaesitum tertio*; the transmission of property; and the scope of constructive trusts. There are many such issues on which competent law teachers could legitimately take different views.

The Best Way of Getting a Firm Doctrinal Foundation.

There are three options. An attempt could be made to achieve a firm doctrinal foundation for Scottish private law first, without legislation; secondly, by scattered legislation or thirdly, by comprehensive legislation in the form of a Scottish civil code.

Without legislation
The proponents of this option usually recognise, explicitly or implicitly, that judges alone cannot do what is necessary, at least in the short term. It is not the judges' job to provide a doctrinal foundation for the law. It is their job to decide specific disputes or grant specific remedies in accordance with the law. They cannot choose areas for development. They are dependent on the hazards of litigation. Many cases which do come forward turn on facts or on the exercise of discretion. Judges cannot prevent interesting cases from being abandoned or settled. They cannot commission research or consult on options for reform. They are often so bound by previous cases or statutes as to have no freedom of action. Any doctrinal development through case law is an incidental by-product.

The non-legislative option would rely mainly on increased analysis by scholars of Scottish private law concepts and increased investigation by scholars of the content and context of Scottish private law. It would involve not only analytical and historical work but also comparative work on the current state of legal doctrine in other legal systems, particularly those with a civilian background. It might involve a rediscovery and redevelopment of a European *ius commune*.[5] It would involve the publication of learned textbooks, going beyond the immediate needs of students and practitioners. All of that would be an excellent thing and indeed the idea of developing a new European *ius commune* is inspirational and exciting. But scholarly activity will

---

[5] See, *e.g.*, R. Zimmermann, "Roman and Comparative Law: The European Perspective", (1995) 16 Journal of Legal History 33, and "Civil Code and Civil Law—The 'Europeanisation' of Private Law within the European Community and the Re-emergence of a European Legal Science", (1994) 1 Columbia Journal of European Law 63.

not be enough. First, scholars tend to disagree. There is no reason why Scottish legal scholars should even agree to place the emphasis on the civilian tradition in Scottish private law. Some might prefer to argue that the true doctrine in parts of the law (for example, in contract, negligence, unjustified enrichment, commercial law or private international law) was to be found in English or Commonwealth or American law.[6] One of the hazards of a mixed system is that people may be attracted to different components of the mix. Secondly, the work would be haphazard, dependent on the interests, energies and preoccupations of individual scholars. There would be gaps and overlaps. Thirdly, publication opportunities would depend on commercial considerations. Fourthly, even agreed doctrines from the European common law background might be unsuitable for contemporary use. Fifthly, even agreed and suitable doctrine from an impeccable source would have somehow to find its way from academic writings into the actual law. Sometimes there would simply be no room for it. Existing firm rules based on statutes or authoritative cases would get in the way. In the few remaining areas, academically agreed doctrine might filter into the law eventually over a long period of time through the scholastic influence on students, practitioners and judges, but in the meantime there would be a lot of drift and, much more importantly, a lot of unnecessary uncertainty, expense and inconvenience for private citizens. The non-legislative option is an option for no change or slow change.

Scattered legislation.
A great deal can be done by this method. It is sometimes not realised how much of the doctrinal foundation of Scottish private law is now in legislation. Legislation is the starting point for any treatment of great parts of the law on the family, employment, succession, trusts, conveyancing, prescription, incapacity, companies, bankruptcy, diligence, consumer protection, sale and supply of goods, unfair contract terms, requirements of writing, occupiers' liability, liability for animals, damages for personal injury or death, partnership, landlord and tenant and many other subjects.[7] However, one disadvantage of scattered legislation is that it tends to deal inadequately with basic concepts which are common to several branches of the law. A fundamental re-examination of the law on sale of goods, for example, would be more satisfactory if certain problems in the general law of contract were resolved.[8] Some problems in the general law of contract are

---

[6] It must not be forgotten that sometimes supposedly English doctrines are themselves derived from Civilian or Canon Law sources. See R. Zimmermann, "Roman Law and European Legal Unity" in A. S. Hartkamp *et al.* (eds.) *Towards a European Civil Code* (1994), pp. 75–80.

[7] Many statutes have replaced parts of the common law. Some of them have given considerable discretion to judges. These statutes have been interpreted and applied just like any other statute. It has been argued that one of the obstacles to codification in this country is that a code would demand an entirely different approach to statutory interpretation. See *e.g.* A. E. Anton, "Obstacles to Codification", 1982 J.R. 15. Experience suggests that there is little or no force in that argument.

[8] The Scottish Law Commission became aware of this when working on implied terms in the law on sale of goods and, for this reason, abandoned work on a more extensive reform of the Sale of Goods Act 1979.

really problems for the even more general law of obligations. The law of obligations has subtle links with the law of property. There are also boundary problems. It may be possible, for example, to leave something out of the law on unjustified enrichment if it can be dealt with in the law on contract but if an Act is dealing only with the former topic an omission would simply leave a gap in the law. A doctrinal foundation for the whole of Scottish private law requires more than scattered legislation.

Comprehensive legislation
The enactment of comprehensive legislation specifically designed to provide a firm doctrinal foundation for Scottish private law would seem to be by far the best way of achieving that aim. The legislation, or code, would not stand alone. It would be supplemented by detailed legislation on specific topics, by writings and by cases. It would be intended to provide the doctrinal foundation, not the whole law.

It could be done

Constitutional considerations
It does not seem unrealistic to suppose that there may, within the foreseeable future, be a Scottish Parliament within the United Kingdom with power to legislate on Scottish private law. An appropriate and worthy activity for that Parliament would be the enactment of a Scottish civil code. It would be less realistic, in the event of there not being a Scottish Parliament, to expect the United Kingdom Parliament to enact a Scottish civil code[9] although, of course, that is not theoretically impossible and might be done more easily by splitting the project into manageable self-contained stages.[10]

Technical considerations
It is clear that, although it would be an ambitious project, there is no technical reason why a Scottish civil code could not be produced and enacted. New civil codes have been produced recently in Quebec and the Netherlands and, with remarkable speed, in the countries of the former USSR. There are international models which could be drawn on for some parts of the code.[11] The Scottish Law Commission has

---

[9] For pessimistic assessments of the prospects for a proper codification from the United Kingdom Parliament see J. Kerr, "Law Reform in Changing Times", (1980) 96 L.Q.R. 515 at pp. 527–530 and Anton, "Obstacles to Codification", *supra*. These assessments are perhaps too pessimistic. If the political will was present codification could be achieved. It would be remarkable, and thoroughly shameful, if the United Kingdom Parliament could not do what many other legislatures throughout the world have done.

[10] This is the approach now being attempted by the English Law Commission to try to achieve the enactment by the United Kingdom Parliament of a criminal code for England and Wales. See *Legislating the Criminal Code—Offences Against the Person and General Principles* (Law. Com. No. 218, 1993).

[11] Notably the Vienna Convention on Contracts for the International Sale of Goods (1980); the UNIDROIT *Principles of International Commercial Contracts* (1994); and O. Lande and H. Beale (eds.) *Principles of European Contract Law—Part 1: Performance, Non-performance and Remedies*, Vol. I (1995).

shown that it is possible to prepare drafts bills which, in effect, codify particular areas of private law. There are well-tried techniques of research, analysis, provisional proposals, consultation, seminars and discussion which could be used, with modifications where necessary. Indeed a great deal of the work has already been done in such areas as family law, incapacity, succession, diligence, bankruptcy and unjustified enrichment. In the area of property law the abolition of the feudal system of land tenure and the statutory reform of the law of the tenement, both of which are well in hand, would provide an ideal start for a codification. The publication of the *Stair Memorial Encyclopaedia* also provides a good basis for codification at this time. There has never been greater strength in depth in the law faculties, the courts and the legal profession. There has never been a greater awareness of what can be done, and of what should not be done, by legislation.[12] The main areas where a lot of work remains to be done are the areas of obligations and property, but those are precisely the areas in which most assistance is to be gained from the civilian tradition and from existing national and international models. The work of the English and Scottish Law Commissions on a British contract code in the 1960s and 1970s is sometimes regarded as a failure and as proof that codification of contract law would not be feasible, but if the work did not result in legislation that was not for technical reasons. In fact the work reached a very advanced stage before it was abandoned.[13] There was a significant input from Scottish Law Commissioners and the draft clauses on the Scottish Law Commission's files could be drawn on, along with more recent models, as a source of ideas. If there was the political will to produce a Scottish contract code quickly it could be done.

The Advantages of a Scottish Civil Code

Functional
The main functional advantages of a code would be ease of reference, ease of use, ease of change, structural strength and doctrinal coherence.[14]

It is obvious that for practical purposes it is easier to find and use the relevant part of the law if it is contained in one well-ordered statute rather than in scattered statutes, often with unhelpful names. However, ease of use also includes ease of use in providing information to others about what Scottish law is. This is likely to be of increasing importance. It is already common for Scottish officials to be asked to provide information about parts of Scottish law for the purposes of work being undertaken by European or international

[12] See A. E. Anton, "Legislation and its Limits", (1979) 5 Dalhousie Law Journal 233.
[13] See H. McGregor, *Contract Code: Drawn up on behalf of the English Law Commission* (1993); C. K. Davidson, "The Scottish Law Commission 1965–95", (1995) 1 Scottish Law and Practice Quarterly, 20.
[14] Or "accessibility, comprehensibility, consistency and certainty". See the carefully balanced article by Sheriff Principal Nicholson on "Codification of Scots Law: A Way Ahead or a Blind Alley?" (1987) 8 Stat. L.R. 173 at pp. 177–179.

organisations. Sometimes the requests are for an exchange of legislation on a topic. Much Scottish law is not in a form which lends itself easily to this sort of exchange. It is a sad reflection on the existing state of our law that its basic provisions are often not fit for showing to others. This contributes to an ignorance of, and undervaluing of, Scottish law outside Scotland.

Ease of change requires slightly more explanation. It is sometimes argued that a disadvantage of a code is that it makes the law more difficult to change. The reverse is true. What is set down in a comprehensive statute can be more easily changed, sometimes by merely replacing a few words, than something which depends on cases or scattered legislation. For one thing, it is easier to see what needs to be changed. For another, it is easier to see how to effect the change. It is significant that the areas of the law which require most frequent changes—taxation and social security—are contained in comprehensive statutes. The existence of civil codes in France and Germany has not prevented French and German family law from being reformed in response to the same social changes as have led to reform of Scottish family law over the same period. Of course, some parts of venerable civil codes now look dated, but so do some parts of the uncodified Scottish law.

Structural strength and doctrinal coherence might be thought to be cultural advantages, and to some extent they are, but they are also important functional advantages. The law is easier to understand and apply, at less cost in time and effort, if it has a clear structure and if it does not contain a great number of gaps and inconsistencies.

It is sometimes claimed that a good textbook would have all the advantages of a code and none of the disadvantages. However, a textbook has to work with the existing law and if the law is undeveloped or confused on any point an honest textbook has to say so. Moreover, there may not be one good textbook. There may be two or more which adopt different structures or interpret the sources in different ways or suggest different solutions to open questions. Textbooks are a valuable part of the doctrinal superstructure, not part of the doctrinal foundation.

Cultural advantages.
The main cultural advantage of a Scottish civil code would be that it would proclaim and fortify the basic concepts of Scottish private law, which are part of the Scottish cultural identity, and preserve its independence. One of the dangers of "drift" is that the doctrinal foundations of the law will be undermined by uncritical use of English cases and writers. In some cases, of course, it may be a good thing for the foundations of an unjust and inconvenient rule to be undermined. The law is not an end in itself, an object of worship to be kept polished and pure for purposes of veneration, without effects on people's lives. But all too often the result of the process of creeping anglicisation has been the replacement of a good Scottish rule by a bad English rule.[15] This sort of thing is a real danger in those parts of

---

[15] See A. Dewar Gibb, *Law from Over the Border* (1950).

the law which depend on cases and writers. It is not a danger in those parts of the law which are embodied in statute. If the statute applies to Scotland only, and is in different terms from any English statute, English cases will not be cited. If the statute applies to Scotland and England in the same terms, English cases may be cited but that is unobjectionable and indeed useful, because the foundation is in the statute and the cases are just part of the interpretative superstructure. The danger of undermining the foundations by citing English cases and writers arises only in the common law parts of the system. Of course, there is always the danger that a statute will itself undermine the foundations but it may be assumed that a Scottish civil code, prepared after full consultation and passed by a Scottish Parliament, would not be open to that criticism.

It is important to note that the cultural advantage would not be distinctiveness for its own sake. A distinctive legal system is as sensible as a distinctive system of air traffic control. The advantage would be a measure of legal independence within the European legal tradition.

The arguments in favour of international harmonisation and unification of parts of private law are as strong now as they ever were and would remain as strong after the advent of a Scottish Parliament. However, the time for bilateral harmonisation of well-established areas of the private law is now past. There would be little point in trying now to achieve harmonisation between, say, Spanish and Portuguese laws, or German and Austrian laws, or French and Belgian laws, or Irish and Northern Irish laws, or English and Scottish laws. It makes more sense now to try for harmonisation at a European or United Nations level. There will undoubtedly be continuing efforts in that direction. Armed with a Scottish civil code, which would itself have taken existing European and wider international developments fully into account, Scottish representatives would be in a much stronger position to play a full and constructive role in such initiatives.[16]

Possible Disadvantages of Codification

People who dislike the idea of civil codes may see them as being wasteful, dreadful, interruptive, inorganic and rigid.

The wastefulness criticism is that a civil code would be enormously expensive to prepare and enact. So far as preparation costs are concerned this does not seem a strong criticism. The work of preparing a code would be neither capital intensive nor labour intensive compared with the work of developing other essential parts of a country's infrastructure. It would still, of course, take a great deal of time and effort but it would be well worth while. Whether the enacting stage was expensive would depend on the approach taken by the Scottish

---

[16] It might be argued that it would be better to wait for a European civil code. However, informed opinion is fairly pessimistic about the prospects for such a code and it might be a long wait. See Hartkamp et al. (eds.) *Towards a European Civil Code*.

Parliament. If the Parliament wished to debate every line of every provision and consider hundreds of amendments, then the process would undoubtedly be expensive, but if the Parliament took the view that the important thing was to repatriate the legislative foundations of Scottish private law as soon as possible and in a coherent and structured way, and if it were accordingly prepared to adopt without excessively detailed debate a code which had been carefully prepared and consulted on, which steered clear of party political issues, and which could be amended later if necessary, then the process need not be expensive at all.[17]

Dreadfulness refers to the fear that a code would embody all that is worst in the Westminster tradition of legislative drafting. That would indeed be dreadful. It would have to be avoided at all costs. There is no reason, however, why a Scottish civil code should not provide an opportunity for the Scottish Parliament to legislate in a more principled and conceptual way, and hence in a more readable and durable way.

The interruption criticism is that a code artificially breaks the continuity of legal development. This criticism is still heard from time to time but is now played down by legal historians.[18] It is based on a misconception. Unless a code is introduced ready-made from a totally different legal tradition it will simply be part of a country's legal development.[19] It would be expected that a Scottish civil code would grow out of the existing law. It would be perfectly possible to provide a commentary to the code to make this clear and to illustrate its provisions by reference to earlier decided cases.

The criticism that a code would be "inorganic" also seems to be based on a misconception. All legal development is the result of human thought. The law does not just grow by itself. The fact that the thought is the result of a deliberate decision to try to systematise and set out clearly certain basic concepts in private law does not make the process any less "organic" than if the stimulus for the thought is the need to decide a case which the hazards of litigation have thrown up or the need to legislate to correct an anomaly caused by a decided case. A code is no less "organic" than a textbook which attempts to introduce some order into the law.

The rigidity criticism takes two forms. One is that a code fossilises the law and prevents further development. This is obviously false.

---

[17] Research commissioned for the English Law Commission has shown that many law reform bills take up very little time on the floor of either House of Parliament. Fifteen smaller Bills from 1984 to 1994 took an average of one hour 49 minutes for all their stages on the floor of the House of Lords and an average of one hour 11 minutes on the floor of the House of Commons. See the English Law Commission's 29th *Annual Report* (Law. Com. No. 232, 1994) at pp. 68–69. The Requirements of Writing (Scotland) Act 1995, which provided a new conceptual basis for an important part of Scottish private law, took just over one hour in total to complete all its stages in both Houses of Parliament.

[18] See *e.g.*, J. W. Cairns, "Comparative Law, Unification and Scholarly Creation of a New *Ius Commune*'", (1982) 32 N.I.L.Q., at pp. 277–280; and "Employment in the Civil Code of Lower Canada: Tradition and Political Economy in Legal Classification and Reform", (1987) 32 McGill L.J. 674.

[19] See R. Zimmermann, "Civil Code and Civil Law", *supra*.

What can be enacted can be amended. Nothing would fossilise a branch of the law more surely than a renunciation of the power to change it by legislation. The other form of the rigidity criticism is that a code would regulate everything in too much detail and leave no scope for judicial or doctrinal creativity. This would obviously depend on the content and style of the code. There are choices to be made. It is a question of degree and of assessing costs and benefits. However, no-one would claim that a code would leave no room for interpretation and comment.[20] Life is complicated. No law can foresee everything. There will always be plenty of room for development by judges and writers. Different types of code could leave more or less room for development. Any decent code would provide a better underlying structure for the development.

What would a Scottish Civil Code look like?

At a general level it might be envisaged that a Scottish civil code would not distinguish between commercial and civil law, but that it would leave many of the details of commercial law to specific statutes outside the code. The same could be done in relation to detailed parts of other areas of the law covered. The code would be most useful if it were confined to the structure, general principles and fundamental rules of private law as much as possible. One advantage of preparing a civil code now rather than a hundred or two hundred years ago is that it is now accepted as normal to have different levels of legislation with different levels of specificity.[21] The contents and arrangement of a civil code would be matters to be worked out but it might be envisaged that there would be at least a general part and parts on persons,[22] obligations, property and succession.[23]

So far as style is concerned a code should be self-standing at its level of generality and should be expressed in conceptual and abstract terms. It should avoid cross-references and other references so far as possible. Administrative and procedural matters should be left for other levels of legislation. Transitional provisions should be in a special part or schedule which could be excised when it had served its function.

---

[20] Lord Wilberforce has said that "codification, intelligently carried out" could revive the spirit of the common law by restoring "to the judges what they may have lost for many years to their great regret: the task of interpreting law according to statements of principle" (H.L. Deb. vol. 264 cols. 1175–1176 (1965)).

[21] What F. H. Lawson called "layers of law" in "Analysing a Legal System", 1982 J.R. 161 at p. 170. On the relationship between an established civil code and special legislation, see H. Kötz, "Taking Civil Codes Less Seriously", (1987) 50 M.L.R. 1 at pp. 12–14.

[22] Including natural persons, legal persons and groupings of persons in families or in associations of various kinds.

[23] This would be a normal structure for a civil code. It would be for consideration whether family law should appear under the law of persons or in a part of its own. See C. Szladits in International Encyclopedia of Comparative Law, vol II, ch. 2, pt. II ("Structure and the Divisions of the Law: the Civil Law System"), pp. 67–75.

Conclusion

There is no doubt that a civil code *could* provide a firm doctrinal foundation for Scottish private law, that it *could* have functional advantages and that it *could* be a significant legal contribution to a resurgent Scottish culture within a European framework. There must be some doubt whether the potential could be realised, but that is not a reason for not trying.

What would Bill Wilson's attitude have been to a proposed Scottish civil code? He was certainly not averse to legislation. Indeed he was unusual in the extent to which he found intellectual fascination in it. He was not averse to the idea of codification, as is indicated by his work on the Lando Commission on the Principles of European Contract Law, and he was himself a master of legal analysis and concise statements of legal principle. Yet he never, so far as I am aware, evinced any enthusiasm for codification of any part of Scottish law. I suspect that he would have had doubts about the idea of a Scottish civil code, that he would have feared that it would be badly done, but that he would have reserved his opinion and kept us all guessing, as he so often did.

The strange thing is that the logic of Bill Wilson's own positions on law, analysis, drift and steer ought to have led him to support the idea of a Scottish civil code. He saw law as a science, an immense and fascinating body of knowledge to be explored, but his approach was also intensely practical.[24] He came to appreciate the value of T. B. Smith's work on the civilian element in Scottish private law, but for much of his career he was critical of the Smith approach, seeing it as selective and remote from the law practised every day in courts and offices in Scotland—at best only part of the picture. He loved legal analysis and legal language, but was critical of the incoherence which he found in existing statutes. He expressed concern about drift, but hated steer—whether from anglicisers, neo-civilians, social welfarists, policy-driven law reformers or politicians of any party. These points of view would in theory have been well met by a code which was scientific and analytical, which used concise, abstract, coherent language, which built on the *whole* tradition of Scottish private law, which served practical needs in a realistic way and which avoided social policy so far as possible and party politics entirely. But attitudes are determined by personality rather than logic, and Bill's was a cautious personality. His most typical gesture in the University of Edinburgh Staff Club was to look dramatically over his shoulder to see if anybody was within earshot before delighting his audience with some amusing story or titbit of information.

One thing is sure. If there had been a Scottish civil code Bill Wilson would have had fun with it.

---

[24] His book on *Debt* is a practitioners' bible.

IF IT AIN'T BROKE, DON'T FIX IT: ON NOT CODIFYING COMMERCIAL LAW

A. D. M. FORTE

In 1982, Bill Wilson predicted that it would shortly be impossible for academic lawyers to discharge their duties properly without having first studied the social sciences.[1] While that prediction has not been fulfilled, the premise on which it was based, namely, that such training would enable us to appreciate how the "civil" law works, retains validity. Moreover, although sociologists were singled out and chided for their reluctance to engage in empirical research, there was implicit in the criticism a warning to all engaged in legal research not "to sit by the fire honing their concepts".[2] The message was for greater pragmatism in our thinking about the law and in this essay I should like to take just such a pragmatic line in discussing the desirability and the probability of codifying commercial law in Scotland. I say "probability", because, although I think that it is unlikely that we will wish to devise a commercial code in the United Kingdom, we cannot entirely dismiss the possibility. There are, I think, three reasons for this. First, there is the statutory duty imposed on the two Law Commissions to keep the systematic development of the law under review; particularly through its possible codification.[3] Secondly, from time to time codification of the law or some branches of it is called for.[4] Thirdly, pressure to codify may come from the European Commission and the growth of a more federalised Europe, in which the great majority of members states have a long history of codified law, may make the case for uniformity hard to resist.[5] But codification through compulsion aside, I believe that voluntary (or self-inflicted) codifi-

---

[1] W. A. Wilson, "Knowing the Law and Other Things", 1982 J.R. 259 at p. 272.
[2] *ibid.*, at p. 271.
[3] Law Commissions Act 1965 (c. 22), s. 3(1).
[4] Lord Cooper, *Selected Papers 1922–1954* (1957), p. 205; D. M. Walker, "La Codification du Droit Ecossais", *Etudes Juridiques Offertes à L Julliot de la Morandiere* (1964), 645; E. M. Clive, "Family Law Reform in Scotland—Past, Present and Future", 1989 J.R. 133; and in this volume "A Scottish Civil Code", at pp. 82–91; R. M. Goode, "The Codification of Commercial Law" [1988] Monash Law Review 135. Note also Lord Rodger of Earlsferry (A. F. Rodger), "The Codification of Commercial Law in Victorian Britain", (1992) 109 L.Q.R. 570, reviewing the nineteenth century movement for codification. Particularly interesting is the willingness with which many Scots embraced the codifying statutes enacted towards the end of that century and the decline in interest in codification as the century closed.
[5] Bill Wilson was a member of the Commission on European Contract Law, part of whose proposals have recently been published: see O. Lando and H. Beale (eds.), *Principles of European Contract Law—Part I: Performance, Non-performance and Remedies* (1995). This is a code and it is grounded in the belief of a former Head of Division of the Directorate General for the Internal Market that "We need a European Code of Obligations": *ibid.*, at p. ix. Ole Lando has himself spoken about a "European Uniform Commercial Code".

cation of commercial law is undesirable and that siren calls to the contrary should not be heeded.

It is as well to be clear at the outset just what it is that is being objected to. We have in the United Kingdom a cluster of commercial statutes of about 100 years' vintage, the Bills of Exchange Act 1882, the Partnership Act 1890, the Sale of Goods Act 1893, and the Marine Insurance Act 1906, which are commonly referred to as "codifying statutes".[6] These are not comparable to codified law as exemplified by the continental European models. Both rest on profoundly different assumptions as to their roles. Continental European codes are characterised by their generalised natures and underwriting this generality is the belief that first, generalisation is necessary if a code is to be comprehensive; secondly, generalisation is needed to prevent the code becoming obsolete too rapidly; and thirdly, generalisation confers wide discretion on the courts in applying a code's provisions and this promotes adaptability.[7] Mackenzie Chalmers, who drafted the 1882, 1893 and 1906 statutes, articulated a very different objective to that of the continental codifiers: "The province of the code ... is to set out, in concise language and logical form, those principles of the law that have already stood the test of time. It co-ordinates and methodises, but it does not invent new principles".[8] There are, of course, other possible models, of which the Uniform Commercial Code (U.C.C.) in the United States is the most obvious and best known example. The U.C.C. is premised on a number of beliefs, but the two which strike the foreign observer most are: first, a faith in the desirability of confining commercial law to a single code; and secondly, a belief that codified law enjoys self-evident advantages over the uncodified variety. I certainly have no quarrel with and, indeed, would advocate systematic and regular legislative restatement of the law applicable to business and commerce. But I do not think that legislation on either the continental or American models is desirable or needed for the United Kingdom.

Commercial law is (and must) be driven by certain imperatives. The checklist may vary to suit individual preferences but high on my list would be the need to ensure that the law is sufficiently flexible to respond to the development of new technologies, new methods of doing business, and changes in the overall economic climate in which business is conducted. This theme has been a constant refrain, often repeated over the past 50 years.[9] The law should also be consistent

---

[6] Might not the Consumer Credit Act 1974 fall into this category?

[7] A. E. Anton, "Obstacles to Codification", 1982 J.R. 15 at pp. 16–17.

[8] Mackenzie D. Chalmers, "Codification of Commercial Law", (1903) 19 L.Q.R. 10 at p. 11. This was an address delivered to the American Bar Association.

[9] In a report submitted on April 5, 1995 to the members of the American Law Institute with a proposal for revising Art. 2 of the UCC, "radical changes" in the U.S. economy whose pace is "likely to accelerate" are cited as reasons for revision: *Uniform Commercial Code Revised Article 2: Transfers of Personal Property*. Grant Gilmore, in a perceptive essay published shortly before the promulgation of the U.C.C., took as his main theme the need for commercial law to adapt and respond to the needs of business: "On the Difficulties of Codifying Commercial Law", (1948) 57 Yale L.J. 1341. Note also, Goode, "Codification"; D. B. King, "Commercial Law: Times of Change and Expansion", in R. Cranston and R. Goode (eds), *Commercial and Consumer Law:*

with the "legitimate practice and expectations of the business community" while also being sufficiently certain as to effect. And, to the extent considered desirable and consistent with the need to protect special interest groups, such as consumers, parties should be free to determine the content of their obligations towards each other.[10] There is, of course, a connecting theme here and that is economic efficiency. A system of commercial law which can satisfy these imperatives is an economically efficient one and does not require to be changed as to the method or form of delivery. I would argue that the present mixture of legislation and common law not only meets these imperatives but does so more efficiently than a commercial code would. In part, this contention can be sustained by refutation of the advantages claimed for a commercial code over the status quo. On a more subtle tack, substantial redress of several of the systemic obstacles in our legal system to codification of the law have had the effect, not of opening it to an increased chance of codification, but of buttressing the argument that change is unnecessary.

Karl Llewellyn, the architect of the Uniform Commercial Code and no stranger to "civilian" legal thinking,[11] based his belief in the desirability of codifying commercial law in the United States on the premise that a mixed system of legislation and case law was unsuited to the development of a satisfactory general commercial jurisprudence. Of the two, legislation was to be preferred since it was prospective in design, proactive in effect, more general in application, and more focused as to consequence.[12] The problem with case law was that judges, perhaps understandably he conceded, were extremely cautious. Particularly where they feel that their decisions will have the effect of innovation, judges have a tendency not to overstate the degree of departure from the law as currently understood. Judicial fear of the prospective consequences of retrospective decisions reflects the unplanned dimension to case law and this compares less favourably with legislation which is consciously forward looking. But Llewellyn's argument against entrusting reform of commercial law to "dumb-bell judges"[13] is itself an illustration of the dangers of generalising about the law.

There are many examples of courts deciding commercial causes in a manner which refutes Llewellyn's point of view. Two recent cases which may be taken as representative of a larger number are *Samuel Hooper v. Royal London General Insurance Co. Ltd and Barclays Bank p.l.c.*

National and International Dimensions (1993), Ch 8; A. D. M. Forte, "A Great Future Behind It? Scottish Commercial Law and the Millennium" (1994) 2 European Review of Private Law 375.

[10] Goode, "Codification", supra, at p. 148, counts three of these ("flexibility", "predictability" and "party autonomy") among his "principles" for a philosophy of commercial law.

[11] W. L. Twining, *Karl Llewellyn and the Realist Movement* (1973). For an overview of possible civilian thinking in Llewellyn's work, see S. Herman, "Llewellyn the Civilian: Speculations on the Contribution of Continental Experience to the Uniform Commercial Code", (1982) 56 Tulane L.R. 1125.

[12] K. N. Llewellyn, *The Bramble Bush: On our Law and its Study* (1960), p. 78.

[13] K. N. Llewellyn, "Why a Commercial Code?", (1953) 22 Tenn. L.R. 779 at p. 782.

v. O'Brien.[14] In the first case the Second Division resolved the uncertainty relating to the proper method of determining the materiality of undisclosed facts in cases of indemnity insurance, declaring this to be (as it already was in England) the test of the reasonable insurer. But whereas the English law of insurance applies this test to *all* types of cover, the Scottish judges emphasised in the case that a different test, that of the reasonable insured, remained applicable to life assurance contracts.[15] Although one may disagree with the judicial reasons advanced in favour of this last test,[16] and although the case may appear to be a paradigm example of Llewellyn's criticisms, I do not see that it fails to do anything that could be better achieved if the appropriate test, even if it were a uniform one, were to be prescribed by statute.[17] Before the decision we were sure, and had been for over a century, as to the law regarding life assurance. Afterwards we were equally sure as to the law regarding indemnity insurance and reassured that the position had not changed for life contracts. Even if we disagree with the end result, we object only to the substance of a rule of law but not to its clarity or certainty. In the second case, the House of Lords imposed a duty on lenders taking security over a matrimonial home from a spouse or partner of the principal debtor to warn of the advisability of taking independent advice. In the leading judgment, Lord Browne-Wilkinson was very much concerned with clarifying "for the future" the circumstances in which lenders would be regarded as having discharged their duty to sureties. His formulation of a principle, that "if the known facts are such as to indicate the possibility of an adverse claim that is sufficient to put a third party on inquiry", and his extension of this to cover all situations where there is an "emotional relationship between cohabitees", whether married or not, homosexual as well as heterosexual, hardly smacks of the narrow containment of innovation attributed to judicial law-making by Llewellyn.[18] Even innovative appellate decisions confined to the issue before the court, such as the decision to award judgment in a foreign currency where the proper law of the contract was not English law, may expressly leave it open to inferior courts to "work out" its application in other contexts.[19] But in *Mumford v. Bank of Scotland; Smith v. Bank of Scotland*[20] the First Division declined to follow *Barclays Bank p.l.c. v. O'Brien*. While this divergence in the treatment of lenders' responsibilities is unfortunate in a unified economy, and the Scottish decision is inconsistent with the banks' own declared position in the *Good Banking* code of practice,[21] it is, nonetheless, based

---

[14] See, respectively, 1993 S.L.T. 679 and [1993] 4 All E.R. 417 (H.L.).

[15] *per* Lord Justice-Clerk Ross at p. 683 C. The test for life assurance was laid down in *Life Association of Scotland v. Foster* (1873) 11 M. 351.

[16] A. D. M. Forte, "The Materiality Test in Insurance" [1993] L.M.C.L.Q. 557.

[17] As it is in marine insurance under Marine Insurance Act 1906 (c.41), s. 18(2).

[18] *The Bramble Bush* at, p. 78.

[19] *Miliangos v. George Frank (Textiles) Ltd.* [1976] A.C. 443: "followed" in *Commerzbank Aktiengesellschaft v. Large*, 1977 S.C. 375.

[20] 1995 S.C.L.R. 839. See also E. McKendrick, "The Undue Influence of English Law", *infra*, 214–223.

[21] See now para. 14.1 of the 2nd ed., 1994.

on a correct interpretation of the Scottish authorities and, arguably, reflects a preferable policy of containment of an ever-increasing liability being visited on business parties. Even if one were to concede that this difference requires eradication, in order to equalise the law relating to the protection of cautioners and sureties alike, codification is quite unnecessary in order to achieve rational uniformity between the commercial laws of England and Scotland.

But one should not be defensive in this debate. The codifiers and their advocates do not have exclusive occupancy of the high ground and neither the substance nor the wording of the provisions of the U.C.C., for example, have been immune from criticism. Indeed, before getting too dewy-eyed about the codification of commercial law, the following views are a useful astringent:

> "No Uniform Commercial Code Article 2 provision has generated more controversy, legal commentary, and litigation than section 2–207. Professor Grant Gilmore once called it a 'miserable, bungled, patched up job' and 'arguably the greatest statutory mess of all time' "[22]

I am not suggesting that the U.C.C. is an unmitigated disaster any more than I should wish to label it the product of "dumb-bell academics"[23]; that would be both unfair and untrue. But it is not so superior in the manner in which it delivers the law as one may be asked to believe. And the case for codification along its lines is very far from irrefutable.[24]

Two further planks in the argument for codifying commercial law are the uncertainty and expense involved in discovering what the law is when it is in an uncodified form.[25] There is uncertainty where the issue is novel, and so the businessman lacks "assurance as to what the law is". There is uncertainty where lawyers are ignorant of the law.[26] And discovering or establishing what the law really is clearly has to be an expensive business. But the picture gets worse for business users because they soon learn to fear commercial law and try to avoid contact with it wherever possible. Uncodified commercial law is to be feared because it is both unfamiliar and, quite frequently, out of date. These are interesting points and, if true, might make me wish to reconsider my opposition to any move to codify commercial law. But one of the acknowledged defects of the U.C.C., at least in its original form, was the absence of empirical data about the needs and prac-

---

[22] M. E. Roszkowski and J. D. Wladis, "Revised U.C.C. Section 2–207: Analysis and Recommendations", [1994] 49 Bus. Law. 1065 at p. 1065. Llewellyn was the original draftsman of Art. 2.
[23] And then hope for some later apologist to excuse my "tone" as being "relaxed and casual": Herman, "Llewellyn", op. cit. at p. 1129.
[24] cf. Goode, "Codification", op. cit. at p. 157, who argues that the case for codification of commercial law was made out long ago by Karl Llewellyn and his colleagues.
[25] K. N. Llewellyn, "Why a Commercial Code?" supra, at pp. 779–780; Goode, "Codification", supra, at p. 138.
[26] A fact gleefully seized on by Llewellyn and graphically demonstrated by a remarkable example of his point: "Why a Commercial Code?", supra, at p. 781.

tices of business.[27] And it is curious that the lawyers who drafted the Code could know what business thought about commercial law without needing to be asked. Since one of the benefits claimed for the Code was that it could be easily used by lawyers who had never used it before,[28] then whatever the ideal, there is a strong inference that the U.C.C. was written by lawyers for lawyers. And even if the practice has since changed in the United States, subsequent revisions of the U.C.C., with its relatively concise provisions and much longer and detailed official comments (sometimes going well beyond what the wording of a provision warrants and sometimes suggesting a narrower interpretation than is justified) have not, if the volume of litigation generated by it is a reliable indicator, made life any easier for business or for the legal profession.[29] And litigation has not dried to a trickle as a consequence of commercial law codification on the Continent.[30] Any businessman who thinks that the codification of commercial law will "effect enormous savings of time, effort and money"[31] is going to find the reality quite different from the aspiration.[32]

We have already noted that continental codes are characterised, *inter alia*, by the generalised nature of their terms. Generalisation, it is argued, renders the code flexible and responsive to new and unimagined situations and is a means of preventing too rapid obsolescence.[33] In the case of the U.C.C., "open-ended" drafting and the requirement to construe its provisions "liberally", and to apply these so as to promote the "underlying purposes and policies" of the Code, combine to achieve the same ends.[34] But codes, even continental ones, still require to be revised or added to,[35] and Gilmore's prediction in 1948 that the proposed U.C.C. would have a shelf-life of around 25 years was too optimistic. As it turned out, it had to be revised three times in its first decade and the work of revision goes on. In their report of April 5 1995 on the revision of U.C.C., Article. 2, Professors Nimmer and Speidel emphasise the need to develop the Code continuously and describe the consequences of not doing so:

> "As new transactions and new types of property dominate the commercial landscape, the U.C.C. should incorporate at least some of these, providing commercially relevant contract law

---

[27] L. M. Friedman, *A History of American Law* (1985), at p. 675.
[28] K. N. Llewellyn, "Why a Commercial Code?", *supra*, at p. 782.
[29] J. White and R. S. Summers, *Uniform Commercial Code* (1988), at p. 13.
[30] Readers can conduct their own examination in verification. It will be a lengthy one.
[31] Goode, "Codification", *supra*, at p. 138.
[32] See the contradictory views of Robert Summers who debunks this as "Uniform Commercial Code Romanticism": *Uniform Commercial Code*, at pp. 21–22. Summers' co-author takes a different view but does not present a stronger case.
[33] Gilmore, "Difficulties of Codifying", *supra*, at p. 1355. Gilmore was at the time the Assistant Reporter for Art. 9 (Secured Transactions) of the draft U.C.C. Note also Anton, "Obstacles", *supra*, at p. 17.
[34] U.C.C. Art. 1–102. Art. 1–106 provides that remedies are to be "liberally administered".
[35] Sometimes reluctantly: Anton, "Obstacles", *supra*, at p. 30, citing Savatier, "Destin du Code Civil Francais", (1954) 6 Revue Internationale de Droit Compare 637 at p. 663.

principles. A failure to do so will attenuate the role of the U.C.C. by leaving outside its scope the most important forms of transaction".[36]

So it would seem that the inclusion of flexible wording or flexible concepts, such as "commercial reasonableness" or "good faith"[37], even when backed up by a battery of Code-declared "liberal" aids, cannot guarantee either its self-sufficiency or organic growth,[38] and, despite the hope that it would do so, there is no evidence to suggest that the role of precedent has been expunged by it.[39] A good system of commercial law must balance the need to be flexible against the need for certainty as to effect. The more generalised the law, the less certain its effect will be, and the less predictable the outcome of recourse to it. If, coupled to the high degree of generality required to ensure comprehensive coverage of the law, there is the intention that all cases decided under reference to the Code have illustrative value only,[40] then any pretence of certainty has to be abandoned.

A commercial code cannot escape its origins. It will be rooted in a particular commercial, economic, or technological *milieu* and drafted by legislators brought up in that climate and whose thinking will reflect the fact. While it will attempt to be as forward-looking as possible, it will inevitably fail in this; just as our existing statutes do from time to time. If it is drafted at a time of rapid developments in communications, finance, technology, or transport, then, unless it is expressed in extremely general terms, it will be out of date almost immediately.[41] Inevitably, it will have to be fairly detailed or it will be unacceptable to those who must work with it, and it will also have to be frequently revised if it is to remain the dominant source of commercial law.[42] In order to be truly that dominant source, there will

---

[36] *Uniform Commercial Code Revised Article 2: Transfers of Personal Property*, p. 3.

[37] Arts. 2 and 9.

[38] Goode, "Codification", *supra*, at p. 150.

[39] White and Summers, *Uniform Commercial Code*, at p. 10.

[40] J. Hawkland, "Uniform Commercial 'Code' Methodology", (1962) U.Ill.L.F. 291 One may contrast this with the following observation on the Sale of Goods Act: "It may be controversial to cite old cases on the meaning of merchantable quality in aid of interpreting an unhelpful definition, but the concept . . . and the difficulties of adapting it to modern conditions cannot be grasped without an enlightened sense of its development." See M. Bridge, "The Sale and Supply of Goods Act 1994", [1995] J.B.L. 398, at p. 399.

[41] Gilmore, "Difficulties of Codifying", *supra*. On the impact of business practices, the growth of credit, new technologies, and consumer protectionism, see King, "Commercial Law", *supra*, at pp. 124–127: this includes a survey of changes to the U.C.C. which will shortly be necessary.

[42] U.C.C. Art. 2, dealing with transfers of personal property, has been said to be the most influential of all the Code's provisions. Its structure has not been revised since the U.C.C. was first promulgated: *Uniform Commercial Code Revised Article 2: Transfers of Personal Property*, p 1. However, the introduction of Art. 2A on leasing reflected acceptance, not confined to the U.S.A., of the premise that possession can be an economically better option than ownership of depreciating assets. It is interesting that the drafters of this new article were more influenced by the law on the sale of goods than by that on the creation of securities: King, "Commercial Law", *supra*, at p. 129. The influence of the law of sale underwrites the Supply of Goods and Services Act 1982, Pt 1A, introduced by the Sale and Supply of Goods Act 1994, s. 6, Sched. 1.

have to be a sea-change in the habits and outlook of judges and practitioners to the role of precedent as a source of law. All of this, and for what benefit exactly? Through case law, through the decisions of commercial courts or of commercial judges, our law has evolved a responsive and highly satisfactory approach to the resolution of commercial disputes. Absence of legislation has not impeded the development of the law applicable to commercial instruments such as contract guarantees,[43] comfort letters,[44] documentary credits, and "swap" agreements.[45] And legislation can be quickly introduced to remedy decisions which, though technically correct, would produce unwanted consequences if allowed to stand.[46]

Among the many obstacles to codification which Professor Anton identified in 1982 was the change which this would require to our rules of statutory interpretation. As Anton observed, recourse might be had to a wider range of aids in interpreting codes than our courts would permit when construing legislation, and argued that it would be difficult to persuade Parliament and the legal profession to break free of the current rules of statutory interpretation and of precedent.[47] But these "obstacles" have been steadily diminishing over the past 20 years.[48] Reference to *traveaux preparatoires* is expressly permitted by a number of statutes implementing international conventions dealing with commercial matters.[49] In the case of the Civil Jurisdiction and Judgments Act 1982, not only is reference to the *traveaux preparatoires* allowed, but the courts are obliged to take notice of principles established by the courts of other states which are parties to the Lugano Convention and they may also consider, *inter alia*, the work of academic lawyers.[50] Even in relation to purely domestic legislation the obstacles have been coming down. The House of Lords has abandoned a "strict constructionist" approach to interpretation in favour

---

[43] See the most recent pronouncement by the House of Lords in *Trafalgar House Construction (Regions) Ltd v. General Surety and Guarantee Co. Ltd* [1995] 3 All E.R. 737 (H.L.).

[44] *Kleinwort Benson Ltd v. Malaysian Mining Corp. Berhad* [1989] 1 All E.R. 785.

[45] *Morgan Guaranty Trust Co. of New York v. Lothian Regional Council*, 1995 SLT 299.

[46] Witness the Insolvency Act 1994 (c. 7), passed to amend s. 19 of the Insolvency Act 1986 (c. 45) regarding the liabilities of administrators and receivers under contracts of employment which they had adopted. The amendment received the Royal Assent on March 24, 1994, in response to the decision of the Court of Appeal in *Powdrill v. Watson* [1994] 2 All E.R. 513 ([1995] 2 All E.R. 65 (H.L.)) delivered on February 22, 1994. The 1994 Act had limited retrospective effect, applying to contracts adopted on or after March 15, 1994. For criticism of this limited retrospectivity see D. McKenzie, "Insolvency", 1995 Bus. L.R. 15–6.

[47] Anton, "Obstacles", *supra*, at p. 25.

[48] M. Kerr, "Modern Trends in Commercial Law and Practice" [1978] 41 M.L.R. 1 at p. 17.

[49] Civil Jurisdiction and Judgments Act 1982 (c. 27), ss. 3(3) and 3B(2): added by the Civil Jurisdiction and Judgments Act 1991 (c. 45); Contracts (Applicable Law) Act 1990 (c. 36), s. 3(3); Law Reform (Miscellaneous Provisions) (Scotland) Act 1990 (c. 40), s. 66(1).

[50] Civil Jurisdiction and Judgments Act 1982 (c.27), s. 3B(1) and (2). The possibility of judges finding assistance in academic writings was stated by the Lord Chancellor, Lord Mackay: Hansard, H.L., Vol. 524, col. 923. In *Bank of Scotland v. Seitz*, 1990 S.L.T. 584, at p. 587 D, Lord President Hope considered the *Reports* by Mr Jenard and Professor Schlosser.

of one which is "purposive" and which emphasises that material relating to the policies underlying legislation may be considered.[51] White Papers and the Law Commissions' reports may be looked at, as may Hansard, all in appropriate circumstances.[52]

In addition to the shift towards a purposive interpretation of legislation, we can also see a commensurate, purposive, approach being taken in relation to the application of the common law. Older, inconvenient, decisions may be explained away as the products of very different economic conditions from those which obtain today,[53] thereby diluting the *stare decisis* doctrine.[54] Moreover, the past 30 years have seen the higher courts repeatedly emphasise the importance in commercial causes of ensuring that decisions do not fly in the face of "commercial reality". Although this attitude may not always be articulated as such, the judgments often reveal an awareness of economic factors which militate in favour of the decisions taken.[55] But a clear example of this approach is that taken by the First Division recently in *Eurocopy (Scotland) p.l.c. v. Lothian Health Board*.[56] In determining the nature of a standard form contract for the supply of two photocopiers (was the contract one of hire or an innominate contract for the sale of unused quantities of paper?), the court rejected an "analytical" approach to interpretation in favour of one according with "commercial reality" and consistent with "business commonsense". It is worth quoting the relevant passage in full, for it is a clear statement of policy and a directive on the proper approach to the interpretation of commercial contracts:

> "It seems to us ... that the result of this analytical approach to the meaning of the contract is far removed from its commercial reality. In *Antaios Compania Naviera S.A. v. Salen Rederierna A.B.* at p. 201D Lord Diplock said[57] that he agreed with a passage in the arbitrators' award in which they stated that a construction should be given to the withdrawal clause in a charterparty which did not defeat the commercial purpose of the contract. He then added these words: 'I take this opportunity of re-stating that if a detailed semantic and syntactical analysis of words in a commercial contract is going to lead to a conclusion that flouts business commonsense, it must be made to yield to business commonsense.' "[58]

---

[51] *Pepper (Inspector of Taxes) v. Hart* [1993] A.C. 593. White and Summers, *Uniform Commercial Code*, at p. 18, indicate that U.S. courts adopt a similar, "rationale-oriented" approach to interpreting the U.C.C. The drafters intended this.

[52] The leading cases in this process of attrition are: *Pepper v. Hart* [1993] A.C. 593; *R. v. Secretary of State for Transport, ex p. Factortame* [1990] 2 A.C. 85; *Pickstone v. Freeman's p.l.c.* [1989] A.C. 66. But in one of Bill Wilson's favourite cases, *Katikoro of Buganda v. Att.-Gen.* [1960] 2 All E.R. 849, the Privy Council indicated that White Papers might be looked at to resolve ambiguities in a statute.

[53] *Commerzbank Aktiengesellschaft v. Large*, 1977 S.C. 375.

[54] See Kerr, "Modern Trends", *supra*, at p. 7.

[55] *e.g.*, *G. M. Shepherd Ltd v. North West Securities Ltd* 1991 S.L.T. 499.

[56] 1995 S.C.L.R. 892.

[57] [1985] A.C. 191.

[58] 1995 S.C.L.R. 892, at p. 898 D.

Common sense told the court that in this case the contract was one of hire.

There is another feature of our uncodified commercial law which may be said to compare unfavourably with the interpretation techniques available to commercial lawyers in the United States and in western Europe. This concerns the role to be attributed to contemporary academic commentators on the law. Should their work, when it is directly relevant to the issue in dispute, be freely referred to and freely considered by the courts? At one time the attitude of the Scottish courts towards non-practitioner writers was notorious. It went far beyond Bill Wilson's pithy summation—"better read when dead"[59]— of the attitude of many Inner House judges and could be contrasted, most unfavourably,[60] with that displayed by the senior judiciary in England and many other jurisdictions.[61] But this attitude is no longer the one which predominates in the Court of Session. A younger generation of judges, the product of full-time legal education, taught by full-time academic lawyers of Bill Wilson's standing, used to the citation of a wide variety of source material, and exposed to broader and more intellectually stimulating courses of study in the law schools, are supplanting the old guard. There may be the occasional, disappointing, outburst of outmoded thought,[62] though nothing that retirement will not eventually cure. But to be effective a change in outlook has to be top-driven. And here again we have had the strongest indication that old attitudes will have to be abandoned. In *Morgan Guaranty Trust Co. of New York v. Lothian Regional Council*, Lord President Hope dealt, at some length, with the help which courts might derive from academic works and concluded that the court was "better placed now than our predecessors were at two critical stages in our history . . . to reach an informed decision as to whether the error of law rule really is part of Scots Law".[63]

Relaxation of the obstacles to codification does not, however, lead us to conclude that we should codify. There is no need for a code of generalised principles when the policy and direction of the law may be ascertained or determined from a broad tapestry of "sources". If the change in attitude towards the use of contemporary legal literature continues to gain acceptance among our newer senior judges, then, when combined with the more relaxed attitude now taken to both statutory interpretation and to the role of precedent, the range of material available to be drawn upon and heightened consciousness of the imperative of keeping commercial law relevant to the needs of the

---

[59] W. A. Wilson, "Knowing the Law and Other Things", 1982 J.R. 259 at p. 267.
[60] The neutrality of academic observers of this phenomenon might be suspect. But the comments of a Lord Advocate cannot be lightly dismissed: see Lord Rodger of Earlsferry (A. F. Rodger), "Mrs Donoghue and Alfenus Varus", [1988] Current Legal Problems 1; "The Bell of Law Reform", 1993 S.L.T. (News) 339.
[61] *Woolwich Building Society v. I.R.C.* [1993] A.C. 70; *David Securities Pty. Ltd v. Commonwealth Bank of Australia* (1991–1992) 175 C.L.R. 353; *Hydro-Electric Commission of the Township of Nepean v. Ontario Hydro* (1982) 1 S.C.R. 347 *per* Dickson J (dissenting); *Willis Faber Enthoven (Pty.) Ltd v. Receiver of Revenue*, 1992 (4) S.A. 202.
[62] *Fortune v. Fraser*, 1995 S.C.L.R. 121 at p. 126B: a Second Division decision.
[63] 1995 S.L.T. 299 at p. 311 B-D.

market and its users (and our commercial law is no stranger to the relevance of custom and trade usage) will continue to ensure that degree of flexibility which is necessary for the smooth operation of that market. At the same time, predictability is not impaired for the effect of these changed attitudes is to render more certain the state of the law at any point.

Today, to talk of "obstacles" to codification is arguably to employ the wrong rhetoric; for this may be misconstrued as suggesting systemic differences which obstruct the progress of a superior methodology but do not refute it. This is not so, and the benefit of codifying commercial law is not *res ipsa loquitur*. If one were to argue for such codification on the model of the U.C.C. then it is difficult to see what such a code could do which cannot already be achieved in the United Kingdom at present. It is not a comprehensive codification of commercial law since many matters are not dealt with,[64] and, as with our statutory codifications, certain issues remain subject to the common law.[65] Nor have the American courts approached the U.C.C. as "a unique source of new law"[66]: they do not find it easy to apply its provisions without paying attention to the interpretations put on these by other courts. The American courts have also been reluctant to refer to prior drafts and official texts of the U.C.C., possibly because these may not be regarded as reliable guides to interpretation.[67] Changing to a commercial code on this model would be a self-indulgent extravagance and wasteful of time and effort which could be better spent dealing with real problems. Changes based on continental models are open to the same basic objection. Is there any evidence to suggest that our continental business counterparts are less litigious because of codification? Is there any evidence to indicate that codification would be more cost-effective than our present system? Principles can be articulated just as easily by the courts as by a code. The courts can probably respond to changing business practices and technology more quickly than a code can. If the rules of precedent were abandoned, predictability would be badly impaired and litigation costs would have to be regarded as a normal item of business expenditure. Ensuring that litigation can swiftly resolve commercial disputes when resorted to, and that arbitration and alternative dispute resolution techniques are available as alternatives, is a real priority and benefits business users of the law. Codification of the substantive law will not confer any comparable benefit. Indeed, it would be profoundly disruptive of a system which works and works well. It should not be attempted.

---

[64] *e.g.*, bankruptcy, some aspects of insurance, security interests in real property with the exception of fixtures, and suretyship.

[65] Bills of Exchange Act 1882 (c.61), s. 97; Partnership Act 1890 (c.39), s. 46; Marine Insurance Act 1906 (c.41), s. 91(2); Sale of Goods Act 1979 (c.54), s. 62(2).

[66] Anton, "Obstacles" *supra*, at p. 24.

[67] White and Summers, *Uniform Commercial Code*, p. 11. American courts have, however, relied heavily on the official comments: *ibid.*, p. 12.

STATUTORY INTERPRETATION: THE WILSONIAN ANALYSIS

GERRY MAHER

I

The topic of statutory interpretation fascinated Bill Wilson throughout his life as an academic lawyer, and was one to which he returned again and again in his teaching and published writings. There is an important link between Wilson's interest in this subject as a teacher and as writer. He took the view that many (though it must be stressed, not all) texts and books on statutory interpretation, especially those prescribed to students in their first years of legal study, were positively misleading in focusing on the unusual aspects of the subject, namely the technical rules and principles of interpretation. Instead, Wilson felt that students should get to know, and as soon as possible in their studies, the normal practices of reading and interpreting statutes. His view was that to tell students, or anyone else seeking guidance on statutory interpretation, about the mischief rule or the golden rule or presumptions against strict criminal liability or the limits of the use of Hansard or Law Commission reports and so on, was to present statutory interpretation as set of technical *legal* rules and principles. For Bill Wilson statutory interpretation did indeed involve rules but the important ones were rules of practice, which reflected the frequent and common activity of lawyers who used statutes as day-to-day tools. Accordingly in his writings he sought to put right this distorted picture of statutory interpretation. In an impressive list of articles and papers, written over four decades, he presented the outline of a general model of statutory interpretation, in an original and incisive approach, to give a more realistic version of the subject.[1] Furthermore, in various other writings which dealt either with statute law in general or other legal topics altogether, he made a long list of perceptive comments on statutory interpretation.[2]

Taken altogether these writings constitute a major contribution to our understanding of statutory interpretation. However there is a further, and typically Wilsonian, twist to the tale of his writings on this subject. At the date of his death, he had written drafts of various papers on statutory interpretation, which were clearly intended for

---

[1] See "A Note on Fact and Law", (1963) 26 M.L.R. 609; "The Complexity of Statutes", (1974) 37 M.L.R. 497; "Questions of Interpretation", (1987) 8 Stat. L.R. 142; "Trials and Try-Ons: Modes of Interpretation" (1992) 13 Stat. L.R. 1; "Oblique Answers to Straight Questions: the Article 177 Procedure" (1994) 15 Stat. L.R. 31; *Introductory Essays on Scots Law* (1st ed. 1978); (2nd ed. 1984), chapter on "Interpreting Statutes".

[2] See especially "Knowing the Law and Other Things", 1982 J.R. 259; "The Progress of the Law 1888–1988", 1988 J.R. 207; "Studying Statutes", 1992 J.R. 213; *Introductory Essays, supra* chapters on "The Study of Scots Law", "Law and Language", and "Reading Statutes".

publication in book form. Much of the content of these papers would not be surprising to anyone who had read his published work but the unity of the writings in book form does give an added dimension to his approach. Yet it may also have been this search for a consistent theoretical unity and coherence which explains (at least in part) why these papers were never published in the form intended for them. Accordingly, although this paper is concerned with examining the major themes of Wilson's general approach to statutory interpretation, the appropriate starting point is with the unpublished papers, for they help to bring out what is truly distinctive about the whole Wilsonian enterprise. And if nothing else they present an interesting story in their own right.

II

It was part of the great Wilsonian legend, even in his own lifetime, that he was in possession of the manuscripts of books which he had written but had not (yet) had published.[3] What was certainly the case was that by the mid-1970s he had completed a draft of a book on statutory interpretation and some time later was actively taking steps to have the book published. But the book on statutory interpretation never reached a form which was mutually acceptable to author and would-be publisher. The explanation for this state of affairs provides a pointer to the originality of Wilson's work in this area.

The unpublished Wilson papers on statutory interpretation can be divided into two distinct categories. I should stress that the only reason for making this distinction is that the state of the papers themselves suggest some such classification. For reasons to become obvious later, nothing necessarily follows from all this as to Wilson's intentions as to how (indeed if at all) the two sets of papers were ultimately to be related to each other in published form. Purely, then, for the sake of exposition in this paper I will refer to the unpublished Wilson writings on statutory interpretation as the "A-papers" and the "B-papers".

The A-papers are the bulkier of the two sets. They amount to 10 chapters, identified and numbered as such, in a coherent order, and clearly set out a complete view of statutory interpretation. The papers are not dated but the revised footnotes refer to cases in the 1991 law reports.[4] The key chapter of the A-papers is the first, where in Wilson's own words he "attempts to formulate a coherent procedure for the interpretation of statutes." A broadly similar version of this paper was published in article form in 1992.[5] In the manuscript chapter, Wilson described the types of questions which arise in statutory interpretation, such as problems of syntactic ambiguity, grammar, and generality of language. However its real focus is on statutory provisions

---

[3] This was certainly true of his book on debt and there was also a similar though perhaps apocryphal story about a book on conveyancing (see above, p. 7, n. 41).

[4] The latest cases to feature in these writings are *R. v. Secretary of State for the Home Department, ex p. Brind* [1991] 1 A.C. 696 and *Att.-Gen. of Trinidad and Tobago v. Whiteman* [1991] 2 W.L.R. 1200.

[5] "Trials and Try-ons: Modes of Interpretation", (1992) 13 Stat. L.R. 1.

where an ordinary word poses some semantic difficulty (either through ambiguity, generality or obscurity of meaning). As regards this sort of problem of statutory interpretation, Wilson proposed a three-stage procedure.

1. The first stage deals with ascertaining the ordinary meaning of the word or words by considering dictionaries, literary works, the judge's own sense of language and the like. Account also has to be taken of a possible range between the word's primary and secondary meanings.

2. The second stage then attempts to find the meaning of the word by locating its narrower or immediate context; at this stage the interpreter looks at other parts of the statute in question, praying in aid such devices as *noscitur a sociis* and *eiusdem generis* as well as considering the mischief the statute was to remedy. This stage involves looking to the intention of Parliament as that intention is disclosed from the words of the Act. It is at this last point that, for Wilson, account is to be taken of a "purposive" approach to statutory interpretation.

3. The third, and final, stage has two different branches. The particular branch to use depends upon whether or not there remains any ambiguity (a term analysed here). The first branch is to be used where there is still ambiguity; if so, the ambiguity is to be resolved by placing the word in a wider context by considering such matters as presumptions, canons of construction, and a whole range of other material.[6] If there is no ambiguity or it has been resolved by using the first branch, what remains is to consider the words by reference to the competing principles embodied in the literal and golden rules.

What Chapter 1 does then is to set out the general model of statutory interpretation. The remaining nine chapters of the A-papers go on to provide the detail of this model, with the appropriate qualifications and difficulties of detail noted.

Stage 1 of the general model is dealt with in Chapter 2, which gives a detailed account of interpretation sections and the Interpretation Act 1978, and Chapter 3, which describes how dictionaries and other expressions of usage can be deployed to determine the ordinary meaning of words.

Stage 2 is covered in Chapters 4 and 5, which provide the detail of the so-called "primary" context and the intention of Parliament.

Chapter 6 then deals with branch 1 of stage 3, that is the wider context, and the same level is considered in Chapter 7 on presumptions.

The last three chapters deal with additional matters. Chapter 9 is concerned with ancillary provisions such as commencement,

---

[6] Wilson's own words here are: "Once an ambiguity has been established, assistance can certainly be sought from further materials—side-notes, punctuation, cross-headings, chapter headings, the short and long title, the preamble, schedules, earlier Acts, later Acts, the legislative history and so on." Each item on this list is extensively footnoted to appropriate judicial pronouncements in decided cases. The manuscript continues: "A distinction can be drawn between the relevance and weight of this material."

retrospectivity, extent, and repeals. Chapter 10 analyses special types of legislation (*e.g.* codifying and consolidation Acts, delegated legislation, E.E.C. (*sic*) legislation, and so on). What is the weakest of the A-papers is Chapter 8, entitled "Implication and Effect". Under "Effect" it considers such matters as the distinctions between mandatory, directory and permissive provisions. Under "Implications" there is a very short account of "implied limitations" based on public policy. Of the A-papers only this chapter, which links the detailed statement of the general model with other issues, can be said to be undeveloped.

This point is of significance once the B-papers are considered. There are four papers in this set. The B-papers, although building upon ideas in previously published articles, are obviously in more of a rough draft form than the A-papers, though they were being revised by Wilson at about the same time.[7] Further, there is no obvious internal indication of the order of these papers.

The first of the B-papers provides a list of the types of arguments used by the courts in dealing with issues of statutory interpretation, by way of examples from decided cases under each head of argument. The second B-paper is a very long paper dealing with the classification of statutory provisions. However written additions to the manuscript indicate that this paper was to form four separate chapters: of these the first deals with non-operative provisions (*e.g.* definitions, factorials, additionals), the others with a very detailed account of operative statutory provisions. This paper is a more detailed and thorough re-statement of many of the ideas previously presented in a published article.[8]

The third B-paper is a very basic anatomy of an Act of Parliament, much more skeletal than the equivalent paper in *Introductory Essays on Scots Law*.[9] The fourth and final paper deals with the different ways in which statutory provisions can be re-arranged or represented, as by flow-charts, logical trees, and decision logic tables. This paper is also a re-working of ideas set out in an earlier published work on statutory classification.[10]

III

Any assessment of the Wilsonian approach to statutory interpretation, both in the published articles and the unpublished papers, must confront the question of what for Wilson were the boundaries of the subject. His writings can be read as adopting either a narrow or a broad conception of statutory interpretation. One complicating factor is that

---

[7] The drafts of the B-papers are dated 1991.
[8] "The Complexity of Statutes" (1974) 37 M.L.R. 497.
[9] "Reading Statutes", p. 87.
[10] "Complexity of Statutes", *supra*. Wilson once made a similar point about methods of presenting facts: "Lawyers tend to assemble facts in strings of prose but there are other methods; we use different information structures in menus, family trees, railway timetables, temperature charts, and for describing naval battles or reporting the results of the Oxford Summer Eights" (*Introductory Essays, supra*, at p. 5).

Wilson was also very interested in the subject of statutes generally, and indeed once wrote that the academic emphasis on statutory interpretation as an aspect of statute law tended to obscure other important issues in the study of statutes.[11] The difficulty then is one of determining the limits of statutory interpretation as part of the study of the more general subject of statute law. This point is of more significance than merely setting out the limits of a book. One of the major themes of recent theories of legal reasoning is precisely the relationship between text, interpretation and interpreter.[12]

Wilson's writings on statutory interpretation can be classified as either descriptive, *i.e.* of the practices of judges as interpreters or as analytical, *i.e.* examining the nature of statutory texts and the concepts used in their interpretation. Broadly speaking, what I have called the A-papers are descriptive, whereas the B-papers are in the main analytical in nature. What then for Wilson was the proper relationship between these two levels of the study of statutory interpretation? Or to put the same point another way, was he writing one book or two books on statutory interpretation (or even one book on statutory interpretation and another on statute law in general)?

As the published papers are to be found in various journals appearing over a period of time, it is difficult to extract any answer from them. In *Introductory Essays on Scots Law* there are two papers in juxtaposition, one on "reading" statutes, the other on "interpreting" statutes, but this treatment is consistent with both approaches to the nature of the subject. The strongest clue is to be found in the unpublished papers, especially in the different states of completion of the drafts of the two different sets of papers. And what these papers suggest is that they were being prepared for publication separately.

However, as far as can be inferred from comments which Wilson made to various colleagues about his plans for his work on statutory interpretation, the position was that he was aware of commercial pressures from potential publishers to write a book on statutory interpretation of an essentially "descriptive" type; and that in due course another book would appear on the analytical aspects of his work, perhaps as part of a more general book on statute law. Yet at the same time Wilson was never happy with this bifurcated approach; for him the descriptive and analytical studies were properly part of the subject of statutory interpretation and both had a place in a book on that subject.

Nonetheless, as I indicated earlier, the descriptive side of Wilson's

---

[11] "Studying Statutes", *supra*, at p. 215. In this paper Wilson included among the other parts of statute law such matters as the user-friendliness of statutes, the effect of E.C. law on the accessibility of U.K. law, the chaotic state of the publication of statutory instruments, and the styles of statutory draftsmen, especially those who drafted Scottish statutes. Interestingly he also included the topic of classification of statutory provisions, of which he wrote that whatever other value it might have, it was a matter of academic interest.

[12] For an account of these theories and their implications for statutory interpretation see D. Miers, "Legal Theory and the Interpretation of Statutes", in W. Twining (ed), *Legal Theory and Common Law* (1986). I revert below to the idea of theoretical context as part of Wilson's approach to statutory interpretation.

writings, especially in their more coherent state in the unpublished papers, by themselves amount to a significant contribution to the subject. It is also easy to sympathise with a publisher who wanted to publish only the A-papers in book form. A first and practical point is that of length: the A-papers take up some 350 pages of manuscript. Further and crucially the papers do form a book which would have obvious commercial attraction. This is so because of two main attributes of Wilson's descriptive writings. The first is that the A-papers impose a structure and order on the subject. Not everyone would agree that the Wilsonian three-stage approach to interpreting statutes captures exactly how judges and other interpreters of statutes go about their task. But there is value in having *some* structure, and Wilson's account is, in my view, sufficiently close to the reality of statutory interpretation to form an acceptable descriptive model of the subject.

A second and related point is that Wilson gets all the disparate parts of the subject, not just into any order (which itself is no mean feat), but in the correct order. As noted earlier, the rules and principles and presumptions beloved of various academic writers play a very secondary role in the Wilsonian approach. What for him is crucial is to appreciate that in interpreting a statute a reader begins by using the same general method which is taken towards reading any text. Only once there has been a failure to determine the meaning of statutory words by deploying the familiar modes of interpreting a text, do we resort to the peculiarly (and at time peculiar) *legal* rules and principles which the courts have devised for reading statutes. In a celebrated passage Wilson once wrote:[13]

> "In the universities when we talk about statutes we tend to talk about the interpretation of statutes. Those of my generation feel a sense of profound shock at the changes which have taken place in statutory interpretation in the last 20 or so years. We are appalled by the crumbling of the massive pillars of principle of statutory interpretation which has taken place."

There is here, I suspect, a considerable dosage of Wilsonian irony. He was not for the wholesale destruction of these "pillars". The technical rules of statutory interpretation had a place but that place was very much at the end-point of the method of statutory interpretation.

The A-papers in book form contain some further Wilsonian oddities. For example, the style is the familiar one of concise and precise statements, followed by footnote reference to detailed case law citations. Accordingly there is little by way of overt argument but, as it were, the accumulation of statements in the text are allowed to speak for themselves and move the reader towards a conclusion without giving rise to the feeling of being argued into one. There is also

---

[13] "Studying Statutes", 1992 J.R. 213 at p. 213. Since the time of this paper another column has fallen, at least for the time being, through the decision of the House of Lords in *Pepper v. Hart* [1993] A.C. 593. See further N. C. Walker, "The Crumbling Pillars of Statutory Interpretation", pp. 126–137, below.

virtually no reference to secondary writings, and where there is, it often relates to matters other than statutory interpretation.[14]

Furthermore, Wilson refrains from making critical comment: his job was to describe, not to censure. Indeed in the whole set of A-papers there are only two occasions where overtly critical points are made. On one occasion a judicial dictum is noted to which is added the comment: "but that seems contrary to principle". On the other the point is put even more briefly, where he noted of a particular view: "It seems wrong".[15] By one of those odd coincidences, it was the same judge on the receiving end of both brickbats, namely Lord Scarman.

Another oddity about the A-papers is that they make reference almost exclusively to English authorities, and virtually ignore Scottish cases. Indeed technical terms of English law are used without explanation. Where Wilson deals with the topic of interpreting a provision by considering the corresponding legislative position in the other jurisdiction, the starting point is that of English law.[16] He did at one time write that "there has been a change in the approach of the Scottish judiciary to the interpretation of statutes; there was a long period when Scottish judges in interpreting statutes very rarely referred to any principles of interpretation".[17] This observation is puzzling. If by principle Wilson meant technical legal rules or principles, this would hardly matter, for these types of rule have only a secondary role in his scheme of things. If he had in mind descriptive rather than technical principles, then again this would not prevent use of Scottish cases as the crucial matter in description is what the courts do when interpreting statutes, not what the judges say they are doing when they do so. Indeed, as a recent and thorough account of statutory interpretation in Scots law brings out, there is now and always has been an abundance of Scottish authority for both the descriptive and technical rules of statutory interpretation.[18]

Perhaps the most surprising feature of the A-papers is the virtual lack of analysis. Technical terms such as syntactic or semantic are used without any detailed explanation. There are, it is true, examples of the typically Wilsonian sort of analysis, such as in his discussion of the brocard *contemporanea expositio est fortissimo in lege*, where he teases out several distinct levels of meaning, and an even clearer example

---

[14] See for example Chap. 10 where there are footnote references to writings on the legislative process in connection with consolidation Acts, and on the issue of the direct effects of E.C. directives. Where there is reference to writings on statutory interpretation, usually the work referred to is Francis Bennion's *Statutory Interpretation*, (2nd ed., 1992). There is also an occasional mention of Maxwell on *The Interpretation of Statutes*, (12th ed. 1969).

[15] These critical comments are made in Chaps. 5 and 6. The first is occasioned by the suggestion that courts may consider the social background of an Act as at the time of interpretation rather than the date of enactment: *Williams & Glyn's Bank v. Boland* [1981] A.C. 487, *per* Lord Scarman at p. 510. The other point is Scarman, L.J.'s view that the European Convention on Human Rights could be considered even in respect of U.K. statutes passed prior to the U.K.'s ratification of the Convention: *Ahmad v. Inner London Education Authority* [1978] Q.B. 36 at p. 48.

[16] A-papers, Chap. 4.

[17] "Studying Statutes", *supra* at p. 215.

[18] J. Fleming Wallace, "Interpretation of Statutes", *Stair Memorial Encyclopedia*, Vol. 12 (1992), pp. 502–565.

where the term "retrospective" is separated out into its various meanings.[19]

Perhaps it is this lack of detailed analysis in the A-papers which provides the strongest support for the view that whatever Wilson may have accepted as realistic proposals for publication, ideally what he wanted was a treatment of statutory interpretation which dealt with both the descriptive and analytical levels of the subject.[20] Yet paradoxically it might also have been his interest in analytical questions which led him to accept that the two aspects of his work would have to be presented separately.

This last point requires some elaboration. As noted before, the two sets of unpublished papers were in different states of completion at the time of Wilson's death. Unlike the descriptive A-papers, the analytical B-papers are very much at the stage of an early draft. At first sight this appears surprising as many of the themes of these papers had appeared in a developed way in his published works. Yet the B-papers were being revised at the same time as the A-papers. What I suspect had happened was that Wilson was fully aware of various theoretical developments which would require substantial re-working of the analytical themes of his statutory interpretation project, and that simply to reproduce the substance of the published analytical papers would not do.

The major theoretical principle to be found in the analytical papers, both published and unpublished, is the idea of classification of statutory provisions, and the related idea that statutes can be represented in a variety of ways to reflect these classificatory schemes. This is a broad theme which Wilson touched upon in one of his earliest pieces on statutory interpretation.[21] However, a significant breakthrough in this area was the publication in 1970 of the definitive version of Bentham's work *Of Laws in General*, which sets out a detailed scheme of the structure of legal systems and the individuation of the single legal units of which legal systems are made up.[22]

The importance of this event was not so much in terms of Bentham's own scheme, which Wilson himself once referred to as the "arid path taken by Bentham in his *Of Laws in General*",[23] but in its effect in revitalising this issue as part of analytical jurisprudence. Indeed within the following 20 years or so the topics of the structure and individuation of law underwent considerable development and refinement.[24]

---

[19] These appear at Chaps. 6 and 9 of the A-papers respectively.
[20] Although this is a matter of speculation, a further factor which may have influenced Wilson's plans was the publication of Bennion's *Statutory Interpretation* in 1984. Bennion's book provides a descriptive "code" for statutory interpretation, and although Wilson's own descriptive model was different from Bennion's in significant respects, Wilson may have felt that his own work should possess the wider boundaries of the analytical writings.
[21] "A Note on Fact and Law", (1963) 26 M.L.R. 609.
[22] For a good introduction to Bentham's detailed and difficult work, see H. L. A. Hart, *Essays on Bentham* (1982), Ch. 5. It is worthy of note that Bentham never finalised the manuscript of this work which was not published in his own lifetime.
[23] "Complexity of Statutes", *supra*, as p. 497.
[24] For a useful account of modern work on the individuation of laws, see R. Susskind, *Expert Systems in Law* (1987), a book with which Wilson was familiar: see "Studying Statutes", *supra*, at p. 224.

There can be no doubt that Wilson was familiar with this modern scholarship, nor any doubt of his ambition to re-think his own approach to take account of it. Indeed the revised B-papers strongly suggest that he was influenced in this area by the writings of his Edinburgh colleague Neil MacCormick, whose institutional theory of law was adapted in Wilson's revised analytical papers.[25]

A further and related analytical issue which Wilson dealt with in his published work was the particular division of statutory terms into operative and non-operative provisions. The recognition that some legal language had operative effects was introduced into mainstream legal theory by H. L. A. Hart, who drew on the writings of the philosopher J. L. Austin.[26] On this issue too there has been considerable theoretical development, especially in the writings of the philosopher John Searle and his theory of "speech acts". The stress placed in these works on the background rules of operative language was a major influence on the theory of legal institutions which Wilson did follow in his own later writings.[27]

A different type of theoretical issue which Wilson used in his approach to statutory interpretation concerned the vagueness of language, especially the sort of language typically to be found in statutes. His writings, both published and unpublished, frequently mention such ideas as ambiguity, generality and vagueness, and he also made explicit reference in this context to the concept of "open texture" associated with the philosopher Friedrich Waismann.[28] However, modern theorists have suggested that these various aspects of language are not variations of one single idea but are rather quite different concepts altogether. As a consequence, different techniques are required for resolving problems posed by each type of linguistic "difficulty".[29]

A final area where revision of the unpublished papers is required in order to take account of developments in legal theory is in what may be called the problem of context. At Chapter 8 of the A-papers,

[25] See D. N. MacCormick, "Law as Institutional Fact", (1974) 90 L.Q.R. 102; D. N. MacCormick and O. Weinberger, *An Institutional Theory of Law* (1986). The first of the Wilson B-papers in particular shows a heavy MacCormick influence.

[26] Hart's main works in this regard can be found in papers in his *Essays in Jurisprudence and Philosophy* (1983), especially at pp. 3–4 and Chaps. 1, 3, and 12. See also his *The Concept of Law*, (1st ed. 1961), Chap. 5. For discussion of J. L. Austin's influence on Hart on this matter, see D. N. MacCormick, *H. L. A. Hart* (1981), pp. 12–19; D. N. MacCormick and Z. Bankowski, "Speech Acts, Legal Institutions, and Real Laws", in D. N. MacCormick and P. Birks (ed), *The Legal Mind: Essays for Tony Honore* (1986).

[27] For the theory of legal institutions, see works referred to at n. 25 above. For a thorough account of speech act theory and its implications for legal theory, see P. Amselek, "Philosophy of Law and the Theory of Speech Acts", (1988) 1 Ratio Juris 187.

[28] Wilson explicitly referred to Waismann in *Introductory Essays on Scots Law* at p. 10 (chapter on "Law and Language").

[29] For an excellent discussion of the range of issues involved in the idea of vagueness see Jeremy Waldron, "Vagueness in Law and Language: Some Philosophical Issues" (1994) 82 Cal. L.R. 509. For discussion of open texture, see B. Bix, *Law, Language and Legal Determinacy* (1993), Chap. 1; N. MacCormick, "On 'Open Texture' in Law", in P. Amselek and N. MacCormick, *Controversies About the Law's Ontology* (1991), p. 72.

under the heading of general implications, Wilson wrote: "statutory provisions which are in terms unqualified may nevertheless be subject to implied limitations based upon principles of public policy accepted by the courts at the time when the Act was passed." He gives as an example the question whether the provisions of the Administration of Estates Act 1925 allowed a murderer to take under his victim's intestacy, and cites three cases on this point.[30] However the authority which springs to the mind of many students of jurisprudence on this general legal question is not an English or Scottish decision but the New York case of *Riggs v. Palmer*, popularised among British lawyers by the theoretical writings of Ronald Dworkin.[31] Dworkin's writings make a major contribution to any study of statutory interpretation. Not only does his theory examine the general legal context of judicial decision-making (including decisions involving the interpretation of statutes) but in his own developed writings the very idea of "interpretation" has a central and crucial place.[32] The debate on interpretive theory has ranged very wide indeed,[33] and some of its themes were touched upon almost incidentally in Wilson's earlier writings on statutory interpretation, but a theoretical approach to the subject would clearly have to make some reference to the developments in this chapter of legal theory.

The final comment on Bill Wilson's work on statutory interpretation must be to highlight a feature which characterised all his contributions to law, whether in lecture form or in the written word. This is the humour which permeated virtually all that he said and wrote. To write well on statutory interpretation is difficult; to avoid making the subject dull is not easy. Bill Wilson managed to make statutory interpretation not just challenging and interesting but also amusing. Where else could we find out about the futility of putting roller-skates under the wheels of a car, or the problems of storing a film in a cave, or the legal pitfalls of parking on a yellow line while collecting a Chinese take-away?[34]

[30] *Re Pitts* [1931] 1 Ch. 546; *Re Sigsworth* [1935] Ch. 89; *Re Giles, decd.* [1972] Ch. 544.
[31] *Riggs v. Palmer*, 115 N.Y. 506 (1889), on which see R. Dworkin, *Taking Rights Seriously* (1977), Ch. 2.
[32] R. Dworkin, *Law's Empire* (1986). In "A Note on Fact and Law", *supra* at p. 619, Wilson accepted that non-linguistic factors had to be taken into account when dealing with questions of statutory interpretation. He referred in this connection to early works of Hart: see H. L. A. Hart, "Theory and Definition in Jurisprudence", (1955) 29 *Proceedings of the Aristotelian Society* (supplementary volume) 239; *Concept of Law*, p. 125.
[33] For further discussion, see Miers, "Legal Theory and the Interpretation of Statutes".
[34] The cases on these points are discussed in "Trials and Try-Ons: Modes of Interpretation", *supra* at pp. 6–9. This paper was first presented by Wilson in lecture form.

WHAT STUDYING STATUTES CAN DO FOR ARTIFICIAL INTELLIGENCE AND LAW

LILIAN EDWARDS

A solicitor sits at his desk. He works in the executry department. It is late and he wants to go home. But his desk is still piled high with work. His next job is the dull task of working out how to distribute the estate of a client who, though well endowed with worldly goods, neglected to make a will before he died. No matter. He pulls his chair close to his desktop computer and selects "Intestate Succession Adviser" from the extensive menu of software loaded on to the firm's local area network. The gaudy title page of the Adviser appears on screen. In a few minutes the program has prompted him via an intuitive question-and-answer dialogue to enter the relevant details of the client: his estate, its heritable and moveable proportions, his relevant close family and his previous relevant transfers and exemptions for inheritance tax purposes. In seconds, the program has called up other relevant details from the inhouse client database (e.g. his client's address), has produced a summary of how the estate will be distributed, has calculated the I.H.T. liability and has transferred the details on to the appropriate form for lodging for confirmation. If the solicitor has any doubt as to the program's efficiency (though he has none, knowing full well its arithmetic is better than his), he can insist on a full trace of the reasoning and calculations that were invoked by the program. A report is printed out for the file. Home is that much nearer.

Such programs are not fantasy but already exist, as research prototypes if not marketed commercial systems. They are called expert systems, and are a product of the hybrid field of study known as artificial intelligence and law. This article will seek to outline what legal expert systems are, how they are constructed and how work on statutory interpretation and the formalisation of law as logic, as exemplified by the work of Bill Wilson, can help them to fulfil their potential to transform the practice of law in the next century.

Artificial Intelligence and Law

The project of artificial intelligence (A.I.), glibly put, is to build machines that can think. More precisely, since (as in humans) machine thinking must be done by the brain and not the body, it is to devise computer programs, whether or not embodied in machines, that can "in some sense think, that is, solve problems in a way that would be considered intelligent if done by a human."[1] By natural implication,

---

[1] D. A. Waterman, *A Guide to Expert Systems* (1986), p. 3.

the field of A.I. and law, which has its origins in the 1950s,[2] but became a visible sub-domain of the A.I. world only in the later part of the 1980s,[3] has as its project the creation of, and study of methods for creating, computer programs that perform intelligent, cognitive or reasoning tasks normally performed by lawyers or those who adjudicate on or argue about legal problems. In particular, one of the principal aims of A.I. and law is to create A.I. programs which can make decisions in a legal case in the same way as a human judge would—the so called "A.I. judge" beloved of science fiction, who will dispense with the need for lawyers, prosecutors, argument, procedure, courtrooms and (of course) legal aid. As may be gathered from the tone of the last sentence, however, there is also a strong critical or sceptical element in the A.I. and law field, emanating from the closely associated world of analytical jurisprudence, which makes it necessary to define as an alternative goal or project disproving the possibility of ever creating programs which can reason with law in the same way as a judge or lawyer.

Building a computerised legal adviser is not the easiest of tasks. Early artificial intelligence projects attempted to write programs which like a human being, could solve a variety of tasks and exhibit common sense reasoning. These enterprises were stymied however by the general (and continuing) absence of firm knowledge about the essential nature of human intelligence and cognition, and thus could could only attempt to mimic human cognitive activity by reference to its external manifestations. These A.I. programs often attempted to emulate human reasoning by breaking activities into a number of generic tasks and using a variety of low level and generalised search strategies to accomplish them. In the end, though, it became plain that such programs, epitomised by the General Problem Solver of Ernst and Newell,[4] could only produce significant results when applied to highly limited, artificial and formally pre-structured domains such as, typically, games-playing. Programs could be built to play chess to grandmaster level but not to work out that if the sun is shining, then the sky will be blue. Certainly such programs could not begin to know how to deal with the problems of natural language understanding and complex reasoning implicit in any higher level domain of knowledge such as law, medicine or science.

Another approach was necessary. A.I. researchers retrenched by turning to the idea of *knowledge representation*. Instead of attempting to build programs that could only reason fairly generally in relation to highly artificial and structured domains, they would instead concentrate on encapsulating detailed knowledge of a certain domain within a program. Essentially, attention was diverted from making

---

[2] See, *e.g.* the work of Layman Allen in formalising statutes as logic which began in 1957.

[3] There has been a regular bi-annual international conference devoted to A.I. and law since 1987; a refereed journal entitled *AI and Law* appeared in 1992; arguably the first student textbook devoted to A.I. and law appeared only in 1994 (J. Zeleznikow and D. Hunter, *Building Intelligent Legal Information Systems* (1994)).

[4] See G. Ernst and A. Newell, *A Case Study in Generality and Problem Solving* (1969); also R. Forsyth, *Expert Systems* (1984), ch. 1.

the program itself behave in intelligent ways—the approach that had failed—to using it as a repository for a creamed-off version of human intelligence, namely, expertise. The new strategy, then, was to capture the high-level knowledge of a human expert, and then to represent it in some kind of symbolic formalisation (the "knowledge base"), from which an appropriately written computer program could then infer conclusions. The process of capturing knowledge from human experts became known as "knowledge acquisition"; that of formalising the knowledge in computer-readable form as "knowledge represen-tation"; and the programmed inference strategy by means of which conclusions, or answers, could be inferred became known as the "inference engine". These three parts together became collectively known as an *expert system*. Expert systems were built by grandly-named "knowledge engineers".[5]

The first true expert system, MYCIN,[6] was built in a medical domain. It consisted of a knowledge base of detailed rules connecting symptoms of blood disease to possible bacteriological causes, and relating these to appropriate antibacterial drug treatment. MYCIN drew conclusions from a computer representation of expert-level medical knowledge and was thus able to give the same kind of advice on how to treat these disorders, given a particular set of symptoms, as a doctor would have. A legal expert system by analogy can be imagined as a system which provides the same kind of advice as a lawyer would in relation to a limited and expert domain of law; and which ideally should overtly exhibit some of the same kinds of reason-ing strategies or justifications in reaching its advice or conclusions as a lawyer would,[7] a property sometimes known as "transparency".

Legal Expert Systems and Statutory Domains

Legal expert systems, and the associated techniques of knowledge rep-resentation, have to a great extent dominated the world of A.I. and law thus far; some systems built in this way have even escaped the world of academe and been used or marketed as commercially viable products.[8] How then does a legal expert system operate? How is law

---

[5] For an interesting critique of this type of metaphorical treatment of knowledge as a substance which can be "bottled" or "engineered", see R. Stamper, "Expert sys-tems—Lawyers Beware!", in S. S. Nagel (ed.) *Law, Decision Making and Microcomputers* (1991).

[6] See E. Shortliffe, *Computer Based Medical Consultations:* MYCIN (1976).

[7] This, it should be emphasised, is a description of the ideal. Most definitions of legal expert systems within the literature are considerably more hesitant and pessimistic. See, for example, Richard Susskind's definition: "[legal] expert systems are computer programs that have been developed with the aid of human legal experts in particular and highly specialised areas of law. These systems are designed to work as intelligent assistants in the processes of legal reasoning and legal problem solving ... It must be emphasised that such an outline today amounts to no more than the research aspirations of workers in the field of expert systems in law." ("Expert Systems in Law: Theory and Practice" (Cambridge Lectures, 1987)).

[8] For example, the VATIA expert system produced and used by Masons, Solicitors; the Pharos environmental law system from NatWest; the E.C. Competition Adviser commissioned by Clifford Chance from Robin Widdison of Durham University.

to be formalised in a computer representation, and what inference strategy is to be embedded in the program? What types of legal domain are particularly appropriate for implementation as legal expert systems? And what does all this have to do with studying statutes?

The most intuitively apparent and technically undemanding way to formalise law is in the form of if-then rules, from which conclusions can be inferred using the process of deduction classically known as *modus ponens*. An if-then rule is one in which if the necessary and sufficient conditions of the rule are met, then the conclusion of the rule must be assumed to be true. The conditions and conclusions— the ifs and the thens—may be formulated as propositions (*e.g.* x has made an offer to y) or in predicate form (*e.g.* offer (x,y)). Both propositions and predicates take only the values true and false. It is possible to draw conclusions of equal validity using either propositional or predicate logic, although the latter has many advantages of flexibility and computational power. So it is equally valid to formalise a rule in the following form:

> IF x makes a legal offer to y
> AND y accepts x's offer
> THEN there is a contract between x and y

as it is to say it this way:

> offer (x,y) ∧ acceptance (y,x) = > contract (x,y)

Of course individual rules do not take us very far in inferring useful legal conclusions. To take another example, it is possible to formalise a meaningful fragment of the Sale of Goods Act in propositional form as follows[9]:

> IF the contract contains a delivery date
> AND the date for delivery has passed
> AND NOT the goods have been delivered
> THEN delivery is late
>
> IF delivery is late
> THEN the seller is in breach of condition
>
> IF the seller is in breach of condition
> THEN the buyer is entitled to reject

These rules can be *chained* by a deductive inference engine.[10] Considering all three rules in turn, it can be assumed that if we establish as

---

[9] This example and formalisation are extracted from C. Reed, "Expert Systems" in C. Reed (ed.) *Computer Law*, (1st ed. 1990.), (omitted from the second edition of the book.)

[10] In A.I. terms, such a system is called a "production rule system", or "blackboard architecture".

legally proven facts that the contract contains a delivery date, that that date has passed and that the goods have not been delivered, then we can infer as a logical and valid conclusion that the buyer is entitled to reject. If more rules were present in the example relating to the Sale of Goods Act, we would be able to draw more useful and legally justified conclusions. The example constitutes a fragment of the knowledge base of a rule-based, deductive expert system on the sale of goods.

Formalisation of law as logic in this way is, of course, hardly novel. It comes naturally both to lawyers and non-lawyers to think of law as a system of rules from which answers can be derived by logical deduction. An entire school of analytical jurisprudence stands or falls on the premise that law confirms to a deductive model. Neil McCormick, for example, offers as substantiation of the deductive model of law, an analysis of the case *Daniels and Daniels v. White & Sons and Tabard*,[11] in which he "formalises" the case in legal propositions. He then demonstrates that the decision in the case can be drawn exclusively from these propositions and the facts established as proven by the court. The susceptibility of particular areas of law to transformation into the style of logical syllogism has been used not only to make jurisprudential points but also to illustrate the precision with which such areas operate. Scottish civil procedure, for example, was formalised by David Walker in 1951 as follows:

"Any pursuer X in circumstances ABCDE against the defender Y is entitled to remedy R. My client P is in circumstances ABCDE as against your client D. Therefore P is entitled from D to remedy R."[12]

Bill Wilson, whose work we are celebrating in this volume, was also interested in the logical character of Scottish pleading, particularly in his introductory essay on civil procedure in which, speaking of possible defences to a civil claim, he defined the concept of relevancy as follows: "Thirdly there is "So what?—even if the facts are true they do not afford the remedy sought—that is exactly the idea of relevancy."[13] Wilson might well have preferred to turn Walker's example on its head to demonstrate the idea of relevancy in logical predicate form, viz.

$$\sim (A\ (x,y) \wedge B(x,y) \wedge C(x,y) \wedge D(x,y) \wedge E(x,y) => R(x,y))$$
$$A\ (x,y) \wedge B(x,y) \wedge C(x,y) \wedge D(x,y) \wedge E(x,y)$$
No inference can be drawn.

but perhaps he felt it kinder to spare the readers of an introductory text their first taste of mathematical notation.

Statute law, in particular, already looks enticingly like logic. Statutes can be regarded as legal texts written in a semi-formalised English

---

[11] [1938] 4 All E.R. 258.
[12] D. M. Walker, "The Theory of Relevancy", 1951 J.R. 1 at p. 14.
[13] *Introductory Essays on Scots Law* (2nd ed. 1984), p. 66.

already akin to the algorithmic language of programming,[14] which enact that if certain factual and legal circumstances occur, then certain legal consequences do or should follow. The advantage of formalising a statute in logical form is arguably that the semantic uncertainty and syntactic ambiguity associated with, and almost inevitable in, natural language texts can be reduced or even banished. This has appeal from the point of view not only of parliamentary draftsmen, but also of anyone who would wish to defend the rule of law by reducing the sphere of discretionary power accruing to both judiciary and executive. Reduction of ambiguity and clarification of meaning was certainly one of the key themes in Wilson's work on statutory interpretation. Transformation of law into logic was one way to achieve this. He asserted that "a statutory provision can be reduced to a proposition that if each set of factual questions is satisfied a legal consequence follows."[15] Considering the problems arising from "the style, intelligibility and logical structure of statutes", he suggested the following:

"One method of simplifying legislation would be to reduce each provision to a set of separate conditions which must be fulfilled for a certain legal consequence to follow. The process can be carried further by reducing the conditions to "unit facts"—if (1) a person (X) gives a thing (Y) to a person (Z), (2) y is an air-gun, (3) Z is under the age of fourteen, X is guilty of an offence unless (4) X believed that Z was fourteen or over and (5) X had reasonable grounds for that belief."[16]

In his note on the Hohfeld analysis,[17] he considered the validity of formalising law in deontic as opposed to ordinary first order predicate logic, with particular reference to legal liberties and warranted interference therewith. Deontic logic is so difficult to analyse and generates so many paradoxical results that to this day few in the A.I. and law community have made serious headway with it.[18]

Statute Law Implemented as Expert System

As explained above, once a legal domain has been converted into a knowledge representation consisting of if-then rules, it can easily be

---

[14] Bob Kowalski of the Imperial College Logic Programming Group commented in relation to s. 1(1) of the British Nationality Act 1981 (formalised by the I.C.G., as discussed below) that "The English of this clause is already close to logic programming form, even to the extent of expressing the conclusion before (most of) the conditions" ("Legislation as Logic Programs" in Z. Bankowski *et al* (eds.), *Informatics and the Foundations of Legal Reasoning* (1995)).

[15] W. A. Wilson, "Questions of Interpretation", (1987) 8 L.R. 142.

[16] W. A. Wilson, "The Complexity of Statutes", (1974) 37 M.L.R. 497 at p. 508.

[17] W. A. Wilson, "A Note on the Hohfeld Analysis", 1972 J.R. 162.

[18] See for a recent encouraging article on the use of deontic logic in law, Jones and Sergot "The Role of Deontic Logic" in Bankowski *et al* (eds.) *Informatics and the Foundations of Legal Reasoning* (1995). Contrast the attack on the practical usefulness and philosophical rectitude of deontic logics in law by D. Hunter in *Representation and*

implemented as a rule-based expert system. Given Wilson's interest in logic, it is unsurprising that he turned his interest in statutes from theory to practice and began to construct working expert systems. He noted that one of the justifications for studying statutes was possible relevance to the creation of computer applications in law.[19] The domains in which he chose to construct systems had been foreshadowed in his earlier work, and were clearly drawn from what have been christened elsewhere as "clear cases of the expert domain".[20] These are typically statutory domains which generate problems requiring the guidance of an expert, not because their resolution is dependent on creative legal reasoning or interpretive skills (which a rule-based system entirely lacks), but because the area of law at hand is extremely complex, and analysis requires a great deal of familiarity with the structure of the statute. Such complexity tends to arise either because, although the law is clear, there are a large number of possible permutations of facts to be analysed in relation to the relevant legal rules; or because there are a large number of interlocking and intertwining rules to be considered in any particular case, as in much modern E. C. legislation, or, typically, tax or welfare law statutes.

Wilson's expert systems on marriage and intestate succession fall very much into the first class. He noted that "complexity depends to some extent on the variety of types of fact ... A rule defining the prohibited degrees of relationship in marriage would also be simple and indeed can be expressed as a matrix".[21] Wilson went on to implement this domain as the expert system "Can John and Mary Marry?", supplying as final coda to the revealed legal answer the bridal march from Lohengrin.[22] His intestate succession system, foreshadowed by the introductory essay on intestate succession,[23] similarly exploited the exponential possible legal outcomes of a domain which is unexpectedly complex, involving as it does interaction between statute and common law rights, the need to take certain steps in a particular order and the need at various steps to choose different paths among the rules according to the composition of the deceased's family and estate.[24] His last project, an unfinished expert system on civil procedure, represents an interesting departure from these paradigm domains, though an obvious one given his interest in the logical structure of Scottish pleadings.

Reasoning in Law, unpublished L.L.M. thesis, University of Melbourne, (1995), pp. 88–96.

[19] "Studying Statutes", 1992 J.R. 213 at p. 224.

[20] R. Susskind, *Experts Systems in Law* (1987), pp. 244–245.

[21] "The Complexity of Statutes", p. 509.

[22] At least in its original implementation on a B.B.C. computer. Wilson later bowed to progress in personal computers and translated the program into the rule based expert system shell CRYSTAL which runs on IBM-compatible PC systems, only to find to his sadness that CRYSTAL's music-playing functionality was somewhat deficient for a full recreation of the original.

[23] *Introductory Essays on Scots Law*, at p. 117.

[24] See for a fuller analysis of the difficulties raised in formalising the intestate succession domain, L. Edwards, "Building an Intestate Succession Adviser: Compartmentalisation and Creativity in Decision Support Systems", (1992) 3 Journal of Law and Information Science 116.

Naturally Wilson is not the only researcher to have been intrigued by the possibilities of statutes as fertile soil for the development of rule based systems. There is a long history of such work in the A.I. and law field, although for varying motives. Wilson, as we have seen, was motivated by a desire to find clarity and logical precision in statutes. Pioneering work, of which Wilson was aware,[25] was done on a similiar basis by Layman Allen and Thorne McCarty from the 1950's on. In recent times, however, probably the most significant and also the most controversial corpus of work on legal expert systems has emerged not out of legal culture, but from the combined efforts of the Imperial College Group (I.C.G.), a group of A.I. researchers working in logic programming and particularly in the specialised predicate logic programming language Prolog (*Programmable Logic*). In 1986, the I.C.G. implemented the British Nationality Act 1981 as a logical formalisation[26] using Prolog, and subsequently went on to build systems dealing with a variety of normative or regulatory texts as far removed from each other as the welfare benefit legislation used by the DHSS[27] (now D.S.S.) and the Imperial College Library Regulations. All these projects were undertaken principally to test the expressive power of Prolog. Law was very much a means to an end.[28] From the I.C.G.'s point of view, statute law represented a source of written down, publicly available, ready-to-order expertise—a happy escape from the usual rather tedious practice of extracting "unarticulated" expertise from experts by slow and painful methods, as usually necessary in domains such as engineering or geology.[29] The British Nationality Act 1981 was selected as a testbed project because it was a new statute and hence "relatively self-contained and free, for the most part, of the many complicating factors that make the problem of simulating legal reasoning so much more difficult". For example, it was "free of the complicating influence of case law",[30] a statement which itself says a great deal about the I.C.G.'s perceptions of the nature of law and legal problems. At no point were any lawyers involved in the project, and the task of interpreting any open-textured terms, such as "settled in the U.K.", or "being of good character" was regarded as extraneous and irrelevant. Nor was there any consideration of the policy factors and other external influences that might influence the effect of a statute solidly enmeshed in the law of immigration. In short, the British Nationality Act project (and its heirs) did a great deal to spread the word about Prolog but did little to explore

[25] See "The Complexity of Statutes", p. 497 *supra*, at n. 7.
[26] The original paper describing this work is Sergot, Sadri, R. Kowalski *et al*, "The British Nationality Act as a Logic Program", (1986) 29 Communications of the ACM 370.
[27] See T. Bench-Capon (ed.), *Knowledge Based Systems and Legal Applications* (1991).
[28] The sub-title of the original paper (cited above at n. 26) says it all: 'The formalisation of legislation and the development of computer systems to assist with legal problem solving provide a rich domain for developing and testing artificial-intelligence technology.' For trenchant criticism of the I.C.G. approach, see especially R. Moles, "Logic Programming: an Assessment of its Potential of A.I. Applications in Law" (1991) 2 Journal of Law and Information Science 137.
[29] In such domains, the process of extracting expertise from the expert is often referred to impatiently as "the knowledge acquisition bottleneck".
[30] "The British Nationality Act as a Logic Program", *supra*, at p. 370.

the nature of statutory interpretation, and was certainly unable to produce a system which might offer useful advice to a client trying to
find out his citizenship status and associated immigration rights.[31]

Other, perhaps more worthy, motivations for building expert systems exist. Richard Susskind's well-publicised project to build an
expert system based on latent damage law, and especially the English
Latent Damage Act 1986, apparently a statute of impenetrable complexity, was primarily designed to expose the legal market to the commercial possibilities of packaging scarce legal expertise for delivery to
clients. High-powered partners would be encouraged to make available in computer form their rarified skills, so that they could be sold
on by less in-demand junior members of the firm. Despite Susskind's
best efforts however, true commercial legal expert systems remain *rara
avis*[32] for multiple reasons. Building a successful expert system is time
and money-intensive and thus requires a degree of speculative capital
investment not often extracted from legal partnerships. In particular,
reducing the fee-earning capacity of a top partner for months on end
while he chats cosily to a knowledge engineer is not often the most
attractive of options. Although lawyers have largely abandoned Ludd-
ite tendencies, and capitulated to the need for new technology, computers are still far more often installed to speed up or replace support
functions such as accounting, time recording and billing rather than
to assist in, or take over true lawyering tasks.[33] It has also been suggested that most solicitors in practice spend very little time offering
high level complex legal advice but rather spend a high percentage
of their time doing routinised business, and thus have little to gain
from expert systems.[34] In fact solicitors only tend to become really
excited by expert systems when they rescue them from their least
favourite activity—mathematics. The Child Support Act 1991, combining the need for "higher algebra"[35] with a classic expert-
system-friendly skein of complex rules, has generated a mini-boom
of computer packages all on its own[36]—something that might have
gladdened Bill Wilson' heart.

Expert systems can also be built for use as educational aids. Since
by their nature they impose logical structure and clarity on complex
and confusing domains of law, they are ideal for teaching students

---

[31] No attempt to turn the B.N.A. formalisation into a working system was ever made.
[32] See n. 8 above. It is commoner to find expert systems in legal offices performing
non-legal functions—e.g. the Mortgage Matcher package devised by Graham Gibson,
a Perth solicitor, which matches house purchaser details to the most suitable mortgage on the market at that date. Expert system techniques have also contributed to
the successful development of quasi-intelligent document-drafting packages, increasingly to be found in computerised legal offices. See V. Mital and L. Johnson *Advanced
Information System for Lawyers* (1992).
[33] See A. Paterson, "Brave New World—When Will Computers Replace Us?" (1991) 36
J.L.S.S. 112.
[34] An analogy can be drawn with the poor uptake by U.K. lawyers of the on-line primary legal materials database LEXIS. Cynics might suggest that more primary law
is exactly what practising lawyers don't need.
[35] W. A. Wilson, "The Bairns of Falkirk: The Child Support Act 1991", 1991 S.L.T.
(News) 417.
[36] See (1994) 39 J.L.S.S. 15 for a review of seven C.S.A. calculational packages.

strategies for working their way through these thickets, especially if they are built to explain and summarise their methodology as they proceed. I have built systems in common law domicile,[37] intestate succession,[38] and inheritance tax law[39] for this purpose, and used them succesfully as tutorial aids. Students are required to solve given problem situations by answering questions as to fact and law posed by the expert system. Such "computerised tutorials" have the advantages over conventional human-led discussion seminars that every student must play an active part and that a logical step by step structure is imposed on the process of reaching a legal answer.[40] It has also been suggested that expert systems could be used more widely to educate the public—by supplying packaged legal advice freely available in environments such as law centres and citizen's advice bureaux, in areas of popular concern such as welfare and unemployment benefits and housing law. The problem with this idea is that the customers using the system are likely to have trouble understanding and interpreting the advice they are given, even if they manage correctly and fully to answer the questions posed by the expert system. It is hard enough to build an expert system for use by lawyers, but more difficult still to build one for general consumption which is more useful than misleading.

The Potential and Limits of Statutory Expert Systems

It is apparent then that expert systems in law have potential. Yet it is also apparent that formalisation of law in expert systems is problematic and that certain aspects of legal reasoning will always be difficult if not impossible to emulate by computerised means. A significant part of the value of work on statutory interpretation such as that undertaken by Bill Wilson is that it offers guidelines as to which parts of the law are implementable as logic, or as rule-based expert systems—and which are not.

We can paraphrase Wilson's definition of a statutory provision, to state that a statute can be viewed as a sequence of propositions each of which states that if a set of factual conditions is met, then a legal effect will follow. The first problem that naturally arises when trying to transform statutes into logical rules, then, is that of trying to decide exactly what propositions the statute should be broken into—what parts it consists of and how they logically relate to and depend on each other. Such questions are usually referred to as *syntactic* issues. In contrast, even if it can be worked out how a statute fits together logically, and any ambiguities have been ironed out, there will still always be problems of interpretation as to what phrases or words

[37] Described in L. Edwards, "Creating a Civil Jurisdiction Adviser" (1992) 1 Law, Computers and Artificial Intelligence 5.
[38] Described in Edwards, "Building an Intestate Succession Adviser", *supra.*
[39] With Sandra Eden, of the Department of Private Law, Edinburgh.
[40] One anonymous student comment in response to the Inheritance Tax Adviser was that "the computer worked through the problems logically which tutors rarely seem to do."

within the language of the statute mean. Such questions are usually referred to as *semantic* issues. The paradigm semantic question is "Is X a Y?" As Wilson once wrote: "The questions abound. Is a safe 'plant'"? Is a Kruggerand 'goods'"? Is an air rifle a 'firearm'?"[41]

Syntactic problems can, in principle, be solved by the builders of statutory expert systems. In fact, it is generally acknowledged that logic programming languages such as Prolog are valuable tools with which to develop skills in clarifying legislation. Eventually drafting support tools might be built to assist draftsmen in creating non-ambiguous legislation. The I.C.G. logic programmers have asserted that

> "Representation in logical form helps to identify and eliminate unintended ambiguity and imprecision. It helps clarify and simplify the natural language statement of the rules themselves. It can also help to derive the logical consequences of the rule and therefore test them before they are put into force."[42]

Personal experience suggests that the process of building and testing an expert system forces into the light of day latent ambiguities and lacunae in the syntax. The rule structure formalised in the expert system can be tested in advance by passing random fact situations through it. The system then acts as a sort of "legal fruit machine", conjugating the legal rules with all kinds of possible permutations of facts, and delivering a spectrum of legal results which can then be examined for absurdity, incompleteness and ineffectiveness.[43]

Wilson catalogued nine different types of problems associated with statutory syntax.[44] Several of these recur as recognised problems in the literature of logic programming. In particular, the difficulty of when an English "or" should be regarded as conjunctive, or an "and" as disjunctive; and what Wilson called the "transfer of additionals", the question of when and how clauses concerning temporal and geographical constraints should be read into statutes, were dealt with at length by the I.C.G. programmers.[45] Such categorisation may then perform valuable spadework in allowing difficulties to be anticipated before future expert systems are built.

Semantic problems on the other hand present a very different challenge. Formalisation of statutory provisions as logic leaves the natural open texture of the language untouched. It is of little use, for example, to build an expert system in the law of income tax allowances if in the end the legal issue most often disputed is whether expenditure is "wholly and exclusively laid out or expended for the purpose of the profession". The problem of deciding how far the meaning of a phrase

---

[41] "Questions of Interpretation", *supra*, at p. 159.
[42] Sergot *et al.* "The British Nationality Act as a Logic Program", *supra*, at p. 371.
[43] For examples of the kind of statutory flaws that can be identified in this way, see Edwards, "Building an Intestate Succession Adviser", *supra*.
[44] "Questions of Interpretation", *supra*, at p. 159.
[45] See for example the discussion of the representation of time in the British Nationality Act in Kowalski, "Legislation as Logic Problems".

can stretch—the problem of the penumbra, in Hartian terms[46]—becomes most visible in the interpretation of terms such as "reasonable care" or "reasonable foreseeability". Words such as "reasonable" are intentionally fuzzy, unable to be deconstructed into a pair of opposite values. Since all the expert system can do is ask questions which take a value of either true or false, it can only throw itself on the mercy of the user and ask for a view whether the facts of the case imply that "reasonable care" was or was not taken. This is of little assistance.

Similiar problems occur in relation to what Wilson termed "factorial" statutory provisions—provisions which require that a list of factors be taken into account in deciding if a statutory description applies.[47] Since these invoke the exercise of human discretion, it is impossible for an expert system to reach a definite conclusion that the factors do or do not justify the description. One obvious example of this type of provision arises in relation to financial provision on divorce under the Family Law (Scotland) Act 1985. The court is directed to make an award of financial provision which is justified by references to the principles in section 9 of the Act and reasonable having regard to the resources of the parties.[48] A financial provision expert system, then, can at best be an interactive checklist of issues to be taken into account. It is impossible to program this kind of evaluative weighting and discretionary thinking into a system based on true/false logic. Factorial provisions are surprisingly common. Indeed, arguably, many examples of "ordinary" open-textured language actually disguise an implicit factorial provision. Taking another family law example, the Children (Scotland) Act 1995 demands that when a court makes an order relating to a child, the "welfare of the child" shall be regarded as the paramount consideration. But the welfare of the child is as long as a piece of string. It is in essence a factorial provision where, to make life more difficult, the exact list of factors that should be taken into account is not clearly delimited.[49]

These problems are not fatal to the project of building statutory expert systems. Lawyers habitually find their way through linguistic vagueness by the use of principles of interpretation and previously decided cases. Expert systems too can go beyond the primary statute to consider the secondary source of case law. The *rationes decidendi* of relevant cases can be incorporated along with the statutory rules as part of the rule base of the system. Such a process is of course, more subjective than the formalisation of the written rules of a statute; in cases with multiple judgments, for example, it may be difficult or impossible to identify the rule the case stands for. More radically still,

[46] See H. L. A. Hart, *The Concept of Law* (1961).
[47] Described as such in "The Complexity of Statutes" *supra*, at p. 504. Wilson noted the inability of factorial provisions to be fitted into binary logic in "Studying Statutes" *supra*, at p. 224.
[48] Family Law (Scotland) Act 1985, s. 8(2).
[49] For further discussion of how an expert system on custody of children might deal with the "welfare of the child" principle, see L. Edwards, "Modelling Law Using a Feminist Theoretical Perspective", (1994) 1 Law, Computers and Artificial Intelligence, p. 101.

advanced techniques such as case-based reasoning (C.B.R.) and neural networks are beginning to allow computer systems to interpret vague and open-textured terms. In C.B.R. the attributes of a current case are compared for similarity to a large selection of prior cases, and conclusions derived by analogical reasoning. Neural networks are highly technical to implement, but essentially work by statistical inference. For example, a neural network might extrapolate from a large sample of cases on "careless driving" whether a current case is likely to be adjudged as fitting into that class of behaviour.[50] Case-based reasoning and neural network modules might be grafted onto rule-based systems to produce hybrid legal reasoning systems capable of dealing with both syntactic and semantic complexity.

But a last general worry relating to the whole project of rule-based expert systems must be voiced. Let us assume that we can iron out syntactic ambiguity in the process of formalising a statutory domain with reference to the principles of construction of statutes. Let us ignore or (aspirationally) find ways to solve semantic vagueness. Do we now know with certainty that our system will generate the "right" result?—that is, will produce, as we stated in our specification of the ideal expert system, the same kind of decision, for the same kind of reasons, that a human judge would have made? Bill Wilson would, it seems, have said yes. His logical view of the law demands that if all the sub-propositions of a statutory rule are proved true, then the rule must take effect as a matter of logical necessity.[51] But many philosophers of law disagree with this point of view. They might disagree that there *is* ever a "right" result, or that legal rulings are ever predictable from the formal sources of law. They might say that such an approach fails to take into account the potential for defeasibility of legal rules, the need to cede to policy and principle, the influence of politics on adjudication and many other factors cited in post-positivist jurisprudence.[52].

Such criticisms may be thought unfair to the memory of Bill Wilson's work. And yet he might well have been the first to admit that the law is not, though perhaps it ideally ought to be, a matter of logic.

---

[50] Case-based reasoning and neural networks cannot be dealt with at length in this article. For an introduction to legal applications involving these techniques, see Zeleznikow and Hunter, *Building Intelligent Legal Information Systems*, pp. 181–195 and 269–273.

[51] See "A Note on Fact and Law", (1963) 26 M.L.R. 609.

[52] These doubts have been extensively canvassed in the A.I. and law field. Hunter, one of the most outspoken critics of the implicit positivist bent of most legal expert system research, asserts that schools of theory which should be taken into account include American legal realism, critical legal theory and post-modernism (see his *Representation and Reasoning in Law*).

THE CRUMBLING PILLARS
OF STATUTORY INTERPRETATION

NEIL C. WALKER

Introduction

In one of his last articles, Bill Wilson remarked that members of his generation were "appalled by the crumbling of the massive pillars of principle of statutory interpretation".[1] He gave a number of examples: the relaxation of the rules against the use of punctuation[2] and marginal notes as aids to interpretation,[3] and also of the rules against the use of regulations made under the Act under construction,[4] and against the use of pre-parliamentary materials such as white papers.[5] He voiced concern at the manner in which methods of interpretation were being stretched and distorted in order to accommodate Community law where it was in tension with domestic legislation.[6] And occupying pride of place at the top of his charge-sheet, he registered disquiet at the gradual qualification of the no-Hansard rule.[7]

In the short period since, a number of these trends have become more pronounced. Pre-parliamentary materials may now be consulted to determine not only the mischief against which an enactment was directed, but also the meaning of particular statutory terms.[8] Although the relevant law is in a state of considerable flux, the pressure to adapt domestic interpretive practice to the needs of Community law may be increasing.[9] Most remarkably of all, the cracks which were begin-

---

[1] "Studying Statutes", 1992 J.R. 213.
[2] *Hanlon v. Law Society* [1981] A.C. 124.
[3] *R. v. Schildkamp* [1971] A.C. 1.
[4] *British Amusement Catering Trades Assoc. v. Westminster City Council* [1989] A.C. 147.
[5] *Att. Gen.'s. Ref. (No. 1 of 1988)* [1989] A.C. 971.
[6] See, for example, *Pickstone v. Freemans p.l.c.* [1989] A.C. 66; *Litster v. Forth Dry Dock Engineering Co. Ltd.*, 1989 S.L.T. 540.
[7] See, for example, *Pickstone v. Freemans p.l.c.* [1989] A.C. 66, in which the Hansard report of a speech by a Minister made when introducing subordinate legislation to give effect to Community law obligations was admissible as an aid to the construction of the primary legislation thereby amended. There were also a growing number of cases in which the judiciary had simply disregarded the exclusionary rule and relied on their own researches into Hansard. See, for example, *Hadmor Productions Ltd v. Hamilton* [1983] 1 A.C. 191.
[8] *Pepper (Inspector of Taxes) v. Hart* [1993] A.C. 593, *per* Lord Browne-Wilkinson at p. 635.
[9] On the one hand, there is increasing pressure on domestic judges to construe domestic legislation in the light of Community obligations wherever possible, even where the domestic legislation long pre-dates the creation of the Community obligation; *Marleasing S.A. v. La Commercial Internacional de Alimentacion S.A.* [1992] 1 C.M.L.R. 305. On the other hand, as the British courts have now conclusively accepted that Community law should prevail over inconsistent domestic law, arguably there may be less need for the application of a strained doctrine of interpretation in order to achieve consistency; *R. v. Secretary of State for Transport, ex p. Factortame (no. 2)* [1991]

ning to appear in the no-Hansard rule opened up considerably in *Pepper v. Hart*,[10] in which the House of Lords held that the rule excluding reference to parliamentary materials as an interpretive aid should be relaxed where first, the legislative provision in question was ambiguous or obscure or led to an absurdity; secondly, the material relied upon consisted of one or more statements by a Minister or other promoter of a bill together where required with such other parliamentary material as was necessary to understand such statements and their effects; and thirdly, the statements relied upon were clear.

As Wilson's lament took the form of a typically arresting overture to a wider analysis of the condition of statute law, he did not develop an explanation for the decline of the traditional edifice, or for his generational antipathy towards this trend. Nevertheless, he identified what is undoubtedly an important set of developments in the approach of the British courts to statutory interpretation. Was his concern justified, and, if so, to what extent? Assessment necessarily involves trying to grasp the dynamic underlying the changes in judicial attitudes. In conducting this inquiry, I seek, where possible to be guided by what Wilson might have intended by his remarks. In so doing, however, I have remained mindful that in the study of academic texts just as in the study of texts generally—including the statute book—it is possible to read too much into the underlying intentions of the author. In the final analysis, it is the words themselves, and the thoughts that they suggest, that remain the most fruitful basis upon which to pursue a deeper understanding.

What, if anything, of value may be lost in the destruction of an established framework of statutory interpretation, and how, if at all, does this inquiry illuminate our understanding of the demise of the no-Hansard rule? These questions may be addressed under two broad heads, each of which is considered in turn.

Departure From Tradition

With its emphasis on the authority of precedent, "[l]aw is a profoundly traditional social practice".[11] Wilson's misgivings about the new approach to interpretation might, therefore, have been rooted in an apprehension of the harm that could come from a break with legal tradition. On this view, the dismantling of a pre-existing structure would be an occasion for regret not for its particular properties but simply because it was there.

Traditions can be adhered to unreflectively, but they may also be rationally defensible. In the first place, they can be defended on cogni-

---

1 A.C. 603; *R. v. Secretary of State for Employment, ex p. E.O.C.* [1994] 2 W.L.R. 409. More generally, the ever-expanding scope of Community law means that there are ever more circumstances in which British courts will be obliged not only to apply Community law, but to construe that law by means of the teleological approach preferred by the European Court of Justice.

[10] *Pepper (Inspector of Taxes) v. Hart* [1993] A.C. 593.

[11] M. Krygier, "Law as Tradition" (1986) 5 *Law and Philosophy* 237 at p. 239.

tive grounds.[12] Traditions distil and retain the knowledge of the ages, providing solutions to recurrent problems and sparing successive generations the tedium of reinventing the wheel. Although the legal system is peculiarly well-suited to the intergenerational transmission of norms, the cognitive advantages of tradition should not be overstated, nor its disadvantages understated—a caution underwriting Wilson's own healthy scepticism about reassertions of the civilian heritage of Scots law.[13] After all, past knowledge may become irrelevant to present problems, and we should not assume that our ancestors, even if eclectically assessed, had a monopoly of either wisdom or virtue.

Tradition in law may also be supported on normative grounds.[14] In particular, the existence of a stable and authoritative framework of norms can resolve social co-ordination problems. A conspicuous framework of rules allows us reasonable foresight of how others might act, and so enables mutually efficient interaction. This appears an altogether more promising line of defence of the existing framework of statutory interpretation, especially if we apply Postema's insight that co-ordination problems pertain to the internal working of the legal system in the same way as they do to any other context of social interaction.[15]

The no-Hansard rule can be seen as anchoring a number of mutually concordant expectations amongst the overlapping "interpretive communities"[16] and "interest communities"[17] constituting our legal system. Parliamentary counsel drafted legislation knowing that other parliamentary materials could not be relied upon as interpretive aids, and that in consequence legal effectiveness had to be achieved through the statutory words alone. Ministers could speak fully and freely to their legislative brief in Parliament, aware that nothing they said could influence judicial interpretation of the text either for or against the Government's preferred reading. Similarly, they could engage in candid private correspondence with parliamentarians seeking supplementary information or explanation, without the need to calculate whether it would be more advantageous if any such exchange were on the parliamentary record. In turn, civil servants charged with briefing their Minister could take a more relaxed view than would be possible if every ministerial word uttered was an interpretive time-bomb. For the practitioner too, the exclusion of parliamentary materials saved the time and expense of exhaustive searches of enacting debates and related materials on behalf of a client seeking to advance a particular statutory interpretation; that this was of considerable practical benefit was underlined by the fact that lawyers

---

[12] *ibid.*, pp. 257–258.
[13] H. MacQueen, "Memoir of Professor W. A. Wilson", *supra*, p. 6.
[14] Krygier, "Law as Tradition", *supra*, at pp. 259–261.
[15] G. Postema, "Co-ordination and Convention at the Foundations of Law", (1982) 11 J. Legal Studies 165, especially p. 182ff.
[16] D. Miers, "Legal Theory and the Interpretation of Statutes" in W. Twining (ed.), *Legal Theory and Common Law (1986)* 115 at pp. 122–129; S. Fish, "Working on the Chain Gang: Interpretation in Law and Literature", (1982) 60 Tex. L. R. 551.
[17] P. Wilmott, *Community in Social Policy*, (1984).

typically did not have direct access to parliamentary materials. Finally, the courts themselves were spared the additional tier of inquiry and debate triggered by a parliamentary search, with benefits in the form of saving judicial time, reduction of expenses incurred by parties, and undistracted focus on the main issues of substance before the court.[18]

The qualification of the no-Hansard rule by *Pepper v. Hart* has set off a chain reaction disturbing all these deeply embedded assumptions and practices, and leaving the affected parties struggling to devise a mutually coherent pattern of readjustment. Parliamentary Counsel may be tempted to make legislation *"too* simple"[19] in the knowledge that Hansard can come to the rescue to secure legal effectiveness. They may also feel obliged to vet more closely the parliamentary briefing materials supplied to Ministers by sponsoring departments, especially since such briefing instruments—in particular notes on clauses and notes on amendments—are not only frequently relied upon as a kind of ministerial autocue but are also now included within the "other parliamentary material" which may be looked at alongside ministerial statements.[20] For their part, Ministers are likely to be less candid both off and on the record, and when they do opt to be forthcoming in Parliament, the suspicion may be that this is intended less to enlighten their parliamentary audience than to influence their judicial audience.[21]

Practitioners are having to learn a new set of forensic skills, and even if advanced information technology makes access to parliamentary materials easier, it still involves greater expense. Furthermore, in the substantial majority of cases, the search is likely to be fruitless; this may be because the enacting Parliament did not foresee the type of circumstance at issue, or because political caution prevented an expansive approach, or because political controversy produced a confused record. Even on the infrequent occasions when valuable nuggets are unearthed, they may be deemed inadmissible in court; but it is a brave legal team that will be prepared to take such a chance and decline to lead evidence of the parliamentary record, since the criteria of admissibility contain such slippery terms as "absurd", "obscure", "ambiguity" and "clear", which, as the subsequent case law demonstrates, can receive expansive treatment in certain judicial hands.[22] In a nutshell, for practitioners, their clients and the courts, the new rules demand a lot of work for a small and somewhat unpredictable return.

---

[18] In this paragraph, I have drawn heavily on the arguments in T. St J. N. Bates, "The Contemporary use of Legislative History in the United Kingdom", (1995) 4 C.L.J. 127 at pp. 132–138, and J. C. Jenkins, "Pepper v. Hart: A Draftsman's Perspective" (1994) 15 Stat. L.R. 23.

[19] Jenkins, "Draftsman's Perspective", *supra*, at p. 25.

[20] *ibid.*, at p. 25.

[21] It is frequently argued that one of the disadvantages of admitting the parliamentary record is that it will allow Ministers the opportunity to make carefully crafted statements intended to exploit the rule; D. Davies, Case Notes: *Pepper v. Hart*, [1993] B.T.R. 172 at p. 173. This seems an unlikely prospect, however, as Ministers and their departments have little to gain and much to lose from manufacturing legislative uncertainty; Jenkins, "Draftsman's Perspective", *supra*, at p. 28. However, the very fact that such a suspicion exists might affect the climate of parliamentary debate.

[22] See nn. 50–53 below.

The co-ordination problems caused by the new Hansard rule are heightened by its retroactive quality. The new assumptions about the status of parliamentary statements pertain to all legislative debates, including those pre-*Pepper v. Hart*, where the participants could not possibly have foreseen that their statements might be relied upon in court one fine day. In such cases there is no scope for adjustment to the imperatives of the new rule, directly flouting assumptions about knowledge, predictability and dependability lying at the heart of the law's co-ordinating function, and indeed of the rule of law itself.[23]

In the final analysis, however, although an argument against change based upon the virtues of social co-ordination can be persuasive, it is never decisive. The law is an open system in which legal norms interact with a changing social environment to provide the structure of constraints and opportunities which guide social action.[24] For instance, no matter how deeply inscribed in the understandings of legislative actors as to the *legal* consequences of their actions, the rule against punctuation was unlikely to survive the development and widespread adoption of the *social* practice whereby the author—including the drafter of statutes—and not, as previously, the printer, supplied the definitive punctuation of a text.[25] Similarly, the easier access to Hansard made possible by its electronic availability undoubtedly shifts the balance of pragmatic arguments about judicial consideration of parliamentary history.[26]

Nor should the law be viewed as a closed system in terms of the substantive moral and political commitments underpinning the norms. It may be that the substantive grounds for changing the structure of legal rules outweigh considerations based upon the law's co-ordination function, or, alternatively, that substantive arguments reinforce the case against change. This points to the second basis upon which Wilson's opposition to the changing face of statutory interpretation may be explained.

Structural Transformation

Bill Wilson evidently disapproved on substantive grounds of some of the changes in statutory interpretation wrought by the judiciary, but why express his disapproval in such pronounced terms? It would have been out of character if his metaphor had not been carefully chosen. The reference to crumbling pillars conjures up the image of an integrated structure, thereby implying that the canons of statutory

---

[23] Even judicial interpretations of statutory terms are not safe from the retroactive operations of the new Hansard rule. This was illustrated in *Sunderland Polytechnic v. Evans* [1993] I.R.L.R. 196, where, upon consulting the parliamentary material, the Employment Appeal Tribunal departed from its own earlier view in *Home Office v. Ayeres* [1992] I.C.R. 175.

[24] Teubner's theory of autopoietic law is the best-known recent example of the application of open systems theory to law. See, for example his *Autopoiesis in the Legal System* (1993).

[25] F. Bennion, *Statutory Interpretation* (2nd ed. 1992), pp. 515–517.

[26] *Pepper (Inspector of Taxes) v. Hart* [1993] A.C. 593.

interpretation were much more than a set of discrete rules, each capable of evaluation on its own merits and without reference to the others. Rather, the structural metaphor suggests that the various rules interlock within a single edifice, supported by pillars of principle. And if a pillar is destroyed or dislodged and the structure becomes unstable or collapses, the other rules may also be affected. Their import, and perhaps even their continued existence, would depend upon their compatibility with a new or modified structure supported by different pillars of principle.[27]

Viewing the rules of statutory interpretation as a coherent whole rather than as a loose aggregation, so that changes in those rules should be viewed in structural rather than incremental terms, is an important insight facilitating a more fundamental critique of the erosion of the no-Hansard rule. In particular, adopting the structural perspective, we may identify "objective" and "subjective" approaches as the two alternative organising principles, or pillars, sustaining statutory interpretation, with the former asserting the primacy of the statutory text and arguments centred on the text, and the latter, in contrast, privileging the views of the author(s) of the text.[28] *Pepper v. Hart* undoubtedly marks a distinct shift from objective to subjective supports. Arguably its potential significance and dangers, which can only be fully appreciated if a structural analysis is further developed, have been widely underestimated.

The failure to grasp some of the broader implications of the decision may be largely attributable to the strong anti-foundational tendency in judicial discourse on statutory interpretation. Questions of statutory construction are typically viewed as involving minor adjustment and application of tried and tested techniques rather than choice among first principles. Accordingly, quite fundamental transformations may be set in train without their consequences being fully apprehended. The value of the structural perspective is that it alerts us to the dangers of false complacency and helps to spell out the full consequences of adherence to existing or alternative frameworks.

Anti-foundationalism has a variety of causes and outlets. Its most basic manifestation is a long-standing judicial tendency to treat statutory interpretation as a craft rather than as the application of a body of rules.[29] The arch-exponent of this view was Lord Wilberforce, who once dismissed statutory interpretation as a "non-subject",[30] later

---

[27] A resilient theme of Wilson's published and unpublished work on statute law was a concern to approach the subject in a highly systematic fashion. This applied equally to his work on procedures of statutory interpretation and to that on the classification of statutory provisions. See, for example, "Trials and Try-ons: Modes of Interpretation", (1992) 13 Stat L.R. 1; "The Complexity of Statutes", (1974) 37 M.L.R. 497. This does not mean, of courses, that he would have developed his structural metaphor in quite the way I have attempted below, but it does reinforce the impression that he was opposed to any approach to the study of statutes which viewed the subject as irreducible to rules and principles—such as the craft approach which I criticise in the text below.

[28] D. N. MacCormick and R. S. Summers, "Interpretation and Justification" in MacCormick and Summers (eds.), *Interpreting Statutes*, (1991) 551, pp. 520–525.

[29] R. Cross, *Statutory Interpretation*, (3rd ed., J. Bell and G. Engle (eds)) (1995), pp. 38–43.

[30] 274 H.L. Official Report (5th series) col. 1294 (November 16 1966).

explaining that he viewed "the interpretation of legislation [as] just part of the process of being a good lawyer; a multi-faceted thing ... not a subject that can be confined in rules".[31]

A number of factors lie behind this attitude. It is partly attributable to the judicial perception of the canons of interpretation as indeterminate in character.[32] These canons tend to be in the form of presumptions or general maxims rather than categorical precepts, and they are often mutually contradictory. They do not, in short, behave like a system of rules, and so there is a temptation to characterise them instead as a form of tacit knowledge bound up with the professional skill and sensibility of the lawyer or judge, and unsuited to articulation within the formal rationality of the legal system.

Anti-foundationalism may also be part of the legacy of the "common law mind"[33] within professional legal culture and education. Coherence and unity have often been viewed as properties exclusive to the common law, with legislation perceived as a marginal encroachment upon this normative universe rather than as an integral component or equal partner. From such a standpoint, statute law lacks internal coherence, and any attempt at the systematic refinement of the canons of statutory interpretation would simply lend a false dignity and artificial rationality to a part of the law in fact driven by the fluctuating demands of public policy and political expediency.

Finally, the projection of statutory interpretation as a craft may be linked to the ideology of legal formalism to which our judges tend to subscribe.[34] This ideology, which helps to secure the legitimacy of law as a source of general social authority, stresses the autonomy of the law from broader political processes. It is grounded in the institutional independence of the key personnel of the legal system, and in their claim to a distinctive working method and mandate—namely, the disinterested application of settled rules with a view to the resolution of disputes between parties. But the systematic elucidation of rules of statutory interpretation and the specification of their theoretical underpinning poses a distinct challenge to the idea of a semantically-ordained right answer which is central to this image of judicial impartiality. In laying bare the complexity and open texture of legal language, it advertises the necessity for the judges to engage in an active choice between different interpretive modalities, the resolution of which might be crucial to the outcome of particular cases. By contrast, the representation of statutory interpretation as an ineffable part of the judicial craft helps to preserve the impression of judicial detachment and of fealty to the law alone.

Another source and manifestation of anti-foundationalism may be

---

[31] 418 H.L. Official Report (5th series) col. 73 (March 9 1981).
[32] Cross, *Statutory Interpretation*, at pp. 38–43; A. Wilson, "The Nature of Legal Reasoning: A Commentary with Respect to Professor MacCormick's Theory", (1982) 2 Legal Studies 269.
[33] D. Sugarman, "Legal Theory, the Common Law Mind and the Making of the Textbook Tradition" in W. Twining (ed.), *Legal Theory and Common Law*.
[34] See, for example, J. H. H. Weiler, "Journey to an Unknown Destination: A Retrospective and Prospective of the European Court of Justive in the Arena of Political Integration", (1994) 32 J. Common Market Studies 1 at, pp. 7–8.

identified in these more abstract concepts and arguments which are typically used by judges engaged in statutory interpretation. Accordingly, although the propensity to view statutory interpretation as a craft is not so strong as to preclude judicial reflection on the deep structure of interpretive schemes, the terminology employed to this end tends to deny or obscure the stark choices of principle shaping this deep structure. Indeed, the craft perspective and the absence of conceptual rigour may be symbiotically related, the vagueness of the available terminology being both a product of the emphasis on craftsmanship and a factor justifying resort to such an approach.

Take for example, the concepts of "statutory purpose" and of "the intention of Parliament". Arguments articulated in these terms are of sufficient generality to have been dubbed "transcategorical".[35] That is, they pervade the various other specific categories of argument used within statutory interpretation, including linguistic arguments, arguments about the systemic coherence of the statute book, and arguments about the values and objectives which the law best represents. Crucially, arguments in these terms also tend to straddle—and so gloss over—the great divide of principle between objective and subjective approaches.[36]

This is particularly pronounced as regards "the intention of Parliament", which provided the key interpretive concept in *Pepper v. Hart*. The history of statutory interpretation reveals a constant tension and slippage between two versions of this idea.[37] On the one hand, there is the objective version, represented in the special sense of an "institutionalised intention",[38] which recognises the words as enacted as the best—and constitutionally prescribed—expression of legislative intent. On the other hand, there is the subjective version, which, applying ordinary linguistic standards, treats intention as a mental predicate, and looks to the concrete motivations of the legislators.[39]

That the subjective version happened to gain ground in *Pepper v. Hart* cannot gainsay the fact that, as a matter of semantics, the notion of the intention of Parliament entirely begs the question as to the choice to be made at the level of principle. Nor are the arguments typically made under the banner of parliamentary intention[40] and invoked in aid of a shift in either direction much more successful in illuminating the question of principle. This is so because both sides of the debate tend to claim precisely the same benefits for their version of Parliamentary intention, so appearing to differ not over ultimate ends, but only over the effectiveness of their respective means.

Thus, one key argument commonly invoked by both sides, and featuring heavily in *Pepper v. Hart*, concerns the constitutional requirement of a balanced relationship between judiciary and Parliament. From an objective viewpoint, reliance on the text demonstrates a

---

[35] MacCormick and Summers, "Interpretation and Justification" *supra*, at p. 532.
[36] *ibid.*, at pp. 518–525.
[37] Bennion, *Statutory Interpretation* at pp. 345–360.
[38] R. Dworkin, *A Matter of Principle*, (1985) at p. 321.
[39] For an extended discussion, see A. Marmor, *Interpretation and Legal Theory*, (1992) Ch. 8.
[40] Cross, *Statutory Interpretation*, at pp. 29–31.

proper deference to the will of Parliament as expressed in a publicly agreed and acknowledged form. In so doing, it avoids the danger of undue deference—of the judges becoming "merely a reflecting mirror"[41] for every Parliamentary whim or caprice, whether or not seriously intended, candidly defended, or genuinely representative of the collective opinion of the legislature. It also avoids the opposite danger, characterised as a threat to Parliamentary privilege,[42] of an eager-to-oblige judiciary intruding too closely upon the freedom of speech and proceedings in Parliament. On the other hand, for those who would supplement the text where necessary with small helpings of subjective intent, including the majority in *Pepper v. Hart*, such an addition reinforces rather than qualifies judicial subordination to the transparent will of Parliament, the narrow qualifying circumstances and the requirement of clarity equally ensuring that this subordination does not slide into undue deference.[43] Further, the spectre of abuse of parliamentary privilege is dismissed since the judicial motive is to empower Parliament rather than to criticise it.[44]

The same pattern of argument is evident over the issue of legal certainty. Defenders of the objective perspective argue that the rule of law demands certain knowledge of and reasonable access to the sources of law, which only a text-based approach guarantees. On the other hand, their opponents argue—and again their view prevailed in *Pepper v. Hart*—that, given the undoubted virtue of legal certainty, the admission of a modest amount of additional material does not unduly exacerbate problems of access, supplies precise answers where the text is unhelpful, and ensures that parties are not unfairly prejudiced before the judge who may be unable to resist the temptation to look at the Parliamentary record even if it is formally inadmissible.[45]

A final argument, which was not joined in *Pepper v. Hart*, concerns the "desire of the judiciary to disavow a large creative role in the interpretation of statutes".[46] Again, both sides might agree on this as an end to be valued in order to avoid the anti-democratic dangers of policy-making by an unaccountable legal élite, but would disagree over the best means to achieve it. For the objectivist, fidelity to the legal text may be the most prudent way to avoid judicial over-reaching, particularly given the pitfalls of deciding who are the true authors of the text and what counts as an authentic and mature statement of their attitude towards the issue in question, even supposing any such attitude had been formed.[47] On the other hand, for those prepared to consider certain statements of authorial intention beyond the text, this may be defended as a way of filling in gaps in the legal

---

[41] *Black-Clawson International Ltd. v. Papierwerke Waldhof-Aschaffenburg* A.G. [1975] A.C. 591, *per* Lord Wilberforce at p. 629.

[42] By virtue of Art. 9 of the Bill of Rights of 1689, which forbids the questioning in any court or other place of the freedom of speech and debates in Parliament.

[43] See especially pp. 634–635 *per* Lord Browne-Wilkinson.

[44] pp. 638–639, *per* Lord Browne-Wilkinson.

[45] pp. 635–636, *per* Lord Browne-Wilkinson. See also n. 7 above.

[46] Cross, *Statutory Interpretation*, at p. 29.

[47] Dworkin, *A Matter of Principle*, at pp. 14–16.

language which meets the test of democratic legitimacy and which prevents judges from ventilating their own prejudices.

In summary, therefore, reliance upon ambiguous concepts such as parliamentary intention, and upon arguments which speak more directly to shared middle-order values than to the deep structure informing a particular approach, combines with more general judicial perceptions of statutory interpretation as craft to consign the pillars of principle to the shadows—rarely acknowledged or explicitly acted upon in judicial discourse. If, however, these pillars are promoted to the foreground, it is not only the style and pattern of reasoning about statutory interpretation that may change. Consideration of the wide ramifications of adherence to a general principle rather than the discrete consequences of reliance upon a particular rule may also alter the balance of substantive argument in a particular case, as *Pepper v. Hart* amply illustrates.

To begin with, we may pursue some of the implications of the choice of principle that the court did make. The point has been well made that once it is conceded that other evidence of the intentions of parliamentarians can supplement their authorised text, it is very difficult to draw a firm philosophical line beyond which such evidence is not permitted.[48] In the first place, although the rule in *Pepper v. Hart* is couched in permissive rather than mandatory terms, it is difficult to see how a non-mandatory approach can be consistent with the underlying logic of the decision. Either subjective intentions are admissible in accordance with the criteria set down or they are not. A more selective approach suggests that the judge's own evaluation of the subjective intention of Parliament in the particular case is a factor in the equation, which would be wholly at odds with the governing idea of judicial subordination to evidence of parliamentary intent. Secondly, once the general principle is conceded, it is also difficult to resist an argument which allows subjective intentions to supplement the text where there is *any* doubt about the adequacy of the text to resolve the issue and *any* prospect that subjective intentions might supply the omission. Thirdly, and much more radically, if subjective intentions now count, on what basis do they nevertheless still count less than the objective evidence of the text? Would it not be more in keeping with a truly subjective approach to place the text and other statements on an equal footing, each viewed as a partial and provisional indication of subjective attitude, and so each, *no matter how clearly stated*, open to revision in light of the overall weight of evidence?

The case law since *Pepper v. Hart* suggests that while the third level of slippage remains remote, the first two levels have already been plumbed. There is no instance amongst the reported cases in which

---

[48] S.C. Styles, "The Rule of Parliament: Statutory Interpretation after *Pepper v. Hart*", (1994) 14 O.J.L.S. 151 at pp. 155–156. Of course, if the rule permitting recourse to parliamentary materials were to be placed on a statutory footing, it might well, if carefully drafted, succeed in specifying the conditions of admissibility with greater clarity than does the judge-made rule in *Pepper v Hart*; see Bates "Contemporary Use of Legislative History" at p. 152. However, the very fact that awareness of the deeper philosophical implications and wider practical ramifications of the new rule tends to be lacking in official circles, and amongst the judiciary in particular, makes it less likely that such a legislative initiative will be actively sought.

parliamentary evidence has been declared inadmissible despite meeting the *Pepper v. Hart* criteria. More significantly, the judges have displayed a willingness to stretch these criteria as far as possible.[49] The idea of ambiguity in particular has been broadly defined, covering not just ambiguity of the immediate terms,[50] but also ambiguity arising from a systematic reading of the words in their statutory context,[51] and even ambiguity derived from concern over the policy implications of applying a particular meaning.[52] Similarly, the scope of admissible parliamentary materials has been broadly defined. In particular, the requirement that statements be clear has been loosely applied,[53] which was perhaps inevitable given that the original criteria explicitly invite consideration of other parliamentary materials for the purposes of clarification of ministerial statements.

If consideration of the broader consequences of the subjective principle exposes hidden dangers, consideration of the broader consequences of the objective principle may, conversely, reveal well-concealed advantages. There is a misconceived tendency, closely associated with the general culture of anti-foundationalism, to equate the objective approach with a narrow literalism.[54] Objectivism may begin with the statutory words, but it does not end with their strict construction. All the "resources of ordinary language argumentation"[55] may be deployed in favour of the objective approach, including looking not only at the immediate words and any special meanings they might carry or general presumptions that may be applied to them, but also at the wider legislative scheme of which they are a part, and additionally, within limits, at the values which might underpin these concepts and the consequences of construing them in one way rather than another.[56] Therefore, despite being found wanting in *Pepper v. Hart*, the objective approach embraces methods of interpretation extending well beyond strict constructivism without resorting to the subjective intentions of the authors of a statute. In short, a return to principle reminds us that the choice of interpretive approach is not so stark or restricted as some partisans of a subjective approach would imply.

Conclusion

I have suggested two reasons why Bill Wilson might have been anxious about changes in the attitude of the courts to statutory interpret-

---

[49] For an extended overview of the post-*Pepper v. Hart* case law, see Bates, "Contemporary Use of Legislative History".

[50] *Att.-Gen. v. Associated Newspapers Ltd.* [1994] 2 A.C. 236.

[51] *Waters (Inspector of Taxes) v. Tickner* [1993] S.T.C. 624.

[52] *Laing v. Keeper of the Registers for Scotland* 1994 S.C.L.R. 135.

[53] See in particular *Islwyn Borough Council v. Newport Borough Council* LEXIS (Ct. of App.); discussed in Bates, "Contemporary Use of Legislative History" at p. 147.

[54] N. Walker, "Discovering the Intention of Parliament", 1993 S.L.T. (News) 121 at pp. 127–128.

[55] R. S. Summers and G. Marshall, "The Argument from Ordinary Meaning in Statutory Interpretation", (1992) 43 N.I.L.Q. 213 at p. 215.

[56] *ibid.* See also MacCormick and Summers, "Interpretation and Justification".

ation. The first concerns the role of the law in solving co-ordination problems, while the second concerns the need to appreciate particular rules in terms of the wider principles and structural arrangements they reflect and sustain. Historically, neither sentiment has figured significantly in judicial reasoning in this area. However, at least as regards the second omission, there is no reason why the courts could not move to remedy this defect and display a greater awareness of structure and principle. Certainly, a healthy recent flow of doctrinal,[57] theoretical[58] and comparative[59] work is heightening academic awareness of and interest in these issues, although there is no strong evidence of this more expansive approach amongst the judiciary, an absence which the restricted reasoning in *Pepper v. Hart* tends to confirm. On the other hand, *Pepper v. Hart* itself has given a further stimulus to academic consideration of these questions.[60] Perhaps even more importantly, as it ordains a significant change of approach to the reception and treatment of certain types of evidence throughout the court system, the decision is bound to generate a new critical awareness of questions of interpretation at all judicial levels. Indeed, it may be that *Pepper v. Hart*, although a model of anti-foundationalism, will in time prove to have been the catalyst for a new judicial concern with questions of fundamental interpretive principle. This is an irony that Bill Wilson would have enjoyed, and an outcome of which he would have wholeheartedly approved.

---

[57] See, for example, Cross, *Statutory Interpretation*; Bennion *Statutory Interpretation*.
[58] See, for example, Dworkin, "A Matter of Principle"; Fish, "Working on the Chain Gang"; Marmor, *Interpretation and Legal Theory*; P. Nerhot (ed.) *Law, Interpretation and Reality; Essays in Epistemology, Hermeneutics and Jurisprudence* (1990); P. Bobbitt, *Constititutional Interpretations* (1991).
[59] See, for example, MacCormick and Summers (eds), *Interpreting Statutes*.
[60] In early 1994, barely a year after the House of Lords decision was reported, over 100 academic articles had already been written on *Pepper v. Hart*; Lord Lester of Herne Hill, "*Pepper v. Hart* revisited", (1994) 15 Stat L.R. 10. Doubtless many more have since been penned.

K. IN SCOTLAND

COLIN MUNRO

"The Law ... should be accessible to every man and at all times."
(Franz Kafka)

"We should know where the law on a subject will be found and
... as far as possible it should be found in one place."
W. A. Wilson, "Studying Statutes", 1992 J.R. 213 at p. 217

Someone must have traduced Joseph K., for without having done anything wrong he was accosted shortly after he arrived at the station
which was his destination. A young man stood in front of him. He
was slim and yet athletic, wore a cap, and his clothing was furnished
with epaulettes, pleats and pockets, as well as a belt, and in consequence looked eminently practical, though one could not quite tell
what purpose it served. "Who are you?" asked K. But the man
ignored the question, as though his appearance needed no explanation, and merely said: "I'm told you've been loitering. That's an
offence under Byelaw 23, and you're liable to be charged."

The man's face was close to K.'s, and with this person confronting
him he could scarcely think. Who could this man be? What was he
talking about? What authority could he represent? K. came from a
peaceful country, with regular laws and guarantees of civil rights in
the Basic Law. He had always been inclined to take things easily, to
believe in the worst only when the worst happened, to take no care
for the morrow even when the outlook was threatening. But that
struck him as not being the right policy here. One could certainly
regard the whole thing as a joke, a joke which perhaps some of the
persons whom he had met on his journey had concocted for some
unknown reason, but his first glance at the man had decided him for
the time being not to do that. There was a slight risk that later on
people might say he could not take a joke, but he had in mind—
though it was not usual with him to learn from experience—several
occasions, of no importance in themselves, when against all his
friends' advice he had behaved with deliberate recklessness and without the slightest regard for possible consequences, and had had in the
end to pay dearly for it. That must not happen again, at least not on
his first day here. If this was a comedy he would insist on playing it
to the end.

And he was still free. "Allow me," he said, slipping past the man,
"if I move away, I can't be loitering, can I?" "See that you keep
moving, then," retorted the man, "and remember we're keeping our
eyes on you." Without replying to this, K. turned and walked away,
and was relieved not to be followed. But relief soon turned into
uneasiness, as he realised that the matter might not have been fully

resolved. "Am I still liable to be charged?" he wondered. He considered going back to ask the man but, when he looked round, he could not see him at the same spot, but only a crowd of people, pushing and shoving, and whispering slyly to each other.

For the first time since his arrival he felt really tired. The long journey he had made seemed at first to have imposed no strain on him, but now the consequences of his exertion were making themselves felt. It was late in the evening and the Castle hill was hidden, veiled in mist. K. stood for a long time on a bridge leading from the main street, gazing into the illusory emptiness above him. Then he went on to find lodgings for the night.

*   *   *   *   *

K. slept badly. He had a nightmare, in which he dreamt of waking up one day as a giant insect, only to find that his family, disgusted at the sight of him, neglected him and shunned him. The landlady's rather greasy breakfast, which included a substance called haggis which he had never previously encountered, did nothing to quieten his stomach or his nerves.

K. meant to visit the Castle on that day. It was easily visible in the bright morning light, far above the streets of the town. First, however, he was most anxious to try to put his mind at rest. He had to find out more about the country's laws and in particular that one which he was accused of breaking.

He soon came upon a bookshop and, as nobody else seemed to be working there, he addressed the young woman who sat by the till. "I should like to buy a copy of your criminal code," K. said. The woman stared at him for a few seconds, as if unsure how to, or even whether to, respond. "I think we have the Highway Code," she said eventually, pointing to a far corner of the shop. "Is that a part of your law?" asked K. "Well, I don't know," she said, "maybe it's more like advice on what you should or shouldn't do." K. was rather irritated by this answer, because already it seemed as if his goal might take longer to achieve than he wished. "How am I to know the law here, if you people don't know what's law or not?" he demanded. A customer in the shop, who had overheard the exchange, intervened. "You should try HMSO," he said to K. When K. looked puzzled, the man went on to explain that he was referring to a special bookshop, run by the Government, and on K.'s request he gave directions to it.

The shop was only a mile or so distant, and for much of the way K. could walk through a park. After about 20 minutes' walk, he saw the sign. Inside the shop, there were rows of maps and displays of books about history and gardens and cookery and such like, but there did not seem to be any collections of laws. K. wondered whether his adviser, who had seemed so helpful, had played a practical joke on him.

"Can I help you?" A bald man, sitting behind a wooden counter which rather resembled the pulpit of a church, had noticed K.'s perplexity. "I hope so," said K., "I would like to have a copy of your laws." "Which laws in particular?" asked the employee. "Can't I have the full set?" K. queried. The man looked appraisingly at K., and his nervous smile became a sneer. "That isn't possible," he said. "There are thousands of laws, not just Acts of Parliament, but statutory instruments and regulations and orders . . . in fact, there's the common law as well, in the judgments of the courts, which we don't stock at all."

"What do you stock?" asked K. "You'll see the kind of thing here," said the man, handing over a booklet entitled *HMSO Annual Catalogue 1994*. "We have many of the items here," he continued, "and we can order the rest." Leaving K. to look at the booklet, the assistant opened a door at his back, and through the opening K. saw that other men and women were working at desks in a larger room behind the shop.

The man returned with two other booklets, revealed by their covers as the Charities Act 1993 and the Railways Act 1993. "These are laws, you see," he said. "They describe the law here?" asked K. The man paused and thumbed through the Charities Act, reading carefully a passage near the end of the booklet. "To be accurate," he replied, "most of this Act doesn't apply in Scotland, only four or five sections of it do out of 100." "But it costs £11," said K., who had noticed the price printed on the front cover. "Are you telling me that a citizen here would have to pay as much as that, even though only five per cent of the Act applies to him?" "Yes, if he wants to buy it," replied the man. "But that's crazy," said K. "Why are they so expensive? In my own country I can buy the entire criminal code for about £5."

"We have to try to make a profit," said the shop assistant. "But I understood that your shops were run by the Government," said K. "Does it not subsidise the publication of laws, so that citizens and advice bureaux may be well informed?" "I'm afraid not," replied the man. "We are an agency operating on a trading fund basis, that is a business-style regime, and we are responsible for service delivery under a framework agreed with the responsible Minister." K.'s head was spinning as he tried to make sense of the answer. "You seem to have a language of your own," he said accusingly, but the man merely shrugged his shoulders.

K. did not pursue the point any further, because the other booklet was of more immediate concern to him. "The Railways Act," he said, "will this give me all the law about railways and stations?" "Well, possibly," said the man doubtfully, "but maybe not", and he started to flick through its pages. "You see," he said, pointing out some passages to K. as he spoke, "it refers to other Acts such as the Transport Act 1962 and the Fair Trading Act 1973 . . . to get the complete picture, you would have to look at all the others it refers to and those it amends, and to check whether there are any others that are relevant." How can I check that, when I don't know what their names might be?" K. asked despairingly. "There are indexes, provided you know what to look for," the man replied, "but there's no sure way. Statutes are not arranged on a rational plan, since the same subject matter may be divided between many statutes, and any one statute may contain bits of several subjects. Sometimes you're fortunate, and there has been a consolidation Act to bring all the Acts together at a certain date. Or, with some subjects, you get the statutes collected together in *Statutes in Force*, although we can't always keep up with the new ones, so it's not as reliable as it ought to be. And, of course, it's only the statute law," he concluded rather lamely.

Perhaps the shop assistant was aiming to be helpful, but K. was finding it difficult to follow the man's disquisition. "Will I find the railway byelaws in here?" he demanded, gesturing to the fatter of the two booklets. "Oh, I don't think so," said the man, "that sounds like delegated legislation . . . I'll try the *Index to Government Orders* . . . No, it doesn't seem to be in here . . . probably they're not statutory instruments . . . the Stationery Office is responsible for numbering and printing the Government's statutory instruments, but there are some other kinds of subordinate legislation which we don't have anything to do with."

"Then where can I see the railways byelaws?" asked K. "I really don't know," replied the man, "perhaps at British Rail's headquarters in London, although it's being broken up and privatised at the moment, so I'm not sure who would be responsible."

Some other customers had come into the shop, and the man was becoming impatient with K. "Do you want this or not?" he said, holding up the Railways Act 1993, "it costs £18." "But then I would have to buy a whole lot of other documents to make sense of it," said K., "and even then it's only part of the law?" "That's right," replied the man more sharply, "of course, you can always consult a lawyer." "I suppose that's expensive," said K. The man shrugged and spread out his hands. "Naturally," he said. He continued: "You might find some legal books in the public library." "Might I?" said K. hopefully. "Would there be a complete collection of laws?" "I don't suppose so," replied the man, "since the libraries don't have so much to spend as they used to." "I'm sorry to hear that," K. said. "I don't think I have any chance of finding out what your laws are, not unless I was a rich man, or I had all the time in the world to hunt around in a hundred different places. But I have better things to do."

K.'s moods had been fluctuating between anger and desolation, but anger was predominant as he summarised his conclusions, and he was shouting the words as he left the shop. In reality, perhaps he had nothing better to do, although he was still hoping to go to the Castle.

But, as he came out of the shop, the Castle was nowhere to be seen, and he was not sure in which direction it lay. He retraced his steps to the park through which he had walked, from where it had been easily visible. He realised, when he reached the entrance to the park, that he had actually been walking further away from it. However, the Castle was then plainly in view and, although he could not see a path going directly to it, he went back into the park in the hope of finding a signpost to indicate the route.

*   *   *   *   *

As Joseph trudged through the park he began to feel a great weariness, and stopped to rest on a bench. Near him, two men whom he thought he remembered seeing on the evening before, were playing a game of sorts, taking turns to pitch empty tins and bottles at a litter bin. They missed the target more often that not, and K. began to smile at their efforts. His reaction seemed to enrage the men. "D'ye think y'could do any better?" asked one of them, bringing his head within an inch or two, so that K. could smell the alcohol on his breath as easily as he could sense the fellow's aggression. But then the man's mood changed. As he swayed back, his features softened to a grin and he invited K., "Go on. Have a shot."

"All right," said K., who was pleased to be included in their game. He took his turns and his efforts were soon shown to be the best, as his aim was good and most of the gold-coloured tins and clear glass bottles landed squarely in the wire basket. His companions were not improving, however, but getting worse. Sometimes the wildest of their throws went over a parapet and the tins or bottles disappeared from view, although they could be heard to rattle or crash on a surface below.

Suddenly there was a commotion below, and K. walked over to the parapet and looked down. He saw that a young girl lay on the ground, a broken bottle beside her, and from a wound on her head a slow stream of blood trickled down her face. The girl was crying, and some adults were trying to comfort her, while others were casting angry glances in K.'s direction. K. realised what must have happened, and turned to reproach his companions, but they were nowhere to be seen. He was still looking around for them or for some other person who might testify to his own blamelessness, when a tall man ran up smartly and seized him by the arm.

"I am detaining you on suspicion of your having assaulted or endangered people," said the man a little uncertainly, and then continued more confidently, "and for breach of the peace, because you have been identified as being responsible." "But I am not responsible," said K., "and as you do not appear to be a police officer, surely you have no right to detain me." "I have every right," replied the man. "I am a police officer, although I'm not in my uniform, as I'm off duty. Now, could I have your name and address, please, sir?" K. told him his name and where he had come from, and the man wrote something in a notebook. "My name is Constable Swann," he said, "I am informing you now that you are not obliged to answer any other questions, but I am detaining you and taking you to the police station."

"Why are you detaining me?" asked K. "So that you can answer some other questions," said the officer with some annoyance, as if it had been unnecessary to ask.

The constable hurried him away, holding his arm in a methodical, practised, irresistible grip. At the police station, which appeared to K. to be just like the other buildings, he was handed over to two men in uniform, introduced as Sergeant Smith and Constable Burnett, who, after conferring quietly with Constable Swann, took him off to a room with no windows, and only a few items of furniture.

The officers asked K. some personal questions, and recorded his replies, and then they ordered him to take his clothes off. "Like a dog," said K. as he stood, shivering a little, and the younger of the two men searched through his pockets. Then he was allowed to dress again, and had his fingerprints taken.

K. did as he was told, although several times he exclaimed that he was entirely innocent and grumbled a bit about the demands made on him. "Do you have the right?" he asked a few times. "Yes, we have the right," the Sergeant replied firmly each time, adding on one occasion, "That is the law. How could there be a mistake in that?" "I don't know this law," said K. "So much the worse for you," said the constable and, after a moment's thought continued: "See, he admits that he doesn't know the law and yet he claims he's innocent."

K. said nothing more for a while. "Must I," he thought, "let myself be confused by the gabble of these functionaries?" He tried to gather his thoughts, and when the two men began to question him about what had occurred in the park, he asked, "May I telephone to a lawyer?" "Certainly," replied the Sergeant, "indeed, you have the right to intimate your position to a solicitor. But I don't see what sense there would be in that, unless you have some private business of your own to consult him about." "What sense would there be in that?" cried K., more in amazement than exasperation. "What sense would there be in telephoning to a lawyer, when I'm supposed to be under arrest?" "But you're not under arrest," the sergeant said. "However, do telephone if you want to," he added, waving an arm towards the corridor outside, "please do telephone." K. was confident that his own efforts could clear up their misunderstanding. "No, I don't want to now," he said. "I'll tell you everything which happened, and then you'll see that I am completely innocent."

The two men listened to K.'s account, interposing questions from time to time, and writing down some of his replies. But they did not seem satisfied. He was required to repeat his account several times, at intervals, as they also left him to sit alone in the room for long periods. The air was stuffy and heavy, and K. was feeling nauseous. The necessity of repeating the same account so many times was causing him to doubt his own faculties.

At the far end of the room, his two interrogators were holding a whispered conversation, but K. could catch some of it. "It might be enough," the sergeant was saying, "but, of course, it all depends what the gentlemen up at the Office think about it." "What Office? What gentlemen?" cried K. The sergeant came over and spoke gently to him: "It's not up to us, you see. We can compile the papers and suggest charges, but it's a gentleman up at the Office who decides whether you'll be prosecuted and for what." K. had a look of vacant melancholy. "And when will I know?" he asked quietly. "In due course," replied the sergeant, "until then the charges hover above you, so to speak."

K. was not sure whether the questioning had finished, but at that moment the sergeant looked at his watch and started slightly. "I must tell you that your detention is terminated," he said. "Does that mean that I'm free to go?" asked K. "I didn't say that," the sergeant rejoined, "I said that your detention was terminated." "Then I'll be going," said K., rising unsteadily from his chair and making for the door. The constable barred his way and forcibly spun him round. "No. You're under arrest," said the sergeant.

*   *   *   *   *

A month had passed since K.'s arrest, and he had been found guilty of a breach of the peace. So far as he could tell from the proceedings, breach of the peace, a concept which did not even derive from legislation, was so vaguely defined that it could be constituted by any behaviour which the authorities didn't like. The judge, who was elderly, had not looked in K.'s direction during the proceedings, but at their conclusion he addressed K. directly and told him that he was deferring sentence, so that it might be seen whether K. could behave himself.

"Don't you want anything more from me?" asked K. "No," said the judge. "The court wants nothing from you. It receives you when you come and it dismisses you when you go."

He continued: "I have decided not to make a recommendation for deportation."

K. had acquired a lawyer called Grace, recommended to him by his Uncle David as being a person of influence, although K. could not see that he had derived any benefit from the association so far. "I was pleased to hear that," K. said to his lawyer as they emerged from the courtroom into a corridor, "because I was not intending to leave just yet. I haven't even reached the Castle yet."

"It's not quite as simple as that," the lawyer warned. "You are still liable to be deported, for example, if the Secretary of State were to deem that your deportation was for the public good."

"But surely my getting into trouble will be dismissed as a factor, when the court made no recommendation?" asked K.

"On the contrary," said Grace. "All factors are relevant, and a decision to deport frequently arises following a conviction."

"A high official like the Secretary of State will surely not be concerned with a trifling affair like this," said K., "so, if the law says that the Secretary must come to a certain view about me, then that will never happen."

The lawyer was reddening as his exasperation with K. increased. "Of course, it is not to be supposed that someone so high as the Minister, as we call him, will deal with your case in person, but there is a whole hierarchy of officials under him, and one of them will have a file bearing your name. If an official of a suitable rank decides that your deportation is desirable, that is quite sufficient. So far as we are concerned, it is all the same whether the Minister decides or his officials decide, for it is not to be imagined that there could be any difference of opinion between them."

In the corridor, where they had sat down, the air was stifling and K., whose state of mind was worsening with every additional thing he was told, felt that he could hardly breathe.

"It's very vague, what they deem 'for the public good' ... He was shouting at the lawyer, who raised his eyebrows in reproof, and waited for K. to calm down. "Yes," Grace agreed. "There is a list of considerations to be taken into account, in the Immigration Rules."

"So there might be some legal grounds in my favour?" asked K. "Perhaps some of them would be in your favour and some of them against you," said Grace dispassionately, then added more confidently, "but they're not exactly legal grounds because the Immigration Rules are not exactly law."

K.'s senses were reeling in the oppressive atmosphere of the court offices, and this last statement, at once astonishing and familiar, enraged him. "They must be law or not law," he said aggressively.

"Not necessarily," replied the lawyer. "Those Rules don't have statutory force. They are rules of practice really, but the court sometimes has regard to them." Seeing that K. was looking disconsolate, he continued: "But they're not exhaustive, anyway. For example, the factors listed as relevant to deportation decisions are only some of the factors that may be taken into account. Besides, there are instructions and policies followed, which account for some decisions outside the rules."

"Can we find out what these are?" asked K. desperately. "In this country, one seems to be condemned not only in innocence, but also in ignorance."

With this last protest, K. was completely worn out. A troubled frown crossed the lawyer's face, while he gave thought to his reply, but K. was to hear little of it. As two men in long coats came into view at the far end of the corridor, K.'s dizziness grew worse and his head drooped. Would his trials ever end?

[Note: Like certain of Franz Kafka's works, including *The Trial*, *The Castle* and *America*, the manuscript of *K. in Scotland* was left unfinished. The fragments published here have been published as they were found, without footnotes. Many readers will recognise, however, that K.'s experiences, inexplicable as they may have been to him, are easily understood by reference to the laws applicable in the United Kingdom, and more particularly in Scotland. In brief, what happened to K. was merely as follows: (i) a British Transport Police officer warned him of a possible offence under the Railways Byelaws; (ii) a shop assistant at an HMSO shop informed him about the repositories of the law; (iii) a police officer used the powers of detention available under the Criminal Justice (Scotland) Act 1980, with the end of the detention period being followed by an arrest; and (iv) a lawyer explained to K. his liability to be deported under the Immigration Act 1971. None of the officials appears to have acted unlawfully. Those who advised K. were perhaps better informed than one might expect to find.]

THE ESCAPE OF HOUDINI AND THE RESTRAINT OF THE NEW APPROACH

SANDRA EDEN

Introduction

Bill Wilson was fascinated by statutory interpretation, and it is no accident that there are a number of papers in this volume concerned with this topic. He was a collector of quirky cases on statutory interpretation, partly for fun, but mostly as part of his search for the intellectual underpinning of the job judges do.[1] His collection was gathered from far and wide and, inevitably, from time to time, his beady eye focused on tax cases, which provides a fertile ground for connoisseurs of statutory interpretation. In 1985 he wrote on the "new approach" to tax avoidance, describing his article as an attempt to clarify in his own mind the implications of the three House of Lords decisions which had by then been decided: *W. T. Ramsay Ltd v. I.R.C.*[2]; *I.R.C. v. Burmah Oil Co. Ltd*[3] and *Furniss v. Dawson*.[4] He concluded that article in typically quixotic style by asking, in response to a statement by Lord Fraser in *Burmah Oil*,[5]

> "Does this suggest that the House of Lords in these three cases has been carrying on an activity other than 'pure construction of the statutory provisions'? Taxation being purely a creature of statute, and the facts being for the commissioners, can the courts do anything other than 'pure construction of the statutes'? Surely they are not legislating?"[6]

The aim of this contribution is to re-examine the role of the judiciary in the development of the new approach over its lifetime[7] against a framework of the anti-tax avoidance options available to the courts,

---

[1] "The Complexity of Statutes", [1974] 37 M.L.R. 497; "Questions of Interpretation", [1987] 8 Stat. L.R. 142; "Trials and Try-Ons: Modes of Interpretation", [1992] 13 Stat. L.R. 1.

[2] [1982] 54 T.C. 101.

[3] [1982] 54 T.C. 200.

[4] [1984] B.T.C. 71.

[5] The extract quoted from Lord Fraser's judgment was, "The appeal raises two issues. The first is one of pure construction of the statutory provisions relating to capital gains tax. ... The second issue raises a question with wider implications as to whether certain transactions, which on the face of them and according to the taxpayer's submission, resulted in an allowable loss, should be regarded as artificial" (p. 215).

[6] "Tax Avoidance—Houdini, Magic and the Luncheon Party" (1985) 30 J.L.S.S. 184 at p. 186.

[7] As the New Approach reaches its fifteenth birthday, its name is as appropriate as that of Edinburgh's New Town, but the tags share the advantages of familiarity generated by use.

and to judge how well they have coped with the conflicts and ambiguities inherent in this task.

Judicial Approaches to Tax Avoidance

Before turning to an analysis of the cases it is helpful to sketch in briefly the range of possible approaches which might be taken by the judiciary in response to tax avoidance schemes. Against this framework, both the impact of the cases and the consistency of the approaches adopted can be assessed. For present purposes, five distinct approaches by the judiciary to tax avoidance can be identified,[8] of which four might be regarded as anti-avoidance strategies. Of these four, two are based on principles of pure statutory interpretation and two focus on the transaction itself but also concern the application of statutory interpretation techniques.

The first approach, which might be described as the doctrinal version, involves the invocation of an over-arching doctrine of tax jurisprudence to the effect that if a transaction is entered for tax avoidance purposes only, the taxpayer cannot claim the relief or exemption sought, because the legislature could not have intended to have applied the relief or exemption to such transactions. In other words, the judge may adopt a general purposive approach to the statute along the lines of "whatever transactions the legislature may have had in mind when creating the exemption, this was surely not included". The difficulties of ascertaining legislative purpose in general are well known but in the context of tax legislation where provisions are often to be found in pockets of labyrinthine complexity, purpose may only be identified by using the broadest of broad brush approaches. Another difficulty is illustrated by *Fitzwilliam v. I.R.C.*,[9] a case concerning a capital transfer tax avoidance scheme. Had the death in that case occurred in 1993, when the case was under consideration by the House of Lords, rather than in 1979, there would probably have been no need to engage in any avoidance device, as little or no tax would have been payable on the estate as a result of various legislative changes in the intervening period.[10] Should a court under these circumstances apply an over-arching doctrine based on policy since superseded?

At a less abstract and more familiar level, the second anti-avoidance approach involves using standard principles of statutory interpretation in relation to particular words of a statute, construing them to exclude activities engaged in for pure tax avoidance purposes. So, for example, when required to determine the meaning of the word "trade", the courts have found that the word has, as part of its natural meaning, an implication that some commercial purpose exists behind the activities in question, and in the absence of such purpose,

---

[8] For further discussion of such approaches, see J. Tiley, "Judicial Anti-avoidance Doctrines: the US Alternatives" [1987] B.T.R. 180 and 220.

[9] [1993] B.T.C. 8003.

[10] A rather similar point is made by Lord Keith at p. 8010.

objectively determined,[11] activities do not constitute a trade.[12] On a similar line, although slightly more adventurously, the U.S. Supreme Court in *Gregory v. Helvering*[13] interpreted the concept of "reorganisation" as not covering a "mere device which put on the form of a corporate reorganisation as a disguise for concealing its real character". Known in the United States as the business purpose test, this approach does not use the existence of a tax avoidance motive as the determining feature of such transactions, but the absence of a commercial purpose. If operated outside the business arena, this approach becomes closer to the doctrinal approach referred to above. There are no direct examples of the application by the U.K. courts of this technique outside the business area, but, as an example, such an approach might have been adopted in *Moodie v. I.R.C.*[14] In that case the question was whether a "self-cancelling" annuity was an annuity for the purposes of the legislation. The business/real purpose approach would there have involved an interpretation of the word "annuity" which would have excluded annuities entered into only for tax purposes. The effect of adopting this approach outside the business area is similar to that of the doctrinal approach, as it has the result that only transactions entered into for non-tax avoidance motives are given fiscal effect. The only difference is that the latter is applied at a general level, whereas the former is applied to individual words.

Turning to the transaction-based approaches, the third approach relevant for present purposes is the doctrine of "substance over form". An attractive notion, the substance approach seeks to tax what has "really" happened, rather than what the parties have contrived to happen. It operates at the stage in judicial reasoning after the primary facts have been ascertained and characterised according to their legal attributes. The fact-finder must then ask whether this concludes the matter, or whether the facts have to be re-characterised in order to get at the substance. Two points may be made. First, stated in this form, the approach becomes one of justification rather than reasoning: it tells us nothing about the conditions under which the answer at the first stage is not conclusive. To allow the judiciary to reinterpret transactions in order to find the "real" result is fraught with difficulties of subjective interpretation. Secondly, in *I.R.C. v. Duke of Westminster*,[15] Lord Wright thought the legal nature determinative of the transaction, leaving no room for a second stage. "And once it is admitted that the deed is a genuine document, there is in my opinion no room for the phrase 'in substance'. Or, more correctly, the true nature of the legal obligation and nothing else is 'the substance'."[16] An argument in favour of Lord Wright's approach is that tax law is

---

[11] *Ensign Tankers (Leasing) Ltd v. Stokes* [1992] B.T.C. 110.
[12] *F.A. & A.B. Ltd v. Lupton*, 47 T.C. 580 H.L.; *Sugarwhite v. Budd* [1988] B.T.C. 189; *Overseas Containers (Finance) Ltd v. Stoker* [1989] B.T.C. 153.
[13] 293 U.S. 465 (1935)
[14] [1993] B.T.C. 85. In fact *Moodie* appears to have been decided on the basis of the step approach, see n. 20.
[15] [1936] A.C. 1.
[16] *ibid.*, at p. 31.

a highly technical area which does not itself in general have regard to the substance. Burmah Oil Co. Ltd., a taxpayer in a subsequent case,[17] had a prior *real* loss which could not be utilised because it did not come within the strict terms of the capital gains tax legislation. The company then engaged in a self-cancelling transaction in an attempt to create an *unreal* loss which *did* come within the terms of the legislation. To be judged according to the reality of the situation in the context of the second transaction but not in relation to the first might, quite justifiably from Burmah Oil's point of view, be regarded as harsh.

The fourth strategy, which is in essence the substance approach with instructions attached, is the step approach.[18] The instructions tell the fact-finder in exactly what circumstances and with what results transactions A, B and C, which are legally separate, can be re-characterised as transaction D. It is fundamentally practical rather than theoretical, as it does not claim that an A followed by a B and a C is a D, unlike the substance approach, but rather determines when they can be so treated. Although it appears to be a way of viewing the facts rather than a technique of statutory interpretation, these matters are mutually interdependent. In the words of Bennion, the "unit of enquiry" in statutory interpretation is "an enactment whose legal meaning in relation to a particular factual situation falls to be determined".[19] In *Ramsay*, for example, Lord Wilberforce thought there was no gain and no loss and Lord Fraser that there was no disposal, both "in the sense required by the statutes".[20]

Of the four approaches, only the doctrinal approach is strictly a tax-avoidance doctrine, and as a consequence is the only one not available to the taxpayer. The business purpose test operates in the absence of a business motive rather than the presence of a tax-avoidance one, so dual purpose transactions are not affected. Both the transaction-based approaches can theoretically be applied wherever a legally circuitous route is chosen by the parties involved, whether the reason behind the route is tax avoidance, criminal intent, legal incompetence or anything else. In relation to the business purpose test, if the intrinsic meaning of the word "trade" contains some commercial purpose, there is nothing to prevent the taxpayer from arguing that a tax-avoidance transaction did not constitute trading. Similarly, the logic of the transaction-based approaches, which are just methods of getting

---

[17] *I.R.C. v. Burmah Oil Co. Ltd* [1982] 54 T.C. 200.

[18] Lord Bridge's judgment in *Furniss v. Dawson* [1984] B.T.C. 71 at p. 75, contains elements of both a general substance approach and a more limited step approach.

[19] F.A.R. Bennion, *Statutory Interpretation*, (2nd ed. 1992) s. 137. Of course, as Wilson pointed out, sometimes problem of interpretation arise before the facts are even considered, whether as a result of syntactic ambiguity or otherwise: see "Questions of Interpretation" *supra*. Much more common, however, are questions about whether the words of the statute cover the factual situation in a particular case.

[20] *ibid.*, at p. 199. According to Lord Templeman in a case with facts indistinguishable from *Plummer*, *Moodie v. I.R.C.*, "it is now plain that Mr Moodie did not pay an annuity within the meaning of the taxing statute because the steps taken under the plan were self-cancelling". In other words, although there was an annuity in the legal sense of the word, applying the step test, there was no annuity. The legal trappings of an annuity are not on their own sufficient.

at the facts, requires neutrality of application as between the Revenue and the taxpayer.[21]

It is evident from the above that the choice between approaches represents a tension between certainty for the taxpayer on the one hand and the flexibility of the judiciary to counter tax avoidance schemes on the other.[22] Ultimately, the pro-certainty proponent would adopt the fifth approach, an entirely literalist response taking no account of anything other than the formal legal structure imposed by the parties on a transaction. In particular, no account would be taken of any motive of tax avoidance. This strategy is usually associated with *I.R.C. v. Duke of Westminster*,[23] which normally provides the starting point against which the new approach is analysed, and is quoted as authority for the principle that a person is taxed according to his true legal position, with no account being taken of any underlying "substance".[24] Support for the literalist approach does not, of course, derive from any desire to facilitate tax avoidance, but rather from a sense of the greater evil caused by uncertainty to the taxpayer, or in the perceived unconstitutionality of the usurpation by the judiciary of the role of parliament in tax matters.

Assuming that, as in most jurisdictions, some degree of purposive construction of tax legislation is permissible, even that some degree of taxpayer uncertainty may not in this context be a bad thing,[25] what potential do the four anti-avoidance approaches hold for the resolution of this tension between certainty and flexibility?

Abstract doctrines are, according to Tiley,[26] like comets rather than stars or planets, in that they are potential rather than actual, unpredictable, and without clearly defined limits. It is also the case that there may be competing abstract doctrines, with no clear hierarchy of application. It is therefore difficult to judge when a particular doctrine will be applied. Moreover, in the tax context at least, it is necessary to be clear about what is left after a doctrine has been applied in order to work out the consequences. If the presence of a tax-avoidance motive causes a transaction is to be treated differently, the doctrine must be able with some degree of precision to say how. This is something for which such general principles are ill-equipped.

A second problem with the adoption of this approach in the tax

---

[21] In fact this argument was used by the taxpayers in *Whittles v. Uniholdings Ltd (No. 3)* [1995] B.T.C. 119 (under appeal to the Court of Appeal at the time of writing). The case was decided in favour of the taxpayers without reference to the *Ramsay* principle, as the transactions entered into were determined to be legally binding from the start, and no re-characterisation was required. Vinelott, J. added, obiter, that if an inference can be drawn that the parties did not intend the arrangements to have binding effect, the *Ramsay* principle would not apply (at p. 138).

[22] On a broader level, to adopt a purposive approach may be regarded as a positive judicial duty in general terms, and not just a piece of anti-avoidance armour.

[23] In this case, the Duke did not pay wages to certain employees, instead entering into a covenant to pay them. This saved the Duke income tax. The Inland Revenue's attempt to treat the covenant payments as if they had been wages failed.

[24] For an account of the approach of the courts to tax avoidance in the years between *Westminster* and *Ramsay*, see W. D. Popkin, "Judicial Anti-tax Avoidance Doctrine in England: a United States Perspective" [1991] B.T.R. 283.

[25] *per* Lord Goff in *Craven v. White* at p. 306.

[26] "Judicial Anti-avoidance Doctrines: the US Alternatives" [1987] B.T.R. at p. 194.

context is the extent to which it oversteps the limits of constitutional behaviour, which has certainly concerned the judiciary.[27] Returning for an instant to the question posed by Bill Wilson, whether the judiciary were legislating in the new approach cases, it was most probably the adoption of a judicial anti-avoidance doctrine that he had in mind.

Similarly, the doctrine of "substance over form", without qualification, provides a hopelessly uncertain indicator of judicial reaction to a set of facts. If there is any sense in which it is legitimate to distinguish between the legal characteristics of a series of events and their underlying form, which some might doubt,[28] there would certainly be no general consensus on how this is to be achieved. Judges of all people would be expected to pay great heed to the formal shape chosen by the parties for a transaction. Serious damage to the principle of legal certainty would be caused by an unqualified acceptance of the substance approach.

Turning to the business purpose test, to the extent its use is restricted to a commercial context a reasonable level of predictability is evident, but of course in this guise the test cannot deal with schemes which are effected in the domestic context, such as those in relation to inheritance tax. One cannot in such circumstances fault the absence of any business purpose. If this test is expanded in its application to words outside the commercial context, it becomes essentially the same as a general anti-avoidance doctrine, as explained above, and subject to the same limitations.

This leaves the step approach, which as outlined earlier is simply the substance test with instructions. The rival perspectives of the doctrinal and the literalist approaches lie at each end of the spectrum of interpretative techniques. The step approach is capable of occupying any point in between, depending on the formula developed for its application.[29] Can a formula be devised which will mitigate the undesirability of legal uncertainty whilst catching "unacceptable"[30] tax avoidance? This not only involves specifying the nexus of the steps for the approach to apply, their timing, and on whether and to what extent the motive of the taxpayer is a relevant factor, but also must provide a basis on which the re-characterised transaction can be taxed. With this question in mind, we turn to the development of the new approach in the U.K.

The New Approach—*Ramsay* to *Craven*

In 1936, when both tax rates and the number of taxpayers were low, the literalist approach to tax avoidance provided an adequate

---

[27] See for example the concerns expressed in *Craven* by Lord Oliver at pp. 289, 295 and 299, Lord Goff at p. 303.

[28] See Lord Wright's view, quoted above.

[29] In *Craven v. White*, for example, whilst all the judges were agreed that the approach being adopted was the step approach, there was a significant gap between the views of the majority and the minority, particularly between Lord Oliver and Lord Templeman, and the conditions for its application.

[30] *per* Lord Scarman in *Furniss v. Dawson* at p. 73.

operating principle. In the 1970s, both these features had changed,[31] and tax practitioners were seeking to run rings around the Inland Revenue with artificial, off-the-peg tax avoidance schemes. With hindsight, *Ramsay*, the first case in which the "new approach" was taken, seems rather narrow and unremarkable. *Ramsay* concerned an entirely artificial self-cancelling scheme designed to create an off-the-peg capital loss. In 1982, Millett Q.C., counsel for the Revenue in *Ramsay*, described the case as "momentous" and a "significant breakthrough for the Revenue",[32] and, viewed in the light of *I.R.C. v. Plummer*,[33] a decision of the House of Lords only two years earlier, so it must have seemed. *Plummer* concerned an "income/capital" scheme[34] by virtue of which the taxpayer was supposed to acquire an income tax deduction by entering into an annuity in favour of a charity in return for a capital sum from that charity. There was no cost to the taxpayer except the fee for fixing up the scheme. The argument for the Crown in *Plummer* was that, although in general the purchase of an annuity turns capital into income, the special features of this scheme meant that the so-called annuity payments represented a repayment to the charity of its own capital. Although this argument is couched in rather different terms from that used in *Ramsay*, the general thrust is the same: the independent parts of a transaction cannot be looked at in isolation. Finding for the taxpayer, Lord Wilberforce was unable to disregard the legal form of the documents to find some underlying substance.[35] Two years on in *Ramsay*, a case concerning an entirely artificial self-cancelling scheme, Lord Wilberforce found himself able to adopt a more robust approach:

> "Given that a document or transaction is genuine, the court cannot go behind it to some supposed underlying substance. This is the well-known principle of *Commissioners of Inland Revenue v. Duke of Westminster* [1936] AC 1. This is a cardinal principle but

---

[31] The top rate of income tax on earned income was, in 1979, 83 per cent, and on investment income, 98 per cent. Interestingly, however, many of the schemes concerned capital gains tax avoidance, which was then taxed at a flat rate of 33 per cent.

[32] P. J. Millett, "A New Approach to Tax Avoidance Schemes", [1982] 98 L.Q.R. 209.

[33] [1980] A.C. 896.

[34] Under this scheme, in return for a capital sum paid by a charity, the taxpayer entered into a five year covenant in favour of that charity for the equivalent aggregate sum. An integral part of the arrangement was that the capital sum was not to come under the control of the taxpayer, but was used to provide security for the annual payments. The advantage to the taxpayer was that the annuity payments were to be treated as an income tax deduction, whilst the charity, taking advantage of the exemption for charitable income, did not suffer a corresponding charge to tax.

[35] He said in *Plummer*, that "if it were possible to disregard the legal form of the documents and to look behind them for an underlying substance, there would be attractions beyond those of ingenuity in this argument. But I do not find it possible to do this. . . . In short, unless we are prepared to disregard the legal structure of these transactions, their nature is clear: a covenant, for a capital sum, to make annual payments, coupled with security arrangements for the payments" (p. 908). It is instructive to compare the difference in approach between the House of Lords in *Plummer* in 1979, and that of the same forum in *Moodie*, which concerned exactly the same sort of scheme, in 1993. In *Moodie*, Lord Templeman, with whom the others agreed, thought that there was no annuity within the meaning of the statute.

it must not be overstated or overextended. While obliging the court to accept documents or transactions, found to be genuine, as such, it does not compel the court to look at a document or a transaction in blinkers, isolated from any context to which it properly belongs. . . . It is the task of the court to ascertain the legal nature of any transaction to which it is sought to attach a tax or a tax consequence and if that emerges from a series or combination of transactions, intended to operate as such, it is that series or combination which may be regarded."[36]

This is an exegesis of the step approach: the "legal" nature of a transaction (not, note, the substance) may emerge from a series of transactions, and is not dependent on the legal characteristics of the individual stages. However, no guidance was given on when it will be appropriate to have regard to the context of a transaction and the judgments give no reasons for denying effect to the intermediate steps. It is primarily this gap which gave rise to the hype following the decision. Until these matters are made clear, the ambit of the approach and the perceived risk to taxpayers (or tax-avoiders, as the case may be) remains unascertainable.

The step approach only becomes an anti-avoidance doctrine when the formula for its application includes the presence of a tax avoidance step. This requirement first appears in the next case, *I.R.C. v. Burmah Oil Co. Ltd*, a case similarly concerning a self-cancelling transaction designed to create a loss.[37] Although the general thrust of *Burmah Oil* was the application of the step approach, the introduction of the need for a tax avoidance purpose suggested judicial drift towards the doctrinal approach, the only one treating a tax avoidance purpose as significant. This, together with some statements[38] possibly embracing a wider tax avoidance strategy than that suggested by *Ramsay*, and a strong sense of the early state of development of the new approach, meant that the precise ambit of the new approach was at this stage extremely uncertain.

The Crown had run a restricted argument in *Ramsay*, relying on the self-cancelling nature of the transactions,[39] but in both *Ramsay* and *Burmah Oil* the judgments were expressed in wider terms and the Revenue appeared to be pushing at an open door when it sought to apply the new approach to transactions which were not self-cancelling: the so-called linear transaction first brought before the House in *Furniss v. Dawson. Furniss* involved a disposal of an asset

---

[36] [1982] 54 T.C. 101 at p. 185.
[37] *per* Lord Diplock at [1982] 54 T.C. 200 at p. 214 "It would be disingenuous to suggest, and dangerous on the part of those who advise on elaborate tax avoidance schemes to assume, that *Ramsay*'s case did not mark a significant change in the approach adopted by this House in its judicial role to a pre-ordained series of transactions (whether or not they include the achievement of a legitimate commercial end) into which there are inserted steps that have no commercial purpose apart from the avoidance of a liability to tax which in the absence of those particular steps would have been payable." A similar formula was coined in *Furniss v. Dawson* at p. 88 by Lord Brightman.
[38] Especially in the judgment of Lord Fraser.
[39] Millett, "New Approach" *supra*.

from A via Greenjacket, an offshore company created especially for this purpose, to B, by two separate contracts. Had the disposal been to Greenjacket, relief would have operated to defer a charge to capital gains tax. Had the disposal had been to B, this relief was not available. Greenjacket was inserted purely to defer tax. After the transaction had been completed, Greenjacket was left holding the cash from the disposal, whilst A held Greenjacket shares. The Revenue argued that the correct construction of the transaction was a disposal from A to B in return for cash to Greenjacket. In the lower courts this argument had been successfully countered because of the existence of the enduring legal consequences, *i.e.* the continued presence of Greenjacket. In the House of Lords this reservation was unanimously rejected as being an unnecessary limitation on the application of the new approach.

The fundamental difference between *Ramsay* and *Burmah Oil* on the one hand and *Furniss* on the other is that in the first two cases, the net result of the activities in question is that nothing had changed and the parties had returned to square one. It is easy to apply a tax statute, or rather not to, where there is nothing to which to apply it: the party does not get the benefit of the loss or deduction or whatever he was trying to create. Rather more sophisticated legal arguments are required where a transaction which does not collapse on itself has taken place, because the shift in the parties' positions must be accounted for in tax terms. In *Furniss*, the concept of "relevant transaction" became important, in terms of which the *actual* transaction was re-characterised according to its end result. The "relevant transaction" in *Ramsay* and *Burmah Oil*, had it been formulated in such terms, would have been a nullity. In *Furniss*, the two separate contracts of disposal from A to Greenjacket and from Greenjacket to B were treated as a tripartite contract from A to B in return for cash to Greenjacket. It was the tripartite contract which underpinned the relevant transaction, and in terms of which the continued existence of Greenjacket could be explained. As will be seen, the search for the relevant transaction to be taxed has become one of the problem areas of the new approach.

The early judgments have a pioneer spirit about them, if not, in some cases, evangelical zeal.[40] They are self-conscious contributions to a process which was not yet finished: the process of ascertaining the limits within which the new approach was to operate. However, a retrenchment towards a more cautious, legalistic approach was clearly

---

[40] "What had been established with certainty by the House in *Ramsay's* case is that the determination of what does and does not constitute unacceptable tax evasion is a subject suited to development by judicial process.... The limits within which [the *Ramsay* principle] is to operate remain to be probed and determined judicially. Difficult though the task may be for judges, it is one which is beyond the power of the blunt instrument of legislation" (per Lord Scarman in *Furniss v. Dawson* at p. 73). "While the techniques of tax avoidance progress are technically improved, the courts are not obliged to stand still. Such immobility must result either in loss of tax, to the prejudice of other taxpayers, or to Parliamentary congestion or (most likely) both.... The capital gains tax was created to operate in the real world, not that of make-belief" (*per* Lord Wilberforce in *Ramsay* at p. 187).

apparent in the judgments of the majority of the House of Lords in the next case, *Craven v. White*.[41] It was made resoundingly clear that the new approach did not give the judiciary general permission to ignore or re-characterise steps taken for tax avoidance motives,[42] merely that composite transactions could be treated as a whole rather than as several separate transactions. In other words, it confirmed beyond doubt that the step approach was being applied, and not some wider version of an anti-avoidance doctrine. Lord Oliver, conscious of the ambiguous relevance of an avoidance motive in the step approach, struggled to explain its presence in the following terms,

> "(T)he absence of any commercial motive underlines the artificiality of the interrelated transactions and entitles the court to disregard them because they are not intended to produce anything other than an artificial fiscal result."[43]

He was evidently attempting to distance himself from any moral standpoint against tax avoidance, but taken out of context, these words seem to suggest approval for the broad application of the business purpose test, a conclusion which is not supported by the rest of his judgment.

Stress was placed on the fact that the application of the *Ramsay* principle was one of statutory interpretation, although, as pointed out by Bill Wilson, there were sparse references to statute in the cases and not a principle in sight,[44] and one reason for the stress on this aspect might be the allegations of unconstitutionality which had been levelled by some who viewed the application of the principle as one of judicial legislation.[45] What can be more natural in an area of pure statute law than to find judges interpreting statutes? Alternatively, this stress on statutory interpretation and the emphatic denial of judicial legislation may just be another way of affirming that a general wider anti-avoidance doctrine was not being imposed.

On a practical level, *Craven* also contained further guidance on when it is appropriate to re-characterise a series of transactions as one. By a majority,[46] the test was tightly drawn to include only transactions which were very closely linked, with emphasis being placed on the "tripartite contract" element of *Furniss*.[47]

---

[41] [1988] B.T.C. 268.
[42] Lord Keith at p. 272, Lord Oliver at pp. 289, 290 and 294, Lord Jauncey at p. 314.
[43] At p. 292.
[44] "Trials and Try-ons", p. 8.
[45] For example, R. K. Ashton, "The Ramsay and Burmah Decisions—A Reappraisal", [1983] B.T.R. 221; G. R. Bretten and F. Stockton, "The Ramsay Doctrine: An Interim Review", [1987] B.T.R. 280; The Monday Club, "Untaxed by Parliament, Taxed by the Judges", Policy Paper TX1 December 1984, referred to in R. White, "The New Approach and the Views of the Law Society", [1986] B.T.R. 18.
[46] With a robust dissent by Lord Templeman, and a less forceful one by Lord Goff.
[47] According to Lord Oliver, who delivered the leading judgment in *Craven*, a series of transactions can be collapsed where
  (i) the series of transactions was pre-ordained at the time the intermediate step was entered into;
  (ii) that the transaction had no other purpose than tax mitigation;

Assessing the four main cases in the light of the earlier discussion of the various approaches to tax avoidance, a fairly well developed strategy to counter the most blatant avoidance schemes has emerged. The intellectual basis of the strategy has been established, namely that it is a method of ascertaining the facts, and the framework for its application placed it towards the literalist end of the step approach spectrum.[48] Those of a more purposive turn of mind thought that the conditions were drawn unnecessarily tightly,[49] but at this stage in its life at least, the new approach provided some kind of reasonable compromise between the literalists and those who perceived the judicial role as a weapon in the armoury of tax anti-avoidance.

The New Approach: Post-*Craven* Developments

Since *Craven*, there have been few victories for the Revenue. A self-cancelling scheme was successfully collapsed in *Moodie*, and a large self-cancelling loop in an otherwise trading transaction was ignored in *Ensign Tankers (Leasing) Ltd. v. Stokes*.[50] But with one limited exception,[51] linear schemes have escaped attack on the basis of the new approach. This is not because they failed the tests of the post-*Craven* framework,[52] but because the framework itself has been drawn in even tighter terms.

In *Fitzwilliam v. I.R.C.*,[53] a five-step capital transfer tax avoidance scheme was entered into which had the effect of passing £3.8 million out of an estate to the deceased's daughter via her mother without the payment of tax. The facts were complex but revolved around the creation and assignation of life interests in the fund.[54]

Lord Keith, giving the leading judgment for the majority, accepted that the transaction was "pre-ordained" in the sense that all the steps would be carried out as part of a pre-planned tax avoidance scheme, but that pre-ordainment was not itself sufficient. In addition, according to Lord Keith, the series has to be "capable of being construed in a manner inconsistent with the application of the exemption" which is being sought.[55] Lord Templeman's 18-page dissenting judgment

---

(iii) there was no practical likelihood that the events would not take place in the order ordained so the intermediate transaction had no independent life; and

(iv) the pre-ordained events actually took place (p. 298).

[48] *ibid*.

[49] *e.g.* Lord Goff at p. 304.

[50] [1992] B.T.C. 110.

[51] The exception is *Hatton v. IRC* [1992] B.T.C. 8024 in the Chancery Division, in which a capital transfer tax avoidance scheme was re-written. The *Hatton* and the *Fitzwillian* scheme share salient features, the major difference between them being the length of time between the various steps: only three days in *Hatton* compared with several weeks in *Fitzwilliam*.

[52] See n. 47 above.

[53] [1993] B.T.C. 8003.

[54] The Inland Revenue sought to treat as one transaction steps 1–5 in the Chancery Division; in the Court of Appeal, in the alternative, they linked steps 1–5, steps 2–5, steps 2, 3 and 4, and steps 3 and 5; and, before the House of Lords, steps 2–5 were presented as the transaction. This does not inspire confidence.

[55] At p. 8015.

engaged in such a construction, but Lord Keith was unable to do so, apparently for two related reasons. First, he was unable to find the relevant transaction by applying the previously used techniques of "running any two or more transactions together or of disregarding any one or more of them".[56] This part of his judgment displays a highly technical approach and is not entirely convincing. However, picking up on a earlier remark made by Lord Oliver in *Craven*,[57] the second basis for his decision is the existence of enduring legal consequences of some of the steps, which were executed over a period of nine weeks, and which included interests in possession for part of that period.[58] Lord Templeman's response to this was that the argument that *Ramsay* did not apply to an inserted step which had enduring legal consequences had been "decisively rejected" by the House of Lords in *Furniss*. What he did not point out is the significant difference between the timing in the two schemes. In *Furniss*, the steps took place so quickly (it may have been all over in time for lunch[59]) that no enduring legal consequences could have occurred *in the course of* the composite transaction. The enduring legal consequence which had worried the lower courts in *Furniss* was the continued existence of Greenjacket, but there is nothing illogical about this if the transaction is rewritten as a tripartite contract from A to B in return for cash to Greenjacket. In *Fitzwilliam*, the legal consequences arose while the more leisurely steps were still taking place and, according to the majority, this prevents the doctrine from applying altogether.

It is not clear why this should be so. The enduring legal consequences which concerned Lord Oliver arose out of the temporary life interest, namely the income arising during the subsistence of the interest and the possibility of the death of the person whilst in possession of that interest and the resultant charge to inheritance tax. To deal first with the intermediate income, take the analogous case of a variation by a beneficiary of an entitlement under a will.[60] The inheritance tax legislation permits a series of events to be re-characterised for one purpose, but not for others, so it is not evident why the

---

[56] *Fitzwilliam* actually involved two side-by-side but independent schemes, the mutual gifts scheme and the revertor-to-settlor scheme, each designed to extract £1.8m, using separate statutory exemptions. It is not clear why two schemes were used; perhaps bets were being hedged. In relation to the revertor-to-settlor scheme, however, it would certainly have been possible to have ignored step 5, subject to the "enduring legal consequences argument".

[57] At p. 294. Lord Oliver speaks of an intermediate transfer which could not be regarded as a real transaction but as merely an element in larger whole *without independent effect*. He was also concerned about the "permanent, legal, practical and fiscal consequences attaching to the intermediate step" which cannot simply be ignored (p. 293).

[58] In particular, the income arising during the subsistence of the interest in possession was subject to income tax in the hands of the person with the interest, and if that person had died whilst in possession of that interest, there would have been a charge to inheritance tax on the value of the fund as a result.

[59] *per* Lord Brightman at p. 78.

[60] An election under s. 142 of the Inheritance Tax Act 1984 writes the variation back into the will, with the effect that the *deceased* is deemed to have bequeathed the property in accordance with its actual destination for inheritance tax purposes. However, any income arising in the pre-variation period will be taxed as the income of the original beneficiary.

judiciary should not similarly be able to do so. The difficulty over the possibility of an intervening death is more easily disposed of. The application of the step approach requires that the contemplated steps actually take place and if the process is permanently halted, one taxes what has happened rather than what might have had the plan proceeded to fruition.

Fitzwilliam marks the most recent analysis of the new approach in the House of Lords, but the tone there set is evident in the subsequent cases in the lower courts.[61] Of particular significance is *I.R.C. v. McGuckian*[62] in which the majority of the Court of Appeal thought that an assignation by a trust of a right to a dividend in return for a capital sum with the aim of avoiding income tax could not be re-characterised under the new approach. The main basis of the decision for the majority was the view that the assignation was not a composite transaction.[63] An alternative argument favoured by the dissenter, Kelly L.J., was that the transaction was the payment of the dividend, the inserted step was the assignation, and when this was ignored, the relevant transaction was a payment of a dividend to the trust. More significantly, the leading judgment cast doubt on whether, in the light of *Craven* and *Fitzwilliam*, the new approach had any continuing relevance for linear schemes.[64] Again, the approach adopted to the scheme in that case was highly technical.

The purpose of the above arguments is to show that on the post-*Craven* formulation it would have been open to the courts to apply the new approach in the most recent cases, particularly in *Fitzwilliam*, but they chose not to, instead drawing back even further from the bold statements in the early cases.

Conclusion

This brief review of the most important decisions which make up the new approach shows that, despite some early uncertainties, it is the step version which has prevailed over competing strategies to combat

---

[61] *I.R.C. v. McGuckian* [1994] B.T.C. 374; *Pigott v. Staines Investments Ltd;* [1995] B.T.C. 90; *Whittles v. Uniholdings Ltd. (No. 3)* [1995] B.T.C. 119.

[62] *ibid.*

[63] In *Moodie*, in which the taxpayer entered into an annuity in return for a capital sum, the self-cancelling nature of the arrangements enabled the court to hold that there was no "annuity". The annuity in *Moodie* was a unilateral obligation which was cancelled by the matching obligation on the charity to pay a capital sum. The court in *McGuckian* were precluded from regarding the assignation as self-cancelling by focusing on its bilateral nature (see Hutton, L.J. at p. 419). It is doubtful if the fine distinction as to whether there are two unilateral obligations or one bilateral one should be regarded as critical to the analysis of a transaction. *McGuckian* is under appeal to the House of Lords.

[64] Carswell, L.J. said at p. 404, "The House of Lords applied the Ramsay principle to a couple of schemes [*Ensign Tankers* and *Moodie*] both of which involved palpably self-cancelling transactions. When asked to strike down transactions on the ground developed in *Furniss* however, the courts have tended to distinguish the earlier cases and to decline to apply the principle to the transactions before them." It appears that the majority regarded the present scheme as linear, although it is no more linear that *Moodie*.

anti-avoidance. In response to the first of Wilson's questions mentioned at the beginning of this contribution, it is evident that the courts have ultimately been involved in a type of statutory interpretation, although the process might more properly be called statutory application. In response to the second question, as to whether the judiciary had been legislating, if this is equated with the introduction of a broad based anti-avoidance doctrine, it is clear that they have not. Prefacing statutory terms with the occasional "real" does not appear to amount to judicial legislation.

However it is more open to question whether the present state of the new approach represents a satisfactory compromise between the view that the proper discharge of the judicial function requires a purposive approach for both practical[65] and theoretical[66] reasons, and the argument that a narrowly formulated text-based approach is the only guarantee of legal certainty. To the requirement that the steps have to be virtually contractual in nature has been added the necessity that there are no intermediate legal consequences, and that in order for re-characterisation to take place, the new transaction must be realistically and intellectually possible.[67] This does not mark a return to the literalist approach of the *Duke of Westminster*, as the self-cancelling circular type schemes exemplified in *Ramsay* are still subject to attack; but it casts doubt on whether any artificial scheme acting as a conduit for a real transaction can be challenged. It is tempting to conclude that an approach which cannot re-characterise the events which took place in *Fitzwilliam* in order to produce a taxable event is of limited value, particularly as the proponents of such schemes will be aware of the need to move steadily. In *Furniss*, had Greenjacket held the assets being disposed of for a few weeks instead of a few minutes, the result today would very possibly be different.

Moreover, an excessively formalistic approach by the majorities in *Fitzwilliam* and *McGuckian* has replaced earlier debates on principle. In contrast with the earlier cases, there were no arguments based on the need for taxpayer certainty or on the proper role of the judiciary. With no sense of irony, a literalist formal approach worthy of the *Duke of Westminster* was applied to the step approach itself. It is as yet too early to judge whether the present position marks the temporary retrenchment not unknown when a significant change has been effected by the judicary, or whether it represents a settled position at the literalist end of the scale. It is likely that the answer lies somewhere in between. The generous amount of time devoted by the House of Lords to tax cases can be a mixed blessing, but it at least provides the opportunity for rapid development, and when the new approach returns to the House in the guise of the *McGuckian* appeal perhaps some further answers will be provided.

---

[65] In order to protect government revenue, for example *per* Lord Wilberforce in *Ramsay* at p. 187, Lord Templeman in *Craven* at p. 279 and Lord Goff in *Ensign Tankers* at p. 128

[66] Namely that the correct approach to statutory interpretation is a purposive one, and that a judge is abdicating his responsibilities if he hides behind the literal words of the statute: see Lord Goff in *Craven* at pp. 303–304.

[67] *per* Lord Keith in *Fitzwilliam* at p. 8015.

OLD BASTARDS AND OTHER CHILDREN

ALAN R. BARR

Introduction

Tales of Bill Wilson's references to bastards are legion; some at least
may be apocryphal. But he undoubtedly lectured on illegitimacy and
began one such lecture by listing the kinds of bastards recognised by
the law. The exact number of types to which he made reference is
open to some doubt, but his starting point was the four kinds detailed
in Craig's *Jus Feudale*.[1] He later pointed out that this analysis had
proved to be insufficient for all purposes, citing a further classification
from the French Civil Code.[2] There were occasions when Wilson
would perhaps have wished to make further, more or less informal,
additions to this list.

In Scots law, it might seem that the status of bastardy has been
swept away for ever. The Law Reform (Parent and Child) (Scotland)
Act 1986 provides that:

> "The fact that a person's parents are not or have not been married
> to one another shall be left out of account in establishing the legal
> relationship between the person and any other person; and
> accordingly any such relationship shall have the effect as if the
> parents were or had been married to one another."[3]

There are indications that Wilson may have disapproved of the virtual
disappearance of the term "illegitimate". In complaining about statutory verbosity in general, he noted that "... instead of 'illegitimate
child', we now have to say 'a child whose parents are not and never
have been married to one another' ".[4]

Bastards have hangovers, however; the statutory provision quoted
above does not apply to any deed executed before its commencement
on December 8, 1986.[5] In fact, earlier legislation repealed by the 1986
Act[6] had achieved much the same effect from an earlier date. The Law
Reform (Miscellaneous Provisions) (Scotland) Act 1968 provided that:-

> "In deducing any relationship for the purpose of ascertaining the
> person or persons entitled to benefit under a provision contained
> in any deed, persons shall, unless the contrary intention appears,

---

[1] 2.18.4. The types listed were heinous, incestuous, adulterine and simple.
[2] "The Importance of Analysis" in D. L. Carey Miller and D. W. Meyer (eds.) *Comparative and Historical Essays in Scots Law* (1992) at pp. 167–168.
[3] Law Reform (Parent and Child) (Scotland) Act 1986 (c. 9), s. 1(1).
[4] "Studying Statutes", 1992 J.R. 213 at p. 220.
[5] Law Reform (Parent and Child) (Scotland) Act 1986, s. 1(4).
[6] *ibid.*, Sched. 2.

be taken to be or, as the case may be, to have been, related to each other notwithstanding that the relationship existing between them is or was an illegitimate one only; and any rule of law to the contrary effect shall cease to have effect".[7]

That provision also only applied to deeds executed after its commencement, which took place on November 25, 1968.[8] Thus, while illegitimacy may have lost much of its legal stigma in relation to many matters in 1968, and even more in 1986, it remains necessary to know the law relating to the subject before these dates. In particular it is necessary to know who may have been illegitimate under the old law when dealing with old deeds. Particularly in relation to wills and trusts, such old deeds remain extremely common. One was the subject of a House of Lords decision in 1993.

Wright's Trustees

Wright's Trustees v. Callender[9] concerned a trust deed coming into operation in 1917, which was varied (as permitted by its terms) by the truster's widow. The widow executed her own trust disposition and settlement in 1925 and died in 1932; on her death one daughter succeeded to the residue of her estate. That daughter had four children. One of these was domiciled in England and had three children at a time when she was not married to their father.

The daughter died in 1953; the relevant granddaughter (domiciled in England) died in 1989. At the latter date, that granddaughter had a life interest in a share of both of the estates of her grandparent trusters. In terms of her *grandfather's* trust (as varied by that of her grandmother), the share of residue liferented by the granddaughter passed to the granddaughter's "issue". In terms of the *grandmother's* trust, her share of that residue passed to the grandmother's "great-grandchildren". Vesting was in each case postponed until the granddaughter's death.

Clearly, the references to relationships were in deeds executed before the 1968 Act came into force. If one had simply been dealing with illegitimate children of any of the types listed by Craig, whose parents had never married, they could not have taken benefit under the trusts—the presumptions against the expressions used including illegitimates would have been too strong.[10]

But the parents of the relevant children had married. This would have been sufficient to make the children legitimate *per subsequens matrimonium* in England or in Scotland,[11] but for the fact that they had not been free to marry at the time of each child's conception, the father being at those times married to another.[12] This particular restriction

---

[7] Law Reform (Miscellaneous Provisions) (Scotland) Act 1968, (c. 70), s. 5(1).
[8] *ibid.*, s. 5(3).
[9] 1993 S.L.T. 556.
[10] See for example *Mitchell's Trs. v. Cables* (1893) 1 S.L.T. 156.
[11] By the Legitimacy Act 1926, (c. 60), s. 1(1), and at common law, respectively.
[12] *ibid.*, s. 1(2), and at common law, respectively.

on the legitimation of children was removed by the Legitimacy Act 1959, s. 1(1), with effect from October 29, 1959, in England; and by the Legitimation (Scotland) Act 1968, s. 4, with effect from June 8, 1968, in Scotland. Both statutes stated that the legitimations achieved by their terms were not to confer any rights under deeds which *came into operation* before their commencement.

The question in *Wright's Trustees* was whether the children of the relevant granddaughter were entitled to the shares of residue liferented by their mother. In other words, were these children disqualified by their undoubted illegitimate status in 1917 and 1932 (when the two trust dispositions first came into effect)?

In the Court of Session,[13] an Extra Division held that a destination to the children of a liferentrix on her death fell to be construed as to her lawful children according to the law of her domicile at her death. By that (English) law, the relevant children had been legitimated by the time of the liferentrix's death and were thus entitled to succeed. The saving provision in the English statute only applied to dispositions which fell to be construed by English law. The court recognised that this produced anomalous results, notably that if the children's mother had died domiciled in Scotland, the saving provision in the Scottish legitimation statute would have preserved their illegitimate status and prevented them succeeding. In the Court of Session, much was made of the private international law issues involved.[14]

The House of Lords cut through such anomalies and reversed the decision of the Court of Session, concentrating on the perceived intentions of the trusters. Lord Keith referred to the fact that there appeared to be no case dealing with a change in the law concerning legitimacy between the coming into operation of an instrument and the opening of the succession (for instance, on the conclusion of a liferent). However, similar issues had been considered in *Cockburn's Trustees v. Dundas*,[15] as to the identification of a testators heirs *in mobilibus* who would take in terms of his will on the expiry of certain liferents. It was held that these heirs should be identified under the law applicable at the testator's death, notwithstanding that before the liferents expired the law had been changed by the Intestate Moveable Succession (Scotland) Act 1855. Lord Keith applied the reasoning of the opinions in that case, which

"indicate that a testator is not to be regarded as having contemplated that there might be a change in the law between his death and the opening of the succession, and that the more natural intention to attribute to him is that the succession should be regulated by the law as it stood at the time of his death. Applying that approach to the circumstances of the present case the conclusion must be that the testator and the testatrix did not intend

---

[13] 1992 S.L.T. 498.
[14] On this issue in particular, and for an excellent commentary on this case and related matters in general, see E. Crawford, "It's a Wise Testator Who Knows His Own Great Grandchildren", 1994 S.L.T. (News) 225.
[15] (1864) 2M. 1185.

that when the succession opened, the class of beneficiaries should include 'issue' and 'great-grandchildren' who answered the description of 'lawful' by reason only of changes in the law occurring after their testamentary dispositions had come into operation."[16]

Both Lord Keith and Lord Jauncey also referred to the case of *Nimmo v. Murray's Trustees*.[17] In that case, a testator died leaving a will dated before the commencement of the 1855 Act, containing a reference to a person's "nearest heirs and successors". It was held that the heirs as ascertained by the 1855 Act were entitled to take.[18]

Lord Jauncey contrasted *Nimmo* with *Cockburn's Trustees*, stating that "these two cases neatly illustrate the different results which may flow from a change in the law affecting the character of a beneficiary between the date of execution of the testamentary document and the date of death of the testator, and a similar change after the death of the testator but before the succession has opened to the beneficiary."[19]

Lord Keith regarded *Nimmo* as:

"no more than a reflection of the established doctrine that a will is ambulatory and speaks from death. As Lord Justice Clerk Inglis said in *Nimmo v. Murray's Trs.* at p. 1149, a testator so long as he is of sound disposing mind must be held to know of changes that have taken place in the law of succession, *and if he does not make any alteration in his will before his death so as to show that he intended the old law to have effect then the new law must have effect*'" (emphasis added).[20]

Wright's Trustees might be thought merely to confirm, and to serve as an example of, the application of two fundamental principles affecting the interpretation of wills and trusts—the constant search for the holy grail of the testator's intentions (the intention principle); and the doctrine of the ambulatory will, speaking only from the death of the testator (the ambulatory principle).

The trouble with fundamental principles of interpretation in relation to private deeds is that statutes can cut across them. Where statutes are not framed in the same way for similar situations, this can cause even fundamental principles to conflict.

The statutes equiparating the rights of illegitimate persons with those of the legitimate are true to the intention principle (as such statutes only affect deeds executed after their commencement), but not to the ambulatory one. If a testator is to be presumed to know the law at the date of his death, the ambulatory principle would demand that he should be forced to alter the wording of his will, where the

---

[16] 1993 S.L.T 556 at p. 559
[17] (1864) 2M. 1144.
[18] The Scottish Law Commission has decided not to recommend any change in the law on the meaning of the term "heirs" in private documents—see *Report on Succession* (Scot. Law. Com. No. 124, 1990), para. 4.81–4.83.
[19] 1994 S.L.T. 556 at p. 561.
[20] *ibid.*, at p. 559.

law has altered the meaning of that wording before the will comes into effect. As *Wright's Trustees* demonstrates, the legitimation statutes (in both Scotland and England) are true to the ambulatory principle, but not to the intention one. If the legitimation rules had come into effect between the execution of a will and the death which brought it into operation for the first time, it would be necessary to assume that the testator had made a conscious decision *not* to alter his will to cope with the new law. This may be a valid assumption, but it is not a *necessary* one.

Salvesen's Trustees

By the laws of coincidence which seem to apply to developments through reported cases, a second decision with a number of similarities to *Wright's Trustees; Salvesen's Trustees, Petitioners*,[21] appeared in 1993. Both cases involved old trust deeds; both involved the interpretation of wording which affected the rights of children other than those born in a married relationship (adopted children in the one case and illegitimate (at least at one time) children in the other); and both involved an attempt to decide what would have been the truster's intentions in relation to those children, when the law had changed considerably over the period spanning the drafting of the trust deeds and the time when certain of their provisions came into effect.

Salvesen's Trustees, a decision of the First Division on May 28, 1992, was decided before the House of Lords pronounced in *Wright's Trustees* (January 28, 1993). There are, perhaps unsurprisingly, difficulties in reconciling both decisions, that in *Salvesen's Trustees* being much more in keeping with the Court of Session's own decision in *Wright's Trustees*.

Salvesen's Trustees dealt with an *inter vivos* trust deed executed in 1947, which was varied by interlocutor of the Court of Session on March 12, 1968. This variation fundamentally altered the terms of the original trust. In effect, it created a new settlement, deemed to be executed as at the date of the interlocutor. This point was of crucial importance in the decision eventually reached.

Neither the original trust nor the variation included adopted children specifically among the beneficiaries. It was noted that in *Pollock-Morris, Petitioners*,[22] the court had refused to give approval to an arrangement introducing express reference to adopted children as beneficiaries, on the grounds that this would prejudice existing and future beneficiaries under the trust as originally drawn. But no such objection was taken in the present case and the court proceeded on the basis that the questions which arose had to be answered without regard to any prejudice which might arise to the beneficiaries of the original trust.

The competing interests in *Salvesen's Trustees* were those of the original truster's natural children and grandchildren on the one hand,

---

[21] 1993 S.L.T. 1327.
[22] 1969 S.L.T. (Notes) 60.

and of two adopted children of one of the truster's sons, on the other. These two children had been adopted in terms of decrees by a United States court in 1989 and 1990. Were these adopted children to be included when considering such terms as "children" and "issue" in the 1968 variation?

In fact, the main issue resolved by the court was a reconciliation of the terms of subsections 23(1) and 23(2) of the Succession (Scotland) Act 1964. Insofar as relevant, these are in the following terms:

> "(1) For all purposes relating to —
> (a) the succession to a deceased person (whether testate or intestate), and
> (b) the disposal of property by virtue of any *inter vivos* deed,
>
> an adopted person shall be treated as the child of the adopter and not as the child of any other person.
>
> (2) In any deed whereby property is conveyed or under which a succession arises, being a deed executed after the making of an adoption order, unless the contrary intention appears, any reference (whether express or implied) —
> (a) to the child or children of the adopter shall be construed as, or as including, a reference to the adopted person; . . .
>
> Provided that for the purposes of this subsection a deed containing a provision taking effect on the death of any person shall be deemed to have been executed on the date of death of that person."

It was accepted that if subsection 23(1) had stood alone, there would have been no difficulty. The question was really whether subsection 23(2) qualified the operation of subsection 23(1) in all cases in which subsection 23(2) applied.

The court held that it did not, explaining subsection 23(2) as follows:

> "Subsection (2) can, and in our opinion should, be read as dealing with a particular situation only, where a deed has been executed in knowledge both of the provisions of the Act and of the existence of an adoption order. It is qualified in the case of provisions with testamentary effect by the proviso that the date of execution is to be taken to be the date of the death of the person on whose death the provision is to take effect. The particular question with which it is designed to deal is whether it was the intention of the person when making the deed, or by leaving an earlier testamentary deed unaltered until his death, knowing of the provisions of the Act and of the existence of the adoption order, that references to a natural relationship were to be construed as including relationships arising from the adoption. The effect of the subsection, on a point which it must be assumed was thought to be liable otherwise to create difficulty, is that a contrary intention must be expressed in the deed in these circumstances if it is not

to have that result. In our opinion, however, it has no other effect. In particular, it cannot be read as restricting the application of subs (1)(a) to only those cases where the inter vivos deed has been executed after the making of an adoption order. There is nothing in the wording of either subsection to indicate that it was the intention that this should be the result. We can think of no good reason why Parliament, having said all that was necessary in subs (4) to prevent the section from having retrospective effect, should have intended that subs (1) was to be further qualified. In our opinion it was intended to have effect, in accordance with its express provisions, for all purposes after the commencement of the Act."[23]

In the passage just quoted, the court made brief reference to subsection (4) of the Succession (Scotland) Act 1964, which did not receive much further attention throughout the opinion. The subsection is in the following terms:

"Nothing in this section shall affect any deed executed, or the devolution of any property on, or in consequence of, the death of a person who dies, before the commencement of this Act."

The commencement date of the 1964 Act was September 10, 1964. Given that the court was dealing, ultimately, with a trust originally executed in 1947, one might have thought that this would have been a matter of great relevance. However, this notion was dismissed, on the ground that the 1968 variation had effectively entirely superseded the 1947 trust. There was no attempt to include adopted children specifically among the beneficiaries of the 1968 variation. On the evidence of *Pollock Morris, Petitioners*,[24] it is likely that any such attempt would have failed. It therefore seems rather cavalier that the 1947 trust should have been ignored in this way. It seems clear that the intentions of the truster in 1947 are unlikely to have included numbering adopted children among his beneficiaries, as was indeed acknowledged by the court.[25]

Reference was made in *Salvesen's Trustees* to the case of *Spencer's Trustees v. Ruggles*.[26] This concerned a trust deed from 1905, in which the beneficiaries included the "lawful children" of a named person. It was held that the intentions of the truster could not have extended to including among such children a child adopted in 1970—indeed, there were no procedures for statutory adoption in 1905. It was however acknowledged that adopted children *could* fall within the description of "lawful children"; and that the absence of adoption procedures at the time the trust was executed did not *necessarily* preclude the

---

[23] 1993 S.L.T. 1327 at p. 1332. See also M. C. Meston, *The Succession (Scotland) Act 1964* (4th ed. 1993) at pp. 91–92.

[24] 1969 S.L.T. (Notes) 60.

[25] 1993 S.L.T. 1327 at p. 1329.

[26] 1981 S.C. 289; 1982 S.L.T. 165. There are references to this case and its emphasis on the intentions of the testator in *Wright's Trs. v. Callender*, 1993 S.L.T. 556 at pp. 559 (*per* Lord Keith) and 562 (*per* Lord Jauncey).

inclusion of adopted children within appropriate classes of beneficiaries. While the result in *Spencer's Trustees* did depend on the terms
of the specific deed under consideration, the key point of principle
was the concentration on the intentions of the testator.

There was a further argument in *Salvesen's Trustees*, on the significance of the fact that the children were adopted in the United States.
As originally enacted, section 23 of the Succession (Scotland) Act 1964
did not extend to overseas adoptions. This was changed by the Adoption Act 1968, s. 4(2) and (3), which did not come into force until
after the 1968 variation of the 1947 trust had taken place (indeed, until
February 1, 1973). It was argued that, even taking the date of the trust
under consideration to be March 12, 1968, it could not have been the
intention at that time to include children adopted by overseas adoptions among the beneficiaries.

This argument was rejected by reference to the Succession
(Scotland) Act 1964, s. 23(5). This provides that:

> "In this Part of this Act the expression 'adoption order' has the
> same meaning as in section 38 of the Adoption (Scotland) Act
> 1978 (whether the order took effect before or after the commence-
> ment of this Act); and 'adopted' means adopted in pursuance of
> an adoption order."

The court went on to say that:

> "The provisions of the 1978 Act reflect those of s. 4(2) of the 1968
> Act, by which references to overseas adoptions were first intro-
> duced. In the result s. 23 of the 1964 Act must be read as
> extending to overseas adoptions, whether they took effect before
> or after the commencement of the 1964 Act, *as respects anything
> done or any event occurring after 1 February 1973* when s. 4 of the
> Adoption Act 1968 came into force" (emphasis added)."[27]

The point to note is that the 1968 variation was surely an event
occurring before section 4 of the Adoption Act 1968 came into force.
Of course, statutory impositions on the meaning of words used in
wills and trusts can have retrospective effect, but this is not the norm.
It would seem that in *Salvesen's Trustees*, the intentions of the actual
truster in 1947, and even of the notional trusters in 1968, may not
have received the attention they deserved. The ambulatory principle
could also be said to have received short shrift, whether the date from
which the trust was deemed to speak was in 1947 or in 1968. However,
it might be argued that the court's explanation of their interpretation
of the main point of the case, on section 23(2), is an example of the
ambulatory principle in action on questions of adopted children in
general, as their decision turned on the presumed knowledge of the
law of any truster at the time when his trust comes into operation,
no matter the changes in that law.[28]

---

[27] 1993 S.L.T. 1327 at p. 1330.
[28] *Salvesen's Trs.* does go a long way towards resolving one matter which was a subject
of heated debate in the pages of the *Journal of the Law Society of Scotland* (see (1979)

Conclusion

The problems which can arise when statutes alter or cut across fundamental rules of interpretation are not confined to issues involving children, although they do seem to be particularly prevalent there. As
well as those mentioned already, reference could also be made to the
Age of Majority (Scotland) Act 1969, which defines majority as the
age of 18 for deeds executed on or after January 1, 1970; and the Age
of Legal Capacity (Scotland) Act 1991. While the latter act does not
deal directly with wills or trusts, its general application combined
with the principles of repugnancy established in such cases as *Miller's
Trustees v. Miller*[29] and *Yuill's Trustees v. Thomson*[30] have enormous
effects on the interpretation of wills.[31]

It could perhaps be argued that *any* such change should always
affect only documents executed after the relevant change comes into
force. Such an absolute rule (which probably reflects the expectation
on such matters already) could (and does) have problems of its own.
Not least of these will be the need to know the state of the law
(perhaps in great detail) over an extended period of time. As the cases
explained above demonstrate, trusts can continue in operation over
many years and even generations. There is of course no perpetuity
period in Scots law.[32] There can be difficulty in ascertaining when the
effective provisions of a will or trust, perhaps with many codicils or
other addenda, were executed.[33] Such an absolute rule would certainly
be in conflict with the ambulatory principle of interpretation, although
it would perhaps take the intention principle to a new supremacy.

At least such a rule, if applied to all statutes affecting the interpretation of deeds, would demonstrate consistency. Careful drafting
would also obviate at least some of the problems mentioned above,
as well as those leading to the litigation which arose (and went as far
as the House of Lords) in *Wright's Trustees v. Callender* because the
legitimation statutes adopted a different approach. Of course, no

---

24 J.L.S.S. (Workshop), lxxxv; (1980) 25 J.L.S.S. (Workshop) 159, 165, 17; (1980) 26.
J.L.S.S. (Workshop) 182, 191, 206; and Meston *The Succession (Scotland) Act 1964*, at
p. 92. The issue was whether the term "issue" was able to include adopted children,
or whether the use of that term "expressed the contrary intention" permitted by s.
23(2) of the Succession (Scotland) Act 1964, as connoting a physical relationship rather
than a legal one. The matter was not specifically addressed in *Salvesen's Trs.*, but the
court did not appear to envisage any basic difficulty in adopted children taking
benefit as "issue". Furthermore, the court's restricted interpretation of the function
of s. 23(2) as opposed to s. 23(1) diminishes the significance of the matter in any
event. The Scottish Law Commission *Report on Succession* (Scot. Law Com. No. 124,
1990, para. 9.1) recommends legislation to put the matter beyond any remaining
doubt.
29 (1890) 18R. 301.
30 (1902) 4F. 815.
31 On this matter, see A. Barr and L. Edwards, "Age of Legal Capacity—Further Pitfalls
(1)", 1992 S.L.T. (News) 77.
32 See W. A. Wilson and A. G. M. Duncan, *Trusts, Trustees and Executors* (1975), p. 81;
also R. Burgess, *Perpetuities in Scots Law* (1979).
33 This and many other valuable points on which this paper draws were first brought
fully to my attention in a paper entitled "Aspects of Testate Succession" delivered
by Professor Michael Meston at a Law Society of Scotland PQLE conference in 1987.

degree of care would eliminate the need for litigation in this or any other field involving statutory interpretation, which by now represents such a very high proportion of reported case law.

Bill Wilson's bibliography demonstrates his lifelong interest in the meaning and structure of statutes, as well as his deep knowledge of wills and trusts. He brought clarity to both of these difficult subjects. It seems unfortunate that where these subjects interact, and the interpretation of trust provisions is affected by statutory developments, such clarity is often lacking.

THE CITATION OF CASES IN COURT[1]

William W. McBryde

Introduction

In his essay on "Dealing with Decisions" Bill Wilson analysed in his inimitable style the use made by judges of reports of cases.[2] Although this article covers some of the same ground, with additional illustrations which might have pleased Wilson, there is a different emphasis.

The novice who is about to plead in a court for the first time—whether as solicitor, solicitor advocate or advocate—will find it difficult to discover written information on how to refer a court to a reported case and what reports should be used.[3] Although it may be that a court will be prepared to look at a vast variety of sources from the *Angler's Mail*[4] to manuscript notes of uncertain authorship made of judges' speeches,[5] there are three problems with the assumption that "anything goes": first, there are ethical duties on a pleader; secondly, there are conventions on which series of reports should be referred to, if there is a choice; and thirdly, there are problems with conflicts between various reports. That last issue—conflicts between reports—is of special interest to anyone who writes on the law; and students of law should be informed about all the issues.

The Duty to Refer the Court to All Relevant Authorities

It is not the function of the pleader to refer the court only to those cases which are in support of the pleader's submission. The standard which should be applied in all courts was explained for the House of Lords by Lord Chancellor Birkenhead[6]:

"It is not, of course, in cases of complication possible for their

---

[1] Thanks are due to W. Stuart Gale, Q.C., who inspired this article and, for helpful comments, to Robert F. Hunter, Peter A. Nicholson, Sheriff Alastair L. Stewart, Sheriff Charles N. Stoddart and Malcolm G. Thomson, Q.C.

[2] W. A. Wilson, *Introductory Essays on Scots Law* (2nd ed. 1984) at pp. 78–86.

[3] A comprehensive guide to the sources available is D. M. Walker, *The Scottish Legal System* (6th ed. 1992) at pp. 470–481; and on citation of cases see pp. 412–413; see also H. L. MacQueen, *Studying Scots Law* (1993) at paras. 10.09 to 10.17.

[4] *Wallace v. Assessor for Perth and Kinross*, 1975 S.C. 92.

[5] *Wills Trs. v. Cairngorm Canoeing and Sailing School Ltd.*, 1976 S.C. (H.L.) 30 at p. 118 *per* Lord Wilberforce; at pp. 130–134 *per* Viscount Dilhorne (dissenting); at p. 138 per Lord Hailsham; at p. 161 *per* Lord Fraser.

[6] *Glebe Sugar Refining Co. v. Greenock Harbour Trs.*, 1921 S.C. (H.L.) 72 at pp. 73–74; the failure to refer to a decisive statutory provision appears to have had an effect on expenses.

170

Lordships to be aware of all the authorities, statutory or otherwise, which may be relevant to the issues which in the particular case require decision. Their Lordships are therefore very much in the hands of counsel, and those who instruct counsel, in these matters, and this House expects, and indeed insists, that authorities which bear one way or the other upon matters under debate should be brought to the attention of their Lordships by those who are aware of those authorities. This observation is quite irrespective of whether or not the particular authority assists the party which is so aware of it. It is an obligation of confidence between their Lordships and all those who assist in the debates in this House in the capacity of counsel."

It will be noted that this ethical duty extends to those who instruct counsel, which had a particular point in the circumstances of that case. The client may not understand why the court is being referred to material apparently harmful to the client's case.[7]

How Many Cases?

The duty is to refer the court to all relevant cases (and other authority, such as statutes), but there is a considerable and increasing problem of—how many cases? There have been judicial strictures in England about first, the multiplication of references to reported cases; and secondly, the use of unreported cases.

Multiple Cases

In one case Lord Templeman protested[8]:

"For the conduct of these appeals, there were locked in battle 24 counsel supported by batteries of solicitors and legal experts, armed with copies of 200 authorities and 14 volumes of extracts, British and foreign, from legislation, books and articles. Ten counsel addressed the Appellate Committee for 26 days. This vast amount of written and oral material tended to obscure three fundamental principles . . ."

His Lordship, with the support of Lord Jauncey, returned to the attack the following year in a case on the duty of good faith in insurance contracts in which their Lordships' speeches referred to 17 cases but an additional 52 cases were cited in argument. There were judicial protests about the obstruction to other litigants, the costs to litigants

---

[7] See discussion of this, and other authority for the duty on counsel, in *Rondel v. Worsley* [1967] 1 Q.B. 443 at p. 502 *per* Lord Denning M.R., at p. 512 *per* Danckwerts, L.J., at p. 517 *per* Salmom, L.J.; on appeal [1969] 1 A.C. 191 at pp. 227–228 *per* Lord Reid.

[8] *J. H. Rayner (Mincing Lane) Ltd v. Dept. of Trade and Industry* [1990] 2 A.C. 418 at p. 483; for an earlier example see *Lambert v. Lewis* [1982] A.C. 225 at pp. 274–275 *per* Lord Diplock.

and "torrents of words, written and oral, which are oppressive and which the judge must examine in an attempt to eliminate everything which is not relevant, helpful or persuasive."[9] The problem is magnified when a case is argued on appeal in several courts, and the clients' advisers charge an hourly or daily rate for their time.

The reasons why there should be a selective citation of authority are, it is suggested:

1. The purpose of oral argument is to convince a court. No more time should be spent on that endeavour than is necessary. If there is a relevant and binding precedent it may be sufficient to refer to it. Selection of appropriate authority is one of the skills of advocacy.
2. In the Scottish system there is a belief that the law is founded on principle. The extent to which that remains so, particularly with statutory incursions, is a matter for debate. Nevertheless an argument which states a principle, backed up by a few key authorities, need not rehearse every reported example of the application, or non-application, of that principle, or trace the history of the law.
3. The judge may have much more experience and knowledge of the area of law than the pleader. Obviously this will vary, but a knowledgeable judge may be impatient to go to the heart of an issue. In any event too much detail will confuse, and weary, any judge.
4. When there may be a written opinion, every pleader should think of the judge's task in writing that opinion. Is it expected that the judge will write, say, 30 or 40 pages with an analysis of all the cases? Some judges might; some cases might merit this treatment.[10] But if the judge can deal with the issue in a few paragraphs, is it necessary for those appearing before the court to say very much more? In general the student of pleading could do worse than read and re-read the opinions of the present Lord President and Lord Justice Clerk to see the structure of their arguments and decide what would be likely to convince them. The expert may also look at the reported opinions of the judge before whom he or she is about to appear.
5. To go through the history of every issue, in every case, would be enormously wasteful of court time and clients' money, which was part of Lord Templeman's complaint. For example in pleading a case of judicial review it may be sufficient to start with the decision of the First Division in *West v. Secretary of State for Scotland*[11] which surveys authorities on the supervisory jurisdiction

⁹ *Banque Financiere De La Cite S.A. v. Westgate Insurance Co. Ltd* [1991] 2 A.C. 249 at pp. 272–273 and p.280 *per* Lord Templeman; at p. 281 *per* Lord Jauncey.
¹⁰ *e.g. Tito v. Waddell (No.2)* [1977] Ch. 106 in which a judgment of Megarry, V.C. occupies 225 pages of the *Law Reports*; see also *Wills Trs. v. Cairngorm Canoeing and Sailing School Ltd, supra.*
¹¹ 1992 S.L.T. 636; reported *sub nom. West v. Scottish Prison Service*, 1992 S.C.L.R. 504, which was the name in the copies of the judges' opinions sent to the editor of S.C.L.R.; differing names cause problems when the attempt is made to check for alternative reports. See also n. 44.

of the court and concludes with propositions on the competency of applications. The history was analysed in that case; only in exceptional circumstances would it be necessary to repeat that analysis with the hope of a different result.

The novice, such as the student in a moot, should be wary of the adoption of the style subconsciously learned from writers and lecturers on the law and from writing essays. Oral pleading, with the background of the rules of precedent and of the facts of a particular case, can use different techniques and is also more limited in scope.

Unreported Cases

Part of the judicial reaction to multiple citation of cases in England has been to require the leave of the House of Lords for a reference to unreported decisions of the Court of Appeal.[12] This provoked a debate, with hostile comments.[13] The Scottish position remains as stated by Lord Guthrie[14]:

"I wish to make it clear that, in my opinion, not only is reference to unreported cases unobjectionable, but it is the duty of Counsel to refer the court to all cases which bear upon the point at issue whether such cases are reported or not. The authority of a case depends not upon whether it is to be found in a series of reports but upon the fact that it is a judicial decision."

All cases must, of course, be unreported for some period and the availability of transcripts in the Faculty of Advocates Library does make compliance with the pleader's duty to the court easier for advocates in respect of Court of Session opinions.[15]

Referring a Court to a Case

Standards may be changing, some would say declining, and there are variations in practice, but there is a right and a wrong way to refer a court to a case. On the first occasion the court should be given the full name of the case.[16] A Scottish case which is *A v. B* is referred to as A against B. An English case which is *A v. B* is referred to as A

---

[12] *Roberts Petroleum Ltd v. Bernard Kenny Ltd* [1983] 2 A.C. 192 at pp. 201–202 *per* Lord Diplock; at pp. 213–214 *per* Lord Brightman; see also *Export Credits Guarantee Department v. Universal Oil Products Co.* [1983] 1 W.L.R. 399 at p. 404 *per* Lord Roskill.

[13] The arguments are summarised in N. Harrison, "Unreported Cases: Myth and Reality", 1984 Law Society Gazette 257.

[14] *Leighton v. Harland & Wolff Ltd*, 1953 S.L.T. (Notes) 34 at pp. 35–36.

[15] Nor do we need the category of the "virtually unreported" case which appears in note form in a journal—*cf. Export Credits Guarantee Department v. Universal Oil Products Co., supra*, at p. 403 *per* Lord Roskill.

[16] On subsequent occasions the case may be referred to in argument by an acceptably abbreviated name.

and B.[17] It is incorrect to refer to A versus B or A v B. This convention may seem inaccurate, even absurd; but refusal to follow the normal rules may show ignorance and produce judicial irritation.

The name of the report should be read out in full.[18] The citation should be provided in a manner, and, in particular, at a speed, which enables the court to write it down. The court will, in general, expect a short account of the facts of the case. A precis of the rubric may suffice. Give an accurate reference to the passage to be relied upon by reference to page and, if appropriate, letter, paragraph or column. Refer to judges by their full titles.

As a careful reading of reports will show, sheriffs and sheriffs principal write notes, Court of Session judges deliver opinions and in England judges give judgments. House of Lords judges make speeches.

Which Series of Reports?

If a case is reported in only one series of recognised reports the problems about to be discussed do not arise. But many cases are reported in several series. A recent Scottish case may, for example, be in any or all of three reports. An English case may be in several of the 70 or so active law reports covering the English jurisdiction which are listed in the *Current Law Year Book*.

The practice is to prefer a citation from the semi-official series of reports, then to accept a citation from an established series of reports and lastly to consider other sources. This may produce problems when the reports differ but as a starting point the pleader (and the writer on the law) should be aware of the convention, and the reasons for it. In exceptional cases the convention may be departed from but with an explanation of why that is necessary.

The result is that the order of priority in citation of a modern Scottish civil case is:

1. *Session Cases*
2. *Scots Law Times*
3. *Scottish Civil Law Reports*[19]
4. Other sources *e.g.* an unreported opinion.

A possible mistake, for example, is to cite a *Scots Law Times* report when the case has been reported in *Session Cases*. *Scots Law Times*

---

[17] The difference reflects the form of the writs used in the case, with the instance of Scottish writs using the word "against" between the designation of the parties and the equivalent of English writs using the word "and". Early reporters of Scots cases used the word "contra". See, for example, *Decisions of the English Judges, 1655–1661*; *Stair's Decisions 1661–1681*; Kames, *Remarkable Decisions 1716 to 1752*.

[18] *i.e.* "Session Cases" or "Scots Law Times", *not* "S.C." or "S.L.T."; subsequent abbreviated references may be acceptable. Thus, for example, the appropriate reference to E.F.T. *Commercial Ltd v. Security Change Ltd*, 1992 S.C. 414 is something like: "I refer your Lordship to the case of E.F.T. Commercial Limited against Security Change Limited which is reported in 1992 Session Cases at page four hundred and fourteen."

[19] See letter from the editor of S.C.L.R., Sheriff Alastair Stewart, complaining about the failure to refer to the reports, particularly in the Court of Session—(1994) 39 J.L.S.S. 83; similarly *Scottish Criminal Case Reports* received some hostile judicial reception initially.

reports often, but not always, in the body of the report change references to prior authority from S.C. to S.L.T. and also suggest that the preferred order is S.L.T. first. There is also a tendency to use the citation used by the judge. All this may mislead the unwary.

An English case would be cited from:

1. The *Law Reports, i.e., Appeal Cases, Chancery Division, Family Division, Queen's Bench*
2. The *Weekly Law Reports*
3. Other recognised reports, *e.g., All England Law Reports, Lloyd's Law Reports,* and many others.

Obvious substitutions are made for a criminal case.

For a European case the order of preference would be:

1. *European Court Reports*
2. *Common Market Law Reports*
3. Other sources, *e.g., All England (European Cases)*

Official Reports

The only official series of reports, in the sense of reports produced by a court, are *European Court Reports* which are the product of the Court of Justice of the European Communities.[20] The tradition in the United Kingdom has been for the courts to distance themselves from reporting their decisions. This has not stopped judges criticising reports and reporters.[21] There is, however, judicial collaboration in the preservation of their words for posterity and this, in part, explains the eminence of certain reports.

The Council of Law Reporting for England and Wales produced reports from 1865 and was incorporated in 1870 with its objects including "the preparation and publication in a convenient form, at a moderate price, and under gratuitous professional control, of reports of judicial decisions of the superior and appellate courts in England."[22] The Council produces the *Law Reports*. When the Scottish Council of Law Reporting was incorporated in 1957 to continue *Session Cases,* previously published by the Faculty of Advocates, its objects appear to have been similar.[23] Several reasons may be advanced as to why the reports of these bodies should have an authority denied to other reports:

---

[20] There are reports produced by HMSO—Immigration Appeal Reports, Reports of Patent Design and Trade Mark Cases, Reports of Tax Cases and Decisions of Commissioners under Social Security Acts and Supplementary Benefits Acts and Value Added Tax Tribunal Reports. The Tax Cases have been accorded special status in the House of Lords. The Commission for Racial Equality publishes the Race Discrimination Law Reports.

[21] *e.g.,* C. K. Allen, *Law in the Making,* (7th ed. 1964) at pp. 221–232; G. Williams, *Learning the Law* (11th ed. 1982) at pp. 35–37; *Warren v. Keen* [1954] 1 Q.B. 15 at p. 21 *per* Denning, L.J.; and see many cases collected in *The Digest,* vol 30, 2nd reissue (1992), cases 4116 to 4175.

[22] *Incorporated Council of Law Reporting for England and Wales v. Att. Gen.* [1971] 3 W.L.R. 853.

[23] (1958) 1 J.L.S.S. 14.

The reports are revised by the judge.
For many years only semi-official reports had the imprimatur of a considered judicial revision of the words. Actually now opinions can be reported in other series at the instigation of, or with the tacit approval of, the judge.

Revision implies that there may be changes. In *Fairman v. Perpetual Investment Building Society*[24] there was a reference to a decision in 1893 of which there were six reports.[25] There were some variations in the reports and the Queens Bench report was accepted as authoritative on the assumption that the judges had revised their judgments. In *Duke of Buccleuch v. Inland Revenue Commissioners*[26] the Court of Appeal had relied on a passage in a judgment of Mr Justice Sankey reported in the *Law Times*; the passage did not appear in the *Law Reports*. In the House of Lords the offending passage was treated as having gone too far and, said Lord Reid, "on second thoughts Sankey J may well have thought the same".[27] A recent Scottish example is *Kildrummy (Jersey) Ltd v. I.R.C.*[28] As mentioned below, however, sometimes the semi-official series is inaccurate or incomplete.

The arguments are reported
The semi-official series may report the arguments. A full report will give the interjections from the bench and, as a result, a comprehensive indication of the points raised, or not made, and the judicial reactions.[29] Arguments give added authority to a report.[30]

Weekly Law Reports, which is produced by the Incorporated Council of Law reporting for England and Wales produces reports with some speed, with the intention that those in volumes 2 and 3 will appear in the *Law Reports*. *Weekly Law Reports* do not contain the arguments.

In present practice neither *Scots Law Times* reports nor *Scottish Criminal Case Reports* or *Scottish Civil Law Reports* have the arguments. The intention was that with more leisure *Session Cases* would report arguments but nowadays not always. From time to time there will be found in *Session Cases* phrases such as "the opinion of the court, within which the arguments of counsel are adequately set forth . . .". The presence of a reporter in court is rarer than it used to be with the effect that judges will deliberately record the arguments in their opinions. From 1995 the *Session Cases* reports will not have formal reporters, and reports will be drafted and edited by the editor.

---

[24] [1923] A.C. 74.
[25] *Miller v. Hancock* [1893] 2 Q.B. 177.
[26] [1967] 1 A.C. 506.
[27] At pp. 526, 527; see also at p. 539 *per* Lord Hodson; at p. 545 *per* Lord Guest; at p. 546 *per* Lord Wilberforce; the Court of Appeal judgments are reported at [1966] 1 Q.B. 851; see also *R. v. Agricultural Land Tribunal for the South Eastern Area* [1960] 1 W.L.R. 911 at p. 914 *per* Lord Parker, C.J.; *Young v. North Riding Justices* [1965] 1 Q.B. 502 at pp. 507–508 *per* Lord Parker, C.J.
[28] *cf.* 1992 S.L.T. 787 at p. 795K and 1991 S.C. 1 at p. 15.
[29] *e.g. Rondel v. Worsley* [1967] 1 Q.B. 443, which is a model of reporting; on appeal [1969] 1 A.C. 191.
[30] Practice Direction Court of Appeal (Law Reports: Citation) [1991] 1 W.L.R. 1.

Preparation of the report by a member of the bar
Only an accurate report is an authority. A report by someone who is legally qualified might be presumed to be more accurate than a report by an unqualified person. The English courts have said that only reports made by barristers with their names attached could be cited in court.[31] The rule was altered to the extent provided by the Courts and Legal Services Act 1990[32] which gave authority to a report by a person who is not a barrister but who is a solicitor or has a Supreme Court qualification.

This problem does not appear to have arisen in Scotland. Dr (now Sheriff) Charles Stoddart reported cases for the *Scots Law Times* from 1979 to 1988, although a solicitor; he appears to have been the first solicitor reporter.

The availability of reports
The Court of Appeal has given the availability of the *Law Reports* as a reason for reference to them.[33] This is a particular problem with English cases because of the multiplicity of citations which might be possible.

Exceptions to the Normal Rules

Although the general rule is to cite cases according to the rules mentioned, problems arise: first, when there is no semi-official report; secondly, when there are conflicts between reports; and thirdly, when one report is more complete than another.

No semi-official report
Obviously a recent case may be reported, if at all, solely in one of the series of reports produced by a commercial publisher. In Scotland some important cases are reported in the *Scots Law Times* only, *e.g. Wordie Property Co Ltd v. Secretary of State for Scotland.*[34] Also a textbook or judge may appear to break the rules but *Session Cases* were spasmodic in appearance in the 1970's and 1980's, and reports do not always even now appear with speed and regularity, although matters are very much improved. It is not easy at a later date to determine what reports were available to a writer, or a judge, at the time of writing.

There is no difficulty in a Scottish case in referring to one of the specialised reports when that is the only report of the subject matter. There is House of Lords authority that *Tax Cases* may now be referred

---

[31] *Re Richards, ex p. Hawley* (1834) 2 Mont. & A. 426; *Francome v. Francome* (1865) 5 New. Rep. 289; *The Queen v. Labouchere* (1884) 12 Q.B.D. 320; *West Derby Union Guardian v. Atcham Union Guardian* (1889) 6 T.L.R. 5; *Geo. Trollope and Sons v. Martyn Bros* (1934) 150 L.T. 376, on appeal [1934] 2 K.B. 436; *Rivoli Hats Ltd. v. Gooch* [1953] 1 W.L.R. 1190.
[32] s. 115.
[33] Practice Direction Court of Appeal (Law Reports: Citation), cited above.
[34] 1984 S.L.T. 345.

to even when a case is also reported in the *Law Reports*, although both references must be given.[35]

Conflicts between reports
The existence of too many reports, with variations, can lead to exasperation. Of one case Warrington, J. complained, "But ... having regard to the various reports, I cannot be sure of what the learned Lord Justice said ...".[36] It can, however, be worthwhile to check the various reports. Perhaps the most famous instance is *Darling v. Gray & Sons*. The report by Rettie[37] gives no arguments and only the speech of Lord Watson. Rettie then observes, "The Lord Chancellor, and Lords Herschell, Morris and Field concurred."[38] The case is reported in *Appeal Cases* under a slightly different name[39] and with an additional speech of Lord Field which was much referred to when *Darling* was overruled in *Dick v. Burgh of Falkirk*.[40]

There may be a misprint in one of the reports. The case of *Humphries v. X and Y* has the word "understandably" in the *Session Case* report in place of the word "undesirable" which appears in the *Scots Law Times* report.[41] The *Scots Law Times* report is correct.[42] It can be important to check if the volume records and corrects a misprint.[43] In one case the *Scots Law Times* gave the pursuer the wrong name.[44]

One report may record circumstances which shed a light on what was decided—and it is not always the semi-official report which does this. In *Adair v. Donaldson*[45] there was a joint minute the terms of which are repeated in full in the *Scots Law Times* report, but not the *Session Cases* report, and the admitted facts affect the construction of what Lord Hunter said.[46]

There is the remarkable story of the case which is reported twice in the *Scots Law Times*, as mentioned by Lord President Hope at the centenary of that publication.[47] The second report of *Stirling v. North of Scotland Hydro-Electric Board* is not an improvement on the first report 10 years earlier.[48] Nor is it easy to discover that there are two

---

[35] *Bray v. Best* [1989] 1 W.L.R. 167 at p. 169 *per* L. C. Mackay (the report at [1989] 1 All E.R. 969 has different, and better, punctuation!); House of Lords Appeal Directions and Standing Orders 19.4, which changes the practice referred to by L. C. Hailsham in *National Bank of Greece S.A. v. Westminster Bank Executor and Tr. Co. (Channel Islands) Ltd* [1970] 1 W.L.R. 1400.

[36] *Stirling v. Burdett* [1911] 2 Ch. 418 at pp. 427–428.

[37] (1891) 19 R. (H.L.) 31.

[38] At p. 33.

[39] *Wood v. Gray & Sons* [1892] A.C. 576.

[40] 1976 S.C. (H.L.) 1.

[41] *Humphries v. X and Y*, 1982 S.C. 79 at p. 83; 1982 S.L.T. 481 at p. 483.

[42] *P. v. Kennedy*, 1995 S.L.T. 476 at p. 481.

[43] e.g. *Hartley v. H.M. Advocate*, 1979 S.L.T. 26 at p. 33, corrected at p. 300—see *Meredith v. Lees*, 1992 J.C. 127 at p. 130 *per* Lord Justice General Hope.

[44] *Morley's Tr. v. Aitken*, 1982 S.C. 73 reported *sub nom Murphy's Tr. v. Aitken*, 1983 S.L.T. 78.

[45] 1935 J.C. 23, 1935 S.L.T. 76.

[46] See *Muir v. Foulner*, 1951 S.L.T. (Sh. Ct.) 88; another example is the report of Lord Clyde's views on an indemnity clause which appear in *Forsyth's C.B. v. Govan Shipbuilders Ltd*, 1988 S.L.T. 321, but not in 1988 S.C. 421.

[47] "The Scots Law Times at 100," 1993 S.L.T. (News) 169 at p. 170.

[48] 1965 S.L.T. 229; 1975 S.L.T. 26.

reports. The *Current Law Citator* does not reveal the first report; the *Scots Law Times Index* does not mention the second report.

Incomplete reports

Unfortunately for Scots lawyers care has to be exercised in the use of *Session Cases* and *Scots Law Times* because there are instances of each series omitting the report of an appeal or reclaiming motion; nor will this always appear from the indices of *Scots Law Times* cases.

Glenlight Shipping Ltd v. Excess Insurance Co Ltd is an Outer House decision of Lord Ross reported in *Session Cases*.[49] The decision of the Second Division affirming Lord Ross is reported only in the *Scots Law Times*.[50] Conversely *Grayston Plant Ltd v. Plean Precast Ltd* was reported in the *Scots Law Times* in 1975 and 1976 soon after Lord Robertson's opinion with useful observations on the "course of dealing" and the incorporation of conditions into a contract.[51] The reader of the *Scots Law Times* is still waiting for a report of the views of the Inner House which eventually appeared in *Session Cases*.[52]

The Outer House decision in a case on gratuitous alienation by a husband to a wife is reported in the *Scots Law Times*[53] but only *Session Cases* reveals that there was a reclaiming motion heard by the Second Division.[54] There is a similar result with a case on a statutory remedy and the *condictio indebiti*,[55] although curiously in this instance *Session Cases* reports the opinion of the Lord Ordinary twice[56] and the second report is not as full as the first. The Lord Ordinary's opinion in *Crown Estate Commissioners v. Fairlie Yacht Slip Ltd* is reported twice in *Session Cases* and once in the *Scots Law Times*,[57] but only *Session Cases* gives us the views of the First Division.[58] Another example is the case of an Aberdeen solicitor's claim for compensation for loss of office following the reorganisation of local government, although on this occasion the *Session Case* reporters thought that the Lord Ordinary's views merited only one report.[59]

The examples given are only those known to the writer. There may be others. The problem for the person who researches on the law is that this difficulty arises only occasionally, but when it does it can have an important effect on an argument. The result is that for Scottish cases both *Session Cases* and *Scots Law Times* must be checked. Whether the appearance since 1981 of *Scottish Criminal Case Reports* and since 1987 of *Scottish Civil Law Reports* adds to the problems, or cures deficiencies in other reports, remains to be seen.

---

[49] 1981 S.C. 267.
[50] 1983 S.L.T. 241.
[51] 1976 S.L.T. 74; 1975 S.L.T. (Notes) 83.
[52] 1976 S.C. 206.
[53] *McManus's Tr. v. McManus*, 1978 S.L.T. 255; 1979 S.L.T. (Notes) 71.
[54] *Henderson v. McManus*, 1981 S.C. 233.
[55] *British Railways Board v. Glasgow Corporation*, 1975 S.L.T. 45 (O.H.); 1976 S.C. 224 (2nd Division).
[56] 1974 S.C. 261; 1976 S.C. 224.
[57] 1976 S.C. 161; 1979 S.C. 156; 1977 S.L.T. 19.
[58] 1979 S.C. 156.
[59] *Gordon D.C. v. Hay*, 1978 S.L.T. 2 (O.H.); 1978 S.C. 327 (O.H. and 2nd Division).

Notes of Cases

It is not, generally, advisable to refer a court to abbreviated notes of cases such as *Greens Weekly Digest*. These extracts exist to inform the profession of the existence of an authority. The proper practice is to produce the full text of the opinion. A similar problem was discussed many times in England with repeated attempts to refer the courts to *Weekly Notes*.[60] The *Digest of Case Law relating to the European Communities* has a special and authoritative status, being produced by the Court of Justice.

Older Reports

For reasons of brevity this article has concentrated on the problems of recent reports. The same problems arise with the older reports. Different reports can have a value because they reveal a varying statements of the facts or the arguments. It is the writer's practice to check several reports if suspicions are aroused or a case is crucial to an argument.

One common trap is the difference between the old and new editions of the first five volumes of *Shaw's Reports*, often placed adjacent to each other on library shelves. An example is a recent article in the *Juridical Review* where the authors discuss *Arrol v. Montgomery* under the heading of fraudulent or unfair preference in bankruptcy.[61] *Arrol* is not a case of fraudulent preference, in the usual sense, but of a bankrupt obtaining agreement of a creditor to a composition contract by secret transactions. The difference from the usual fraudulent preference is critical to an understanding of the case, because it affected the title to sue.[62] The authors referred only to the original report of the case in the first edition of *Shaw*.[63] The revised edition of *Shaw* has a report of two opinions of the Lord Ordinary which make clearer what the case was about and why the Second Division altered his interlocutor.[64] Similarly the Lord Justice Clerk in *Arrol* founded on the

---

60 *Newson v. Pender* (1884) at 27 Ch.D. 50n; *Bridgend Gas & Water Co. v. Dunraven* (1885) 31 Ch.D. 219 at p. 221; *Pooley's Tr. v. Whetham* (1886) 33 Ch.D. 76 at p. 77; *Loveridge, Drayton v. Loveridge* [1902] 2 Ch. 859 at p. 865; *Smith's Settlement, Wilkins v. Smith* [1903] 1 Ch. 373 at p. 375; *Stirling v. Burdett* [1911] 2 Ch. 418 at p. 429; *Re Howell, Re Buckingham, Liggins v. Buckingham* [1915] 1 Ch. 241 at p. 243; *Chaplin and Staffordshire Potteries Waterworks Co. Ltd's Contract* [1922] 2 Ch. 824 at p. 829. See also the fate of the reference to the *Angler's Mail* in *Wallace v. Assessor for Perth and Kinross*, *supra*.

61 R. Evans-Jones and D. McKenzie, "Towards a Profile of the Condictio ob Turpem vel Injustam Causam in Scots Law", 1994 J.R. 60 at pp. 71–77.

62 A bankrupt cannot challenge his or her own fraudulent or unfair preference; it is different with a corrupt agreement to obtain a composition contract as the case demonstrates; there will be other differences in the effect of knowledge of insolvency and the defences available to a creditor, which is why it is misleading to treat the case under the same heading as fraudulent preferences.

63 (1826) 4 S. 499; whether this would have affected the authors' argument on the condictio indebiti is not the point for present purposes, although it is the writer's belief that the treatment of *Arrol* would have benefited from a fuller appreciation of the case.

64 (1826) 4 S. 504 (n.e.)

case of *Junner v. Caddell* and there are material differences between the two *Shaw* reports, with the second being the version which should be referred to.[65]

Conclusion

In the end the search is for an accurate record of, not what a judge said, but what he or she intended to say. A report can be judicially dismissed as inaccurate.[66] An opinion once delivered can be revised. And, of course, an opinion can be ignored by the reporters for a long time,[67] or for ever.[68]

---

[65] (1822) 1 S. 325; (1822) 1 S. 301 (n.e.). As might be expected, old reports pose many problems and there are long-forgotten controversies around *Morison's Dictionary* and the *Faculty Collection*: see the notes to W. Tait, *Index of Decisions* (1823).

[66] *Hamilton v. Hamilton*, 1954 S.L.T. 16, rejecting the accuracy of the report in *Robb v. Robb*, 1953 S.L.T. 44, which case is omitted from the *Faculty Digest Supplement 1951– 1960*; see also *Straker v. Reynolds* (1889) 22 Q.B.D. 262 at p. 264 *per* Wills, J., who refused to accept a report from the *Times Law Reports* on the grounds that the publication did not always accurately report his own judgments; later in the same year the Master of the Rolls stated that *Times Law Reports* were acceptable—*West Derby Poor Law Guardians v. Atcham Poor Law Guardians* (1889) 6 T.L.R. 5 at p. 6.

[67] *e.g. Cremin v. Thomson* (1941), 1956 S.L.T. 357; *Brown v. Redpath Brown & Co.* (1952), 1963 S.L.T. 219; *Hunter v. Bradford Property Trust* (1960), 1970 S.L.T. 173; (1957), 1977 S.L.T. (Notes) 33.

[68] For example, as the writer has mentioned elsewhere, *Donoghue v. Stevenson*, 1932 S.C. (H.L.) 31, has never been fully reported: "Donoghue v. Stevenson: The Story of the 'Snail in the Bottle' Case," in A. J. Gamble (ed.), *Obligations in Context: Essays in Honour of D. M. Walker* (1990); reprinted with revisions in P. T. Burns and S. J. Lyons (eds.), *Donoghue v. Stevenson and the Modern Law of Negligence: The Paisley Papers* (1991), which, however, at the editors' insistence, does violence to the normal methods of Scottish case citation.

TRUST AND PATRIMONY

George L. Gretton

Introduction

In the autumn of 1978 I was sitting in a basement room at 57 Queen
Street Edinburgh, the law offices of Messrs Ketchen & Stevens. I was
reading the first chapter of W. A. Wilson and A. G. M. Duncan, *Trusts
Trustees and Executors* (1975). I had taken my LL.B at Edinburgh and
had learnt that ownership was undivided, and that it lay in the trustee.
This made sense to me. But I accepted this on trust, so to speak, and
I had not read for myself the first chapter of the book. Now I did so.
I followed the analysis with interest and appreciation. On page 15 I
came to a sentence which at once fixed itself in my memory. The sentence is laconically Wilsonic, or Wilsonically laconic, and might not
seem particularly exciting: "It must be accepted that the property in
the normal sense is vested in the trustee." Though this was what I
had been taught, only now did I fully understand it. It proved a key
to many locks. The influence of Bill's analysis was widespread. The
sentence which I have quoted was also quoted with approval by the
Lord President in *Sharp v. Thomson*.[1]

The Problem of the Nature of the Trust

The problem of interpreting the trust in a civilian or mixed system is
notorious and has over the years attracted some attention from com-
paratists. Maitland wrote that "the trust could hardly have been
evolved among a people who had clearly formulated the distinction
between a right *in personam* and a right *in rem*.[2] Later in the same
essay he wrote:

> "If a foreign friend asked me to tell him in one word whether
> the right of the English *Destinär* (the person for whom property
> is held, in trust) is *dinglich* or *obligatorisch*, I should be inclined to
> say: 'No, I cannot do that.' If I said *dinglich*, that would be untrue.
> If I said *obligatorisch*, I should suggest what is false. In the ultimate
> analysis the right may be *obligatorisch*, but for many practical pur-
> poses of great importance it has been treated as though it were

---

[1] 1995 S.L.T. 837; 1995 S.C.L.R. 683. For Bill Wilson's posthumous influence on this
case, see p. 1. of this volume.

[2] F. W. Maitland, "Trust and Corporation", in *Collected Papers of Frederic William Maitland* (1911), vol. iii, at p. 325. This remark is typical of Maitland's insight, but at the
same time it might be questioned. The trust is elusive, and much depends on what
you mean by "trust." In Roman law both *fiducia cum amico* and *fideicommissum* are
at least trust-like, and the same can be said of the German *Treuhand*.

dinglich, and indeed people habitually speak and think of it as a kind of *Eigenthum*."[2a]

Maitland's "ultimate analysis" did not however persuade other Anglo-American lawyers, who speak not merely of concurrent ownership but also of the beneficiary having a "right *in rem*." In the *International Encyclopaedia of Comparative Law*[3] Professor Fratcher writes:

> "The interest of a beneficiary is also a property interest in the subject matter; it is not a mere personal or contract claim against the trustee. Neither trustee nor beneficiary has a mere *jus in re aliena*. In other words, the interests of both the trustee and the beneficiary in the subject matter are interests *in rem*."

Fratcher is here supposedly not writing of Anglo-American trusts in particular but of trusts as such.[4] Fratcher's apparent identification of "personal" and "contract" claims is baffling to the civilian.[5] The view that neither trustee nor beneficiary has a *jus in re aliena* is true of Scots law but is clearly not an essential truth of all trust systems. Fratcher then says that *both* rights are *in rem*. If, like Fratcher, we use civilian terminology, a real right must be either *in re propria* or *in re aliena*. It cannot be both. It is an impossibility that *both* trustee *and* beneficiary should have a real right *in re propria*.[6]

In Anglo-American law these problems do not cause much loss of sleep even to theoreticians. "Ownership" is not a traditional concept among Anglo-American lawyers, though it is a term which sometimes passes their lips. The doctrine of real and personal rights has never been received. The question of the juridical nature of the trust is simply not a pressing one. Indeed, in a system where law divides into "law" and "equity" it is difficult even to put into words just what the civilian is worried about. The trustee is owner in law, and the beneficiary is owner in equity. So what is the difficulty?

The rights of the beneficiary are evidently more extensive than one would associate with ordinary personal rights. If the trustee becomes insolvent, the beneficiaries prevail over his creditors. If he dies, the property is not administered by his executor[7] and does not pass to his heirs and legatees. In some types of case if the trustee transfers trust property in breach of trust the property can be recovered by the beneficiaries.[8] Such considerations move one to say that the right of the beneficiary is real, and perhaps even some sort of ownership. On

---

[2a] At p. 326.

[3] Vol. vi, Chap. 11 (at p. 3–4).

[4] For criticism of the assumption that trusts everywhere must be Anglo-American see H. R. Hahlo "The Trust in South African Law" (1961) 78 S.A.L.J. 195.

[5] Contract claims are personal but most personal claims are not contractual.

[6] The Court of Justice has held, in *Webb v. Webb* [1994] E.C.R. 1–1717, that a beneficiary's right is not a real right under Art. 16 of the Brussels Convention. This decision, which looks correct from a Scottish standpoint, has caused upset in England.

[7] Subject to the Executors (Scotland) Act 1900, s. 6.

[8] Thus at least the received wisdom. The topic is obscure. One clear point however is that a beneficiary's claim can never be *vindicatory*. The action is personal, not real.

the other hand, for most purposes connected with third parties the law treats the trustee as owner. In Scottish conveyancing practice, immoveable property is registered as owned by the trustee. Whilst it is the norm for his title to disclose that he holds the property in trust, this is not a legal requirement. When the time comes for the trustee to denude, a conveyance to the beneficiary is necessary: that looks strongly like a personal right in the beneficiary to receive a conveyance. Even if the fact of trust does appear in the registration, the identity of the beneficiaries almost never does. It would be surprising if beneficiaries could have a real right in immoveables without registration. Similar considerations apply to other kinds of property. The rights of beneficiaries do not behave like ordinary personal rights, but at the same time they do not look like real rights either. Functionally, they are something in-between.[9] But if the law is to aspire to coherence, matters cannot be left thus. Conceptual analysis is needed.

Possible Responses

I turn now to some possible ways of conceptualising the trust for a legal system that does not have the division between law and equity and which does have a more or less civilian system of rights. My treatment will be short, disorderly and incomplete.[10] I have a few preliminary remarks.

First, the pragmatist, not to say the legal realist, may ask whether it matters how one conceptualises the trust. Is this not legal metaphysics? Is this not the "heaven of concepts" satirised by von Jhering? The question is a large one. In brief, my own experience of handling trust problems, as problems in other areas, is that a conceptual framework is absolutely necessary. A rule is a key for one lock. A principle, or a conceptual structure, is a master key for a hundred locks. There is nothing so practical as a good theory. Secondly, I do not wish to suggest that a single framework must be adopted by all civilian or mixed systems. Thirdly, language is slippery. "Trust" is a word used in many ways. One might be tempted to suppose that priority in the trustee's insolvency is an essential quality of trust. But English law did not develop this until the seventeenth century. South African law did not fully accept this doctrine until 1988.[11] At the same time, it is commonly said that German law does not know the trust, yet the *Treuhand* in fact has this quality. Should one say that before 1988 Germany did and South Africa did not have the trust? Again, is it of the essence of a trust that "title" be in the trustee? The South African legislation[12] defines "trust" to include an arrangement in which the

---

[9] For the sake of brevity I shall say no more. Anyone who has wrestled with the concept of trust will be aware of the complexity of this in-between status.
[10] For instance I do not discuss Honoré's conception of trust in terms of "office." See A. M. Honoré and E. Cameron, *Honoré's South African Law of Trusts* (4th ed. 1992).
[11] Trust Property Control Act 1988.
[12] *infra.*

beneficiaries are the owners but administration is in another person.[13] Fourthly, in what follows I am chiefly concerned with private trusts. Public trusts involve some special difficulties.

Mandate

In the past, when issues of international private law involving the trust came before the French courts, there was great difficulty.[14] One common approach was to regard the trustee as a sort of agent for the beneficiary. At one stage Mexican law did the same.[15] If this seems odd it should be recalled that this approach was once popular in Scotland. I refer of course to the now abandoned view that trust is a combination of mandate and deposit. However, in Stair and Erskine it looks as if the trustee is conceived of as the agent not of the beneficiary but of the truster, and moreover I think that what Stair meant by deposit may have been misunderstood. Stair writes:

> "Trust is also a kind of deposition, whereby the thing intrusted is in the custody of the person intrusted, to the behoof of the intruster, and the property of the thing intrusted, be it land or moveables, is in the person of the intrusted, else it is not a proper trust."[16]

In deposit, the depositor remains owner. Stair knew that as well as we do. Read as a whole, it seems that Stair is using the term loosely. The trustee is owner. But the relationship between him and the truster is similar to that of depositor and depositee. Imagine a contract of deposit, add a transfer of title, and you have a trust. It is striking that Stair takes it for granted that the truster and the beneficiary will be the same person. For Stair trust is *fiducia cum amico*.[17] This is embryonic trust law only. It would be difficult, I think, to distinguish Stair's trust from German *Treuhand*.

Lord Watson

The "mandate" theory of trusts has long been discredited both in Scots law and elsewhere. But Lord Watson seems to have believed

[13] Our own legislation sometimes calls non-trustee fiduciaries "trustees": see notably Trusts (Scotland) Act 1921 s. 2. Nevertheless, in its usual sense, trust does imply title being in the trustee.

[14] See *e.g.* L. T. Bates, "Common Law Express Trusts in French Law", (1930) 40 Yale L.J. 34.

[15] R. M. Pasquel, "The Mexican Fideicomiso: The Reception Evolution and Present Status of the Common Law Trust in a Civil Law Country", (1969) 8 Columbia J. Transnatl. Law 54.

[16] I, xiii, 7.

[17] As Lapaulle—see below, n. 32—rightly observed, *fiducia* is closer to trust than *fideicommissum*. See his "Civil Law Substitutes for Trusts", (1926) 36 Yale L.J. 1126 at p. 1127.

something of the sort. He was no property lawyer, and it is perhaps unfair to analyse too closely what he says in the landmark case of *Heritable Reversionary Co. v. Millar*.[18] "An apparent title to land or personal estate,[19] carrying *no real right of property*[20] with it, does not, in the ordinary or in any true legal sense, make such land or personal estate the property of the person who holds the title."

Lord Watson developed the theory that the beneficiary is the sole owner. The trustee has a mere *apparent* title. In law that title is an absolute nullity. If this is so, how can it be that the trustee can pass title to a third party? Lord Watson has an answer: personal bar against the beneficiary. "A true owner who chooses to conceal his right from the public and to clothe his trustee with all the indicia of ownership is thereby barred from challenging rights acquired by innocent third parties . . ."

I do not wish to spend time discussing this theory, which can only be described as bizarre.[21] But I have two observations. First, if the beneficiary is owner, how is it that he cannot give good title? The theory should require that result. Of course, a beneficiary can *assign*, but that lets the cat out of the bag, for *assignation* is of *incorporeals*. What the beneficiary transfers is his right *against the trustee*. Secondly, while Watson's theory might perhaps have some superficial plausibility in the sort of case which arose in *Heritable Reversionary Co.*, namely where X holds as nominee, or bare trustee, for Y, it could never work with most trusts, where there are many beneficiaries, and where some or even all of the beneficial rights are unvested. If a man conveys, *mortis causa*, a house to trustees to hold for his widow in liferent and in fee for his daughter whom failing to her children and the survivor of them, who, on Watson's theory, is owner? The question would be unanswerable even if the beneficial fee were a vested fee: here it is unvested.

I have said that Lord Watson's theory was a variant of the mandate theory. It could also be classified under the next response.

Coming Out With Your Hands in the Air

Another approach which the civilian might adopt is simply to come out with his hands in the air, *i.e.* to abandon the structure of his system and accept the dichotomy of law and equity. Other civilian or mixed systems have not, I think, been much tempted to do this, but this temptation has certainly existed in Scotland. For instance in what was once a standard work A. Mackenzie Stuart[22] in the very first sentence

---

[18] (1892) 19 R.(H.L.) 43.
[19] His choice of this expression is striking. Andrew Dewar Gibb characterises Lord Watson as a "doughty angliciser": *Law From Over the Border* (1950) at p. 90.
[20] Emphasis added.
[21] Wilson and Duncan, *Trusts*, quote the above passage at p. 7, and T. B. Smith does the same at p. 225 of his *Studies Critical and Comparative*. But Watson's statement is inconsistent with Wilson's own views. T. B. Smith's views of the nature of trust were similar to Wilson's and indeed Wilson is thanked in the footnotes of the essay cited.
[22] *Law of Trusts* (1932).

explained trusts as something "enforceable in a court of equity" and in the third sentence explained that where there is a trust, "estate is owned by two persons at the same time."

One of the difficulties in writing about contributions such as those of Lord Watson, is that they are—with respect—too confused to classify. The same is true of J. (Lord) McLaren's *Law of Wills and Succession*.[23] McLaren quotes[24] with approval Lord Chancellor Westbury's statement that a beneficiary has an "equitable estate" but at the same time he also suggests (see below) that it is a subordinate real right and, yet again, that it is a personal right. Finally, to make his position perfectly clear, he tells us that trust is "quasi-contract."[25]

Trustee is Owner and Beneficiaries have Personal Rights

Another approach is that the trustee is owner and that the beneficiaries' rights are personal rights against him. This has become Scottish orthodoxy.[26] This approach does have its difficulties. As has already been remarked, the rights of the beneficiaries, if they are personal rights, are rather odd personal rights. Moreover, the trustee's right, if it is ownership, is a strange sort of ownership. In the *jus commune* ownership came to be conceived as *usus, fructus et abusus*. Evidently in that sense a trustee is not an owner. But this theory is nonetheless correct. In legal theory ownership is curious because you can subtract from it but however much you subtract what you have left is always ownership. It is a well that can never quite be emptied. *Inland Revenue v. Clark's Trustees*[27] is the leading case in support of this view, and this approach was consolidated by the academics. What remains is to develop it. This should be done in terms of the concept of estate or patrimony, of which more below.

Subordinate Real Rights

Yet another approach is that while the trustee is owner, the beneficiary's rights are nonetheless real, not personal. This is actually quite an interesting idea because it attempts to resolve the problem in a respectably civilian manner, by making use of the conception of the *jus in re aliena*.[28]

McLaren writes[29] that the beneficiary's right is "a right of property

---

[23] 3rd ed. 1894.
[24] Para. 1528.
[25] Para. 1508.
[26] In South Africa the Trust Property Control Act 1988 offers a double definition of trust. Both, interestingly, use the word *ownership*. In the sense which corresponds to our trust, *ownership* is said to be in the trustee.
[27] 1939 S.C. 11.
[28] That is, the theory that while the trustee is owner, the beneficiary's right is a subordinate real right. I will not here go into the strange theory that in some trusts the *truster* has ownership and the *trustee* a subordinate real right, for which see my "Radical Rights and Radical Wrongs", 1986 J.R. 52, 192 (two parts).
[29] Para. 1527.

in the same sense that a ground-annual, real burden, or other right be reservation, or an estate standing upon a decree or minute of sale, is a right of property" and that "equitable estate in personal property is a real and preferable right." This is muddled. He may have been groping for the idea of a subordinate real right. But if so, he lacked the knowledge of property law to say so. His list of analogies is strange. A purchaser's right under a minute (*i.e.* contract) of sale is purely personal.

Bill Wilson seems to have had some inclination towards the view that the right of the beneficiary, though not one of ownership, is nevertheless real. In *Trusts and Trust Like Devices*[30] he writes:

> "In their anxiety to stress that the beneficiary does not have a right of ownership, the Scottish judges have displayed a regrettable tendency to assert that the beneficiary has merely a personal right or *jus crediti*. For example, in *Inland Revenue v. Clark's Trs*[31] Lord President Normand described the beneficiary's right as 'no more than a personal right to sue' the trustees and to compel them to administer the trust in accordance with the directions which it contains. The beneficiary's right, as McLaren argues must be something more than a personal right, or *jus crediti*, because the trust estate does not pass to the trustee in the trustee's sequestration."

But Wilson never developed this idea. He was right to complain that the formula "no more than a personal right to sue" is inadequate. For one thing, a right to sue is not the *content* of a substantive right, but the *consequence* of a *breach* of a right. For another, Lord Normand's formulation disregards certain special features such as priority in insolvency. However, the idea that the beneficiary's right is real, not personal, has never established itself.

Lepaulle and Patrimony

In North and South America the trust has been more or less universally adopted, chiefly because of U.S. influence. And the mode of conceptualising the trust has been much influenced by the work of Lepaulle,[32] whose significance has not been realised in Scotland. Lepaulle argued that a civilian system cannot accept the trust in the form of legal and equitable ownership, nor in the form of agency. Moreover he argued that to say that the trustee was owner and that the beneficiaries had personal rights was unsustainable for various reasons, some of which I have outlined above. Lepaulle accordingly developed a theory of his own, using the concept of patrimony.[33]

---

[30] (1981); edited by Wilson himself.
[31] 1939 S.C. 11.
[32] Pierre Lepaulle was Professor at the Institut de Droit Comparé, Paris. Among his various qualifications was a doctorate from Harvard.
[33] His writings on trust are so extensive and subtly argued that what is said here is a mere caricature.

Patrimony is not a doctrine but an organising concept. Like other organising concepts, one employs it to the extent that it is useful. On the European continent it is regarded as useful, though it has been criticised. It means the totality of a person's economic rights.[34] We also have this concept. The term we tend to use is *estate*. When someone dies, we say that the *estate* is to be administered. The executor confirms to the *estate*.[35] Again, a trustee in sequestration winds up the bankrupt *estate*. The word is useful, for in the conceptual scheme of things there is a slot here which needs a name. But *estate* is a poor choice, and its use has hindered the development of our law. For *estate* is commonly used to mean something quite different, namely a large tract of land. Even when the word puts a wig on, it brings to mind the English doctrine of estates in land. The word has been used in statutes to mean real and personal rights in immoveables.[36] The story is all the stranger since we began to use the term *patrimony* and then stopped half way. For we speak of *patrimonial loss*, meaning a loss to the patrimony, and of *patrimonial interests*. A more intelligent use of terminology would help us in many a tight spot. When we acquire rights, we tend to say that they come into our ownership, and then we end up in a muddle when we consider that many of these rights are not rights of ownership at all. Everything in our patrimony is ours, but not everything in our patrimony is a real right of ownership. A failure to distinguish patrimony from ownership underlies many of the muddles about trust,[37] and indeed other matters.[38]

Patrimony (*patrimonium*, *patrimoine*, *Vermögen*) has in fact two senses. "Estate" indeed shares this quality. In one sense it is the totality of assets, but in a wider sense it means the totality of assets and liabilities. This latter is the more usual on the continent, though the Germans, while using the word thus in the 19th century, nowadays use it in the narrower sense. The broader sense is especially valuable for trusts, because in a trust there is segregation not only of assets but also (albeit subject to certain qualifications) of liabilities. So when we say that a trustee has two estates (or, better, two patrimonies), his personal patrimony and his trust patrimony, we are using a rather effective concept.

Lepaulle says that while in general one person has one patrimony, in a trust there is a separate patrimony. He called this a *patrimoine affecté*[39] or a *patrimoine indépendant de tout sujet de droit*.[40] In Lepaulle's view, nobody owned the assets in this patrimony. The trustee had power to deal with them, and he is *titulaire*, but not *propriétaire*.

Lepaulle's theory grew out of German doctrines about special kinds of patrimony, the *Sondervermögen* and the *Zweckvermögen*. K. W. Ryan

---

[34] "Economic" rights because some rights are non-patrimonial.
[35] In fact we nowadays use "estate" to include *haereditas jacens*.
[36] *e.g.* Conveyancing (Scotland) Act 1874, s. 3.
[37] G. L. Gretton, "What is Vesting?" (1986) 31 J.L.S.S. 148.
[38] In *Sharp v. Thomson*, 1995 S.L.T. 837 the personal right was in the patrimony of the buyers and the real right in that of the sellers.
[39] An earmarked patrimony.
[40] *Traité theorique et pratique des trusts* (1932) at p. 31.

has argued[41] that Lepaulle misunderstood his German sources. One may also argue that Lepaulle's theory did not really solve all the problems,[42] and in particular, the distinction between *titulaire* and *propriétaire* seems evasive, though no worse than when we say that a trustee has *title*. Whatever its defects, the theory became the basis on which trusts were adopted in most of Latin America.[43] In Québec trusts have existed for a long time, with an unclear juridical basis, until the new Civil Code, when Lepaulle's approach was adopted:

> "Le patrimoine fiduciare, formé des biens transférés en fiducie, constitue un patrimoine d'affectation autonome et distinct de celui du constituant, du fiduciaire, ou du bénéficiare, sur lequel aucun d'entre eux n'a de-droit réél. [Official translation: The trust property, consisting of the property transferred, constitutes a patrimony by appropriation, autonomous and distinct from that of the settlor, trustee or beneficiary, and in which none of them has any real right."[44]

Louisiana however held aloof. The Lousiana Trust Code states that: "A trust . . . is the relationship resulting from the transfer of title to property to a person to be administered by him as a fiduciary for the benefit of another."[45]

Separate Personality

One approach which has occasionally been mooted is that a trust should be regarded as a distinct juristic person. This is not such a bad idea. Long-running trusts with their own premises and staff are functionally indistinguishable from organisations with juristic personality.[46] But as far as I am aware no legal system has ever adopted this approach. A trustee may have two capacities, but he is one person. Later in his career Lepaulle argued for this approach: "La solution la plus efficace et la plus simple est de doter le trust de la personne morale."[47] But this suggestion has seemingly had no influence. That

---

[41] "The Reception of the Trust", (1961) 10 I.C.L.Q. 265.

[42] One objection, that ownerless assets would fall to the state as *bona vacantia*, is anticipated by Lepaulle.

[43] His book was eventually issued in a Spanish translation: *Tratado teorico y pratico de los trusts* (1975).

[44] Art. 1261. For discussion, see J. E. C. Brierley, "Regards sur le Droit des Biens dans le Nouveau Code Civil du Quebec", (1995) 47 Revue Internationale de Droit Comparé 33.

[45] Actually not a bad definition, if incomplete. For history, see J. Dainow, "The Introduction of the Trust in Louisiana", (1961) 39 C.B.R. 396.

[46] That juristic personality could arise without state grant would be unacceptable in some systems, but in many countries including Scotland partnerships have personality.

[47] (1952) 4 Revue Internationale de Droit Comparé 377, in a review of R. M. Pasquel, *La Propriété dans le Trust*. He had however already suggested the idea in his "An Outsider's Viewpoint of the Nature of Trusts" (1928) 14 C.L.Q. 52 at p. 57. See also what seems to have been Lepaulle's final—and superb—essay: "The Strange Destiny

Lepaulle reached this conclusion is perhaps not surprising, for patrimony has historically shown a tendency to develop into personality. The *haereditas jacens* of Roman law began as patrimony and ended up as something like an autonomous person. One sees the same development in the German *Zweckvermögen*. Indeed, it is arguable that the concept of juristic personality and the concept of autonomous patrimony are essentially identical. This is something which needs examination.

The Hague Convention

The Hague Trusts Convention was not intended to transplant trusts around the world, but to deal with cross-border issues. It is the only international attempt to define trust so as to make sense in all legal systems. I quote Article 2:

"Aux fins de la présente convention, le terme "trust" vise les relations juridiques créées par une personne, le constituant—par acte entre vifs ou à cause de mort—lorsque des biens ont étés placés sous le contrôle du trustee dans l'intérêt d'un bénéficiare ou dans un but déterminé. Les biens du trust constituent une masse[48] distinct et ne font pas partie du patrimoine du trustee."

This definition, or explanation, has a fairly low theory-content, probably inevitably, since it had to command international acceptance. Patrimony is there, but in the negative. We learn that the assets form a *masse*. The choice of term is interesting. *Masse* is the name given to a *patrimoine* upon bankruptcy.[49] The statement that trust assets do not form part of the trustee's estate (*patrimoine*) is not a happy one, for it would be natural to say that a trustee has two estates, namely his own estate and the trust estate. The Recognition of Trusts Act 1987 says that the trust assets "are not part of the trustee's own estate" which, by the addition of the word "own," seems to go beyond the French text. The translator must have felt instinctively that a trustee has a double *patrimoine* and that accordingly the French text was not well expressed at this point: hence the additional word "own."[50]

---

of Trusts", in Roscoe Pound (ed.), *Perspectives of Law: Essays for Austin Wakeman Scott* (1964).

[48] It has the same inclusive meaning, covering both the *masse active* and the *masse passive*, though here the active meaning only seems to be used.

[49] In the Recognition of Trusts Act 1987 this becomes "estate."

[50] There has been a recent *projet* to introduce trusts to French law. The text runs: La fiducie est un contrat par lequel un constituant transfère tout ou partie de ses biens et droits à une fiduciare qui, tenant ces biens et droits séparés de son patrimoine personnel, agit dans un but déterminé au profit d'un ou plusieurs bénéficiares conformément aux stipulations du contrat. (Text from F. Sonneveldt (ed., *Trust: Bridge or Abyss between Common and Civil Jurisdictions?* (1992) at p. 68.) Here we are told that the separation is from the *personal* patrimony. This is to be applauded.

Final Thoughts

The orthodox view of trusts is as set forth in *Inland Revenue v. Clark's Trustees*.[51] Wilson accepted this view and elaborated it, and thus helped stabilise the law. It is infinitely preferable as a model to some of its rivals. But difficulties remain. We have yet to confront all the conceptual problems of trusts: many of the challenges laid down by Lepaulle have never been addressed, let alone answered, in our law. But we would at least do well to develop our concept of the estate, preferably under its better name, patrimony.

---

[51] 1939 S.C. 11.

THE FUTURE OF FAMILY LAW: EMPOWERMENT: RHETORIC OR REALITY?

Anne Griffiths

Family law was one of the many areas of law in which Bill Wilson expressed an interest during his long and distinguished career.[1] However, he was critical of what he perceived of as a growing trend towards delegalisation and the disenfranchisement of courts and lawyers. His concern over the displacement of law by administrative bodies, such as the Child Support Agency, was not limited to the family arena but extended more widely to cover employment and property relations. He viewed this move towards bypassing courts and the legal profession as raising important constitutional issues concerning the exercise and extension of state power and control.[2] These concerns have been shared by other scholars who have been sceptical about the move away from courts in favour of alternative dispute resolution with its claims to less coercive forms of ordering and greater party empowerment.[3] In this essay I shall consider Wilson's comments on delegalisation in the light of ongoing developments in family law.

As the end of the twentieth century approaches, what stage has family law reached and where is it going? Developments over the last two decades point towards minimal court intervention in family affairs, particularly with respect to separation and divorce and the parenting of children. The whole thrust behind legislation such as the Children Act 1989 in England and the Children (Scotland) Act 1995, and underlying recent proposals for divorce reform,[4] is towards enabling parties to reach their own decisions on financial provision, and on residence and contact arrangements with respect to children. As family law has become more focused on children, so the traditional emphasis on marriage as the predominant paradigm for ordering family relationships has come under critical scrutiny. Such scrutiny is pertinent in the light of statistics which reveal that 32 per cent of all live births in 1993 were extra-marital ones[5] and that 79 per cent of these born to women aged over 30 were jointly registered by parents

---

[1] W. A. Wilson, "The Bairns of Falkirk: The Child Support Act 1991", 1991 S.L.T. (News) 417.

[2] W. A. Wilson, "The Progress of the Law, 1888–1988", 1988 J.R. 207 at p. 230.

[3] R. L. Abel (ed.), *The Politics of Informal Justice*, 2 vols (1982); A. Sarat and S. Silbey, "The 'New Formalism' in Disputing and Dispute Processing", (1987–88) 21 Law & Soc'y. Rev. 695.

[4] *Looking to the Future: Mediation and the Ground for Divorce the Government's Proposals*, Cm. 27990 (1995).

[5] *Birth Statistics England & Wales: Review of the Registrar General on Births and Patterns of Family Building in England and Wales*, Office of Population and Censuses and Surveys (1993) at p. xxii.

living at the same address.[6] While we have not yet attained Dr Clive's ideal of recognising marriage as an unnecessary legal concept,[7] positive moves have been made towards the legal recognition of cohabitation contracts.[8]

The rhetoric underlying these developments is one of empowerment. The trend is towards self-regulation where the emphasis is placed on individuals taking responsibility for their actions and for reaching their own agreements. Where they experience difficulties in achieving consensus, or even outright conflict, government now actively promotes mediation as an alternative to court-based systems of dispute processing and adjudication.[9] This is because:

> "Unlike current legal processes, mediation is a flexible process which can take into account the different needs of families, and differing attitudes and positions of the parties."[10]

This flexibility involves:

> "a process in which an impartial third person, the mediator, assists couples considering separation or divorce to meet together to deal with the arrangements which need to be made for the future."[11]

As such, it represents:

> "an alternative to negotiating matters at arms length through two separate lawyers and to litigating through the courts."[12]

Through comments such as these mediation is set apart from the sphere of courts and lawyers and identified as having other more positive features. The legal process is characterised in terms of lack of flexibility, impersonal treatment and adversarial relations pursued through litigation, while mediation is presented in terms of all these qualities which the legal system is said to lack and which do not favour party empowerment. However, the notion of empowerment, which promotes the image of individuals maintaining control and autonomy over their own affairs, requires critical analysis.[13] To what

---

[6] *ibid.*, at p. xxiii. Of the 67 per cent of extra-marital teenage births in 1993 that were jointly registered, 55 per cent were to parents living at the same address.

[7] E. M. Clive, "Marriage: an Unnecessary Legal Concept?", in J. M. Eekelaar and S. M. Katz (eds.), *Marriage and Cohabitation in Contemporary Societies: Areas of Legal, Social and Ethical Change* (1980) at pp. 72–73.

[8] See *Report on Family Law*, Scot. Law. Com. (No. 135, 1992), draft bill, cl. 42 at p. 127.

[9] This is not only in the family sphere but in other areas.

[10] *Looking to the Future, supra,* para 5.5 (p. 38).

[11] *ibid.*, para 5.4 (p. 37).

[12] *ibid.*, para 5.8 (p. 39).

[13] See the debates between Roberts and Dingwall and Greatbach over this issue in the *Journal of Social Welfare and Family Law*: M. Roberts (1992), "Who is in Charge? Reflections on Recent Research on the Role of Mediator" at pp. 372–387; R. Dingwall and D. Greatbach (1993), "Who is in Charge? Rhetoric and Evidence in the Study of Mediation", pp. 367–385; M. Roberts (1994), "Who is in Charge? Effecting a Productive Exchange between Researchers and Practitioners in the Field of Family

extent and under what conditions does such an image conform to the reality of the world people inhabit? Issues of power and control arise in every type of social setting, comprising personal encounters between individuals, as well as their interactions with officials and institutions (including those associated with law). The important question is, how are they handled?

Unfortunately debates on self-regulation in family law in Britain have tended to become polarised around the pros and cons of mediation, as distinct from those attributed to the legal system. They have much in common with the old debates concerning informal and formal justice. What these earlier debates demonstrated was the inadequacy of characterising justice or law in terms of dichotomies which set up the informal as a sphere of non-specialist, non-coercive ordering based on consensus and party control, as contrasted with the formal arena which was presented in exactly opposite terms.[14] Research on forms of justice has progressed beyond this kind of analysis to examine the relationship that exists between the various agencies which are said to represent differing forms of justice, and their impact on one another as parts of regulatory processes overshadowed by the State.[15]

When applied to families and their regulation on divorce or separation, this approach allows for a more integrated examination of the processes at work and more complex analysis of their characteristics. This is valuable because first it raises issues about our conception of law and thus what is meant by the term "delegalisation" and secondly, mediation in reality, whether in or out of court,[16] takes place in the shadow of the law and is inextricably linked with the legal process.

Empowerment—the Role of Law and Lawyers

To present law wholly in terms of a combative, adversarial system geared to handling conflicts in courts is to focus on one aspect of law and to elevate it above all others. What is ignored in this account is the facilitative and prescriptive role that law may play which may serve to pre-empt or diffuse conflict by establishing normative frameworks for action in other arenas. These aspects become apparent when we shift our focus away from court proceedings, which represent only a minority of cases, to the work carried out by lawyers in the ordinary

Mediation" at pp. 439–454; R. Dingwall and D. Greatbach (1995), "Family Mediation Researchers and Practitioners in the Shadow of the Green Paper: a Rejoinder to Marian Roberts" at pp. 199–206.

[14] See Abel (ed), *The Politics of Informal Justice*; P. Fitzpatrick, "The Impossibility of Popular Justice", in R. Matthews (ed), *Informal Justice?* (1988).

[15] A. N. Allott and G. R. Woodman (eds.), *People's Law and State Law: The Bellagio Papers* (1985); (1992) 1(2) Social and Legal Studies, Special Issue on State Transformation, Legal Pluralism and Community Justice

[16] In England there is provision for mediation to take place in court through the auspices of a court welfare officer as well as out of court. In Scotland, while parties may be referred to mediation by the courts, it is an independently organised and funded service which is provided outside the courts.

course of business. It is well known that cases going to court are the exception rather than the rule.[17] It is true that in divorce parties are processed through the courts, but this does not necessarily mean that they are in conflict with one another. By far the majority of divorce cases are undefended and undisputed. The parties are not engaged in adversarial proceedings. This is because most couples do reach agreement on the terms of their divorce, including arrangements for child care and distribution of property. Where they do so, such agreements are usually embodied in minutes of agreement drafted by solicitors and merely approved by the courts.

What is the role of the lawyer in this context? He or she may be presented with an agreement which merely requires transcription into the appropriate legal form. However more active assistance may be required in terms of providing the relevant legal information that will frame the basis for any agreement, as well as pursuing negotiations on the client's behalf. What little research has been done in this area[18] indicates that the role of the lawyer in this context is not as, is commonly believed, geared towards litigation or towards depriving the other party of their share in any assets in a "winner take all" mentality. The research suggests that in this area, lawyers are concerned with what is "fair" and that they take account of this in terms of the family situation as a whole and not just from their client's perspective.[19] A number of instances are recorded where lawyers had to prevail on their clients not to act on emotional grounds but to consider their children's position and that of their spouse.

Power and Control—Lawyer/Client

Where parties reach agreement and thus enter into a form of self-regulation, is it appropriate to talk in terms of their empowerment, and where does this leave issues of power and control? The circumstances under which agreements are concluded vary from those where the parties work together from the start and where the role of the lawyer is very much a facilitative and administrative one aimed at producing the necessary legal paperwork, to those where the relationship between the parties is much more tenuous or even hostile and where much more active engagement in negotiation is required by the lawyer. Within this range of lawyer/client interactions differing degrees of power and control are exercised on both sides. While the lawyer has the advantage of special expertise and knowledge which

---

[17] See M. Galanter, "Justice in Many Rooms: Courts, Private Ordering and Indigenous Law", (1981) 19 Journal of Legal Pluralism and Unofficial Law 1.

[18] R. Ingleby, "The Solicitor as Intermediary", in R. Dingwall and J. Eekelaar (eds.), *Divorce Mediation and the Legal Process* (1988); W. L. Felstiner and A. Sarat, *Divorce Lawyers and Their Clients: Power and Meaning in the Legal Process* (1995); F. Wasoff, R. Dobash and D. Harcus, *The Impact of the Family Law (Scotland) Act 1985 on Solicitors' Divorce Practice* Central Research Unit Papers, Scottish Office (1990).

[19] Wasoff, *et al, Impact of Family Law (Scotland) Act, supra,* found that solicitors tended to quantify aliment in terms of figures that had little to do with the particular circumstances of the case and which had nothing to do with maximising their client's claim.

can be used to manipulate the client, the client is not powerless but may circumvent such manipulations through avoidance, withdrawal, stalling behaviour or even by terminating the relationship.[20] The dynamics of power within this relationship are fluid and vary during the course of negotiations.

Power and Control—the Clients

In addition to these considerations, there is the question of empowerment as between the parties themselves and the degrees of power and control that operate within their own relationship. These concerns have come to the forefront through feminist discussions over the role of contract in domestic relations. There are long-standing debates about how far marriage represents a contractual or a status relationship. In examining the role of law in this context, general debate has centred on the advantages and disadvantages of upholding freedom of contract, as compared with the imposition of certain legal provisions which are non-negotiable.

The Gender Dimension

Feminists have added another dimension, that of gender, to these discussions.[21] They argue about the extent to which either approach benefits women. On the one hand, the image of contract representing freedom and equality for individuals is challenged on the basis that women, as individuals, do not have the same economic and social bargaining power as men. This imbalance is systematically replicated as a result of the way in which society is structured and the role that is allotted to women in the domestic sphere. What appears to be "voluntary" may in reality represent the product of coercive power relations. On the other hand, it is argued that adopting a legal interventionist position based on status has the danger of reinforcing the very type of relationship, founded on women's economic dependence upon men, that feminists and others are striving to eliminate.

These concerns are not confined to marriage but are pertinent to the growing number of women who are cohabiting. While many feminists are against assimilating cohabitation with marriage, on the ground that most cohabitants reject marriage as a paradigm for ordering their relationship, they continue to have disputes over the viability of contract as a means of self-regulation in this context.

---

[20] For a discussion of the range of techniques employed by both sides see Felstiner and Sarat cited in n. 18.
[21] M. A. Fineman, "Implementing Equality: Ideology, Contradiction and Social Change—A Study of Rhetoric and Results in the Regulation of the Consequences of Divorce", (1983) Wis. L. Rev. 789; S. M. Okin, *Justice, Gender, and the Family* (1989); C. Smart, *The Ties That Bind: Law, Marriage and Reproduction of Patriarchal Relations* (1984).

Olsen,[22] for example, while recognising that some women might benefit from the use of cohabitation contracts, considers that they are generally undesirable so long as they continue to promote equality within the family by making it more like the market place. In her view the predominant Western legal paradigm is one upholding a dichotomy between public and private arenas and between the market and the family. Each has its own characteristics, and the public arena which embraces the market, competition and the world of free enterprise, upholds contract as a means of regulation. Olsen's concern is that the ideology underpinning this sphere of public life which promotes equality is and will continue to be used to legitimise substantive forms of inequality and domination not apparent on the surface but derived from women's unequal earning capacity and their psychological socialisation and conditioning.[23]

However, other scholars consider contract from another perspective. For Freeman and Lyon,[24] contract is a facilitative device that enables women to structure the terms of their relationship to suit their needs. It provides flexibility and accommodates a diverse range of options, so that women need not have a marital model of relationship imposed on them in the mistaken belief that marriage protects women or through treating cohabitants as spouses. Weizman[25] also subscribes to the view that contract may be used to promote more egalitarian relationships, as parties are empowered to order their own personal relations. From this perspective, any refusal by the courts to uphold cohabitation contracts,[26] appears an unnecessary interference with personal freedom.[27] Deech[28] challenges the construction of women as "weak" and in need of protection, especially where this is used to undermine arguments in favour of cohabitation contracts.

These differing perspectives on the advantages and disadvantages of contract are grounded in historical debates over the role of contract as a means of empowering individuals which go back to Adam Smith and Sir Henry Maine. Such discussions led the latter to declare "that the movement of progressive societies has been uniform in one respect ... [in that] it marks the shift from status to contract."[29] Taking up this theme, the varying feminist views on whether or not this represents a progressive measure for women derive from specific models of women and gender relations that are applied at the level of the ideal as well as in the real world.[30] The difficulty in adopting a position

---

[22] F. Olsen, "The Family and the Market: A Study of Ideology and Legal Reform", (1983) 97 Harv. L.R. 1497.
[23] For a critique of Olsen see E. Kingdom, "Cohabitation and Equality", (1990) 18 International Journal of the Sociology of Law 287.
[24] M. D. A. Freeman and C. M. Lyon, Cohabitation Without Marriage (1983).
[25] L. Weizman, The Marriage Contract (1981).
[26] There is uncertainty as to whether such contracts fall foul of the immorality doctrine: see Report on Family Law, supra, at para. 16.46, and L. M. Parry, The Law Relating to Cohabitation (3rd ed. 1995).
[27] A. Bottomley et al, The Cohabitation Handbook (1981).
[28] R. Deech, "The case against legal recognition of cohabitation" (1980) 29 I.C.L.Q. 480.
[29] Sir Henry Maine, Ancient Law (new ed., 1906) at pp. 180–182.
[30] For a summary of the equality/difference debates see B. Brown, "Feminism", in R. Bellamy (ed.), Theories and Concepts of Politics: An Introduction (1993).

that is either for or against the use of contract in domestic relations is that it presupposes a pattern of uniformity in women's relations with men. But neither women nor men represent a homogeneous category. They embody a range of persons who come from varying economic, social, and ethnic backgrounds.

Failure to acknowledge this can lead to the false assumption that the interests of one particular group of women represent the interests of all women. It is this kind of conflation that has led to criticism of Deech, on the basis that her account of legal strategies for women is formulated solely in terms that relate to professional, white, middle-class women.[31] This is not to say that such groups are to be ignored. As Kingdom[32] argues, contract need not always operate to the detriment of women, but can be used to their advantage. What is needed is an analysis of the conditions which render contract a viable option and which ensure that power and control are not vested in one party to such an extent that this seriously undermines the other's position.

Part of this analysis involves examining legal techniques for dealing with the issue. These include the ordinary law of contract under which agreements procured under force and fear (or duress) or undue influence may be set aside. There is also the statutory ground of challenge contained in section 16 of the Family Law (Scotland) Act 1985, relating to separation agreements, where the test is whether the agreement was "fair and reasonable at the time it was entered into".[33] The binding nature of these contracts[34] raises questions about how to deal with changes in a family's circumstances. These may have altered radically since the agreement was first made.[35] While there is some scope for varying contractual provisions on periodical allowance contained in minutes of agreement or joint minutes, this is limited to cases where the parties have made appropriate express provision[36] or where there has been a material change of circumstances.[37] However the material change in circumstances is only open for consideration where the agreement forms part of a court decree.[38]

Mediation

Promoting agreement between parties is one of the key aims of mediation. It initially focused on assisting:

---

[31] K. O'Donovan, "The Principles of Maintenance: An Alternative View" (1978) 8 Family Law 180, challenges R. L. Deech, "The Principles of Maintenance" (1977) 7 Family Law 229. O'Donovan is critical of Deech for promoting a policy that is based on the supposition that all women are, or ought to be, employed and she argues that this approach ignores the reality of many women's lives.

[32] E. Kingdom, What's Wrong with Rights? Problems for Feminist Policies of Law (1991) at pp. 101–113.

[33] s. 16(1)(b).

[34] Jongejan v. Jongejan, 1993 S.L.T. 181.

[35] Drummond v. Drummond, 1992 S.C.L.R. 473.

[36] s. 16(1)(a) of the 1985 Act.

[37] s. 13(4) of the 1985 Act.

[38] This occurs where the court interpones authority and grants decree in terms of the arrangement arrived at in the settlement. For the complexities surrounding the effect of an order interponing authority and whether or not the agreement is to be

"divorcing and separating couples to reach agreements amicably, especially over the arrangements for their children."[39]

From one centre, The Scottish Family Conciliation Service (Lothian)[40] established in 1984 and based in Edinburgh, the organisation has expanded to cover regions throughout Scotland,[41] as well as the foundation of a national body, Family Mediation Scotland (formerly SAFCOS),[42] established in 1987. As the service has developed, so its remit has extended to cover mediation on all issues, and it is now Family Mediation Scotland's policy to start mediation on the once controversial areas of finance and property,[43] bringing it into line with services in England and other jurisdictions.

Does this development signal the delegalisation that Bill Wilson was so concerned about? For as long as the state has existed, family relationships have been subject to regulation of some kind. As part of the state, the role of law has involved creating frameworks for regulation, as well as being a mode of control over other forms of state power by subjecting them to various tests of accountability. Delegalisation in Wilson's terms implies both a dismantling of the regulatory frameworks associated with law and a withdrawal from certain forms of control related to this accountability. To what extent does this apply to mediation?

As currently structured, mediation in Scotland forms part of a process closely connected to the legal system. Courts may refer cases to mediation,[44] and any agreements reached there may then be embodied in minutes of agreement or joint minutes (although this is not mandatory). While mediation is handled independently from the courts and its sessions are guaranteed confidentiality[45] (except for a statement of outcomes), the legal framework which governs divorce and separation is always in view. For those who are divorcing and who participate in mediation, referral to a lawyer is necessary at some stage in the process to institute court proceedings. This may occur before or after mediation, or may even form part of a more extended lawyer/client relationship in which mediation represents a stage in the overall process of divorce. However the Lord Chancellor's pro-

---

superseded by decree or not, see E. M. Clive, *The Law of Husband and Wife in Scotland* (3rd ed. 1992) at p. 508.

[39] *The Scottish Family Conciliation Service (Lothian)*, Scottish Office Central Research Unit Papers (1986), para 2.19 (p. 7).

[40] The term mediation has been substituted for conciliation in order to avoid any confusion with reconciliation which has different aims.

[41] For an up-to-date account of mediation in Scotland see S. Matheson, "Family Mediation in Scotland", in S. R. Moody and R. E. Mackay (eds.), *Greens Guide to Alternative Dispute Resolution in Scotland* (1995).

[42] The Scottish Association of Family Conciliation Services.

[43] See para. 4.11 p. 20 of the 1986 report cited above at n. 19 for comment on solicitors views, observing that "(there has been much discussion in conciliation circles as to whether finance should be dealt with)".

[44] See O.C.R. 33.22 and R.C.S. 49.23. The wording of these rules is different. It is clear that the Court of Session Rules require the parties to consent to mediate before the court can refer them to mediation whereas the Sheriff Court Rules make no reference to the parties' consent and are more ambiguous on this point.

[45] Civil Evidence (Family Mediation) (Scotland) Act 1995.

posals for England and Wales move towards displacing lawyers with mediators, on the grounds of cost and better practice.

There is presently no move to oust the jurisdiction of lawyers in Scotland. Indeed, a number of lawyers are training as mediators so that they can combine both legal knowledge and mediation skills in dealing with family relationships.[46] Mediators are also extending their training in law to have the knowledge that is required to frame party negotiations over finance and property. What is emerging is a new form of expertise that draws on a range of fields, including law. The fact that this expertise adopts a new form of procedure, involving direct negotiations between the parties in the presence of a third party who lacks judicial powers, does not mean that it is "non-legal" in character because it fails to follow a model of party representation and adjudication associated with courts. What is important is that the legal norms that govern the regulation of family relationships, including the "best interests of the child" and "fair sharing of matrimonial property" continue to feature as reference points in mediation.

There is a concern, however, that while these norms continue to function their content and meaning will be transformed in the course of mediation. In a process where it is the parties who "control the content and the outcome", social pressure will operate to a far greater extent than it would in a system where both parties have legal representation which can act as some form of check on the power relations and inequalities of bargaining power that exist between the parties. There are fears that what is expedient will carry greater weight in a system geared toward consensus and accommodation rather than the upholding of individual rights. This is especially so where the third party role is defined in terms of facilitation rather than adjudication. For some feminists these features of mediation represent a major issue, for they see women as structurally located in a set of social relations denying them power.[47]

While the power of an adjudicator is openly acknowledged, that of a facilitator is less so. The role of a mediator who "controls the process"[48] raises questions about the nature, extent and form of her interventions in framing and upholding the appropriate context for negotiation. Given the expert nature of a mediator's training, is there not a danger that she may direct discussion around such issues as "the best interests of the child" to meet criteria established by specialist discourses, such as child psychology and development, of which the parties have little or no knowledge?[49]

These concerns raise issues of accountability, especially with regard to control. To turn to courts, however, will not necessarily dispense with these issues. In the first place, as already mentioned, although

---

[46] In 1993 there were 26 trained lawyer/mediators in Scotland. They belong to CALM (Comprehensive Accredited Lawyer Mediators), a specialist group of lawyers who charge commercial rates for their services.

[47] See A. Bottomley, "Resolving Family Disputes: A Critical Review", in M. D. A. Freeman (ed.), *The State, the Law and the Family Critical Perspectives* (1984).

[48] See Matheson, "Family Mediation", *supra*, at p. 44.

[49] R. F. Kandel, "Power Plays: A Sociolinguistic Study of Inequality in Child Custody Mediation and a Hearsay Analog Solution", (1994) 36 Ariz. L. Rev. 879.

adjudication is associated with courts, the great majority of family cases coming before them are uncontested.[50] This means that the role of the court, in this type of case, is essentially an administrative one geared to processing what has already been negotiated.[51] Despite a power and a duty to intervene, where for example agreements do not sufficiently provide for the interests of children,[52] courts prefer to uphold what the parties have agreed, regarding them as the most appropriate judges of the situation.[53] It is true that the court plays a more active role where parties are in dispute. However, when it comes to assessing parties' claims, particularly with regard to residence and contact (formerly custody and access), judges are inclined to rely on the reports of experts who come from a range of disciplines outside law. Legal expertise is not immune from the pressures of social norms which form part of the construction of what is deemed fair or appropriate in family relationships. Thus lawyers advising and assisting clients to reach agreements may well bring social pressure to bear within a legal framework of negotiation.

As the twentieth century comes to a close, Wilson's fears of delegalisation, in terms of ousting the jurisdiction of courts or lawyers over the handling of property and children in the dissolution of family relationships in Scotland, have not yet materialised. Self-regulation and party empowerment still occur within a legally structured framework. But this does not mean that there is no cause for concern either with regard to the current system or over future developments. For what is at issue is accountability for the decisions that are reached. Such accountability arises, not only with respect to the parties who must live with decisions reached, but also in terms of public interest and the state.

What underlines all these interests, as highlighted in this essay, are issues of power and control which are not necessarily addressed adequately just because courts and the legal profession exist as overseers of family dissolution. Nor can it be argued, on the other hand, that such issues in family matters are better removed from the legal domain altogether because of its association with coercive and adversarial relations. The role that law plays in the ordering of family relationships is a multi-faceted one, of which only one aspect involves dealing with conflict. But where conflict arises, it is important to provide a number of options for its resolution, including mediation and recourse to the courts. If debates over power and control in terms of self-regulation and party empowerment are to be meaningful, they must go beyond an analysis focused on the dichotomy between legal and non-legal approaches to dissolution. What is required is an understanding of the ways in which the two dimensions come together to

---

[50] Around 80 per cent of ordinary divorce actions were undefended in the years 1989–1991: E. Morris, G. Gibson and A. Platts, *Untying the Knot: Characteristics of Divorce in Scotland*, Scottish Office Central Research Unit (1993) at p. 15.

[51] See Wassoff, *et al*, *Impact of Family Law (Scotland) Act*, at p. 5; J. M. Eekelaar and E. M. Clive, *Custody After Divorce* (1977) at p. 42.

[52] Formerly Matrimonial Proceedings (Children) Act 1958, s. 8, now repealed and replaced by Children (Scotland) Act 1995, s. 12.

[53] Royal Commission on Legal Services, Cmnd. 7846 (1980), vol 1, p. 157.

create an overall framework for governing separation. This under-standing derives from an analysis of both social and legal factors which give rise to power and control among and between individuals, as well as experts and institutions. It is only through this form of analysis that the reality of family law can be set apart from its rhetoric.

THE ANALYSIS OF NEGLIGENCE:
ECONOMIC LOSS AND ASSUMING RESPONSIBILITY

Douglas Brodie

It seems safe to say that Bill Wilson's best-known contribution to the literature on delict is to be found in his *Introductory Essays on Scots Law*, where he provides an analysis of negligence. This has stood the test of time remarkably well, and seems likely to continue to do so. It provides a succinct, clear and thoroughly sound analysis. More recent cases tend to be readily accommodated within its framework. One aspect which Wilson might have returned to, however, is the question of duty of care. At the time he wrote, *Dorset Yacht Co. Ltd v. Home Office*[1] and *Anns v. Merton London Borough Council*[2] were in the ascendancy, with the result that reasonable foreseeability provided a *prima facie* test for the existence of a duty. This led Wilson to question whether the concept of duty was a "fifth wheel on the wagon" of negligence, because foreseeability was also a requirement of other areas of negligence. Nevertheless he felt that there were four aspects of the law of negligence which were best explained by the concept of duty: nervous shock, pure omissions, pure economic loss and animals. Indeed Wilson later reviewed the vexed question of recovery for pure economic loss in an essay entitled "Mapping Economic Loss".[3] This is a highly analytical piece of work, setting out a most original classification of the case law. It offers limited assistance, however, in predicting how future cases will be decided. It also does not attempt to prescribe how such cases should be decided. In this essay I wish to examine the development of the pure economic loss debate and, in particular, the evolution of the criteria which must be satisfied before liability will be imposed.

Assistance from the Civil Law?

Reference has already been made in this volume to the fact that latterly Bill Wilson became more concerned with Scots law's civilian roots. However, if one turns to civil law for assistance on the question of pure economic loss, the position appears to be ambiguous.[4] In South Africa the development of the law has taken place against the background of the *lex Aquilia*. But the South African courts have not found this area straightforward:

---

[1] [1970] A.C. 1004.

[2] [1978] A.C. 728.

[3] A. J. Gamble (ed.), *Obligations in Context: Essays in Honour of D. M. Walker* (1990) at p. 141.

[4] R. Zimmermann, *The Law of Obligations: Roman Foundations of the Civilian Tradition* (1990), Chap. 30.

"[A]lthough the contrary view had long been held by many authorities, it seems clear that the fact that the patrimonial loss suffered did not result from physical injury to the corporeal property or person of the plaintiff, but was purely economic, is not a bar to the Aquilian action".[5]

Have matters been made easier by the more extensive resort to Roman law on the part of South African jurists than their Scottish counterparts? One suspects both that the answer is no and that such a conclusion is also not surprising.[6] The features of economic loss recovery which the courts have found most intractable are in the realms of "indeterminacy": that is, the fear of unlimited liability to an unlimited class of persons for an unlimited period of time.[7] Roman society, being pre-industrial, did not have to grapple with the legal consequences of activities such as the publication of the accounts of a limited company or the disruption of the power supply to an industrial estate.

Assuming Responsibility

In the absence of significant help from long-standing doctrine, whither Scots law? Bill Wilson's analysis of negligence owed a large debt to the judical pronouncements of Lord Reid, who gave one of the speeches in the landmark case of *Hedley Byrne & Co. v. Heller & Partners*.[8] Lord Reid's subsequent judgment in *Dorset Yacht* also contains a most influential dictum on the approach to duty of care. In *Hedley Byrne* he looked to the notion of "assumption of responsibility" in determining whether a duty arose from the giving of a reference. For a number of years *Hedley Byrne* tended to be viewed as a case about negligent misrepresentation only. But of late Lord Goff has indicated that the ratio of *Hedley Byrne* is best regarded as being about assumption of responsibility in general.[9] Do these recent judgments suggest that Lord Reid was correct in looking to the notion of assumption of responsibility to provide a basis for liability rather than reasonable foreseeability? This might be tested against, on the one hand, cases where economic loss recovery has been allowed and, on the other, those where it has not.

In *Hedley Byrne* itself Lord Reid found the foreseeability principle laid down by Lord Atkin in *Donoghue v. Stevenson*[9a] of little assistance: "I do not think that it has any direct bearing on this case".[10] It must be said that since the representation was treated as being made face

---

[5] *Coronation Brick (Pty.) Ltd. v. Strachan Construction Co. (Pty.) Ltd*, 1982 S.A. (4) 371 at p. 377.
[6] One may note that the German courts have also found this a difficult area of law. See B. S. Markesinis, *The German Law of Torts* (3rd ed. 1994) at pp. 42–59.
[7] *Ultramares v. Touche*, 174 N.E. 441 (1931) (Cardozo, C.J.).
[8] [1964] A.C. 465.
[9] *Spring v. Guardian Assurance* [1995] 2 A.C. 296; *Henderson v. Merrett Syndicates* [1995] 2 A.C. 145; *White v. Jones* [1995] 2 A.C. 207.
[9a] 1932 S.C. (H.L.) 31.
[10] *Hedley Byrne, supra* at p. 482.

to face, the resulting loss was clearly reasonably foreseeable. At the same time, had there been resort to the Atkin dictum, there would have been no reason to restrict its operation because there was no issue of indeterminacy. However, instead a duty was held to arise on the basis of the assumption of responsibility, reinforced by the view that the relationship of the parties had been close to contract. Lord Devlin believed that the issue in the case was "a by-product of the doctrine of consideration. If the respondents had made a nominal charge for the reference, the problem would not exist".[11] Had the case been Scottish, there might have been a contract "to be careful".[12] Lord Reid went on to conclude that an assumption of responsibility arose where "the party seeking information or advice was trusting the other to exercise such a degree of care as the circumstances required, where it was reasonable for him to do that, and where the other gave the information or advice when he knew or ought to have known that the inquirer was relying on him".[13]

Such references to reasonableness and reliance in *Hedley Byrne* might be taken to indicate that the detail of the duty would have been otherwise formulated had the test for duty been reasonable foreseeability. This can be doubted. One might, for example, readily say that it is not reasonably foreseeable that someone would rely on advice given in a social context.

Obviously reasonable foreseeability would also embrace situations beyond face to face representation. However, the current law also accepts that there may be a duty not to misrepresent despite the absence of such direct communication: a duty exists where

> "the defendant knew that his statement would be communicated to the plaintiff, either as an individual or as a member of an identifiable class, specifically in connection with a particular transaction or transactions of a particular kind . . . and that the plaintiff would be very likely to rely on it for the purpose of deciding whether or not to enter upon that transaction or upon a transaction of that kind.[14]

The cases in which house purchasers claim against surveyors in respect of mortgage valuation reports provide excellent examples.[15] In *Smith v. Bush*,[16] as in *Hedley Byrne* itself, there was no problem over indeterminacy. Again there was some suggestion that matters were akin to contract; the fact of payment by the mortgagee being crucial here.[17] On the other hand, Lord Jauncey was of the view that there was no room for contract because one already existed between the

---

[11] *ibid.* at p. 525.
[12] See the judgment of Viscount Haldane in *Robinson v. National Bank of Scotland*, 1916 S.C. (H.L.) 154.
[13] *Hedley Byrne, supra* at p. 486.
[14] *Caparo Industries v. Dickman* [1990] 2 A.C. 605 at p. 621.
[15] The position of the "indirect" names in *Henderson v. Merrett Syndicates* [1995] 2 A.C. 145 may also be placed here.
[16] [1990] 1 A.C. 831.
[17] See the judgment of Lord Templeman, *ibid.* at p. 846.

building society and the valuer. This might be thought a more realistic view, involving less in the way of contractual fictions. It also indicates that, in holding that there has been an assumption of responsibility, one is not necessarily concluding that there was almost a contract between the parties.

Moving on, one comes to a group of cases which it is more difficult to categorise and in which several judges have resorted to the notion of assumption of responsibility. It is to be hoped that *White v. Jones*[18] has ended the debate in the U.K. on the position of the "disappointed beneficiary".[19] Recovery was allowed on the basis of an extension of the notion of assumption of responsibility. However, the same result had previously been arrived at by applying the Wilberforce dictum in *Anns*: "Prima facie a duty of care was owed by the defendants to the plaintiff because it was obvious that carelessness on their part would be likely to cause damage to her."[20] Again it may be noted that it has been argued in South Africa that the *Aquilian* action can and should be extended to allow the disappointed beneficiary's claim.[21]

In *Spring v. Guardian Assurance*[22] Lord Goff regarded the basis for liability for character references as being assumption of responsibility, although the other judges in the majority regarded it as an extension of the misrepresentation cases. The basis of this extension was to be found in the presence of the requisite degree of foreseeability and proximity, and in the absence of considerations that would make it unjust to impose a duty. However, the same result had been arrived at 10 years previously by an application of *Donoghue* principles.[23]

It is submitted that, in terms of providing an underlying principle to explain cases where liability has been established, assumption of responsibility offers nothing more than reasonable foreseeability does.

No Assumption of Responsibility

What of the situations where there is no duty? Can it be said with conviction that the defender has not assumed responsibility in such cases? *Spartan Steel & Alloys v. Martin & Co. (Contractors)*,[24] where there was a claim for damage to machinery and loss of profit caused by a contractor's negligence, the pursuer was owed a duty as regards the physical loss which had arisen; and it must be said that the economic loss was just as foreseeable as the physical.[25] How can the contractor be found to undertake responsibility over the one but not the other? "The solution to such borderline cases has so far been achieved

---

[18] [1995] 2 A.C. 207.
[19] However in Scotland the decision of the House of Lords in *Robertson v. Fleming* (1861) 23 D. (H.L) 8 still presents a major obstacle.
[20] *Ross v. Caunters* [1980] Ch. 297 at p. 310.
[21] O. Rogers, "The Action of the Disappointed Beneficiary" (1986) 10 S.A.L.J. 583 at p. 614.
[22] [1995] 2 A.C. 296.
[23] *Lawton v. B.O.C.* [1987] 2 All E.R. 608.
[24] [1973] Q.B. 27.
[25] See the dissenting judgment of Edmund Davies, L.J., *ibid*; at p. 45.

pragmatically . . . not by the application of logic but by the perceived necessity as a matter of policy to place some limits—perhaps arbitrary limits—to what would otherwise be an endless, cumulative causative chain bounded only by theoretical foreseeability."[26]

Clearly where loss has been suffered as a result of injury to the person or property of someone else, the indeterminacy factor looms large.[27] Where the pursuer has suffered economic loss because of the acquisition of a defective product or the careless performance of work on his property, a duty of care will normally not be owed, though there is unlikely to be any problem of indeterminacy.[28] *Murphy v. Brentwood District Council*[29] tells us that such a loss may well be fore-seeable: "it can reasonably be foreseen that if an inherently defective . . . chattel is manufactured some future owner will be likely to sustain loss when the defect comes to light, if only because it is less valuable than it was thought to be when he bought and paid for it."[30] As the case of *Junior Books v. The Veitchi Co.*[31] demonstrates, a finding of an assumption of responsibility is possible in this situation. It seems, however, virtually certain that *Junior Books* will be overruled if an opportunity arises.[32] There is judicial disquiet on the basis that the decision intrudes on the province of the law of contract. So in *Murphy* Lord Keith was of the view that a finding of duty would be equivalent to a "transmissible warranty of quality". Again Lord Brandon's dissent in *Junior Books*, arguing that the approach of the majority was "wholly undesirable" in that it imposed "what are really contractual obligations", has also proved influential. Such arguments, it must be said, have not been found persuasive by all academic commentators.[33]

But in situations such as those contained in *Murphy* and *Junior Books*, why is it more than likely to be held that the defender no longer assumes responsibility? The approach taken in recent judgments seems to be that the contractual relationships involved are, when viewed in the round, inconsistent with a duty of care arising. In *White* Lord Mustill noted that

> "where the act or omission complained of occurs between persons who have deliberately involved themselves in a network of commercial or professional contractual relationships, such as for example may exist between the numerous parties involved in contracts for large building or engineering works, the contractual framework may be so strong, so complex and so detailed as to exclude the recognition of delictual duties between parties who are not already connected by contractual links".[34]

---

[26] *Murphy v. Brentwood D.C.* [1991] 1 A.C. 398 at p. 486.
[27] See, for example, the decision of the House of Lords in *Leigh and Sillivan v. Aliakmon Shipping Co.* [1986] A.C. 785.
[28] *cf. Parkhead Housing Association v. Phoenix Preservation*, 1990 S.L.T. 812.
[29] [1991] 1 A.C. 398.
[30] *ibid.* at p. 487.
[31] 1982 S.C. (H.L.) 244.
[32] But see J. M. Thomson, *Delictual Liability* (1994) at pp. 76–81.
[33] See, for example, P. Cane, "Economic Loss in Tort: Is the Pendulum out of Control?" (1989) 52 M.L.R. 200.
[34] [1995] 2 A.C. 207 at p. 279.

More specifically, in *Henderson v. Merrett Syndicates*[35] Lord Goff dealt with

> "the common case of an ordinary building contract, under which main contractors contract with the building owner for the construction of the relevant building, and the main contractor sub-contracts with sub-contractors or suppliers (often nominated by the building owner) for the performance of work or the supply of materials in accordance with standards and subject to terms established in the sub-contract."

Where the work or materials do not conform to standard, a duty of care will not be owed as a rule because "there is generally no assumption of responsibility by the sub-contractor or supplier direct to the building owner, the parties having so structured their relationship that it is inconsistent with any such assumption of responsibility".[36] It would be appear to be the case then that the determining factor in denying liability is the judical evaluation of the contractual matrix.

One difficulty with the "contractual matrix" approach is that, so far, there has been limited judicial elaboration of why different networks of contractual relationships should have particular implications for the law of delict. In relation to *Junior Books* Fleming has asked "whether it is wise to let tort intrude into so complex a relationship as that of the various participants in a building project under the umbrella of long-tested standard contracts."[37] The judicial answer appears to be no. However, one might go on to argue that the "matrix" approach could also be deployed to deny a remedy in negligent misrepresentation cases (other than where the misrepresentation was made "face to face"). Might not the pursuer in a case like *Smith v. Bush* be met with the defence that he has no remedy in delict because he could have contracted with the surveyor? This suggests that the contractual matrix, *per se*, reveals relatively little. It may be worth recalling the *obiter* view in *Smith* that the decision might have been different at the top end of the property market. This perhaps suggests that while the key to all this may lie in an overall evaluation of the contractual matrix, there is clearly the possibility of a period of uncertainity until there has been greater judical discourse as to why various networks of relationships should be treated differently.

Whilst negligent misrepresentation is clearly the core area for pure economic loss recovery, the existence of such a misrepresentation does not always give rise to a duty. The most famous example of this is probably *Caparo*.[38] However, this is not because of a lack of foreseeability:

> "It is, of course, equally foreseeable that potential investors having no proprietary interest in the company might well avail

---

[35] [1995] 2 A.C. 145 at pp. 195–196.
[36] *ibid.* at p. 196.
[37] J. Fleming, "Comparative Law of Torts", (1984) 4 O.J.L.S. 235 at p. 241.
[38] [1990] 2 A.C. 605.

themselves of the information contained in a company's accounts published in the newspapers or culled from an inspection of the documents to be filed annually with the Registrar of Companies ... in determining whether or not to acquire shares in the company."[39]

The denial of the existence of a duty is because of a fear of imposing liability of "an indeterminate amount for an indeterminate time to an indeterminate class."[40] What of assumption of responsibility? One is very much reminded of the judicial doubts as to whether "voluntary assumption of responsibility is a helpful or realistic test for liability."[41] It would be perfectly possible to argue that auditors do owe a duty in such a case; an argument that had proved persuasive to a majority of the Court of Appeal in *Caparo*.[42] One can only deny that a duty exists by making a value judgment on the merits of such cases. Indeed arguably the notion of assumption of responsibility is only of utility here in so far as it describes the result arrived at.

A Convenient Phrase?

It does not seem unduly cynical to conclude that the concept of "assumption of responsibility" is merely a useful device to link the group of cases where recovery for pure economic loss is permitted. Thus *Spring* suggests that there will be an assumption of responsibility "where the plaintiff entrusts the defendant with the conduct of his affairs, in general or in particular".[43] Does the concept merit anything more than the description of "convenient phrase"?[44] In most reported cases where pure economic loss has been at issue, whatever the outcome, the loss has been reasonably foreseeable. However, as Lord Oliver noted in *Caparo*, in such cases the imposition of a duty based on foreseeability is "untenable without the imposition of some intelligible limits to keep the law of negligence within the bounds of common sense and practicality".[45] The fundamental limitation of foreseeability is its inadequacy in determining the cut-off point. Does asking the question, "Has the defender assumed responsibility?", assist in this regard? This has been doubted: "it was not intended to be a test for the existence of the duty".[46]

Further evidence that the concept of assumption of responsibility is little different from foreseeability can be gleaned from some of the dicta defining the former. Lord Nolan has said that "a professional man or an artisan who undertakes to exercise his skill in a manner which, to his knowledge, may cause loss to others if carelessly per-

---

[39] *ibid.* at p. 632, *per* Lord Oliver.
[40] *ibid.* at p. 621, *per* Lord Bridge who was quoting from Cardozo, C.J. (see n. 6).
[41] *Smith v. Bush, supra, per* Lord Griffiths at p. 862.
[42] [1989] Q.B. 653.
[43] *Spring, supra, per* Lord Goff at p. 318.
[44] [1990] 2 A.C. 605 *per* Lord Oliver at p. 637.
[45] *ibid.* at p. 633.
[46] *ibid.* at p. 637.

formed, may thereby implicitly assume a legal responsibility towards them".[47] If one scrutinises this dictum more closely, it does not seem radically different from the Atkin dictum. After all, the requirement of carelessness takes us back to foreseeability, and the case law also tells us that the word "undertake" does not mean that there must be a contract.[48] It is worth highlighting the fact that any assumption of responsibility may be implicit:

> "the assumption of responsibility referred to is the defendant's assumption of responsibility for the task, not the assumption of legal liability. Even in cases of ad hoc relationships, it is the undertaking to answer the question posed which creates the relationship. If responsibility for the task is assumed by the defendant he thereby creates a special relationship between himself and the plaintiff in relation to which the law (not the defendant) attaches a duty to carry out carefully the task so assumed."[49]

In *Donoghue* Lord Atkin refers to those who are so "closely and directly affected" by one's behaviour that one ought to have them in contemplation. Equally it seems that by engaging in certain acts which cause someone else economic loss one is taken to have assumed responsibility. The similarity in role is also evident in the following dictum, expressing a duty in respect of physical injury in terms of assumption of responsibility:

> "If the defendant drives his car on the highway, he implicitly assumes a responsibility towards other road users, and they in turn implicitly rely on him to discharge that responsibility. By taking his car on to the road, he holds himself out as a reasonably careful driver."[50]

The obligation said to be owed is entirely uncontroversial, but one might have expected it to be couched in the language of reasonable foreseeability.

The Duty of Care Question

The plethora of economic loss cases and the difficulties they have given rise to in terms of producing criteria for liability lead one to reappraise the approach to duty of care in general. In *Dorset Yacht* Lord Reid stated that the Atkin dictum ought to apply "unless there is some justification or valid explanation for its exclusion".[51] Are we

---

[47] *White v. Jones, supra* at p. 294.
[48] So in *Hedley Byrne* itself while it was held that the defendant would have assumed responsibility towards the plaintiff, had it not been for the disclaimer, there was no question of there being any contract between the parties.
[49] *White v. Jones, supra* at p. 273 *per* Lord Browne-Wilkinson.
[50] *ibid.* at pp. 293–294, *per* Lord Nolan.
[51] [1970] A.C. 1004 at p. 1027.

any further forward now in testing the existence of any duty of care? Both the Atkin dictum and the concept of assumption of responsibility provide much more guidance in terms of inclusion rather than exclusion. Both tell us little about the boundaries of recovery. This is not to say that no progress has been made in this area. The volume of economic loss cases has made it much easier to predict the result in any given case. The reaction to *Anns* and *Dorset Yacht* is to a large extent explained by their slant in favour of expanding liability. But this can be corrected without becoming embroiled in the cumbersome and often opaque three-stage approach adopted in recent cases such as *Marc Rich v. Bishop Rock Marine*.[52] Twenty-five years after *Dorset Yacht*, I would submit that there is no reason why foreseeability should not be able to play the role of *prima facie* test of liability. What is required is an element of refinement making it clearer that policy factors may outweigh a conclusion reached simply on the basis of foreseeability. It might also be argued that reasonable foreseeability is not adequate even as a tool of inclusion. After all, the Law Lords tell us that before a duty over misrepresentation is owed the situation must fall within Lord Bridge's definition in *Caparo*. However, once a situation is recognised as giving rise to liability, it is likely to be subject to more detailed definition. This process will be undergone irrespective of whether the basis of liability was assumption of responsibility or foreseeability.

Mapping the Policy?

Bill Wilson's analysis of negligence commendably rejects unnecessary detail and clearly identifies and expounds the core concepts. On the test for duty, it is suggested that Lord Reid's judgment in *Dorset Yacht* may require refinement but is essentially sound. Moving to "Mapping Economic Loss", there is limited reference to the policy considerations that arise in economic loss claims. Might it be profitable to map them too? The idea in doing so would be to identify areas in which the rules of economic loss recovery might be liable to change. Where might such areas lie? What would happen if loss is suffered as a result of injury to another's property on which you are dependent and where you are the only foreseeable victim? Given the importance of indeterminacy in misrepresentation cases, one might have thought that this was a volatile area. Thus in the *Coronation Brick (Pty)*[53] case, where the situation was similar to *Spartan Steel*, the South African court applied the *Caltex*[54] approach, *viz*, the requisite degree of proximity arose by virtue of the fact that the plaintiff was foreseeable as a specific individual or at least as a member of an ascertained class. Again the language of *Caltex* is similar to that used in the misrepresentation cases to mark the boundaries of recovery. Nevertheless indeterminacy is not the only policy consideration. It may well be that in

[52] [1995] 3 W.L.R. 227 (H.L.).
[53] 1982 S.A. (4) 371.
[54] *Caltex Oil (Australia) Pty. Ltd v. Dredge "Willemstad"* (1976) 136 C.L.R. 529.

a situation like *Spartan Steel* the loss should lie where it falls.[55] Moreover, the reasoning in *Caltex* has not proved attractive to the British courts so far: "is the single company which uses a bridge for the purposes of its business to recover damages when the bridge is damaged and rendered unusable, but not a number of companies which use another bridge similarly damaged?"[56] Again, in *Candlewood Navigation Corporation v. Mitsui OSK Lines* the Privy Council took the view that "apart from cases of negligent misstatement . . . they do not consider that it is practicable by reference to an ascertained class to find a satisfactory control mechanism which could be applied in such a way as to give reasonable certainty in its results".[57]

What of a situation involving "transferred loss"? This idea was floated by Lord Goff in *Leigh and Sillivan*, but was rejected by his brethren in the House of Lords.[58] It is similar to the German doctrine of *Drittschadensliquidation* "which allows a creditor to a contract to claim (in contract) for loss resulting from the non-execution or bad execution of the contract, which falls not upon him (the creditor) but upon a third party."[59] The problem which particularly troubled Lord Goff in the case has been solved by the Carriage of Goods by Sea Act 1992. However, might the principle be resorted to elsewhere? Analogous reasoning might be invoked in a situation such as arose in *Candlewood*. One might regard the 1992 Act as legislative endorsement of the concept of transferred loss. A further possibility for development lies in the concept of a joint venture.[60] This might be supported by the decision in *Morrison Steamship v. Greystoke Castle*[61]; in *Murphy* Lord Keith stated that "there is room for the view that an exception [to the irrecoverability of economic loss] is to be found in *Morrison Steamship* . . . That case, which was decided by a narrow majority, may, however, be regarded as turning on specialities of maritime law concerned with the relationship of joint ventures at sea".

Probably of greatest interest is the disparity of treatment between defective product/work cases and other cases involving professional services. Would it be convincing to deny recovery in a situation such as the one in *Greater Nottingham Co-operative Society v. Cementation Piling and Foundations*[62] on the basis of the contractual matrix while allowing the plaintiff in *Smith* to recover? How principled is it to say that it is legitimate to interfere in one network of contractual relations but not in the other? It is suggested that greater elucidation of the relevant policy factors is called for. There is undoubtedly a danger that unless the courts can provide more detailed elaboration of the material differences between such relationships then the law will enter a rather volatile phase.

---

[55] *e.g.*, see the policy reasons articulated by Lord Denning in *Spartan Steel*.
[56] *Leigh and Sillivan v. Aliakmon Shipping Co.* [1985] 2 All E.R. 44 *per* Goff, L.J. at p. 74 (CA).
[57] [1986] 1 A.C. 1 at p. 24.
[58] [1986] A.C. 785.
[59] Markesinis, *German Law of Torts*, p. 55.
[60] *e.g.*, see *Main v. Leask*, 1910 S.C. 772. Oddly enough this case is not mentioned in Wilson, "Mapping Economic Loss".
[61] [1947] A.C. 265.
[62] [1989] Q.B. 71.

THE UNDUE INFLUENCE OF ENGLISH LAW?

EWAN MCKENDRICK

Clarity of analysis was one of the hallmarks of Bill Wilson's work. It was a quality which we have all admired but have found impossible to emulate. Allied to his analytical skills was a concern, especially latterly, for the preservation of Scots law as a distinctive system and to draw attention to the dangers of inappropriate borrowing from English law. These two issues go together. A legal system which has no concern for principle and which borrows uncritically from other jurisdictions will always be in difficulty or, in Wilson's words, "a legal system which has no doctrinal foundation must drift".[1]

These observations prompt me to begin with a confession. As a graduate of the University of Edinburgh who has "defected" to the extent that I now bear the title of Professor of English Law at University College London, I must concede that I am not the best qualified person to discuss the future of Scots law as a distinctive system. Indeed, the charge of being an "angliciser" may not be far from the minds of some readers. Yet I believe that it is not "borrowing" which is the evil but *inappropriate* borrowing. In an increasingly interdependent world we have much to learn from each other and one would expect citations from other jurisdictions to increase, not decrease.[2] A rule should not be rejected simply because of its jurisdictional origin. It must stand or fall in the light of its ability to withstand analysis and in the light of its "fit" within the existing legal framework.

The subject-matter of this essay is, in fact, an example of Scots law refusing to borrow from English law. Its focus is on the decision of the House of Lords in *Barclays Bank p.l.c. v. O'Brien*[3] and the recent refusal of the First Division of the Inner House of the Court of Session to follow it in *Mumford v. Bank of Scotland*.[4] *O'Brien*, together with its sister case, *CIBC Mortgages p.l.c. v. Pitt*[5] has given rise to a deluge of

---

[1] "The Importance of Analysis" in D. L. Carey Miller and D. W. Meyers (eds.) *Comparative and Historical Essays in Scots Law* (1992) p. 171.

[2] An excellent example of "borrowing" from or drawing on the learning of other jurisdictions (as well as careful analysis of the historical development of Scots law itself) is provided by the decision of the Inner House of the Court of Session in *Morgan Guaranty Trust Co. of New York v. Lothian Regional Council*, 1995 S.L.T. 299.

[3] [1994] 1 A.C. 180.

[4] 1995 S.C.L.R. 839, affirming the decision of Lord Johnston in the Outer House (1994 S.L.T. 1288). The Second Division had previously referred to *O'Brien* without disapproval in *McCabe v. Skipton Building Society*, 1994 S.L.T. 1272, but the reference was held by Lord Johnston to be *obiter* and it was not considered by the First Division on the reclaiming motion in *Mumford*.

[5] [1994] 1 A.C. 200.

case law[6] and academic commentary[7] in England and it could be said
that Scots law has done well to avoid being caught up in the mael-
strom. But it is suggested that *O'Brien* and its successors do give rise
to some difficult issues both of analysis and of policy and that Scots
lawyers can look with some profit at the issues which have been aired
in the recent English case law.

O'Brien and *Mumford*: The Facts

The fact situation in *Barclays Bank v. O'Brien* was relatively straightforward. Mr O'Brien negotiated an overdraft with Barclays for a
company in which he had an interest. It was agreed that Mr O'Brien
would guarantee the company's indebtedness and that his liability
would, in turn, be secured by a second charge on the matrimonial
home. The bank manager asked the branch at which the security
documents were to be signed to ensure that the O'Briens were
"fully aware of the nature of the documentation to be signed and
advised that if they are in any doubt they should contact their
solicitor before signing."[8] These instructions were not complied with
and Mrs O'Brien was given no explanation of the effect of the
documents before she signed them, nor was she advised of the
need to take independent advice. When the company's indebtedness
rose to £154,000 the bank demanded that Mr O'Brien honour the
guarantee. When he failed to do so, the bank sought to enforce the
charge which Mrs O'Brien had signed and to obtain possession of
the house. Mrs O'Brien sought to defend the claim on the ground
that she had been induced to sign the charge by the undue influence of her husband and by his misrepresentation that the charge
was limited to £60,000 and that its duration was to be confined to
a short period of time. The claim based on undue influence was
rejected in the Court of Appeal and was not pursued in the House
of Lords, where the claim to set aside the transaction was based
on the misrepresentation of Mr O'Brien, of which it was argued, in
the event successfully, that the bank had constructive notice so that
it could not enforce the charge against Mrs O'Brien.

---

[6] A recent LEXIS search threw up over 30 citations of *Barclays Bank v. O'Brien*. The
leading post-*O'Brien* cases include *Halifax Building Society v. Brown* [1995] 3 F.C.R.
110; *Midland Bank p.l.c. v. Serter* [1995] 1 F.L.R. 1034; *Castle Phillips Finance Ltd. v.
Piddington* [1995] 1 F.L.R. 783; *Banco Exterior Internacional v. Mann* [1995] 1 All E.R.
936; *Midland Bank p.l.c. v. Massey* [1995] 1 All E.R. 929; *Bank of Baroda v. Rayarel* [1995]
2 F.C.R. 631 and *Goode Durrant Administration v. Biddulph* [1994] 2 F.L.R. 551.

[7] Useful examples of such analysis are provided by, amongst others, R. Hooley,
"Taking Security After O'Brien", [1995] L.M.C.L.Q. 346; A. Lawson, "O'Brien and its
Legacy: Principle, Equity and Certainty?" [1995] C.L.J. 280; G. Battersby, "Equitable
Fraud Committed by Third Parties", (1995) 15 L.S. 35; S. H. Goo, "Enforceability of
Securities and Guarantees after O'Brien", (1995) 15 O.J.L.S. 119, and S. Cretney, "Mere
Puppets, Folly and Imprudence: Undue Influence for the Twenty-First Century",
[1994] R.L.R. 3.

[8] [1994] 1 A.C. at p. 184.

On the other hand, in *Mumford v. Bank of Scotland*[9] the two pursuers were two wives who were induced to execute a standard security over the matrimonial home in favour of the defender bank as a result of false or misleading misrepresentations made by their husbands. It was held that, in the absence of actual notice of the husbands' misrepresentations, the bank was not affected by their wrongdoing and was not prevented from enforcing the security.

The Basis of *O'Brien*

There are three essential stages to the reasoning of the House of Lords in *O'Brien*.

Setting aside "the transaction" against the husband

At the first stage, the defendant must show that she is entitled to set aside the transaction against her husband. Any vitiating factor would probably suffice, but the two which have featured in the case law are misrepresentation and undue influence. Misrepresentation is relatively straightforward in the present context but undue influence has given rise to greater difficulty and a number of significant points have been clarified in the course of this line of authority. The first is that in cases of actual undue influence, the party seeking to set aside the transaction is not required to show that the transaction was manifestly disadvantageous.[10] The basis for this conclusion is that actual undue influence is a species of fraud and that, once a plaintiff has proved actual wrongdoing, there is no need to assume the additional obligation of showing manifest disadvantage. The second is that the requirement of manifest disadvantage has come under pressure, even in the context of cases of presumed undue influence.[11] The third is that, although the relationship of husband and wife does not, of itself, give rise to what in English law would be termed a presumption of undue influence, the courts now appear to be readier to conclude that a wife has reposed trust and confidence in her husband in relation to their financial affairs, so that undue influence can be presumed.[12]

When is the bank put on notice?

The second stage is to show that the bank has been put on notice of the possibility of wrongdoing on the part of the husband. It is not every transaction between husband and wife which puts the bank on notice. The transaction must "on its face"[13] not be to the financial

---

[9] 1995 S.C.L.R. 839.
[10] *CIBC Mortgages p.l.c. v. Pitt* [1994] 1 A.C. 200.
[11] In his judgment in *Pitt* Lord Browne-Wilkinson drew attention (at p. 209) to the "abuse of confidence" cases where there is no such requirement and the onus of proof is on the party seeking to uphold the transaction to show that it was a fair one. There would appear to be a significant degree of overlap between the two groups of cases and the difference in treatment appears hard to justify.
[12] *Barclays Bank p.l.c. v. O'Brien* [1994] 1 AC at p. 190; *Banco Exterior Internacional v. Mann* [1995] 1 All E.R. 936.
[13] [1994] 1 A.C. at p. 190.

advantage of the wife. The bank does not appear to be under an obligation to look beyond the papers to the real purpose or motive behind the application for a loan. Thus a joint loan application, the stated purpose of which was to fund the purchase of a second home, did not suffice to put the bank on notice, even though the money was, in fact, used by the husband to finance his investment activities on the Stock Exchange.[14] While this requirement has been criticised,[15] it does have the merit of laying down a relatively clear rule without putting the bank on notice of undue influence in every transaction between a husband and a wife.[16] But it should not be thought that banks are only put on notice where the parties are married. The test to be applied is that there must be a substantial risk that one party has committed a legal or equitable wrong that entitles the weaker party to set aside the transaction.[17] While this most obviously applies within the context of the marriage relationship, it is not so confined. In *O'Brien* Lord Browne-Wilkinson appeared to indicate that cohabitation, whether heterosexual or homosexual, was a pre-requisite,[18] but the Court of Appeal has since held that it extends to cases whether there was no cohabitation between the debtor and the surety, but there was "a stable sexual and emotional relationship over many years" and the parties had two children.[19] It may also apply to a case, such as *Avon Finance Co. Ltd v. Bridger*,[20] where an adult son persuaded his elderly parents to act as a surety for his debts. But in such cases it would appear that the creditor must have actual knowledge of the fact that the surety reposes trust and confidence in the principal debtor: constructive notice will not here suffice.

What must the bank do once it has been put on notice?
The third stage relates to the steps which a bank must take, once it has been put on notice, to ensure that the agreement of the wife to the charge was properly obtained. In his judgment in *O'Brien*, Lord Browne-Wilkinson distinguished between "past transactions"[21] and "future transactions", laying down more onerous requirements in the latter than in the former. The emphasis in his speech was on the steps which the bank itself must take to bring home to the wife the risk which she is running by standing as surety. In relation to "future

---

[14] *CIBC Mortgages p.l.c. v. Pitt* [1994] 1 A.C. 200 at p. 211.
[15] See, e.g. B. Fehlberg, "The Husband, the Bank, the Wife and her Signature", (1994) 57 M.L.R. 467 at pp. 473–474 and, with rather more hesitation, Cretney, "Mere Puppets", *supra* at pp. 7–8.
[16] Although difficulties have begun to emerge in cases where the wife is (nominally) a director and shareholder of the family company the loans to which are the subject of the guarantee: see, *e.g.*, *Bank of Credit and Commerce International S.A. v. Aboody* [1990] 1 Q.B. 923 and the different approaches taken in *Goode Durrant Administration v. Biddulph* [1994] 2 F.L.R. 551 and at first instance in *Halifax Mortgage Services Ltd v. Stepsky* [1995] 3 W.L.R. 701 at p. 708.
[17] [1994] 1 A.C. at p 196.
[18] *ibid.*, at p. 198.
[19] *Midland Bank p.l.c. v. Massey* [1995] 1 All E.R. 929 at p. 933.
[20] [1985] 2 All E.R. 281, as approved by Lord Browne-Wilkinson in *O'Brien* [1994] 1 A.C. 180 at p. 198.
[21] That is, transactions entered into before October 21, 1993.

transactions" this required the bank to hold a private meeting with the wife at which she would be told of the extent of her liability as surety, warned of the risk she was running and urged[22] to take independent legal advice. But the Court of Appeal has since noted that the "guidance" which was offered by Lord Browne-Wilkinson was "not intended to be exhaustive", nor was it to be "mechanically applied".[23] In subsequent cases, the vital issue has proved to be, not the role of the banks themselves in advising the wife, but the role of the solicitors appointed to advise the wife. The attitude which has been adopted by the Court of Appeal in a number of cases has been that it is sufficient for the bank to advise the weaker party to obtain independent legal advice and the bank is then "entitled to assume (in the absence of clear indications to the contrary) that the solicitor who did advise was honest and competent.[24] This has been held to be the case even where the solicitor was chosen by the principal debtor[25] and in cases where the principal debtor has attended the interview between the solicitor and the surety.[26] The bank is entitled to assume that the solicitor will decide for himself whether or not he can act in the best interests of the surety and, if he takes it upon himself to carry out the task of advising the surety, the bank is entitled to assume that he has done it honestly and competently.[27]

Criticisms of O'Brien

There are a number of technical problems with the reasoning of the House of Lords in O'Brien. The first is that it adopts a "two transaction" approach rather than a "one transaction" analysis. Lord Browne-Wilkinson insists that the wife must first be able to set aside "the transaction" as against her husband before she is entitled to set it aside against the bank. Yet it is not at all clear what transaction has

[22] In certain "exceptional" cases where the creditor has knowledge that undue influence is not only "possible but probable", the creditor to be safe will have to "insist" that the wife is separately advised, per Lord Browne-Wilkinson in O'Brien at p. 197.
[23] Midland Bank p.l.c. v. Massey [1995] 1 All E.R. 929 at p. 934. See to similar effect the judgment of Morritt, L.J. in Banco Exterior Internacional v. Mann [1995] 1 All E.R. 936 at p. 943.
[24] per Morritt, L.J. in Banco Exterior Internacional v. Mann [1995] 1 All E.R. 936 at p. 944.
[25] As was the case in both Midland Bank p.l.c. v. Massey [1995] 1 All E.R. 929 and Banco Exterior Internacional v. Mann [1995] 1 All E.R. 936.
[26] As was the case in both Midland Bank p.l.c. v. Massey [1995] 1 All E.R. 929 and Banco Exterior Internacional v. Mann [1995] 1 All E.R. 936.
[27] But it should be noted that in both cases the bank sent the instructions directly to the solicitor and required the solicitor to witness the charge and return it directly to the bank. The position may well be otherwise if the bank entrusts the relevant documentation to the principal debtor. Difficulties may also arise for banks in future cases if it can be maintained that the solicitor is the agent of the bank and his knowledge should be attributed to the bank. The latter argument was rejected by the Court of Appeal in Midland Bank p.l.c. v. Serter [1995] 1 F.L.R. 1034 and in Halifax Mortage Services Ltd v. Stepsky [1996] 2 W.L.R. 230 (in the latter case the court based its decision, not on common law or equitable principles, but on s. 199(1) (ii)(b) of the Law of Property Act 1925), but found rather more favour in Bank of Credit and Commerce International S.A. v. Aboody [1990] 1 Q.B. 923 and in Allied Irish Bank p.l.c. v. Byrne [1995] 2 F.L.R. 325.

taken place between the husband and wife. This is especially so where the wife is the sole owner of the matrimonial home and it is used to guarantee her husband's debts. In such a case, is there any transaction at all between the husband and the wife? The focus should be on the transaction between the wife and the bank and not on some fictitious transaction which is created as between the husband and the wife. The second is that the invocation of notice has been criticised on two distinct grounds. The first is that it is alleged that notice is being used in an unnatural sense[28] and the second is that objections have been raised to the extension of constructive notice into the realm of commercial transactions.[29] The third problem is that the requirements imposed by the House of Lords in *O'Brien* and *Pitt*[30] seem more apposite for cases of misrepresentation than for cases of undue influence. The requirement that more information be disclosed to wives should reduce the incidence of misrepresentations of the type which were made in *O'Brien*.[31] But the guidelines do not appear to be particularly well suited to freeing the wife from the influence of her husband. And that is the problem which wives face in cases of undue influence; it is not a lack of comprehension but the inability to bring an independent mind to the wisdom of entering into the transaction.[32] Had the position of the bank been equated with the position of the party alleged to have exercised the undue influence, it is clear that banks would not have been able effectively to shift the obligation to advise the wife on to the shoulders of solicitors but would have had to take greater steps to ensure that the wife was independently advised prior to entering into the transaction.[33]

The final problem with *O'Brien* concerns the remedial consequences of a finding that the bank has constructive notice and has failed to take reasonable steps. This point did not emerge with any clarity from *O'Brien* itself, but it has subsequently been held that the charge must be set aside in its entirety as the court has no power to rewrite the terms of the guarantee.[34] This can result in the over-protection of the

---

[28] See, *e.g.* J. Mee, "Undue Influence, Misrepresentation and the Doctrine of Notice", [1995] C.L.J. 536, esp. pp. 541–543, and W. Swadling, [1993] All E.R. Review, pp. 366–367; *cf.* the discussion by Battersby, "Equitable Fraud", *supra*, at pp. 41–43.

[29] The courts have traditionally been reluctant to accord constructive notice a significant (or any) role in commercial transactions (see, *e.g. Joseph v. Lyons* (1884) 15 Q.B.D. 280 and *English and Scottish Mercantile Investment Co. Ltd v. Brunton* [1892] 2 Q.B. 700). What is generally required is actual notice, not constructive notice.

[30] And by the Court of Appeal in *Midland Bank p.l.c. v. Massey* [1995] 1 All E.R. 929 and *Banco Exterior Internacional v. Mann* [1995] 1 All E.R. 936.

[31] Although it may not affect the type of misrepresentation in *Massey* which related to the financial viability of the company in which the principal debtor had an interest, rather than the nature of the charge itself.

[32] As pointed out by Hobhouse, L. J. in his dissenting judgment in *Banco Exterior Internacional v. Mann* [1995] 1 All E.R. 936 at p. 948.

[33] See, *e.g. Inche Noriah v. Shaik Allie Bin Omar* [1929] A.C. 127 at pp. 135–136 where inadequate legal advice given to the party seeking to set aside the transaction and obtained by the party alleged to have exercised the undue influence was held not to be sufficient to rebut the presumption of undue influence.

[34] *T.S.B. Bank p.l.c. v. Camfield* [1995] 1 W.L.R. 430. The point had previously been the subject of conflicting first instance decisions. In *Bank Melli Iran v. Samadi-Rad* [1995] 2 F.L.R. 367 it was held that the charge could be set aside in part, while in *Allied Irish Bank v. Byrne* [1995] 2 F.L.R. 325 it was held that the court could not set aside

wife to the extent that she can be given full relief even though she would have entered into the transaction on more limited terms had the true position been made known to her.

The *Mumford* Analysis

Two points can be made about *Mumford* by way of introduction. The first is that it was a misrepresentation, not an undue influence case.[35] The second was that the court did not employ a "two transaction" analysis of the type used in *O'Brien*. Rather, it analysed the issues in terms of the relationship between the bank and the cautioners and did not consider first whether the wives were entitled to set aside the "transactions" as against their husbands.[36]

Thus the vital question for the court was whether the circumstances were such as to put the bank on inquiry. If they were, and the bank failed to carry out that inquiry, the court would have held that the bank was in bad faith and so was barred from enforcing the securities as against the cautioners. However the court held that it was only where the bank had actual knowledge of misrepresentations by the principal or of other circumstances leading to a suspicion of fraud that the duty of inquiry arose. Neither requirement was satisfied on the facts of the case. The fact that the transactions were not on their face to the financial advantage of the wives and that English law regards the relationship between husband and wife as one in which there is a substantial risk of wrongdoing by the husband were not sufficient to trigger the existence of a duty of inquiry on the part of the bank, at least as far as Scots law is concerned.

The merits of this analysis are that it is consistent with two generally accepted principles of law. The first is that a cautioner is expected to satisfy himself or herself as to the extent of the risk proposed to be undertaken and it is not the responsibility of the creditor to explain to the cautioner the nature of the obligation which he or she has assumed.[37] The second is that, as a general rule, a person is bound by his signature.[38] On the other hand, *O'Brien* is difficult to reconcile with these principles and could be said to have imposed by the back-door

the charge on terms. The latter view has now prevailed. But contrast the views of P. Ferguson, "Partial Rescission for Misrepresentation Rejected" (1995) 111 L.Q.R. 555 who points out the different route which equity has taken in the line of cases beginning with *Bristol and West Building Society v. Henning* [1985] 1 W.L.R. 778 and suggests that there is room for the argument that the wife should be estopped from claiming rescission except in so far as her liability exceeds the sum which she was prepared to guarantee.

[35] Although the same could be said of *O'Brien*, the House of Lords did have some justification for engaging in an analysis of the law of undue influence given that its sister case, *Pitt*, was an undue influence case.

[36] One reason for this may have been that it was so clear that the wives had such a right that the point was simply assumed.

[37] *Young v. Clydesdale Bank* (1889) 17 R. 231 and *Royal Bank of Scotland v. Greenshields*, 1914 S.C. 259. The same principle applies in English law: see *Barclays Bank p.l.c. v. O'Brien* [1994] 1 A.C. 180 at p. 193.

[38] *L'Estrange v. F. Graucob Ltd* [1934] 2 K.B. 394.

a "limited duty of explanation and advice" owed by creditors to "a limited class of non-commercial, would-be sureties".[39]

Criticisms of *Mumford*

Yet the decision in *Mumford* is not free from criticism either. The first criticism can be dealt with quickly. It relates to the fact that the court chose not to develop the common law rules but left any reform of the duties owed by creditors to prospective cautioners to Parliament after detailed consideration of the issues by the Scottish Law Commission. But the English experience post-*O'Brien* suggests that such judicial caution has much to commend it. For *O'Brien* has given rise to an unsatisfactory degree of commercial uncertainty but done little for the plight of women in that they still lose their homes to the banks, albeit for different reasons. Nevertheless there is an issue of some importance to be explored here. It concerns the scope of the judicial function in the development of the common law in an era when legislation tends to be the dominant source of law. The perceived judicial conservatism in developing private law stands in stark contrast to the much-criticised activism of the judiciary which is being demonstrated in the public law arena. Has the appetite of legislators for intervention and the availability of the Law Commissions as law reform bodies had the effect of reducing the willingness of the judiciary to develop and adapt private law? The decision of the Inner House in *Morgan Guaranty Trust Co. of New York v. Lothian Regional Council*[40] shows that a reference to the Scottish Law Commission need not impede the development of the common law and can, in fact, assist in its rational development. But in other areas the picture is not so clear.[41] More analysis of this relationship is required.

The second criticism is of more substance. It relates to the court's analysis of undue influence. In the first place, undue influence was not strictly speaking in point. The issue should have been framed in terms of whether the bank was put on notice of the husbands' misrepresentations. Secondly, the court's analysis of undue influence itself is somewhat disappointing. Too much is left to the facts of the case and insufficient attention is paid to the juridical basis of the doctrine. Yet the existence and scope of the doctrine of undue influence in Scots law is in desperate need of analysis.

In relation to the *existence* of the doctrine, the point could be taken that undue influence is an alien doctrine in Scots law, having been imported from the English chancery courts.[42] But jurisdictional origins

---

[39] *Chitty on Contracts* (27th ed. 1994), vol. II, para. 42–019.

[40] 1995 S.L.T. 299.

[41] *e.g.*, it could be argued that the English Court of Appeal in *Re Selectmove* [1995] 1 W.L.R. 474 used the existence of the Law Commission as a partial excuse for not addressing a thorny issue head-on (see, in particular, p. 481), although, in fairness to the court they could do little else consistently with the doctrine of precedent.

[42] See, *e.g.*, T. B. Smith, "English Influences on the Law of Scotland", in *Studies Critical and Comparative* (1962), and W. H. Winder, "Undue Influence in English and Scots Law" (1940) 56 L.Q.R. 97.

should not be allowed to mask difficult substantive issues. For the fact remains that all legal systems, Scotland included, must address the grounds on which a contract can be set aside. And that requires the courts to grapple with such potential grounds of invalidity as "influence", "pressure" "domination" and "exploitation". In relation to the *scope* of undue influence, it must be said that the law is shrouded in uncertainty. Substantially the same point can be made about English law. Take the word "undue". What does it mean? Does it mean "too much" or does it mean "illegitimate" or "wrongful"? And what about "influence"? Is it the same as pressure or does it encompass more subtle forms of domination? Further, is the focus of the doctrine upon the "excessive dependency" of the weaker party or does its basis lie in some wrongful conduct or exploitation on the part of the defendant? These are difficult questions and they cannot be answered within the scope of this essay. But it is suggested that there are three principal bases for intervention in these cases. The first is that the defender has applied "illegitimate pressure" to the pursuer. These cases should be dealt with under the heading of duress (or force and fear if one wishes to retain traditional terminology). They are not the stuff of the undue influence cases. The second is that the defendant has been guilty of unconscionable conduct or has exploited the weakness and vulnerability of the pursuer. The invocation of a doctrine of unconscionable conduct as a ground of relief in the *O'Brien* type case has proved popular in the southern hemisphere[43] but has not enjoyed much success elsewhere. There are some suggestions in the Scottish cases on undue influence that there must be some "abuse of a position of trust"[44] for there to be undue influence, although the doctrine of "facility and circumvention" seems rather more apposite for the task of identifying unconscionable conduct which seeks to exploit the weakness of another. It must be a question for further discussion whether the doctrine can be expanded so as to encompass all forms of exploitation of positions of weakness.[45] The third possible basis for intervention is the pursuer's excessive dependence upon, or reposing of trust and confidence in, the defender. If the latter view is accepted then the undue influence cases can be aligned with the capacity cases where knowledge by the other party of the inapacity is not generally required.[46] A powerful case has recently been made in England for the recognition of such a plaintiff (or pursuer)-sided version of undue influence.[47] Of course there is no need for a legal system to choose between these three bases. It can recognise all three. But, if it does

---

[43] See, *e.g.*, *Commercial Bank of Australia Ltd. v. Amadio* (1983) 151 C.L.R. 447 and *Akins v. National Australia Bank* (1994) 34 NSWLR 155.

[44] See, *e.g.*, *Forbes v. Forbes's Trs.*, 1957 S.C. 325 at p. 335, and *Honeyman's Ex. v. Sharp*, 1978 S.C. 223 at p. 230.

[45] The definition of "facility" would appear to be too narrow at present to achieve a broader role, although it may yet be open to development, as demonstrated by *Anderson v. The Beacon Fellowship*, 1992 S.L.T. 111; but see n. 48 below. See also W. W. McBryde *The Law of Contract in Scotland* (1987), paras. 11–01–11–29.

[46] See, *e.g.*, *John Loudon & Co. v. Elder's C.B.* 1923 S.L.T. 226.

[47] P. Birks and Chin Nyuk Yin, "On the Nature of Undue Influence", in J. Beatson and D. Friedmann (eds.), *Good Faith and Fault in Contract Law* (1995).

so, it must be made clear in each individual case which ground of intervention is being invoked: otherwise the result will be a muddle.[48] And here Scots law would be wise to continue to avoid reliance upon the "presumption" of undue influence which English law employs because the cases are not always clear about what it is that is being presumed: is it the excessive dependence or is it the wrongful conduct of the defender? The court must spell out the basis of its relief, not hide it behind a presumption.

Conclusion

While the development of the law relating to undue influence is of importance to both Scots and English law, in the final analysis it must be said that the vital issue in both *O'Brien* and *Mumford* is the relationship between the bank and the cautioner and not the relationship between the cautioner and the principal debtor. Unless the principal debtor is the agent of the bank, a construction which is unlikely to be adopted in either Scotland or England,[49] the principal debtor should not loom large in the inquiry. *Mumford* is therefore right in its choice of focus but more questionable in its characterisation of the relationship between cautioner and creditor. The bargaining weakness and relative ignorance of many cautioners today may suggest that more onerous obligations both of disclosure and explanation should be placed upon the shoulders of creditors (although it is a matter for consideration whether such a duty should give rise to a claim for damages or only prevent enforcement of the security). Alternatively, what may be required is some form of "legislative restriction on the granting of security on a family home for purposes other than its acquisition."[50] In the resolution of these difficult questions of analysis and policy, the voice of Bill Wilson will be sorely missed.

---

[48] A muddle was arguably the outcome in *Anderson v. The Beacon Fellowship*, 1992 S.L.T. 111, where the relationship between undue influence and facility and circumvention was not at all clear, nor was it clear what the relationship was between the pursuer-sided factors (such as weakness) and the defender-sided factors (such as exploitation). The relationship between these factors must be spelt out with much greater clarity.

[49] In Scotland see *McCabe v. Skipton Building Society* 1994 S.L.T. 1272 and in England see *Barclays Bank p.l.c. v. O'Brien* [1994] 1 A.C. at p. 195.

[50] *Chitty on Contracts*, Vol. II, para. 33–320.

PUBLIC LAW—IN PERIL OF NEGLECT?

C. M. G. Himsworth*

Introduction

"So a private lawyer neglects public law at his peril."[1]

This was how Bill Wilson concluded his chapter on "The Study of Scots Law" in his *Introductory Essays on Scots Law*. He was concerned to explain that, in many important areas, rules with a private law origin were greatly affected by public law rules governing the relationship between the state and the individual and he went on to say that, "although public law is on the whole United Kingdom law, points peculiar to Scotland do crop up from time to time because public law cannot be completely separated from private law."[2]

The aim of this article is to explore briefly what it has meant for the public law of Scotland to be "on the whole United Kingdom law"; to take account of continuing points of divergence between Scots law and English law in matters of public law; and to consider how far the surviving distinctiveness of Scots law rules can or should be sustained in the face of demands for uniformity of provision across the United Kingdom and much more importantly across Europe.

Underlying these questions are other more general questions about the coherence and co-existence of systems of law. The case for the sustainability of Scots law as a distinct system of law focuses almost exclusively on Scots law in its private law aspects and, in the making of that case, there is an assumption that no problem is raised simply by virtue of the co-existence within the same state of two or more bodies of private law. It is a phenomenon well-known in other parts of the world where the meeting of civilian and common law systems or of "modern" and "traditional" or of religious and secular systems also produce the circumstances of co-existence. These are by no means always happy circumstances and there is often a need for quite complex rules for governing relationships at the interface between systems, varying according to whether the divisions are geographically or community based. No one appears to doubt, however, that states can accommodate systemic diversity of private law. But, in relation to a state's own law—its public law, can one sensibly talk of a diversity of "systems", each capable of internal coherence, within the same state? Or is one instead confined to noting a limited diversity of pro-

---

* I am very pleased to acknowledge the help of my colleagues, Peter Cullen, Robert Lane, Colin Munro and Neil Walker in the preparation of this essay.
[1] W. A. Wilson *Introductory Essays on Scots Law* (2nd ed. 1984) at p. 9.
[2] *ibid.*

vision, whether imposed or merely tolerated, whether relatively unstructured or (as in a federal state) more structured, within a single "system" of public law? How far, for these purposes, is the European Union best regarded as a state?

Scots Public Law in the United Kingdom

It will be helpful to start by identifying a number of strands which have been detectable in discussion of the distinctiveness of Scottish public law:

1. There has, in the first place, been the position from which, historically at least, it has been argued that there is not and cannot be any serious difference between the public law of Scotland and England. This view is associated with the hostile and offensive attitude which the nineteenth-century House of Lords adopted towards Scots law and, whilst better known for its effects on private law, also made a deep impression on public law. It reflected a form of imperial domination, a certain "tyranny of closeness"[3] but also the specific assumption that one necessary effect of the Treaty of Union was to dissolve differences between Scotland and England. It produced the famously unattractive dicta of the House of Lords in *Duncan v. Findlater*[4]; *Heriot's Hospital v. Ross*[5] and other cases.[6] The court, in strongly assimilative mode, was determined, in the area of what we would now recognise as public authority delictual liability, either to be ignorant of Scots law or, to the extent it was known, deny its compatibility with the practice of civilised countries.[7] In the earlier case of *Macao v. Officers of State for Scotland*[8] this "imperial" approach had come through strongly in the (lamentable) speech of Lord Redesdale as he distinguished between the Court of Session's powers, since the Union, to deal with matters of "local law" and its exclusion from "public law"—the "public law of the whole empire . . . a great constitutional question and a question which can be decided by the Court of Session, as, since the Union, it must be decided on just public grounds".[9] No-one who has read Sir Thomas Smith's polemic on the "Pretensions of English Law as 'Imperial Law' "[10] can be in any doubt about the contempt in which the law of Scotland was held in this period.

---

[3] To acknowledge but invert the title of Geoffrey Blainey's history of Australia, *The Tyranny of Distance* (1966).

[4] (1839) Maclean & R. 911

[5] (1846) 5 Bell 37.

[6] For discussion of these cases, see A. Dewar Gibb, *Law from over the Border* (1950), Chap. III.

[7] See Cottenham, L.C. in *Heriot's Hospital v. Ross, supra* at p. 47. For the aftermath in the House of Lords in *Mersey Docks Commissioners v. Gibbs* (1866) L.R.I. H.L. 93 and its reception in the Court of Session in *Virtue v. Alloa Police Commissioners* (1873) I.R. 303; see Dewar Gibb, *supra*, at pp. 110–112.

[8] (1822) 1 Shaw's App. 138.

[9] *ibid.*, at p. 149. He had earlier expressed the same sentiments in the *Strathmore Peerage Case* (1821) 6 Pat. 645 at p. 655.

[10] See *Stair Memorial Encyclopaedia*, Vol. 5, paras. 711–800. See also his "English Influences on the Law of Scotland", in *Studies Critical and Comparative* (1962); "Special

Hidden behind the offensive rhetoric of the House of Lords, however, are questions which, though it may be unacceptable to have them resolved by judges of ignorance and insensitivity, do demand serious attention. Questions of citizenship (as in *Macao*) and questions of public authority liability cannot, it may be argued, fall to be answered differently in the several parts of the same state without careful justification of the differences and their effects.

2. The justification (or lack of justification) for difference where it occurs is something to which we return but, in the meantime, some undoubted differences between Scotland and England in matters of public law should be noted. A full catalogue would be unhelpful and, within the confines of this essay, impossible but a loose classification identifying some five categories of difference might be given broad recognition. There would be the institutional differences which into modern times have sustained a different judicial system, some different mechanisms for Scottish legislation at Westminster and a separate Law Commission, and, in the executive, the Scottish Office, a different local government tradition and some differences in the way that police administration and intermediate government (including the health service) have developed. Secondly, there is probably a difference between the approach adopted by the Scottish and English courts to the status to be accorded, against the admittedly general background of a principle of legislative supremacy of Parliament (subject to the supereminence of the law of the European Community), of the Treaty of Union 1707.[11] Thirdly, there appear to be continuing differences in the treatment of Crown liability and Crown privilege—or, as it is more often called today, public interest immunity. Once to be derived from a tradition in Scots law which accorded much less generous immunity to the crown in legal proceedings, remaining distinctions are drawn from interpretation of the Crown Proceedings Act 1947[12] or from an apparently more restrictive view of crown privilege.[13] Fourthly, there

Aspects of Scottish Constitutional Law", in *A Short Commentary on the Law of Scotland* (1962), at p. 61; "Scottish Nationalism, Law and Self-Government", in N. MacCormick (ed.), *The Scottish Debate* (1970).

[11] Although the subject is not to be treated in detail here, this is not to deny that, for many, the claimed "higher law" status of the Treaty of Union is *the* important distinguishing characteristic of Scots public law. See *MacCormick v. Lord Advocate*, 1953 S.C. 396 and then J. D. B. Mitchell *Constitutional Law* (2nd ed. 1968), Chap. 4; Sir Thomas Smith, "Fundamental Law", in *Stair Memorial Encyclopaedia*, Vol. 5, and his earlier "The Union of 1707 as Fundamental Law," in *Studies Critical and Comparative* (1962); N. MacCormick, "Does the United Kingdom have a Constitution?", (1978) 20 N.I.L.Q. 1. For a discussion of the Treaty in relation to the poll tax and generally, see N. Walker and C. M. G. Himsworth. "The Poll Tax and Fundamental Law", 1991 J.R. 45. An interesting phenomenon has been the taking of Treaty issues in *English* cases. See *R. v. Lord Chancellor, ex p. The Law Society*, June 21 1993, unreported, and the cases referred to at nn. 25 and 26 below. Colin Munro challenges the Smith/MacCormick approaches in P. Hodge (ed.), *Scotland and the Union* (Hume PPP, 1994).

[12] See *McDonald v. Secretary of State for Scotland*, 1994 S.L.T. 693 in which the more liberal approach to remedies against ministers in *M. v. Home Office* [1994] 1 A.C. 377 was distinguished. See below.

[13] See *Parks v. Tayside Regional Council*, 1989 S.L.T. 345—perhaps paradoxical especially in the light of the liberal contribution a generation earlier of *Glasgow Corporation v. Central Land Board*, 1956 S.C. (H.L.) 1. But see F. M. McShane, "Crown Privilege in Scotland: The Demerits of Disharmony", 1992 J.R. 256 and 1993 J.R. 41.

is a clear divergence between the two jurisdictions in some matters of civil liberties and in the regulation of police powers.[14] And, fifthly, there are some important continuing distinctions in the law of judicial review.[15] Although the Court of Session[16] has declared a broad similarity between the grounds of review, there are procedural differences and, important in ways to be discussed, differences in the rules defining the scope of review and *locus standi*.

3. A full list of rules differing between Scotland and England which fall within and perhaps beyond these categories would be endless and pointless. Most such differences are of little consequence because they derive solely from the practice of enacting much (substantially uniform) regulatory law in separate codes with only small differences of detail between them. Some, however, are of much greater consequence and there have already been indications of these more important areas of divergence. In a state, treated for most political purposes as unitary, there are interesting questions to be asked about rules which expose a Secretary of State to significantly different sanctions because a different view is taken of the relationship of a minister to the Crown in the courts of the jurisdiction in which a case is heard[17]; which afford public authorities different degrees of protection from the production of documents in a trial[18]; which expose the police to different degrees of civil liability[19]; and which give to international obligations under the European Convention on Human Rights a different status in domestic courts.[20]

4. The interest in those questions is heightened in circumstances where differences between rules prompt an element of forum choice and, therefore, forum shopping for the resolution of disputes. The expansion of judicial review in both jurisdictions has produced the conditions in which not only may the same types of decision be exposed to challenge in either or both[21] but the same minister or public

---

[14] For a comparative discussion see W. Finnie, "Public Order Law in Scotland and England 1980–1990", in W. Finnie, C. M. G. Himsworth, N. Walker (eds.), *Edinburgh Essays in Public Law* (1991).

[15] See A. W. Bradley, "Administrative Law" in Vol. 1 of the *Stair Memorial Encyclopaedia* (1987). For discussion of inter-jurisdictional differences, see C. M. G. Himsworth, "Judicial Review in Scotland" in M. Supperstone and J. Goudie (eds.), *Judicial Review* (1992) and "Judicial Review in Scotland" in B. Hadfield (ed.), *Judicial Review: A Thematic Approach* (1995).

[16] See Lord President Hope in *West v. Secretary of State for Scotland*, 1992 S.C. 385 at pp. 402 and 413 and also, in the House of Lords, Lord Fraser in *Brown v. Hamilton District Council*, 1983 S.C. (H.L.) 1 at p. 42.

[17] See *McDonald v. Secretary of State for Scotland, supra.*

[18] See n. 13 *supra.*

[19] The authorities point to a clear line on police liability in neither jurisdiction but there is very little correspondence between the Scottish case law down to *e.g. Wilson v. Chief Constable of Lothian and Borders Police*, 1989 S.L.T. 107 and *Ward v. Chief Constable of Strathclyde Police*, 1991 S.L.T. 292 and the English cases to *e.g. Ancell v. McDermott* [1993] 4 All E.R. 355 and *Osman v. Ferguson* [1993] 4 All E.R. 344.

[20] *Kaur v. Lord Advocate*, 1980 S.C. 319. But see also *Lord Advocate v. Scotsman Publications*, 1989 S.C. 122. See further W. C. Gilmore and S. C. Neff, "On Scotland, Europe and Human Rights", *infra*, p. 265.

[21] Examples of cases which have by chance raised issues in Scotland before a parallel case has arisen in England have included *Colas Roads Ltd. v. Lothian Regional Council*, 1994 S.L.T. 396 (local authorities and C.C.T.) and *Highland Regional Council v. British*

body may be similarly exposed. The Social Fund Commissioner's decisions have, for instance, been reviewed in Scotland.[22] More importantly Home Office decisions on immigration matters are increasingly being challenged in the Court of Session and it has become apparent that interim liberation is more readily available in that court than its equivalent in the English High Court. This produced the case of *Sokha v. Secretary of State for the Home Department*[23] in which a litigant with no previous Scottish connections whatever and imprisoned in England prior to probable deportation sought to challenge the detention in the Court of Session. Following a concession by counsel for the Home Secretary to this effect, Lord Prosser took the view that, whilst the court did have jurisdiction—the Home Secretary was for the purposes of the Civil Jurisdiction and Judgments Act 1982 domiciled in both Scotland and England—the application for judicial review should not proceed in Scotland in accordance with ordinary principles of *forum non conveniens*. These pointed clearly towards England as the appropriate jurisdiction and that conclusion should not be displaced merely by evidence that interim liberation or its equivalent might be less readily available. Lord Prosser did emphasise, however, that it could not possibly be said that the petitioner would not obtain justice in England. It was not one of those "countries in whose courts there is a risk that justice will not be obtained in particular kinds of suits, whether for ideological or political reasons, or because of inexperience or inefficiency of the judiciary or excessive delay in the conduct of the courts, or (which is in a sense the present petitioner's contention) the unavailability of appropriate remedies".[24]

It has not been in Scottish cases alone that interjurisdictional issues in judicial review have arisen. In the recent English case of *R. v. Secretary of State for Scotland, ex p. Greenpeace*[25] the concession made on behalf of the Home Secretary in *Sokha* was treated as mistaken—as was any reliance in judicial review proceedings on the Civil Jurisdiction and Judgments Act 1982. This was the case which concerned the proposal by Shell U.K. to dispose of the Brent Spar by sinking and the challenge by Greenpeace to decisions made in Scotland by the Secretary of State for Scotland and the Chief Inspector at Her Majesty's Industrial Pollution Inspectorate. Popplewell, J. held that the English High Court did not have jurisdiction. The 1982 Act did not apply to "administrative matters" and did not, therefore, give an English domicile to the Secretary of State. Furthermore, the guarantees contained in Article XIX of the Treaty of Union operated as an additional means of ensuring that the English courts do not deal with cases in which there is a right of action in Scotland. It would be "quite

---

Railways Board, 1996 S.L.T. 274 (rail closures and "ghost trains"). An example with a higher constitutional profile was *Monckton v. Lord Advocate*, 1995 S.L.T. 1201 (challenge to Crown payments in respect of the E.C. Agreement on Social Policy).
[22] *Murray v. Secretary of State for Social Security*, 1994 G.W.D. 23–1436 and *McKim's Curator ad litem v. Collinge*, 1994 G.W.D. 13–864.
[23] 1992 S.L.T. 1049.
[24] *ibid.*, at p. 1054.
[25] May 24, 1995, unreported.

improper for an English court to seek to review the making of what is essentially a foreign administrative decision".

In the rather different context of *R. v. Commissioner of Police, ex p. Bennett*,[26] Article XIX of the Treaty was also successfully invoked to persuade the English High Court that it did not have jurisdiction to interfere by judicial review with the execution of a Scottish warrant—issued in circumstances where courts in England and in Scotland had earlier reached different views on whether the treatment of the applicant by the English and South African police was such as to require them to prevent criminal prosecutions from proceeding.[27]

Another point of divergence in the law of judicial review which may come to have inter-jurisdictional consequences relates to the core issue of the scope of review. Which bodies (and which functions) are reviewable? It has been of some amusement north of the border to see the Court of Session's rejection in *West v. Secretary of State for Scotland*[28] of a test based on a public/private distinction so warmly welcomed by English commentators,[29] perhaps without full regard for the continuing problems raised in Scotland and without regard too for the disparity of treatment which divergence may bring. It is not clear why questions such as whether the unreasonableness of allowances paid to prison officers (the issue in *West*) may be reviewed should fall to be decided by different standards. This possibility arises because of the insistence by the First Division in *West* that access to the supervisory jurisdiction of the Court of Session by judicial review should be determined, not by reference to the criteria the English High Court seeks to apply (and towards which the Court of Session had shown earlier signs of moving), but by reference instead to whether or not a tripartite relationship (of a sort elaborated but not without ambiguity by the court) exists between the relevant parties. This may be expected to produce different answers in Scotland and in England to the question of which bodies are subject to review and in respect of which of their functions.[30]

Of even greater significance may be an apparently increasing divergence between the effect of the rules of *locus standi* in the two jurisdictions. There is no reason why, despite the use of tests cast in the different language of "title and interest" and "sufficient interest", broadly the same degree of access to judicial review should not be assured and it may be that this has generally been the case. But, in the particular circumstances of applications for review by pressure groups, it may

---

[26] [1995] 3 All E.R. 248.

[27] See *Bennett v. Horseferry Road Magistrates' Court* [1994] 1 A.C. 42 and *Bennett v. H.M. Advocate*, 1995 S.L.T. 510.

[28] 1992 S.C. 385; 1992 S.L.T. 636.

[29] H. W. R. Wade and C. F. Forsyth, *Administrative Law* (7th ed. 1994) at pp. vii, 667 and 682; J. E. Alder, "Hunting the Chimera—the end of *O'Reilly v. Mackman*" (1993) 13 *Legal Studies* 183.

[30] See W. Finnie, "Triangles as Touchstones of Review", 1993 S.L.T. (News) 51; W. J. Wolffe, "The Scope of Judicial Review in Scots Law" [1992] Public Law 625; C. M. G. Himsworth, "Public Employment, the Supervisory Jurisdiction and Points *West*"', 1992 S.L.T. (News) 257; "Further *West*? More Geometry of Judicial Review", 1995 S.L.T. (News) 127, and "Judicial Review in Scotland", in B. Hadfield (ed.), *Judicial Review: A Thematic Approach* (1995).

be that a considerable gap has opened up between the restrictive doctrine of the *Age Concern*[31] case in Scotland and the apparently much more liberal approach recently adopted by the English High Court in the *Greenpeace (THORP)*[32] case and the *World Development Movement*[33] case. The divergence received recognition in *R. v. Secretary of State for Scotland, ex p. Greenpeace*[34] already referred to. Although deciding the jurisdictional issue on the basis discussed above, Popplewell, J. went on to deal with arguments which had been put forward in debate on the assumption that the jurisdiction of the High Court was upheld and that an issue of *forum non conveniens* could arise. In essence, Greenpeace had suggested that the High Court should hear the review because it was unlikely that their title and interest to sue would be recognised in Scotland. Popplewell, J. decided first[35] that Scotland was *prima facie* the appropriate forum but then that this should be displaced by evidence produced to him in memoranda prepared by two Scottish Queen's Counsel[36] and leading him to conclude that there would indeed be "very real difficulties in Greenpeace establishing a right of interest, as such, before a Scottish court". He did not, however, accept that this conclusion should be viewed as a criticism of the way in which the Scottish courts proceed—"it merely observes that there is, or may well be, a substantial difference between our practices. The Scots courts seem to proceed on the basis that if Greenpeace wish to pursue a case in Scotland it will be necessary for them to find a person, or persons, prepared to litigate, even though it may be a token applicant and Greenpeace must still bear the burden of the case". Whilst acknowledging that this approach would not adversely affect the quality of the arguments Greenpeace would wish to develop, he concluded nevertheless that the different rules on *locus* were in this case sufficient to persuade him that Greenpeace should on grounds of *forum conveniens*, if these had become determinative, succeed in their claim to have the judicial review heard in London. On the jurisdictional grounds already discussed, however, that option was to be denied to them.

5. The feature common to these examples of rules in different fields of public law is that of acknowledged differences between the position in Scotland and that in England and then, in those cases where choice of law issues are important and can be raised, the mechanisms available to courts for resolving them. Returning, however, to the ideas introduced at the beginning of this essay, the question posed by these signs of divergence within a system which is, on the whole, a system

---

[31] *Scottish Old People's Welfare Council, Petrs.*, 1987 S.L.T. 179. On standing in Scotland in general, see C. R. Munro "Standing in Judicial Review", 1995 S.L.T. (News) 279 and, I. Cram "Towards Good Administration—The Reform of Standing in Scots Public Law", 1995 J.R. 332.

[32] *R. v. Inspectorate of Pollution, ex p. Greenpeace (No. 2)* [1994] 4 All E.R. 329.

[33] *R. v. Secretary of State for Foreign and Commonwealth Affairs, ex p. World Development Movement* [1995] 1 All E.R. 611.

[34] May 24 1995, unreported.

[35] Following the approach laid down by Lord Goff in *Spiliada Maritime Corporation v. Cansulex Ltd* [1987] 1 A.C. 460.

[36] Messrs. J. J. Mitchell and N. F. Davidson.

of law common to the United Kingdom is how far they are sustainable. Pressures towards uniformity do not come from an imperial intolerance equivalent to that evinced by the nineteenth-century House of Lords, but it is becoming difficult to sustain historically-based justifications for peculiarly Scottish or English rules of public law. This is partly because many of the historical threads in this area have long since been broken and lost any contemporary force, and partly because there are much stronger pressures bearing down on the system. For the same reason, the opportunities for a dispassionate weighing of the relative merits and demerits of legal harmony[37] are declining. What is replacing them is the spirit of uniformity illustrated in the path-breaking (or path-restoring) recent case of *Morgan Guaranty*[38] where the Lord President made clear that he thought it right that, by overruling *Glasgow Corporation v. Lord Advocate*,[39] Scots law would be brought in line with the English rule established in *Woolwich Equitable Building Society v. I.R.C.*[40] in the matter of recovery of a tax payment made under error of law: "[W]e will be achieving the same result by reference to the principles of Scots law. I regard that as satisfactory, because it would be inequitable that a remedy which is now available in England in this important field of transactions between the citizen and a public authority should be denied here on the ground that it was not permitted by our law."[41] The question this raises is how far the principle of equivalent treatment should extend across relations between citizens and public authorities, eliminating, if necessary, any distinctions between rules in the different UK jurisdictions.

Scots Public Law and Europe

Bill Wilson would have been the first to remind us that there is now an important European dimension to all of this. The question becomes one of how far the level playing field of the European Union demands rules of public law which apply equally not just from Shetland to Sussex but also from Sweden to Spain.

The *Woolwich Building Society* case is instructive here. The Court of Appeal and House of Lords were reviewing cases which, in line with the view expressed in due course by the Lord President in *Morgan Guaranty* confirmed that, all other things being equal, it was desirable that the laws on recovery of tax paid in England and Scotland should be the same.[42] It was also acknowledged, however, in the speech of Lord Goff that there was a Community aspect to this—"at a time when Community law is becoming increasingly important, it would be strange if the right of the citizen to recover overpaid charges were

---

[37] *cf.* J. D. B. Mitchell "The Merits of Disharmony", [1956] Public Law 6.
[38] *Morgan Guaranty Trust Co. of New York v. Lothian Regional Council*, 1995 S.L.T. 299.
[39] 1959 S.C. 209.
[40] [1993] A.C. 70.
[41] 1995 S.L.T. 299 at p. 315.
[42] See Lord Wheatley in *Glasgow Corporation v. Lord Advocate*, 1959 S.C. 203 at p. 220 quoted at [1993] A.C. 70 at p. 132.

to be more restricted under domestic law than it is under European law".[43]

Insofar as the cases of *Woolwich* and then *Morgan Guaranty* concern the substantive rights of citizens in relation to the state, dicta such as these are in the broader context of European law unsurprising. We are becoming entirely used to the idea that the underlying principles of the European Union demand parity of treatment in the fields to which they apply and that the mechanisms are in place to ensure that the supremacy of these principles when expressed in law is sustained. Although less direct in its methods, the European Convention on Human Rights has introduced similar tendencies towards uniformity. Whilst some of the rights assured by the Convention may have a procedural character (notably Article 6 providing for the right to a fair trial),[44] and certainly much of European Community law prescribes administrative procedures intended to be followed in a broadly uniform manner, important outstanding questions concern the degree to which the same spirit of parity of treatment throughout the Union (including, of course, parity between Scotland and England) will be applied to administrative law. There are good reasons why, in the interests of sustaining the level playing field of substantive rules, they should. If parity of effect of those rules is to be achieved, there are clearly strong arguments that the supporting rules needed to ensure their enforcement and to enable challenge to their enforcement should be similar across the Union. This principle is, of course, of very broad effect and extends much more widely than the area conventionally regarded as that of "public" law. Parity of treatment in the prosecution and punishment of criminal offences is clearly involved and so too are many aspects of civil procedure.

But certainly public law issues loom large and much of administrative law may be expected to become vulnerable to European pressures. We have already seen the *Factortame* case[45] forcing a rethinking of the vulnerability of the Crown to injunctive relief in matters relating to Community law rights in England and as the trigger of a wider consideration of relief against ministers generally in the case of *M. v. Home Office*.[46] Plainly the force of the principal reasoning in *Factortame* must apply equally in Scotland although, as already noted, the Court of Session has diverged from the line taken in *M*.[47] Meanwhile it has become clear that European pressures are having a harmonising influence on *locus standi* issues in judicial review[48] and it seems certain

---

[43] [1993] A.C. 70 at p. 177.
[44] See, in particular, A. Boyle, "Administrative Justice, Judicial Review and the Right to a Fair Hearing under the E.C.H.R.", [1984] Public Law 89 and A. W. Bradley, "Administrative Justice—a Developing Human Right?", (1995) 1 European Public Law 347.
[45] *R. v. Secretary of State for Transport, ex p. Factortame Ltd (No. 2)* [1991] 1 A.C. 603.
[46] [1994] 1 A.C. 377.
[47] *MacDonald v. Secretary of State for Scotland*, 1994 S.L.T. 692, interestingly reviewed by D. J. Edwards at (1995) 111 L.Q.R. 34 where he explains that the basis for the difference of approach in the Court of Session was already laid by that of the English courts.
[48] *R. v. Secretary of State for Employment, ex p. Equal Opportunities Commission* [1995] 1 A.C. 1.

that there will be a similar impact on the grounds of review themselves. In particular, Lord Diplock's prediction of an expanded role for the doctrine of proportionality in administrative law[49] will come to be justified as British courts become increasingly familiar with the need to apply the doctrine not only where Community law already undoubtedly demands it[50] but also where a broader need for parity of treatment is recognised.[51]

Some may say that this has already been achieved. Most prominent in the judgment of Sedley, J. in *R. v. Ministry of Agriculture, Fisheries and Food, ex p. Hamble (Offshore) Fisheries Ltd.*[52] were the dicta affirming that English (and presumably, therefore, Scottish) principles of legitimate expectation are the same as those propounded by the European Court of Justice but the reason for upholding the minister's decision to refuse a fishing licence was that "[t]he means adopted bore a fair proportion to the end in view".[53] The relevance of proportionality as an aspect of fairness in the assessment of a person's legitimate expectations was acknowledged.[54]

A recent further manifestation of the same trend was the publication in 1994 of the Storme report on the *Approximation of Judiciary Law in the European Union.* This was the product of a group of experts from a number of European countries which was set up in 1990 at the request of the European Commission to "draw up a study on the approximation of the laws of procedure" in the member states.[55] In the English-language preface written by Professor Jolowicz it is explained that "if a market is to flourish, disputes arising out of business conducted in the market must be resolved consistently with one another, and that requires more than a uniform substantive law. The idea of a single 'internal market' requires for its complete realisation a single system for the judicial resolution of disputes."[56] The published report contains the group's proposals for new rules extending not to every single aspect of civil procedure but, under a number of fairly discrete headings, to an important selection on *e.g.* the commencement of proceedings, discovery, evidence, costs, provisional remedies and enforcement of judgments.

The report has attracted a certain amount of hostile flak, some of it

---

[49] *CCSU v. Minister for the Civil Service* [1985] A.C. 374 at pp. 410–411.
[50] *Walkingshaw v. Marshall*, 1992 S.L.T. 1167 is a Scottish illustration.
[51] For signs of this see *e.g.* the dicta of Neill, L.J. in *R. v. Secretary of State for the Environment, ex p. NALGO*, November 26 1992, unreported. See also D. Williams, "The Influence of European Union Law", in G. Richardson and H. Genn (eds.), *Administrative Law and Government Action* (1994) for a very helpful and interesting discussion of the problems emerging through differences between U.K. and European law.
[52] [1995] 2 All E.R. 714.
[53] *ibid.* p. 735.
[54] There are, of course, other pressures in the direction of an expanded role for courts in judicial review, including an expansion of the grounds of review. See *e.g.* the concerns voiced recently by Lord Mustill in *R. v. Home Secretary, ex p. Fire Brigades Union* [1995] 2 All E.R. 244 at p. 268.
[55] From the Notice to the Reader by the group's chairman Professor Marcel Storme at p. 1.
[56] p. xiii.

well-deserved.[57] It is very poorly edited and its general presentation anarchic. The lack of a Scottish representative on the group, leaving Scotland to be either lumped in with England or ignored as part of a wider United Kingdom, inevitably raises hackles. The quality of some of the detailed points made is not good. But what the report does achieve is the renewal of debate about the limits of subsidiarity and the extent to which the European order must indeed infiltrate the procedural and remedial aspects of the legal systems of member states.

No doubt those critics who point out the great difficulties of procedural harmonisation are right. No doubt they are right too to demand as much sensitivity as possible (and that may not be very much) to the peculiarities of national legal orders. But it is clear that this report is no "Storme in a teacup". By reaching down into the detail of civil procedure and insisting on harmonisation there, the report's logic must also carry with it the prior need for harmonisation on a broader canvas. The private lawyer may be able to envisage a common market allowing commercial organisations to choose from a variety of differently operating legal systems to suit their needs[58] but in matters of public law, regulating the market to prevent uneven discrimination, or to ensure equal environmental protection, the demand for uniformity is clear. Systems of rule enforcement, access to the courts, the powers of courts to control "emanations" or "manifestations" of the state[59] similarly defined across the Union, remedies available to both sides—all demand harmonisation, not now on the whim of an imperial England or United Kingdom but as a prerequisite of European public law.

An expression of the need for uniformity in the application of Community law and the penalties applicable for breaches of the law is to be found in a recent council resolution[60] which insists on the need for the effective application of the law and for penalty provisions which are effective, proportionate and dissuasive. But the European Union, as well as sustaining the common market, is exerting a broader influence on British legal culture[61] and this is a phenomenon very interestingly discussed by Professor van Gerven, formerly Advocate General at the E.C.J.[62] Not only does he trace the developments which have led from the E.C.J.'s earlier position in which it took the view that member states alone were responsible for ensuring the enforcement of Community law through the remedies of their own systems to the

---

[57] See, from Scotland, N. Morrison, "Approximation of Judiciary Law in the European Union", 1995 S.L.T. (News) 183, and M. Upton, "European Harmonisation of Court Procedure" (1995) 40 J.L.S.S. 197.

[58] See Morrison, "Approximation", *supra*, at p. 183.

[59] See *e.g. Foster v. British Gas p.l.c.* [1991] 2 A.C. 306 and *Kincardine and Deeside District Council v. Forestry Commissioners*, 1992 S.L.T. 1189.

[60] Resolution of June 29 1995, O.J. 1995 C188/1.

[61] For an interesting discussion of its different aspects, see J. E. Levitsky, "The Europeanisation of the British Legal Style", (1994) 42 A.J.C.L. 347.

[62] W. van Gerven, "Bridging the Gap between Community and National Laws: Towards a Principle of Homogeneity in the Field of Legal Remedies", (1995) 32 C.M.L.R. 679.

need for a harmonised response,[63] a process which he identifies as a move from a less "gratuitous" to a more "operational" function for comparative law,[64] but he goes on to see this as requiring a Europe-driven homogeneity of law *within* member states.[65] It will become unacceptable for there to be a drifting apart of national laws depending simply upon whether they fall within or outside the sphere of Community law. Ways must be found, he writes, to keep the two sets of rules together. In making this point he invokes the dicta of Lord Woolf to the same effect in *M*.[66]

The logic of this position is one which has a compelling force right across the member states of the Union but it has a particular poignancy in the United Kingdom where it must be taken to insist upon the matching of the law of Scotland and of England not only with that of other member states but also with each other.

As Bill Wilson said, a private lawyer neglects public law at his peril. Today, however, that public law which was "on the whole United Kingdom law" is in the process of becoming on the whole the law of the European Union with consequences for the further integration of the law within the United Kingdom which have still to emerge but which will undoubtedly affect many of those points peculiar to Scotland which, in Wilson's words, do at present "crop up from time to time".

---

[63] See also T. Koopmans, "European Public Law: Reality and Prospects", [1991] *Public Law* 53; R. Caranta, "Judicial Protection against Member States: a New *Jus Commune* Takes Shape", (1995) 32 C.M.L. Rev. 703; G. Tesauro, "The Effectiveness of Judicial Protection and Co-operation between the Court of Justice and the National Courts", (1993) 13 Yearbook of European Law 1.

[64] "Bridging the Gap", *supra*, at p. 695.

[65] *ibid.*, at p. 700.

[66] *M. v. Home Office* [1994] 1 A.C. 377 at p. 422.

FLEXIBLE RULES

R. A. A. McCall Smith

Bill Wilson's interest in interpretation rarely took him into the area of criminal law. This need not be a matter of particular note; he was a civil lawyer who, like many other distinguished jurists, found more than enough material in private law to satisfy his intellectual appetites. Yet the fact that the more general issues of criminal law have occupied relatively few academic Scots lawyers is one that might be remarked upon. Scots criminal law has undoubtedly been the poor relation in legal studies. Why is this so? Are there signs that matters are changing?

Modern Scots criminal law begins, of course, with Hume, who in his *Commentaries*[1] introduced a degree of system into the criminal law and extracted from a morass of cases that vital spark of principle which is needed for reasonably coherent development. Hume's work survived for an extraordinarily long period and, with Alison,[2] effectively provided the main source of Scots criminal law until the wide adoption of Macdonald's *Practical Treatise*.[3] Macdonald's work similarly had an extraordinarily long life, and its extensive use by the judiciary effectively dominated criminal law practice until some time after the publication of Gordon's magisterial *Criminal Law* in 1967.[4] This latter work, which evoked considerable respect in jurisdictions outside Scotland, was somewhat slow to be adopted within Scotland itself. For many years, where judicial reference was made to a textbook, it was to Macdonald (a book rightly described by Gordon as "confused and inaccurate"), and it is only comparatively recently that the authority of Gordon's work has come to be more widely acknowledged within Scotland. This tardiness is puzzling; in other jurisdictions, works of this stature are regularly quoted in judgments and their assistance frankly acknowledged. One only has to glance at decisions of the Supreme Court of Canada or the High Court of Australia to see the difference in this respect.

For most of this century, then, Scots criminal law has been served by very little commentary.[5] The criminal law became a common law

---

[1] David Hume, *Commentaries on the Law of Scotland Respecting Crimes* (4th ed., 1844; reprinted 1986)

[2] A. J. Alison, *Principles and Practice of the Criminal Law of Scotland* (1832–33).

[3] J. H. A. Macdonald, *A Practical Treatise on the Criminal Law of Scotland* (1st ed., 1867); (5th ed., 1948).

[4] G. H. Gordon, *The Criminal Law of Scotland* (1st ed., 1967); (2nd ed., 1978).

[5] The position has now clearly changed. In addition to Gordon's *Criminal Law*, there are several other modern textbooks available, including the most useful work of T. H. Jones and M. G. A. Christie, *Criminal Law* (1992). There is also a series of monographs on criminal law, edited by Lord McCluskey, which has provided a useful forum for the treatment of special topics.

system par excellence; there was comparatively little criminal law legislation (in contrast to the position in England), and very few decisions which fundamentally reformed the law. Indeed, the decisions of note—until recently—were those which actually set the clock back. One thinks, in particular, of decisions such as *H.M. Advocate v. Cunningham*[6] (automatism) and *Brennan v. H.M. Advocate*[7] (intoxication). An external observer, contemplating Scots substantive criminal law during the first eight decades of this century, might have been forgiven for describing it as a somewhat conservative system of criminal jurisprudence unmarked by any features of note. This is not to say that it was a flawed system of criminal justice; in many respects, particularly in relation to procedural and evidential matters, it was quite the opposite, with its admirable dispatch, its espousal (in theory at least) of corroboration, and its attachment to the flexible principles of fairness in evidence generally. The integrity of its administration, too, has generally been above approach.

What were the features of Scots criminal law which could have imparted an impression of undue conservatism? The most striking of these is the way in which important issues of principle were dealt with. There was, quite simply, in most of the decisions of this period very little elaboration of principle. The rules of criminal law were presented in an extremely terse way, with an implication that they were simply not in need of elucidation. Very little explanation of the rules was given, and indeed they were often stated in the simple form given them in the pages of Macdonald.

Stating the rules in a simple, concise fashion can be a good thing. The criminal courts do not exist to give lengthy, academic expositions of the law; and yet, if there is too little exposition, the rule becomes opaque. There may also be areas where the law is simply not discernible to anyone, because the courts have not adequately developed the theoretical foundation of the law to an extent which will allow it to be applied to new situations. This leads to uncertainty and obscurity, which are conditions which offend the basic principles of legality.

Examples of the tendency of the courts to give inadequate explanation of a rule can be found in many branches of Scots criminal law. The law of attempts, for instance, is by no means clear. Gordon examines a range of theories which have have been applied in Scotland in the nineteenth and twentieth centuries and provides a useful analysis of the most important ones.[8] But what rule is actually endorsed by Scots law? In a sense, one can take one's pick, because the High Court has not settled the issue by stating unequivocally that a particular theory of attempts is endorsed in Scotland. We are left with the impression that most courts favour the preparation/perpetration distinction, but this is not specifically endorsed to the exclusion of those other options for which authority may be found. The result is that the law is unclear, and although this may cause little practical inconvenience, there is surely an argument for certainty should the issue

---

[6] 1963 J.C. 80; 1963 S.L.T. 345.
[7] 1977 J.C. 38; 1977 S.L.T. 125.
[8] *Criminal Law*, at p. 163 *et seq.*

arise in the future. Also in the same area, there is the question of attempts to do the impossible. This may not be an everyday problem, but it is a real one, as English and other Commonwealth experience has shown in troublesome cases such as *R. v. Shivpuri*[9] and *Anderton v. Ryan*.[10] The earlier Scottish authorities are frankly irreconcilable, for the very reason suggested above—a disinclination by the court to address the issue of principle and to give an exposition of the law— and it is only very recently, in *Docherty v. Brown*,[10a] that a Full Bench has resolved the matter. It is therefore very difficult, if not impossible, to say with any confidence whether in Scots law the courts would punish a legally impossible attempt.

In the area of defences, the position is similarly uncertain. That intoxication is not a defence to a criminal charge in Scots law would be a widely endorsed proposition. The leading case on the subject is *Brennan*[11] which makes it unequivocally clear that this is so, at least in relation to murder. The ratio of *Brennan*, however, is opaque. Is intoxication not a defence on policy grounds (which would be quite understandable), or because it has never been a defence, or because in becoming intoxicated the accused manifests that degree of wicked recklessness which is sufficient mens rea for murder? There is a suggestion of each of these in the decision, but it is not clear which is the governing ratio. If recklessness provides the grounds for exclud- ing the defence, then what is the position when it comes to an offence for which recklessness would not suffice for *mens rea* purposes (such as theft)? Then there is the question of the specific/general intent dis- tinction which has been developed in English law and which appears to be accepted in *Brennan*. Is this really a part of Scots law, and if the defence of intoxication is available in relation to offences requiring specific intent, then is assault properly placed in that category? Obvi- ously, intoxication cannot be a defence to an assault charge as that would be quite unacceptable to victims and to society at large; and yet the basis of its exclusion in such cases should at least be made clear.

The defence of error is another area in which the law became less than clear because of a failure to address the relevant theoretical issues. There is a strong line of authority to the effect that an error of fact, in order to form the basis of a defence, must be reasonable. Then, in the case of *Meek and Others v. H.M. Advocate*[12] the proposition was stated that in relation to rape a mistaken belief in consent would elide the *mens rea* requirement even if this belief was unreasonable. The basis on which this view was taken was that Scots law on this point was in line with the English decision of *D.P.P. v. Morgan*.[13] This gave rise to doubt: had the reasonableness requirement in error been replaced, or was it inapplicable merely in relation to rape? These doubts have now been settled by the decision of the High Court in

---

[9] [1987] A.C. 1; [1986] 2 All E.R. 334.
[10] [1985] A.C. 560; [1985] 2 W.L.R. 968.
[10a] 1996 S.L.T. 325.
[11] *Supra,* n. 7.
[12] 1983 S.L.T. 280; 1982 S.C.C.R. 613.
[13] [1976] A.C. 182

Jamieson v. H.M. Advocate,[14] where it is made clear that the rule stated in cases such as *Crawford v. H.M. Advocate*[15] survives. For an error to be a defence it must therefore be reasonable, at least in matters such as self defence; rape, however, is an exception.

The lack of clarity in defences shows itself in relation to the the defences of coercion and necessity. It is really quite difficult to identify the scope of these defences in the law of Scotland, and, in the case of necessity, it is open to doubt whether the defence even exists. As far as coercion is concerned, there is the authority of Hume for the existence of the defence, although his recognition of it is grudging.[16] The requirements of the defence, however, have not been set out at any length in any of the cases, in marked contrast to the situation in other comparable legal systems. Such systems identify requirements of immediacy and of reasonableness, as well as the requirement that the accused should not have demonstrated fault by placing himself in a position where he is likely to be subjected to coercion. One of the few modern cases on the subject in Scotland, *Thomson v. H.M. Advocate*,[17] stresses the requirement of immediacy, but does not go further, with the result that all that one can say with any certainty about the defence in Scotland is that immediate coercion may be recognised by a court in suitable circumstances. But what those circumstances are is not clear.

Necessity is even murkier. Both the first and second editions of Gordon's *Criminal Law* were not able to identify any Scottish cases in which the defence of necessity was specifically discussed,[18] and also pointed out the hostile attitude of Hume to the concept.[19] Yet, since then, in three recent cases, *Tudhope v. Grubb*,[20] *McNab v. Guild*,[21] and *Morrrison v. Valentine*,[22] the matter has been raised where the accused has been charged with driving offences; in each case the accused argued that he had to commit the driving offence to escape an imminent physical threat. In *McNab*, where the accused drove recklessly in his attempt to get away from persons who were threatening him in an hotel car park, the court declined to pronounce on whether there was such a thing as a defence of necessity, further pointing out that even if there were such a defence, the circumstances in question would not be of the sort in which the defence could be made out.

While it is easy to appreciate why the courts should feel anxious about a broadly-based defence of this sort—an uneasiness that is certainly shared by other systems—it might be argued that a developed system of criminal jurisprudence should not be in doubt as to whether or not a defence exists. The occasions for its invocation may be few and far between, particularly in a small jurisdiction, but when they arise the matter might best be settled to the greatest possible extent.

---

[14] 1994 S.C.C.R. 181
[15] 1950 J.C. 67; 1950 S.L.T. 279.
[16] *Commentaries*, i, at p. 53.
[17] 1983 J.C. 69
[18] *Criminal Law*, at p. 428.
[19] *Commentaries*, i, at p. 55.
[20] 1983 S.C.C.R. 250.
[21] 1989 S.C.C.R. 138.
[22] 1991 S.L.T. 143.

If this cannot be done by the courts, then it should be done through organised law reform.

If necessity is a recondite matter, the same cannot be said for provocation, which is a fairly common feature of homicide, as it is of assault, where it has a mitigating effect. In Scots criminal law there has long been a rule that provocation must be physical (at least in homicide cases); verbal provocation alone will not suffice. In *Stobbs v. H.M. Advocate*[23] and *Berry v. H.M. Advocate*[24] chinks appeared in this robust rejection of provocation by words or gestures; in the latter case sexual taunts were allowed to go to the jury. Then, in *Thomson v. H.M. Advocate*[25] the court said that verbal provocation was not excluded; it all depended on the circumstances of the case.

There was by now a small number of cases in which verbal taunts appeared to have been accepted as forming a possible basis for a plea of provocation. These cases were clearly incompatible with the rule expounded in Macdonald, and relied upon by the courts, to the effect that provocation must be based on assault. In *Cosgrove v. H.M. Advocate*[26] the question arose as to whether a jury instruction in traditional terms (excluding verbal provocation) would be objectionable. The High Court held that it would not be; it was open to the court to give an instruction which excluded verbal provocation or one which allowed it. Either would be acceptable.

The courts clearly favour discretion in these matters but it is difficult to see how the two approaches can be reconciled. If the traditional instruction excludes verbal provocation, and is correct, then it is wrong to allow verbal provocation to go to the jury. This would appear to be an example of a defence in Scots law which is now so widely stated as to include two irreconcilable positions, both of which are correct, and which allow a choice to be made by the court as to which of the two interpretations should be applied. As a result, it is impossible to say whether verbal provocation suffices in Scots law to reduce murder to culpable homicide. The only answer is that it does sometimes, but not always. Bill Wilson would have been interested in this.

The opacity which is apparent in relation to defences has its counterpart in the way in which some offences are defined. The breadth, or openness, of the definition of certain offences is one of the features which most distinguishes Scots law from comparable systems. In the typical common law jurisdiction, the last 50 years have seen an increase in the exactitude with which offences are defined. To a great extent this has been the result of a testing, by both defence and prosecution, of the boundaries of the law, but it has resulted from a concern on the part of the courts that the principle of legality be observed, and that only such conduct which is clearly stated in advance to be criminal should be punished. An example of this process of refinement is the debate in many common law jurisdictions

[23] 1983 S.C.C.R. 190.
[24] 1976 S.C.C.R. (Supp) 156.
[25] 1985 S.C.C.R. 448.
[26] 1991 S.L.T. 25; 1990 S.C.C.R. 358.

over the precise categorisation of homicide and the *mens rea* of the offences of murder and manslaughter. Many common law systems allow conviction for manslaughter where death has followed an unlawful and dangerous act. The term "dangerous act" is broad one, though, and this has led to the elucidation by the courts of the circumstances in which danger will be inferred. In some jurisdictions the test has been settled as being one that of whether the reasonable person would have anticipated the risk of injury, however slight, to another; other courts have opted for the test of whether the serious injury was foreseeable. Whichever option is chosen, the issue has at least been canvassed, and the definition refined either way. Manslaughter therefore has its clear limits, which can be identified. By contrast, the Scots crime of culpable homicide has not been defined by the courts with anything like the same degree of precision. It is difficult, in fact, to find clear statements of the law in any particular case, with the result that any proposition as to what is culpable homicide is going to be very general. As a result, our crime of culpable homicide is very broad, embracing any death which results from a criminal act or from negligence of a sufficient level. Death following upon a very minor assault is therefore culpable homicide, even if the death is a freakish and completely unforeseeable result of the act. It may be that this is desirable, but the question of its desirability or otherwise has never been raised, largely because the definition has been so unrefined that it is capable of embracing any non-accidental death.

The offence of shameless indecency is another example of a broad definition which can be used to control a wide range of activity. The proposition advanced in *McLaughlan v. Boyd*,[27] the case which effectively established this offence, is an example of a sweeping definition which has given the criminal law a compass which some might regard as excessively wide. In this case the court observed that "all shamelessly indecent conduct is criminal", a formula which could hardly be more expansively expressed. Obviously the criminal law must have power to punish certain forms of indecent conduct, but the range of such a power can easily be controlled by defining the crimes of indecency which may be punished. By creating and defining such crimes as obscenity in publication or display, or public indecency, the scope of the law in this area is kept within bounds, and it would be difficult for it to intrude into what might be considered the private domain. Shameless indecency, however, is so broadly defined that it is possible to invoke it in cases in which although the conduct is distasteful in the extreme, its punishment is arguably a matter for the legislature to decide upon. This was so in *H.M. Advocate v. R.*[28] in which a father was convicted of shameless indecency with a daughter (of the age of consent) with whom he had engaged in sexual activity falling short of intercourse. The aspect of this case which caused disquiet is the fact that his conduct was not covered by the law of incest (which requires sexual intercourse) and would therefore seem not to have been covered by the criminal law—were it not for the catch-all

[27] 1934 J.C 19.
[28] 1988 S.L.T 623; 1988 S.C.C.R. 254.

offence of shameless indecency. Then, in *H.M. Advocate v. K.*[29] the same approach was taken in relation to a case involving a foster daughter; again the scope of the law was considerably extended to deal with conduct which had little connection with any existing common law crime.

Not every offence has been broadly defined. The *mens rea* of theft has long been recognised as specifically requiring that there be an intention permanently to deprive the owner of the property. There was some authority which implied that an intention to take temporarily—for a nefarious purpose—could be sufficient *mens rea* for the crime, but the bulk of modern authority endorsed the permanent deprivation view, enabling Gordon to state: "Whatever the semantic problem . . . it is clear that Scots law requires an intention to deprive the owner permanently of his goods. In the absence of this intent, there can be no theft."[30]

A definition of theft as circumscribed as this may have been thought to be too restrictive, and in several cases, beginning with *Milne v. Tudhope*[31] in 1981, the definition of theft in Scots law has been extended to embrace cases where an intention permanently to deprive may be absent but where there is nonetheless a nefarious purpose in depriving the owner of access to his goods. But what is a nefarious purpose? This was not explained in *Milne v. Tudhope*, where the court said: "Whether 'nefarious' means 'criminal' in this context or unlawful does not matter for present purposes."[32] A clear, defined rule has thus become broad, and, it might even be said, rather fuzzy. The process by which this occurred did not involve a discussion of the desirability or otherwise of such an important shift in the meaning of the law, and there did not appear to have been any legal argument on the point. Later, in the important case of *Black v. Carmichael; Penrice v. Carmichael*,[33] the nefariousness issue was to return, this time to allow wheel-clamping to be treated as theft. This decision did not rely on theft alone—there was the extortion element as well—but it demonstrates the far-reaching consequences of the change that occurred in *Milne v. Tudhope*.

The discarding of an apparently well-established rule without much ado can also be seen in the marital rape saga. The rule that a husband cannot be convicted of the rape of his wife—a rule stated (not particularly firmly) by Hume and subsequently echoed by Macdonald—strikes the modern mind as anachronistic. Yet the process by which it was abandoned in Scots law is a curious one. The door was first opened by Lord Robertson in *H.M. Advocate v. Duffy*.[34] In *Duffy* Lord Robertson said that rape was merely a form of assault and there was no reason why a husband should not be convicted of the crime. There was no further discussion of the matter in that case, and it was not

---

[29] 1994 S.C.C.R. 499.
[30] *Criminal Law*, at p. 500.
[31] 1981 J.C. 53; 1981 S.L.T. (Notes) 42.
[32] *Supra*, n. 28.
[33] 1992 S.C.C.R. 709.
[34] 1983 S.L.T. 7; 1982 S.C.C.R. 182.

until *Stallard v. H.M. Advocate*[35] that the court addressed Hume's marital exception head-on and formally discarded any rule that might have existed.

Conclusion

The cases on marital rape show the flexibility of Scots criminal law, in this case in the context of an overdue and welcome reform. This flexibility may be attributed to a variety of factors. To a very great extent, it proceeds from a feature of Scots law identified above, namely, the marked preference for broadly-framed rules, which allow for a great deal of latitude in their application. A concomitant of this has been a reluctance on the part of the courts to engage in an analysis of the substantive rules of Scots criminal law and to develop a coherent body of principle to underpin them. Does this have to be done? Is it a matter of real concern for the courts? The answer must be that it does matter that the criminal law is unambiguous, consistent, and, most importantly, knowable. Major issues of principle are involved in the matter of defences and definition of crimes, and most systems do address these. The Scottish Law Commission has not been encouraged to concern itself much with substantive criminal law, although it has recently made a major contribution in evidential matters. Law reform commissions in other jurisdictions have paid a very great deal of attention to criminal law, as will be seen by the sheer volume of reports they have issued on the subject. Why should Scotland be any different?

That the criminal law of Scotland has shown signs over the last few years of entering a new period of its history—a period in which there will be major re-assessments and important developments by the courts—is now apparent. The decision in *Ross (Robert) v. H.M. Advocate*[36] is an example of this; here the court laid to rest the legacy of the *Cunningham* decision,[37] one of the more regrettable decisions of the High Court, but not before its baneful influence had been felt for almost 30 years. There have been other decisions which, in some views, constitute a real revolution. In particular there are the implications for the doctrine of art and part of the decision in *Brown v. H.M. Advocate*.[38] There is undoubtedly today a new willingness on the part of the courts to explain and develop the criminal law, and this is very much to be welcomed. It is also possible that at some time in the future, the Scottish Law Commission or the Government will consider the possibility of formulating a draft criminal code for Scotland.[39] Codification respects the principle of legality, and provides an accessible and clear statement of the criminal law. It is not always a simple

---

[35] 1989 S.L.T. 469; 1989 S.C.C.R. 248
[36] 1991 S.L.T. 564; 1991 S.C.C.R. 823.
[37] *Supra*, n. 6.
[38] 1993 S.C.C.R. 382.
[39] See C. G. B. Nicholson, "Codification of Scots Law: A Way Ahead or a Blind Alley?", (1987) 8 Stat. L.R. 173 for discussion of the possibility of a Scots criminal code.

panacea, but it is a matter of remark that virtually every jurisdiction in the English-speaking world, including England, now has either a penal code or a draft available for discussion and adoption. Again, why should it be so unthinkable for Scotland to follow suit?[40]

---

[40] There is currently an informal Committee on Codification, working within the Universities of Edinburgh and Aberdeen, and including outside membership, which is drawing up a draft code of Scots criminal law. This document, which will be published for discussion, attempts to show what a code of Scots criminal law would look like, and will be available for debate should a future Scottish Parliament wish to embark on a codification exercise.

SCOTTISH PRIVATE INTERNATIONAL LAW:
A STATUS REPORT

R. D. Leslie

The Purposes of Conflict of Laws Rules

Before assessing the current state of the law in this area, it may be useful briefly to recall the purposes of this branch of the legal system. The main purpose of these rules, we are told, is to do justice to the individuals concerned.[1] Justice here relates to the choice of the appropriate system rather than to the fairness, by our standard, of another legal system's rules of law; emphasis is on selections of system rather than on choice of solution. This is justice in the choice of law context; its applications in other branches of conflict of laws are rather different. Thus, in the area of the recognition of foreign decrees, what justice generally requires is that a claimant should not be put to the expense and inconvenience of a second trial where the matter has already been the subject of a decision by a court in another country.[2]

This concern for justice to individuals should not mislead one into thinking that conflict is a field of private law in which state or community interests are seldom of any real relevance. Conflict is, in fact, an area where state interests not infrequently legitimately intrude. Examples are to be found in fields such as state and diplomatic immunity and the enforcement of the laws of unrecognised governments. Even in domicile, public policy considerations may preclude the acquisition of a domicile of choice where the propositus is residing illegally in the country in question.[3]

In the context of factors relevant to the formulation of conflict rules, a simple clear rule may favour ease of application and predictability of result; the latter aids meeting the expectations of the parties, an important element in private justice. In contrast, a simple clear rule may not do justice to the complexity of a situation and its application could sacrifice justice to certainty. Lord Hodson in *Chaplin v. Boys*[4] in deciding there was a flexible exception to the English choice of law rule in tort, commented:

> "I reach this conclusion not without reluctance since rules of law should be defined and adhered to as closely as possible lest they lose themselves in the field of judicial discretion where no secure foothold is to be found by litigants or their advisers. The search

---

[1] See *e.g.* A. E. Anton with P. R. Beaumont, *Private International Law* (2nd ed. 1990) p. 5. This work will be referred to as "Anton".
[2] Anton, at pp. 4–5.
[3] *Puttick v. Att.-Gen.* [1980] Fam 1.
[4] [1971] A.C. 356 at p. 378.

for justice in the individual case must often clash with fixed legal principles especially perhaps where choice of law is concerned".

It is important for different countries to have the same choice of law rules so that a person's rights and duties continue to be determined by the same legal system regardless of the country in which it is sought to enforce them. This is the important aim of international harmonisation, often achieved through international convention. Conflict, then, is an area where to have distinctive laws is, generally, not a good thing; being the same as others is here a virtue, not a vice. Conflict is, thus an area where other countries' solutions are particularly relevant to solving our problems.

Such harmonisation of internal private law rules as has taken place, for instance, in the fields of unfair terms in consumer contracts[5] and intellectual property, is also relevant to conflict situations because such harmonisation may obviate the need for the application of choice of law rules.

There is a third type of harmonisation that is very relevant in the conflict context. It is important as a general proposition that the scope of our own internal rules be compatible, or in harmony with, our choice of law rules. Thus, if Scots law governs the succession to the moveable estate of a person domiciled here, we should view the domiciliary law of a person not domiciled here as the system applicable to the devolution on death of his, or her, moveable estate. There may be exceptional situations in the conflict field where this harmony cannot be maintained, but they should be rare; a foreigner could well feel aggrieved to discover that a scope of application is provided for a domestic law which is denied to a similar foreign law. This could undermine confidence in the ability of our courts to give fair decisions, particularly where the rights of foreigners are concerned, and this could be detrimental to our own interests in that it may inhibit overseas trade and the free movement of workers and other skilled persons between countries.

It is clear, then, that in propounding conflict rules competing interests and considerations need to be balanced. These factors can be listed and a conflict rule assessed on whether it expresses a sensible balance between relevant interests; the relevance and weight of individual considerations will, of course, vary from rule to rule. A rule-by-rule assessment of our conflict laws on this basis would be a mammoth task and will not be attempted here. However, examples can be given of alleged imbalance in respect of individual rules. For instance, at one time a broad flexible rule was developed by the courts to the effect that a foreign divorce would be recognised if either party had a real and substantial connection with the country in which the divorce had taken place.[6] The test was criticised as being too vague and creating uncertainty.[7] It was replaced in 1971 by legislation based on

---

[5] M. Upton, "European Unfair Contract Terms Law", 1995 S.L.T. (News) 295.

[6] *Indyka v. Indyka* [1969] 1 A.C. 33, *Galbraith v. Galbraith*, 1971 S.C. 65; 1971 S.L.T. 139, *Bain v. Bain*, 1971 S.C. 146; 1971 S.L.T. 141.

[7] Lawrence Collins (ed.), *Dicey and Morris on the Conflict of Laws* (12th ed. 1993) at pp. 731–732.

an international convention, which used rules of alternative references, applying the more specific connecting factors of domicile, habitual residence and nationality.[8] Then the approach to the application of the laws of unrecognised governments adopted in cases like *Adams*[9] and *Bilang*[10] has been criticised as being too concerned with state interests and approaches giving more weight to the interests of the individuals concerned have been suggested.[11]

Sources

Until the nineteenth century the main source of our conflict rules was the writings of jurists, mainly continental jurists. Indeed, as late as 1885 one finds Lord McLaren averring, "private international jurisprudence is not a positive and ascertained thing like municipal law, but it is only the prevailing opinion of authors and jurists".[12] Even today judges place greater reliance, in this area, on textbooks and other writings than in most other branches of the law. In England *Dicey and Morris* has particular authority and in Scotland, Professor Anton's work is often relied on in conflict cases.

The nineteenth century saw a growth in local case law in this area with borrowing from English law, not all of it wise. Until the last 30 years or so, this was an area where there was little legislation. This lack of enacted law was thought by some to be an advantage. Thus Cheshire commented in 1935 that English conflict was a subject "only lightly touched by the paralysing hand of the Parliamentary draftsman".[13] This implicit criticism of legislation as a means of developing the law in this area was unjustified; the extent of the reforms required and their complexity, the need for radical change and the need for harmonisation all indicated legislation as the appropriate means of reform in most cases. The correctness of this latter view has been confirmed by developments in Scotland and England in recent years; in this period there has been a great deal of legislation in the conflict area, much of it based on conventions aimed at harmonisation. This too is a field where the Law Commissions have been promoting legislative change. A number of attempts at reform in this area by the courts have not been successful. One thinks in particular of attempts to adopt a more flexible approach to the recognition of divorces,[14] to reform choice of law in delict,[15] and to develop the rules on polygamous marriages abroad by local domiciliaries.[16] In all these areas the legislature

---

[8] Recognition of Divorces and Legal Separations Act 1971. See now Family Law Act 1986, Part II.

[9] *Adams v. Adams* [1971] p. 188.

[10] *Bilang v. Rigg* [1972] N.Z.L.R. 954.

[11] *Hesperides Hotels Ltd v. Aegean Turkish Holidays Ltd* [1978] Q.B. 205 at pp. 214–222 (C.A.).

[12] *R. Waygood & Co. v. Bennie* (1885) 12 R. 651 at p. 655.

[13] G. C. Cheshire, *Private International Law* (1935), Preface.

[14] See the cases cited in n. 6.

[15] *Red Sea Insurance Co. Ltd v. Bouygues S.A.* [1994] 3 All E.R. 749 (P.C.); *Chaplin v. Boys* [1971] A.C. 356.

[16] *Hussain v. Hussain* [1983] Fam. 26 (C.A.)

favoured other solutions which it enacted.[17] Not all legislative changes have been sound, but on the whole, the legislation has much improved our law in the conflict area. In some instances where the legislation has been based on international convention new approaches to ascertaining the law have been adopted. Thus the consulting of commentaries by learned jurists may be permitted,[18] or a matter of construction may be referred to the European Court of Justice.[19] Then different language texts of a convention may be viewed as being equally authoritative.[20] This certainly is a novel and interesting dimension.

No doubt, the future will see more legislation on conflict matters, much of it aimed at harmonisation. Then one can safely predict that some of the existing legislation will be revised in the light of experience of its working.[21]

Influences

Though there are differences, English law and Scots law tend to have the same conflict rules, especially those on choice of law. This is partially due to these systems sharing sources, but there has, undeniably, been a very substantial English influence on Scots law in this area. Compared to Scotland, England is an area of much greater economic activity with a substantially larger body of case law and there has been a tendency for the Scottish courts to use English authority where Scottish case law is absent, sparse or dated. Then new issues tend to reach the courts earlier in England than they do in Scotland.[22] Much legislation in the conflict area harmonises the law of the United Kingdom, enacting the same provisions for Scotland, England and Wales and Northern Ireland. Frequently the purpose of such legislation is to give effect to international conventions or to joint recommendations of the English and Scottish Law Commissions.

It is rare for foreign materials other than English to be referred to by the Scottish courts. The English courts are, perhaps, a little less parochial in this regard.[23] It is probably fortunate that the new

---

[17] On recognition of divorces see the legislation referred to in n. 8. On delict see the Private International Law (Miscellaneous Provisions) Act 1995, Pt III. and on capacity to marry polygamously see this Act, Pt II.

[18] See, *e.g.*, Civil Jurisdiction and Judgments Act 1982, s. 3(3).

[19] See, *e.g.*, Civil Jurisdiction and Judgments Act 1982, Sched. 2, art. 3.

[20] See, *e.g.*, Contracts (Applicable Law) Act 1990, Sched. 1, art. 33.

[21] As already occurred in respect of the Brussels Convention. Some think further amendment of this convention is required. See, *e.g.*, J. G. Collier, "Conflict of Laws", 1994 All E.R. Rev. at p. 79.

[22] See, *e.g.*, *Hyde v. Hyde* (1866) L.R. 1 P. & D. 130 and *Muhammed v. Suna*, 1956 S.C. 366; 1956 S.L.T. 175; *Miliangos v. George Frank (Textiles) Ltd* [1976] A.C. 443, *Commerzbank Akt. v. Large*, 1977 S.C. 375; 1977 S.L.T. 219.

[23] Australian cases on choice of law in tort were considered by the Privy Council in the recent case of *Red Sea Insurance Co. Ltd v. Bouygues S.A.* [1994] 3 All E.R. 749, an appeal from Hong Kong where the common law is English. See too *Chaplin v. Boys* [1971] A.C. 356.

approaches to conflict problems of jurists and courts in the United States of America have had little influence in the U.K.[24]

With the close contact between the U.K. and Western Europe the influence of continental law on our legal systems has increased and will continue to do so. Several Hague and E.C. conventions are now part of our law. Thus, along with other E.U. countries, we have, through the Rome Convention, introduced to rules on choice of law in contract the Swiss concept of "characteristic performance".[25] Also introduced, where the law is derived from an E.C. convention, are continental methods of ascertaining the law.[26] Then, in certain areas, as a result of adopting international conventions, we now apply "the national law" as a connecting factor.[27]

Is There a Distinctive Scottish Conflict System?

As noted earlier, distinctiveness of laws in the conflict context is a vice rather than a virtue. In choice of law, in particular, harmony of rules as between legal systems is highly desirable, the aim being to ensure that the same legal system is applied wherever rights are sought to be enforced. This is particularly the case in the Scottish/English context.

It was also observed earlier that the Scots law in the conflict area is very similar to the English. There are differences, however. Some of these are the result of relatively recent legislation. An example is provided by the provisions of the Matrimonial and Family Proceedings Act 1984 giving the courts jurisdiction to make financial provision for a spouse after a foreign divorce. There are separate provisions for Scotland which are materially different from those for England and Wales. On this the Scottish Law Commission has commented as follows:

> "It is here that we find ourselves differing from the Law Commission (for England and Wales). They prefer a solution in which there are wide grounds of jurisdiction and in which it is left to the courts, guided by a list of factors to be taken into account to sift out cases where an award would be inappropriate. We prefer a solution in which there are stricter grounds of jurisdiction and the legislation identifies certain cases as inappropriate in advance. In our view, a system based on rules is likely to be fairer to defenders and less objectionable to other countries than a system which depends almost entirely on judicial self-restraint. We

---

[24] The American approaches are more appropriate where inter-state as opposed to international conflict problems are concerned. See Anton, at pp. 39–41. There has been some American influence in England in choice of law in tort. See the speeches of Lords Hodson and Wilberforce in *Chaplin v. Boys* [1971] A.C. 356 and the *Red Sea Insurance* case cited in previous note.

[25] Contracts (Applicable Law) Act 1990, Sched. 1, art. 4(2).

[26] See the provisions cited in nn. 18 and 19, *supra*.

[27] See, *e.g.*, Wills Act 1963, s. 1 and Family Law Act 1986, s. 46(1)(b)(iii).

accept that strict rules on jurisdiction may exclude some cases which a judge in his discretion might allow to proceed. A power to award financial provision after a foreign divorce is, however, a new and exceptional one in our law, and we would rather proceed with caution."[28]

A further example of differences in approach is provided by Schedule of 8 of the Civil Jurisdiction and Judgments Act 1982 which deals with the residual jurisdiction of the Scottish courts. There is no equivalent consolidation of the English provisions. In some areas, English law has moved towards Scots law. Thus the doctrine of *forum non conveniens*, long known to the Scottish courts, has relatively recently been discovered by the English.[29]

Some cases suggest that the Scottish courts are more conservative in the conflict area than the English,[30] others suggest the opposite.[31] A generalisation is probably unwise. Then it is sometimes said that the Scottish courts are strong on principle; they will apply the rule with little regard to the individual result. This was a view expressed by Lord Denning in the famous English case on choice of law in tort, *Boys v. Chaplin*.[32] He said, "We were referred to general Scottish cases where the Scottish judges, insistent as ever on principle, rigorously applied the law of the place (*lex loci delicti*) without exception. But I cannot help noticing that this has led to injustice, so much so that I am not inclined to follow them". This same criticism may, I consider, fairly be made of the decision of an Extra Division in *Wright's Trustees v. Callander*.[33] But the general validity of the criticism may be doubted. At most, it can, perhaps be said that, where certainty and particular justice have to be balanced, there is a general, if slight, tendency for the Scottish courts to give more weight to certainty than would an English court. Scottish equivalents of English cases like *Radwan v. Radwan (No. 2)*[34] and *Hussain v. Hussain*[35] where precedent was abandoned in the interests of justice, do not readily come to mind.

Structure

Some characteristics of the structure of our conflict system have already been observed. For example, it has already been noted that its rules are increasingly in legislative form. Other broad changes in structure can be seen. Thus, there is a steady growth in the number

---

[28] *Family Law: Report on Financial Provision after Foreign Divorce*, Scot. Law. Com. No. 72 (1982) at para. 2.13.
[29] Anton, at pp. 213–214.
[30] See, *e.g.*, *Muhammed v. Suna*, 1956 S.C. 366; 1956 S.L.T. 175 and *Ali v. Ali* [1968] P. 564.
[31] See, *e.g.* *Inland Revenue Commissioners v. Bullock* [1976] 3 All E.R. 353 (C.A.) and *McEwan v. McEwan* 1969 S.L.T. 342.
[32] [1968] 2 Q.B. 1 at p. 26.
[33] 1992 S.L.T. 498, overruled 1993 S.L.T. 556 (H.L.). See R. D. Leslie, "Private International Law, Characterisation and *Wright's Trustees v. Callander*'", 1995 S.L.T. (News) 264, and A. R. Barr, "Old Bastards and Other Children", *supra*, pp. 161–164.
[34] [1973] Fam. 35.
[35] [1983] Fam. 26.

and complexity of rules in this area, reflecting both a growth in the complexity of the area and an increasing realisation of this complexity. Another example of increasing complexity is provided by the growth in the use of rules of alternative reference. A common approach in conflict is to refer a single issue to a single legal system. However, in several areas such as the formal validity of wills[36] and the recognition of divorces,[37] it is the case that compliance with either or any of two or more alternative systems will suffice. Rules permitting this are called "rules of alternative reference" and their use has increased over the years. There is also development in the processes involved in the solution of conflict problems; these too are becoming more numerous and more complex.

Another trend, in some areas, has been the abandonment, in whole or in part of certain inflexible single-element connecting factors[38] like the place of a contract or the place of the delict, using instead more flexible connecting factors, such as the most closely connected system.

It is clear, then, that this is an area of growing complexity. This is compensated for by consideration that there has in general been, in my view, an accompanying improvement in quality.

Degree of Development of Scottish Conflict

Although conflict is not a new or young subject, much of its development is relatively recent, and in some important respects, the law in this area remains rather primitive. There is considerable scope for growth and development.[39] Some areas like contract and delict have received considerable attention; future development here is likely to be in respect of specific contracts or delicts[40] rather than in general fields. Some areas, the subject of considerable attention, are thought still to be in need of reform. An example here is the field of the recognition of foreign divorces, particularly talak divorces. Despite a Hague Convention,[41] two joint reports of the Law Comissions[42] and major legislation in 1971[43] and 1986,[44] the law in this area is still thought to

---

[36] Wills Act 1963.

[37] Family Law Act 1986, Pt. II.

[38] The meaning of this expression is explained in the *Stair Memorial Encyclopaedia*, Vol. 17 (1989), para. 125.

[39] These views are an amended version of those expressed by the author in the *Stair Memorial Encyclopaedia*, Vol. 17 (1989), para. 123. A valuable area-by-area survey of developments in conflict in the period 1958–1990 may be found in Elizabeth B. Crawford, "What Happened to Indyka? A Survey of Developments in International Private Law 1958–1990" in A. J. Gamble (ed), *Obligations in Context: Essays in Honour of D. M. Walker* (1990).

[40] See P. R. Beaumont, "Private International Law of the Environment", 1995 J.R. 28 at pp. 28–31.

[41] Hague Convention on the Recognition of Divorces and Legal Separations (1968) Cmnd. 6248 (1970).

[42] Hague Convention on Recognition of Divorces and Legal Separations, Law. Com. No. 34, Scot. Law. Com. No. 16 (1970); Recognition of Foreign Nullity Decrees And Related Matters, Law. Com. No. 137, Scot. Law. Com. No. 88 (1984).

[43] Recognition of Divorces and Legal Separations Act 1971.

[44] Family Law Act 1986, Pt. II.

require attention.[45] Then domicile, particularly that of children, is in urgent need of reform. Sensible reforms were suggested by the two Law Commissions in 1978,[46] but no legislation has followed. The fact that Anglophonic systems use domicile as the personal law while the continentals favour the national system impedes harmonisation. Attempts to overcome this problem have been made in specific areas; not all of them have been felicitous. I think, in particular on the negative side, of the Hague Convention on Succession 1988[47] which, happily, is still not part of our law.[48] In a number of important areas the Scottish conflict rules are not as developed as they should be. One thinks, in this context, of the rules on patents, securities, bankruptcy and the winding up of companies.[49] There are a number of areas in which there is English case law, but a dearth of Scottish authority. Examples of such areas are the laws of unrecognised governments[50] and "transmission and remission".[51]

Conclusion

At one time my over-view of the conflict field was as follows. There are, in this area, a large number of legal problems requiring solution. Many of these problems have been addressed and solved over the years, although some remain. The amount of attention given to a particular problem was determined mainly by its social or economic significance at the relevant time, but the problems, whether active or dormant, were constants. Thus the legal problems posed by the polygamous marriage were always with us, though their solution became more urgent when immigration brought many persons, parties to such marriages, to our shores.

A conclusion reached by Professor Wilson in an article in 1988 suggested to me that this model was defective; a more dynamic model is required. He wrote:

"It is easy enough to trumpet about examples of progress made in the century—sexual equality in family relationships and succession, the removal of discrimination against illegitimate children, the abolition of capital punishment, the strengthening of the

---

[45] J. Young, "The recognition of extra-judicial divorces in the United Kingdom" (1987) 7 L.S. 78; L. Edwards, "The Family Law Act 1986: A Lost Opportunity", 1988 Fam. Law 419.

[46] *The Law of Domicile*, Law. Com. No. 168; Scot. Law. Com. No. 107 (1987).

[47] Hague Convention on the Law Applicable to Succession to the Estates of Deceased Persons (1988).

[48] The Convention is thought to be defective because it favours the application in succession matters not of the domiciliary law but that of the deceased's country of habitual residence. However, there is a strong argument that domicile not habitual residence is the appropriate connecting factor here: *The Law of Domicile*, Law Com. No. 168; Scot. Law Com. No. 107, paras. 3.5–3.8 and 3.12.

[49] See, *eg*, D. P. Sellar, "The Insolvency Act 1986 And Cross-Border Winding Up" (1995) 40 J.L.S.S. 102.

[50] *Stair Memorial Encyclopedia*, Vol. 17, paras. 148–151.

[51] *ibid*, paras. 152–158.

rights of consumers, and so on. Progress, however, is relative. The conferring of succession rights on illegitimate children or rights to damages on cohabitees may appear to represent progress today but in 1888 these would have been regarded as dangerous attacks on the family and its values."

"The important question is whether the law at a given time has responded to the needs of the society and the economy at that time."[52]

There is, then, no *numerus clausus* of problems needing legal solutions; over the years old problems will change or disappear and novel situations, social, economic and technological, will arise requiring new laws to deal with them. One may conclude, then, that, despite all the good work already done in the conflict area, a demanding future lies ahead. It is a fascinating, if challenging, prospect.

---

[52] W. A. Wilson, "The Progress of the Law, 1888–1988", 1988 J.R. 207 at p. 233. The only publication of Professor Wilson which deals, to any extent, with conflict matters is his essay "Nothing But a Border" in his *Introductory Essays on Scots Law* (2nd ed 1984).

EUROPEAN COMMUNITY LAW AU PAYS DU TARTAN

CHRISTINE BOCH AND ROBERT LANE

"Psychiatrists have suggested that a student who enters upon the study of law is in search of the security provided by certainty. He expects to find a fixed and unchanging body of unambiguous rules which, once absorbed, will furnish a clear solution to any legal problem which arises in a professional lifetime. It is not at all like that. In the first place, there are many areas of law where it is doubtful what the rule is and, where there is a rule, there is often dispute as to its meaning or effect . . . In the second place the law is changing all the time."[1]

Bill Wilson was reflecting, in his customarily wry manner, upon the qualities necessary to become a good student of law, and in the full-ness of time a successful lawyer. It is also an acute observation, as the received image of the lawyer is often that of a rather dull, (arch)conservative and excessively conformist individual. Some—out-with the confines of the Old College—doubtless are. But Wilson was an eminent lawyer yet certainly none of these things, and his prop-osition that in order to be a good lawyer it is essential to be inquisitive, supple and open-minded—verging in some aspects on the revolution-ary—is well taken. More importantly for the sake of the present argu-ment, these qualities which have long been a necessary part of the armoury of the Scots lawyer are needed more than ever, for the Scots lawyer, long "forced to pay attention to what is happening elsewhere in the world",[2] is now required to become a Community lawyer. When concerned with matters of Community law—a system of law to which Wilson's *cri du coeur* applies with far greater force—the solici-tor, advocate and judge, from the meanest district and sheriff courts to the giddy heights of Parliament House, must now shed some of their Scottish carapace. They must urge or allow a construction of statutes which runs contrary to their apparent meaning[3]; they must seek or supply remedies which do not exist in national law or pro-cedure—for example, declaratory relief in an application for judicial review that provisions of an Act of Parliament are incompatible with the requirements of Community law[4]; they must ignore national statu-tory rules, and even constitutional bars, which limit the effective exer-cise of a Community right.[5] In short, they must from time to time think the unthinkable and require the impossible. This is not to say that every Community law case requires a fresh tilt at windmills or

[1] W. A. Wilson, *Introductory Essays on Scots Law*, (2nd ed. 1984) at p. 1.
[2] *ibid.*, p. 2.
[3] *Marshall v. Southampton and South West Hampshire Area Health Authority (No. 2)* [1994] 1 A.C. 530.
[4] *R. v. Secretary of State for Employment, ex p. E.O.C.* [1995] 1 A.C. 1, discussed below.
[5] *R. v. Secretary of State for Transport, ex p. Factortame* [1991] 1 A.C. 603, discussed below.

254

frontal assault upon constitutional fundamentals. Frequently a little ingenuity will suffice. But lawyers must be aware they are playing the game to a different set of rules. The purpose of this essay is to provide the Scots lawyer with a journeyman's guide to the pitfalls, and opportunities, of those rules.

The Context and Challenge of Community Law

Community law can baffle the neophyte, and not only the neophyte. Like any legal system it has its unique features which must be taken on board by the lawyer in order merely to become literate. It can properly be understood only in its wider political and economic context, and presupposes the acquisition of a substantial body of contextual knowledge. Its principles and rules are applied adopting canons of intepretation significantly different from those to which Scottish lawyers' training and instincts would direct them; they must begin to *think* differently. And the rules of Community law, more so than those of Scots law, can be difficult to find, may be ambiguous, and are subject to change. Wilson once said, after contriving to draw upon Robert Service, Dangerous Dan McGrew and the law of the Yukon, that the statute law of Scotland is far from being clear.[6] Community law is no clearer. It is unclear in its terms; it is unclear in its application; and it is unclear because of the pace of change of both. The Community legal system is a relatively fluid and unstable system, and the practitioner must be wary that he may find himself standing on shifting sand.

The Community system has of course one obvious problem. It is language. It is, for good or ill, a fact of life in the Community, and it goes far beyond "the inherent features of language which create difficulties for the lawyer".[7] The Treaty exists in 12, Community legislation in 11, equally authentic language versions,[8] and Scottish judges and lawyers, not all of whom are fluent in Finnish and Greek, may be required to take notice of all of them.[9] The Community comprises 15 member states, some having more than one legal system, and perhaps again as many different legal traditions, and must draw inspiration from them in defining Community rules, concepts and principles. The meaning of legal concepts can, and does, vary widely amongst legal systems, and it is difficult for any judge or lawyer to stray from the distinct tenets and principles in which his or her own jurisdiction is grounded. To cite one example, the English version of the E.C. Treaty refers at a number of important junctures to a right of national derogation from Community rules justified upon grounds of "public policy".[10] This is an anodyne and misleading rendering of what the original language texts call *ordre public, öffentliche Ordnung, openbare orde* and *ordine pubblico*, all of which have well-established

---

[6] "Studying Statutes", 1992 J.R. 213 at p. 213.
[7] Wilson, *Introductory Essays on Scots Law* at pp. 10–20.
[8] The Treaty exists in an authentic Irish version but Community legislation is not adopted in Irish.
[9] See Case 283/81 *CILFIT v. Ministero della Sanità* [1982] E.C.R. 3415.
[10] E.C. Treaty, Arts. 36, 48(3) and 56(1).

and specific meanings in the national law of other member states which are neither rendered by "public policy" nor necessarily equivalent to the meaning to be given to the term in Community law. So in a Community case before him the Scottish judge may be required to divine and distil a Community law meaning not only of public policy but also of *an beartas poiblí* (perhaps, fortuitously, just manageable if he hails from Lewis), *yleinen järjestys* and δημόσια τάιξη. And this is but one term drawn from the Treaty. Multiply this by the sheer volume of the Official Journal which in English alone occupies at the moment some 43 yards (or, with the entry into force of the Units of Measurement Regulations,[11] 39.32 metres) of shelf space, consider the impenetrability and ambiguity of some of it, the duty to interpret it in its Community, not national, law context, and the enormity of the task becomes clear. To give an even simpler example: pivotal to the evolution of Community law, and so to the interpretation and enforcement of Community rights, is the *acquis communautaire*, yet it is a principle so elusive that it cannot be rendered in any language other than French. All this is of course precisely why the national judge wrestling with a question of interpretation might well wish to seek in aid the "panoramic view" of the Court of Justice by means of an Article 177 preliminary reference[12]—although Scottish judges seem particularly reluctant to do so.[13]

This is only the starting point. Having begun to come to terms *with* Community law, the lawyer must then address contradictions *within* Community law. In the Community legal system, just as Wilson observed in the context of Scots law, there are many areas in which it is difficult to trace a rule, as rules frequently develop and become redefined as the system evolves. Even where there is an ascertainable rule disputes as to its meaning or effect can arise, and the Community system is certainly not the least of those marked by ambiguity and volatility. Whilst it is no longer seriously questioned that it boasts competences, in limited albeit ever widening fields,[14] rules and principles which constitute a legal order, it is not (yet) a fully elaborated system. Furthermore, in the Community, even where there is a rule and it is relatively clear and precise, this is no bar to the ingenious

---

[11] S.I. 1994 No. 2867.

[12] *Customs and Excise Commissioners v. ApS Samex* [1983] 1 All E.R. 1042, *per* Bingham, J. at p. 1055.

[13] Since British accession in 1973 to the end of 1995 only five references have been made from Scottish courts (three from the High Court, one from the Outer House and one from a sheriff court). This compares with 192 from the rest of the UK, 61 from Denmark (with a population size comparable to that of Scotland) and 32 from Ireland. Sweden, a member state since January 1995, has already overtaken Scotland with six references in its first 12 months. This lack of (direct) exposure of the Scottish courts to the methods of interpretation practised by the Court of Justice may be part of a vicious circle: the less the direct contact and so exposure to those methods, the less the inclination to seek further contact and exposure.

[14] Compare the well-known dictum of the Court of Justice in Case 26/62 *van Gend en Loos* [1963] E.C.R. 1 at p. 12: "the Community constitutes a new legal order of international law, for the benefit of which the states have limited their sovereign rights, albeit within limited fields . . ." with its subsequent reformulation in Opinion 1/91 *re the Draft E.E.A. Treaty* (No 1) [1991] E.C.R. I-6079 at p. 6102, in which the Court substituted "in ever wider fields" for "albeit within limited fields".

lawyer arguing for a different meaning or effect. Many of the rules of Community law, be they in the Treaty—*traité cadre*—or in legislation made under the Treaty, are formulated and drafted in opaque and ambiguous terms, reflecting in part the political compromise which led to their adoption.[15] This style has been cited by Lord Templeman as both a strength and a difficulty of Community legislation.[16] Moreover, in many instances the issue of subsequent application of and compliance with the rule is deliberately left unaddressed and arises only if and when the rule comes up for enforcement. In the process of enforcement, the content of the rule is in turn clearly affected and/or altered through the judiciary clearly defining and/or expanding upon the substance of the rule.

> "Thus a decision that a provision produces direct effect makes the Court of Justice responsible for fine tuning the application of the provision in concrete cases, which in turn leads to a judge-made gloss on the provision, determining its *real content and relevance*."[17]

In the same way, when a matter arises before a Scottish judge he may himself be required to perform that very function: to expand upon or define the substance of the rule or refer back to an interpretation of the Court of Justice. Even where the Community rule is directly effective—in British terms, of itself an "enforceable Community right"[18]—the task is not straightforward. Indeed, interpretation in Community law goes far beyond the received British understanding of the task of statutory interpretation, for it is a means of ensuring that rights created within a purposive scheme enjoy effective protection. At the moment the House of Lords seeks to square the circle either by applying the Community rule directly as best it can or, where it cannot, by relying upon a (generous) purposive interpretation of British legislation in order that such rights are protected:

---

[15] The quality of Community drafting, for many years overlooked, is now the subject of significant attention in the Community institutions. At the 1992 Edinburgh Summit the European Council demanded that practical steps be taken to make Community legislation simpler and clearer, and the Council subsequently adopted a resolution on the quality of drafting (O.J. 1993 C166/1) which contains guidelines against which Community legislation is to be measured. Although concern has been expressed as to whether this will bring about any improvement, as indeed "the quality problem of Community legislation is above all a matter of *substance*. Its imperfectness is strongly related to the subject matter of the rules and the particularities of the Community's institutional structures. It is and will be a fact of Community life that Member States and operators are fully confronted with, and to a large extent liable for, the negative effects of low quality legislation"; R. Barents, "The Quality of Community Legislation: Some Observations on E.C. Legislation in the Agricultural Sector", (1994) 1 Maastricht Journal of Comparative Law 101 at p. 114 (emphasis added); see also A. E. Kellermann, "The Quality of Community Legislation Drafting", in D. Curtin and T. Heukels (eds), *The Institutional Dynamics of European Integration: Essays in Honour of H. G. Schermers* (1994), p. 251.

[16] *Dule v. G.E.C. Reliance Ltd* [1988] AC 618 at p. 641.

[17] K. Lenaerts, "Interaction between Judges and Politicians", (1992) 12 Yearbook of European Law 1 at p. 11; emphasis added.

[18] European Communities Act 1972, s. 2(1).

"If the legislation can reasonably be construed so as to conform with those obligations—obligations which are to be ascertained not only from the wording of the relevant Directive, but from the interpretation placed upon it by the European Court of Justice at Luxembourg—such a purposive construction will be applied even though, perhaps, it may involve some departure from the strict and literal application of the words which the legislature has elected to use."[19]

Or, in the Lords' more generous and most recent brush with Community rights:

"The ruling of the European Court proceeds on an interpretation of the broad principles dealt with in articles 2(1) and 5(1) of the Directive Council 76/207/EEC. Sections 1(1)(a) and 5(3) of the Act of 1975 [the Sex Discrimination Act] set out a more precise test of unlawful discrimination, and the problem is how to fit the terms of that test into the ruling."[20]

The requirement for the Scots lawyer to think the impossible extends even further. Even where Community rules appear to be relatively straightforward or even precise, it ought not to dissuade the lawyer from arguing for an interpretation which by instinct might be dismissed outright. In the Treaty, some rules require implementing measures in order to achieve their "*effet utile*". Sometimes they are not adopted through lack of political consensus. But this does not mean that the rules cannot be enforced. This is best illustrated by the case law on the direct effect of Articles 52 and 59 of the Treaty. When these provisions first arose for enforcement, counsel seeking to ascertain their clients' rights under them were sufficiently ingenious to argue that the Treaty rules had to be operative notwithstanding the absence of implementing measures provided for in the Treaty.[21] They were not dissuaded by arguments to the contrary that, the Treaty having provided for implementing measures, and the implementing measures not having been adopted, the rules could not be operative or enforceable just yet. In these cases, the Court of Justice dismissed and by-passed the need for such measures, qualifying them in its case law as mere facilitating measures, the absence of which could not affect the existence and exercise of the rights provided for by the Treaty. Implementation was not accepted as a valid prerequisite for operation and enforcement; what matters to the Court of Justice is ensuring that the rules are operative and effective in practice. In this respect the Community system, like the Scottish legal system, strives for efficiency.[22] As the Court of Justice consistently observes, rules are designed to achieve a precise result. Therefore they must be made

---

[19] *Litster v. Forth Dry Dock Ltd*, 1989 S.C. (H.L.) 96 *per* Lord Oliver at p. 105.
[20] *Webb v. Emo Air Cargo Ltd* [1995] 1 W.L.R. 1454 *per* Lord Keith at p. 1459.
[21] Case 2/74 *Reyners v. Belgium* [1974] E.C.R. 63; Case 33/74 *van Binsbergen v. Bestuur van de Bedrijfsvereniging voor de Metaalnijverheid* [1974] E.C.R. 1299.
[22] See P. Pescatore, "The Doctrine of 'Direct Effect'; An Infant Disease in Community Law", [1983] E.L.R. 155.

effective. And it is courts, whether Community courts or national courts, which must provide the means by which to achieve that result. For national courts the obligation is now drawn expressly from Article 5 of the Treaty,[23] a principle which has been enunciated by the Court of Justice thus:

> "[W]here Community legislation does not specifically provide any penalty for an infringement or refers for that purpose to national laws, regulations and administrative provisions, Article 5 of the Treaty requires the Member States to take all measures necessary to guarantee the application and effectiveness of Community law."[24]

Just as the Court of Justice undertook to ensure the independent operation of Community rules notwithstanding the absence of political agreement to make them operative, it now falls to national courts—organs of the member states[25]—to take all steps necessary and appropriate to afford Community rights the protection they require so as to render their exercise effective. The task facing national courts therefore extends not only to giving effect to directly effective provisions of Community law (which in the United Kingdom is in any event a statutory duty under section 2(1) of the European Communities Act 1972), but also to inverting the plain meaning of national legislation in order that non-directly effective rights are protected (*interprétation conforme*),[26] and even to overriding the detail of a national legislative scheme in order to give effect, "as far as is at all possible", to general objectives of broad principles of Community law.[27] And where the national court is empowered and charged with this uncommon task of ensuring the effective protection of a Community right, it falls to the lawyer to submit uncommon means by which it ought to do so. But daring lawyers must be prepared to show humility as, on occasion, they are likely to encounter resistance from a court which may not be entirely sympathetic, and may in truth be bluntly hostile, to this uncomfortable and unfamiliar approach. This is not the case only when appearing before a lower court; the House of Lords has itself wrestled with it on a number of occasions.[28]

---

[23] See J. Temple Lang, "Community Constitutional Law: Article 5 EEC Treaty", (1990) 27 C.M.L. Rev. 645; O. Due, "Artikel 5 van het EEG Verdrag—een bepaling met een federaal karakter?", (1992) 40 S.E.W. 355.

[24] Case 68/88 *Commission v. Greece* [1989] E.C.R. 2965 at p. 2984.

[25] Community law does not distinguish amongst the various authorities of the member states; whatever their constitutional status in national law, each is bound by the obligations of Art. 5. See Case 96/81 *Commission v. Netherlands* [1982] E.C.R. 1791; Cases C-1 & 176/90 *Aragonesa de Publicidad Exterior v. Departmento de Sanidad y Securidad Social de la Generalitat de Cataluña* [1991] E.C.R. I-4151.

[26] Case 14/83 *von Colson and Kamann v. Land Nordrhein-Westfalen* [1984] E.C.R. 1891; Case C-106/89 *Marleasing v. La Comercial Internacional de Alimentación* [1990] E.C.R. I-435; Case C-91/92 *Faccini Dori v. Recreb* [1994] E.C.R. I-3325.

[27] Case C-165/91 *van Munster v. Rijksdienst voor Pensioenen* [1994] E.C.R. I-4661.

[28] Compare the judgments in *Pickstone v. Freemans* [1989] A.C. 66; *Litster v. Forth Dry Dock Ltd*, 1989 S.C. (H.L.) 96; *R. v. Secretary of State for Employment ex p. E.O.C.* [1995] 1 A.C. 1 and *Webb v. Emo Air Cargo Ltd* [1995] 1 W.L.R. 1454 with those in *Duke v. G.E.C. Reliance Ltd* [1988] A.C. 618 and *Finnegan v. Clowney Youth Training Programme*

A Moving Target

Wilson wrote of the development of Scots law outwards and down-wards.[29] Community law can be said to be beset by rapid change, the pace of which is both quantitative and qualitative. Quantitatively, there is simply the rapid growth of Community legislation, both within established Community spheres and in its "ever wider fields" of competences.[30] There is also in the Community context the phenom-enon of abrupt, sometimes seismic, expansion with constitutional amendment, as with for example the Single European Act, the Maas-tricht Treaty, and whatever the 1996 intergovernmental conference may bring. These are both relatively straightforward aspects to which Wilson referred as expansion, or volume of change. Further, whilst as a legal system not yet 50 years old, Community law has already devel-oped into a remarkably comprehensive system. This is evolution and development of legal principles far more rapid than that which type-fies other, more venerable legal systems. It is also a system given substance in large measure by judge-made law, which discomfits our continental friends far more than it does us.

The pace of change is also qualitative. As is well known, the Com-munity legal system owes much, if not everything, to the Court of Justice. Whilst Scottish lawyers may be perfectly comfortable in recog-nising case law as an important if not pre-eminent source of law, they may nevertheless be bewildered by the manner in which the Court of Justice wields it. This can best be illustrated by two different aspects of the Court's jurisprudence. First, the instinct of the Scottish lawyer is to look for consistency in case law as a means of safeguarding legal certainty. But the Community is a new adventure, without precursor, and in shaping its legal system the Court of Justice is required to adapt to rapidly changing circumstances. This has produced inconsistency: evolution, but not linear evolution. Just as there is an ebb and flow to political integration, periods of what is referred to (usually disparagingly) as "judicial activism" tend to be followed by periods of consolidation. The Scottish lawyer will look for logic and precision in developing case law—but will sometimes be disappointed. The Court of Justice is blessed/cursed to be a collegiate body, with the reasoning of judgments the product of judicial compromise. And there has not traditionally been seen the necessity, self-evident to the Scot-tish lawyer, to be absolutely consistent with previous case law. Indeed, until recently the Court of Justice made no effort to take notice of its own case law; previous judgments were cited only very rarely and appeared not to form a component of the Court's reasoning. This left the Court of Justice free to depart from a previous (apparent) line of authority without requiring or bothering to justify doing so.[31] This

---

[1990] 2 A.C. 407. In the former the Lords allowed a purposive construction of British statutes but in the latter refused so to construe (or "distort") British legislation where there has been no attempt by Parliament or the government to give effect to the Community right in question.

[29] *Introductory Essays on Scots Law*, at p. 2.

[30] See n. 14 *supra*.

[31] *e.g.*, the early rule on standing to raise an action under Art. 215(2) absent a previous action under Art. 173 as established in Case 25/62 *Plaumann v. E.E.C. Commission*

has changed slowly. The Court of Justice began to buttress its reasoning with earlier judgments in the 1970s—although it must be said that it tended to cite only that "well established case law" which supported its conclusions, and case law which went the other way was not cited, not addressed, and not distinguished. This may be an improvement but it is still overruling implicitly and by stealth, and does not assist legal certainty. Latterly however the Court of Justice has tightened up and begun to cite apparently contrary authority and to justify not following it.[32] And it has now admitted to fallibility by expressly overruling its own case law on two occasions.[33] This willingness to recognise a *cursus curiae* implicitly as a source of law and to reason by it ought to be welcomed by Scots lawyers, leads to greater clarity and legal certainty, and is a mark of the maturity of the legal system. Yet they must be sensitive to the fact that even with these developments the precision of the Court of Justice is less than that to which they are accustomed, and some (what appears to Scottish eyes to be) woolly reasoning still surfaces.[34] And they must of course be aware that when the tectonic plate shifts with Treaty amendment, the game can start anew with fresh fundamental principles.

The second illustration of qualitative change lies in the context of enforcement of Community rights. Again, Community law is an improvised system which is still incomplete and evolving. Early case law of the Court of Justice recognised the enforceability (direct effect) of Community rights, but left the mechanisms to achieve it to national rules and procedures, in deference to a principle of the institutional autonomy of the member states in which sphere the Community generally did not interfere.[35] Remedies in Scots law were created and

---

[1963] E.C.R. 95 was "reversed" in Case 44/69 *Lütticke v. Commission* [1971] E.C.R. 352 without mention of *Plaumann* or the "precedent" it set.

[32] *e.g.* Case 175/84 *Krohn v. Commission* [1986] E.C.R. 753, this time distinguishing Case 25/62 *Plaumann*, ibid; Case 70/88 *Parliament v. Council* (Chernobyl) [1990] E.C.R. I-2041, distinguishing Case 302/87 *Parliament v. Council (Comitology)* [1988] E.C.R. 5615; Case C-188/92 *T.W.D. Textilwerke Deggendorf v. Germany* [1994] E.C.R. I-833, distinguishing Case 216/82 *Universität Hamburg v. Hauptzollamt Hamburg-Kehrwieder* [1983] E.C.R. 2771; and Case C-410/92 *Johnson v. Chief Adjudication Officer* [1994] E.C.R. I-5483, distinguishing and narrowing significantly Case C-208/90 *Emmott v. Minister for Social Welfare and Att. Gen.* [1991] E.C.R. I-4269.

[33] Case C-10/89 *S.A. C.N.L.-Sucal N.V. v. Hag G.F. A.G.* [1990] E.C.R. I-3711; Cases C-267–8/91 *Criminal Proceedings against Keck and Mithouard* [1993] E.C.R. I-6097. The Court of Justice has now been invited by the English High Court, Chancery Division expressly to overrule its judgment of Case 187/80 *Merck v. Stephar* [1981] E.C.R. 2063 in Case C-267/95 *Merck v. Primecrown*, pending.

[34] *e.g.*, in Case C-188/92 *T.W.D. Textilwerke Deggendorf* (n. 32 *supra*) a previous case arguably more directly in point was Case 314/85 *Foto-Frost v. Hauptzollamt Lübeck-Ost* [1987] E.C.R. 4199 but it was not mentioned; and in Cases C-6 & 9/90 *Francovich and Bonifaci v. Italy* [1991] E.C.R. I-5357 the Court of Justice effectively overruled its previous judgment in Case 60/75 *Russo v. AIMA* [1976] E.C.R. 45, yet cited *Russo* in a manner which implies full agreement with it.

[35] *e.g.*, Case 45/76 *Comet v. Productschap voor Siergewassen* [1976] E.C.R. 2043; Case 33/76 *Rewe-Zentralfinanz und Rewe-Zentral v. Landwirtschaftskammer für das Saarland* [1976] E.C.R. 1989; Case 158/80 *Rewe-Handelsgesellschaft Nord v. Hauptzollamt Kiel* [1981] E.C.R. 1805. See C. Boch and R. Lane, "European Community Law in National Courts: A Continuing Contradiction" (1992) 5 Leiden Journal of International Law 171.

developed in order to give effect to Scots law rights. They are not necessarily compatible with, or equal to the task of, giving effect to Community law rights. So long as they are the means by which Community rights are to be enforced in Scottish courts, lacunae will exist and the pursuer may be left without a remedy. This problem has now been addressed by the Court of Justice by, some would argue, a gradual and still evolving frontal assault upon the constitutional prerogative of the member states to order their own judicial mechanisms. Far from not interfering, over the years the Court of Justice took note of the lacunae in national laws and the consequent threat to the effective and uniform protection of Community rights, and so began filling them in. So, where a remedy did not exist in national law or procedure it had to be created *ex proprio motu* by the national court, and a national statutory or even constitutional bar to its exercise had to be set aside.[36]

In this area more than others, practitioners will find themselves confronting new challenges. Submission of uncommon or innovative pleadings based upon Community law rights before a Scottish judge may well be required "to be made with some eloquence, not to say courage".[37] But it has succeeded elsewhere, simply by virtue of emboldened lawyers trying it on in national proceedings. Given Crown immunity in English law, counsel for the Anglo-Spanish "quota hoppers" were certainly not confident of their application for interim injunction.[38] The Equal Opportunities Commission were venturing into the unknown when seeking declaratory relief in an application for judicial review.[39] Mr Francovich's *avvocati* urging recognition of a principle of state liability and so for a remedy in damages for failure to implement a directive, at the time a revolutionary proposition, must surely have thought they were grasping at straws.[40] Yet

---

[36] Case 222/84 *Johnston v. Chief Constable of the R.U.C.* [1986] E.C.R. 1651; Case C-271/91 *Marshall v. Southampton and Southwest Hampshire Area Health Authority (Marshall II)* [1993] E.C.R. I-4367; Case C-213/89 *R. v. Secretary of State for Transport, ex p. Factortame* [1990] E.C.R. I-2433.

[37] M. Upton, "European Unfair Contract Terms Law", 1995 S.L.T. (News) 295 at p. 299.

[38] *R. v. Secretary of State for Transport ex p. Factortame* [1990] 2 A.C. 55, in which the House of Lords found it unconstitutional in English law to grant an interim injunction against the Crown, but subsequently ([1991] 1 A.C. 603) granted the injunction following a reference from the Court of Justice (Case C-213/89 *Factortame*, n. 36 above). This Crown immunity rule has now been reversed in English law (*M. v. Home Office* [1993] 3 All E.R. 537) but not in Scots law (*McDonald v. Secretary of State*, 1994 S.L.T. 692), on which see in this volume C. M. G. Himsworth, "Public Law: In Peril of Neglect?", pp. 224–238 above.

[39] *R. v. Secretary of State for Employment, ex p. E.O.C.* [1995] 1 A.C. 1, in which petitioners sought a declaration that some provisions of the Employment Protection (Consolidation) Act 1978 were incompatible with Art. 119 of the Treaty and the equal pay directive. Lord Browne-Wilkinson said (at p. 34) that the relevant question was whether an English court "has ... jurisdiction to make a declaration that the domestic law of the United Kingdom is not in conformity with European law", which their Lordships answered in the affirmative; see also the speech of Lord Keith at pp. 26ff. For an (unsuccessful) application for declarator in comparable circumstances in a Scottish case see *NUPE v. Grampian Regional Council*, March 11, 1993, Outer House, unreported.

[40] Cases C-6 & 9/90 *Francovich and Bonifaci v. Italy* [1991] E.C.R. I-5357. This remedy in damages has now been recognised (*obiter*) by the House of Lords in *Kirklees Municipal Borough Council v. Wickes Building Supplies Ltd* [1993] A.C. 227 *per* Lord Goff at

they all prevailed. Practitioners must therefore be aware that they are addressing an evolving, moving target. It is a brave or foolish solicitor who advises a client: sorry, that won't wash before the Court of Justice. Yet at the same time, even if the case ends up before the Court of Justice courtesy of a brave or puzzled Scottish judge, counsel must still be prepared to be humbled when advocating a proposition which has doctrinal support, is on one view irresistible, yet the Court of Justice, perhaps in a consolidating phase, refuses the fence.[41]

These are all examples of ways in which Scots lawyers must learn to think on a Community wavelength. But there is more. When faced with the application of a Scottish rule they may ask whether the rule has a Community origin, in which case the court might, and should, be prepared to allow an expansive construction of the Scottish rule. Even more daring, can a Scottish rule, even with no apparent link with Community law, be brought within the material scope of the Treaty? However apparently preposterous the proposition, it can pay useful dividends. As Lord Mackenzie Stuart observed, Community law has a habit of emerging in unlikely corners.[42] The argument that those provisions of the Shops Act 1950 which prohibited Sunday trading in England and Wales constituted an infringement of the Treaty rules on the free movement of goods was far-fetched in the extreme, yet it won a partial victory from the Court of Justice[43] before ultimately failing,[44] and in any event had the effect of permitting clients to continue trading on Sunday for a number of years pending the final outcome. More successful and durable were arguments by which the concepts of indirect discrimination as developed by the Court of Justice in relation to Article 119 of the Treaty and the equal pay and equal treatment directives were used to bring within the scope of Community law the precarious status of part-time workers,[45] arguments since recognised and applied by the House of Lords.[46] Again, this was

---

p. 282 and *R. v. Secretary of State for Employment, ex p. E.O.C.* [1995] 1 A.C. 1 *per* Lord Keith at p. 32.

[41] The phrase ("*La Corte rifiutò l'ostacolo*") is (then) Advocate-General Mancini's in Case 204/86 *Greece v. Council* Racc. 1988, p. 5323 at p. 5344, commenting upon a refusal by the Court of Justice in an earlier judgment to pronounce upon the availability to member states of the Art. 184 plea of illegality. See more recently Case C-91/92 *Faccini Dori v. Recreb* [1994] E.C.R. I-3325, in which the Court of Justice, notwithstanding the urging of Advocate-General Lenz in the case and of Advocates-General van Gerven and Jacobs in previous, related cases (C-271/91 *Marshall v. Southampton and Southwest Hampshire Area Health Authority (Marshall II)* [1993] E.C.R. I-4367; Case C-316/93 *Vaneetveld v. Le Foyer* [1994] E.C.R. I-763 respectively), adopted a textual interpretation (!) of Art. 189 and refused to recognise that directives were capable of creating rights enforceable between private parties.

[42] *The European Communities and the Rule of Law*, 29th Hamlyn Lectures (1977), p. 1.

[43] Case 145/88 *Torfaen Borough Council v. B & Q p.l.c.* [1989] E.C.R. 3851, in which the Court of Justice indicated that in some circumstances, by application of a quite incomprehensible test, a prohibition of Sunday trading might infringe Art. 30.

[44] Case C-169/91 *Stoke-on-Trent City Council v. B & Q p.l.c.* [1992] E.C.R., I-6635; and even then the Shops Act escaped the prohibition of Art. 30 not on the ground that the matter fell outwith the scope of Community law, rather that the purpose of the Sunday trading rules was compatible with Community law.

[45] See *inter alia* Case 171/88 *Rinner-Kühn v. FWW Spezial-Gebäudereinigung* [1989] E.C.R. 2743; Case C-33/89 *Kowalska v. Freie und Hansestadt Hamburg* [1990] ECR I-2591.

[46] *R. v. Secretary of State for Employment ex p. E.O.C.* [1995] 1 A.C. 1.

at odds with a *prima facie* interpretation of these texts which did not appear at first sight to cover such issues, issues which are still the subject of much contention.[47] In a similar manner the Court of Justice was also forced to intervene in relation to pregnancy and maternity issues, before any specific legislation in the field was adopted and implemented.[48]

It should by now have become apparent that Bill Wilson's warning to intending students of law must be taken to heart. Even more so than in Scots law, the search for security in the Community is elusive in the extreme. Wilson did not write as much in the area of Community law as he could and should have,[49] to our loss. But he was very sensitive to its challenges and opportunities, and could often be found in the Europa Institute library in the Old College poring over Community law materials, in search certainly not of certainty, but of adventure. Or perhaps of mischief. He developed a theory that the simplest way to understand Community law was by reference to the Court's copious case law on food and drink.[50] Whilst he never committed this theory to paper, it was always one of the great joys and privileges of life in Old College to join him whenever possible in his field work.

---

[47] A directive on part-time work is still in draft form. Its adoption is being most vehemently resisted by the government of one member state.

[48] See Case 177/88 *Dekker v. Stichting Vormingcentrum voor Jong Volwassenen Plus* [1990] E.C.R. 1–3941 and Case C–32/93 *Webb v. Emo Air Cargo Ltd* [1994] E.C.R. I–3567, which pre-date the implementation of Directive 92/85 O.J. 1992 L348/1 on the protection of pregnant women.

[49] He wrote a number of articles on Community law matters in the *Scots Law Times* at the time of British accession, which duly became the chapter on "Community Law in Scotland" in his *Introductory Essays on Scots Law*. For a more recent foray see his "Oblique Answers to Straight Questions: The Article 177 Procedure", (1994) 15 Stat. L.R. 31, reflecting in some measure his keen interest in statutory interpretation.

[50] He even alluded, in his half-joking manner, to writing a comprehensive piece on Art. 95 of the Treaty exposing the issues raised by the compatibility with Community law of national taxation systems of alcoholic beverages.

ON SCOTLAND, EUROPE AND HUMAN RIGHTS

WILLIAM C. GILMORE AND STEPHEN C. NEFF

Introduction

A number of scholars—with W. A. Wilson prominent amongst them—
have struggled to maintain the coherence and distinct character of
Scots law. The principal concern in this regard has been, of course,
with respect to the actual influence of English law. But other "foreign"
legal systems have also had an impact, or at least a potential impact,
on the law of Scotland. The present discussion will focus on one of
these: the law of the European Convention on Human Rights (ECHR),
to which the United Kingdom has been a party since its entry into
force in 1953, and the relevant case law as developed by the European
Court of Human Rights.

The first section will look at the various attempts which have been
made, or which might be made, to import the ECHR into Scots law,
with an assessment of their viability. The second part will look at two
of the principal areas in which, to date, the Scottish legal system has
been held by the European Court of Human Rights to fall short of the
standards laid down in the Convention: legal aid in criminal appeals,
and the conduct of children's hearings.

Attempts to Import the European Convention into Scots Law

Given the refusal of Parliament to date to enact a bill of rights which
would render the provisions of the ECHR directly enforceable in
national law, the focus has been on the extent, if any, to which the
Convention can indirectly influence the domestic legal order.[1] In Scotland there have been several attempts to introduce the Convention
through the "back door."[2] While, as will be seen below, most such
attempts have failed, there have been some limited successes and certain avenues continue to provide potential for positive developments.[3]

---

[1] See *e.g.* D. J. Harris, M. O'Boyle and C. Warbrick, *Law of the European Convention on
Human Rights* (1995) at pp. 23–24.
[2] This paper is not concerned with the indirect impact of the Convention on Scots
law resulting from United Kingdom membership of the European Union. For a brief
discussion of this matter, see *ibid.*, pp. 27–28. See also A. Evans, "Treaties and United
Kingdom Legislation: The Scottish Dimension" (1984) 29 J.R. 41 at pp. 52–61; and A.
Clapham, "A Human Rights Policy for the European Community" (1990) 10 Year
Book of European Law 309 at pp. 317–37.
[3] For comparative purposes, a useful analysis of the role of the Convention in English
law is C. Warbrick, "Rights, the European Convention on Human Rights and English
Law" (1994) 19 E.L. Rev. 34.

Jus quaesitum tertio
One strategy was to invoke, by analogy, the contract law principle of *jus quaesitum tertio*. In the leading case of *Kaur v. Lord Advocate*,[4] it was argued that the states parties to the Convention intended the provisions to benefit private persons in the various contracting states. Consequently, individuals in Scotland should be held to possess the Convention rights—and the ability to invoke them in Scottish courts. The court conceded the argument to be "superficially attractive"[5] but declined to endorse it. One reason was that *jus quaesitum tertio* requires an intention on the part of the contracting parties to confer the benefit onto the third party. The court contended that the United Kingdom, in becoming a party to the Convention, did not have the intention to confer the rights directly onto those in its jurisdiction. Since *jus quaesitum tertio* is not a principle of English law, the effect would have been to institute a radically different civil-liberties regime in Scotland as distinct from England and Wales. The British government, it was contended, surely could not have intended that. In addition, it was doubted whether the principle of *jus quaesitum tertio* could operate to confer a benefit onto the public at large, as distinct from specific, identified third parties.

The principle of quod fieri debet infectum valet
According to this principle, courts will sometimes treat an unperformed legal duty as if it had been duly performed, with a view to ensuring that innocent third parties do not suffer prejudice from some party's culpable non-feasance. Applying the principle to the ECHR, the proposition would be that, even though Parliament has failed to incorporate the legislation into domestic law, the Scottish courts should nonetheless proceed as if it had done so—with the result that Scottish courts would enforce Convention rights for the benefit of individuals.[6]

In the *Kaur* case, this argument was rejected, along with that of *jus quaesitum tertio*, on the ground that there was no legal duty which had not been performed. The European Court of Human Rights has itself held explicitly that there is no legal duty on the part of states parties to incorporate the Convention into their domestic legal systems[7] (although it may be noted that most of the parties have done so by one means or another).[8] The Convention only requires states parties to provide an effective remedy to persons under their jurisdiction whenever there is an "arguable" violation of a Convention right.

---

[4] 1980 S.C. 319; 1981 S.L.T. 322.
[5] *ibid.*, p. 330.
[6] For a discussion of this issue, see Evans, "Treaties", *supra*, at pp. 42–44.
[7] For the leading decision to this effect, see *Swedish Engine Drivers Union v. Sweden*, 1 E.H.R.R. 617 (1976), para. 50. For British cases to this effect, see *James v. United Kingdom*, 8 E.H.R.R. 123 (1986), paras. 84–85; *Observer and Guardian v. United Kingdom*, 14 E.H.R.R. 153 (1991), para. 76; and *Costello-Roberts v. United Kingdom*, 19 E.H.R.R., 112 (1993), para. 40.
[8] See generally R. Bernhardt, "The Convention and Domestic Law", in R. St J. Macdonald, F. Matscher and H. Petzold (eds), *The European System for the Protection of Human Rights* (1993), pp. 25–40.

Therefore, since there is no duty on Britain's part to incorporate the Convention into its domestic law, there can logically have been no failure on its part to perform such a duty—and consequently no scope for applying the *quod fieri* principle.[9]

The Convention as an aid to interpretation of domestic law
Another strategy is to use the Convention as a means of interpretation of domestic legislation. At best, this approach is of only limited utility, since it would not come into play unless domestic law was in a state of uncertainty. Here, the position may differ somewhat as between England and Scotland. In English law, the House of Lords has accepted that the ECHR can be an aid to interpretation.[10] In Scotland, however, the *Kaur* court intimated that the Convention could not play even that modest a role, although it may be noted that, strictly speaking, the point was not before the court.[11] Lord Ross found the position as articulated in the English case law "extremely difficult to comprehend."[12] In his view, the Scottish courts were "not entitled to have regard to the Convention either as an aid to construction or otherwise."[13]

The learned judge, however, went further. The ECHR was not "in any way" part of the law of Scotland[14] and was "irrelevant in legal proceedings unless and until its provisions have been incorporated or given effect to in legislation."[15] This seemingly absolute view of the irrelevance of the Convention was subsequently adopted by the Inner House. In *Moore v. Secretary of State for Scotland*, it was held that Lord Ross "was perfectly correct in holding that the Convention plays no part in our municipal law so long as it has not been introduced into it by legislation."[16]

The *Kaur* and *Moore* cases present, as just noted, an absolutist view on the part of the Court of Session against the use of the ECHR in Scotland as an aid to statutory interpretation. One writer has gone so far as to characterise these two decisions as "twin watchdogs at the doors of the legal system prohibiting entry of the Convention without legislative authority."[17] These cases do not necessarily, however, rep-

---

[9] *Kaur v. Lord Advocate* 1980 S.C. 319 at p. 329.
[10] *Waddington v. Miah* [1974] 2 All E.R. 377; [1974] 1 W.L.R. 683. See also the leading case of *Brind v. Secretary at State for the Home Department* [1991] 1 A.C. 696; [1991] 1 All E.R. 720; [1991] 2 W.L.R. 588. This approach gives effect to the presumption that Parliament does not intend to legislate in a manner inconsistent with the treaty obligations entered into by the Crown. On this presumption, see *Mortensen v. Peters* (1906) 8F. (J) 93.
[11] The reason was that, in that case, the court clearly stated that there was no ambiguity in the law in question (the Immigration Act 1971). *Kaur v. Lord Advocate*, 1980 SC 319 at p. 329.
[12] *ibid.*, at p. 328.
[13] *ibid.*, at p. 329.
[14] *ibid.*, at p. 324.
[15] *ibid.*, at p. 329. For a critical analysis of the judgment, see T. St J. N. Bates, "Treaties in the Courts", (1981) 2 Stat. L.R. 40. For a more supportive academic perspective, see W. Finnie, "The European Convention on Human Rights: Domestic Status" (1980) 25 J.L.S.S. 434.
[16] 1985 S.L.T. 38 at p. 41.
[17] J. Murdoch, "The European Convention on Human Rights in Scots Law" [1991] P.L. 40.

resent the final disposal of the question, because the House of Lords, as the final court of appeal in Scottish civil cases, has not yet pronounced on the question. When it does, it might adopt a more flexible stance.[18] Some indication that it might do so is provided by the case of *Lord Advocate v. Scotsman Publications Ltd*.[19] The case arose out of the efforts of the Lord Advocate to prevent the disclosure or publication in Scotland of any information contained in the unauthorised memoirs of a former member of MI6.[20]

The House of Lords held unanimously that the Crown was not entitled to an interdict restraining publication by a third party unless it was required in the public interest. The importance of this case for present purposes is that, in determining what the public interest required, their Lordships made extensive reference to the right of liberty of expression as embodied in Article 10 of the ECHR.[21] The approach of the House of Lords in that decision appears consistent with the position as it has evolved south of the border: that, "where judges, in contradistinction to officials, are exercising a discretionary power . . . they should take the Convention into account."[22]

In judicial review cases—as a standard of reasonableness
English case law has established that, when the Executive is exercising a discretion conferred upon it by statute, the ECHR cannot act as a fetter upon that discretion (*i.e.* it cannot limit the scope of the discretion to a narrower ambit than Parliament conferred).[23] Some attempt has been made, however, to compel the judiciary to have regard to the Convention in cases of judicial review. The principal area in which this has been attempted in Scotland has been in cases of expulsion of aliens when issues of family separations have arisen. Attempts have been made to persuade the courts to consider Article 8 of the Convention, which protects private and family life.

So far, these attempts have not succeeded. The Scottish courts have confirmed that they will review the reasonableness of executive action in the light of "the obvious humanitarian principle of respect for family life."[24] But recent case law has confirmed that this humanitarian principle of respect for family life is strictly a principle of domestic law, with no resort to the Convention called for.[25] Nevertheless, it would appear that Scottish courts have not, at least as yet, entirely closed the door on using the Convention in the context of a judicial review setting if an appropriate fact setting should arise.[26]

[18] See, for example, K. D. Ewing and W. Finnie, *Civil Liberties in Scotland: Cases and Materials* (2nd ed. 1988) at pp. 49–54; and Bates, "Treaties in the Courts", pp. 42–43.
[19] 1989 S.C. (H.L.) 122; 1989 S.L.T. 705; [1990] 1 A.C. 812. Our thanks are due to Professor Colin Munro for bringing this case to our attention.
[20] This notwithstanding the admission that it did not contain material capable of damaging national security.
[21] See, *e.g.*, 1989 S.C. (H.L.) 122 at pp. 166 (Lord Keith), 167 (Lord Templeman), and 172 (Lord Jauncey).
[22] See, *e.g.*, Warbrick, "Rights", *supra*, at p. 36.
[23] *Brind v. Secretary of State for the Home Department* [1991] 1 A.C. 696.
[24] *Re Budh Singh*, 1988 S.C. 349.
[25] *Re Irfan Ahmed*, October 26, 1994, Outer House unreported.
[26] It may be noted that the English Court of Appeal has held, in its recent judicial review of the British government policy of excluding homosexuals from the armed

In judicial review cases—as a basis of legitimate expectations
A slightly different strategy also involves utilising the judicial review
process, not as a standard of reasonableness in judging the Executive's
action, but as a means of protecting legitimate expectations, in the
manner pioneered by the English case of *Council of Civil Service Unions
v. Minister for the Civil Service.*[27] The issue has been raised in Scotland,
in the Outer House case (as yet unreported) of *Hamilton v. Secretary
of State for Scotland* (1990). The pursuer, a convicted criminal, sought
judicial review of a revocation of a licence to remain at liberty. In
support of his case, he attempted to invoke principles on deprivation
of liberty from the jurisprudence of the European Court.[28] Knowing
of the failure of the various arguments just pointed out, the pursuer
contended that, as a national of a state party to the Convention, he
had a legitimate expectation that his government would adhere to the
convention in its treatment of him, and that the Government accordingly should honour that expectation. Such an expectation could be
based on either a promise by the British Government or an established
practice.

The Outer House readily conceded that this argument was a
"clever" one, but it rejected it on a number of grounds. For one thing,
it distinguished this case from the European Court case on which the
pursuer was relying. More notably for present purposes, the court
denied that such a legitimate expectation actually existed. The British
Government, it pointed out, had never made an express promise to
its nationals that it would adhere to the convention. Furthermore, the
court held that there is also no established "practice of the courts" in
Scotland supporting adherence to the Convention (referring to *Kaur*
as evidence of this lack).[29]

There is room for argument whether the *Hamilton* court was correct
in asserting that the British Government has made no express promise
regarding adherence to the Convention. Even if the Government has
made no such promise *to its nationals*, it certainly has made a commitment, and a very public and solemn one at that, to its fellow state
parties. Seen in this way, the argument becomes analogous to the *jus
quaesitum tertio* argument referred to above—with the third parties
(*i.e.*, persons under British jurisdiction) being the beneficiaries here
not of rights in the strict sense, but rather of expectations, which in
turn can be the source of rights. Notice, however, that there is one
important distinction between this expectations-based form of *jus
quaesitum tertio* and the right-based form of the argument considered
above. Here, the principle would operate substantially even-handedly

---

forces, that the ECHR is relevant "as background to the complaint of irrationality" (*R.
v. Ministry of Defence, ex p. Smith* [1996] 1 All E.R. 257. See also Murdoch, "European
Convention", pp. 49–51.
[27] [1985] 1 A.C. 374; [1984] 3 All E.R. 935; [1984] 3 W.L.R. 1174.
[28] In particular, the case of *Weeks v. United Kingdom*, 10 E.H.R.R. 293 (1987).
[29] It should be noted that *Kaur* was significant not as a legally binding precedent for
the court, in the *res judicata* sense, but rather as evidence of the non-existence of a
"practice of the courts" to adhere to the European Convention. In this same connection, the court also referred to the case of *Moore v. Secretary of State for Scotland*, 1985
S.L.T. 38.

in England and Scotland, since the legitimate-expectations principle, unlike *jus quaesitum tertio* properly speaking, operates on both sides of the border.

Furthermore, there is room for arguing that, since the *Hamilton* decision was handed down, the British Government has now given an express promise of adherence to the convention. In 1994, Lord Lester of Herne Hill put a written question to the Government as to whether "Ministers and civil servants, in discharging their public functions, have a duty to comply with the European Convention on Human Rights. . . ."[30] The response was that the British Government "must comply with its obligations" under treaties to which it was a party. The response went on to state that "[i]n so far as acts of Ministers and civil servants in the discharge of their public functions constitute acts which engage the responsibility of the United Kingdom, they must comply with the terms of [such] treaties."[31] Whether this statement will suffice to found legitimate expectations which give rise, in turn, to legal rights is a question yet to be answered in the law of Scotland.

The Scottish Legal System Seen from Strasbourg

It remains to observe some instances in which the law of Scotland has been judicially considered by the European Court of Human Rights. The focus will be on cases which have dealt with aspects of the Scottish legal system as such, as distinct from matters (such as corporal punishment and wiretapping) which merely affect Scotland along with the rest of the U.K. Only two areas, so far, offer much instruction in this regard, with quite recent developments in both: the provision of legal aid in criminal appeals and certain procedural aspects of children's hearings.[32]

Legal aid
The provision of legal aid in Scotland is governed by the Legal Aid (Scotland) Act 1986, which empowers the Scottish Legal Aid Board to grant assistance to indigent litigants in various designated circumstances. The crucial Convention provision is Article 6(3)(c), which guarantees to everyone charged with a criminal offence the assistance of free legal services, provided that two express conditions are met: that the person lacks sufficient means to pay for legal representation

---

[30] Hansard, December 7, 1994, at W-84.
[31] *ibid.* Our thanks are due to Mr C. M. G. Himsworth for bringing this material to our attention.
[32] The subject of censorship of prisoners' correspondence is, strictly speaking, a peculiarly Scottish matter, since prisons in Scotland operate under a different set of prison rules from those in England and Wales. In reality, however, the issues involved do not differ significantly from those that have arisen south of the border. For the principal European cases in area that have originated in Scotland, see *Boyle and Rice v. United Kingdom*, 10 E.H.R.R. 1 425 (1988); and *Campbell v. United Kingdom*, 15 E.H.R.R. 137 (1992).

from his own resources, and—more significantly for present purposes—that "the interests of justice so require".

The *Pakelli* case of 1983 laid down the basic guidelines regarding when "the interests of justice . . . require" the provision of legal aid.[33] The situation in Scotland first came to the European Court of Human Rights' attention in the *Granger* case of 1990.[34] The applicant had been duly convicted of perjury and sought to exercise the right of appeal to which he was automatically entitled under Scots law. There was one crucial barrier: the lack of any reasonable prospect of success in his appeal. This lack led directly to two distinct material consequences. One was a denial of legal aid, by decision of the Scottish Legal Aid Committee. The other was the fact that no advocate was willing—or indeed able—to act on the applicant's behalf, because the *Guide to Professional Conduct of Advocates* barred advocates from appearing in cases in which there was no reasonable prospect of success.[35] The applicant chose nonetheless to proceed with his appeal and to conduct it himself. In such cases, the practice in the High Court of Justiciary is for the Crown to be present at the appeal but to remain silent unless called upon by the court itself to present its views on some aspect of the case. The basic policy, in other words, is to leave the appellant unmolested to make of his own appeal the best he can.

In this instance, the appeal did not succeed; but it threw up a legal issue of some interest and complexity, which led the court to call for a transcript of the trial proceedings. It also led the court to call for the views of the Solicitor-General, who proceeded to address the court for some 90 minutes. The appellant's complaint in Strasbourg was, in essence, that the appeal was seriously unbalanced, in that he, a lay person, was left on his own without legal assistance to face no less a legal power than the Solicitor-General of Scotland on a legal point of some difficulty.

In its defence, the British Government pointed to a number of features in the case. One was the two independent determinations that the appeal had no reasonable prospect of success—the one by the Legal Aid Committee and the other by the various advocates who had declined to act. Moreover, it was observed that the advocates had not merely declined of their own volition to act—they were positively forbidden to do so by the rules of their profession. A grant of legal aid, accordingly, would not have resulted in representation. No advocate could appear, because of the relevant professional rules. Nor could any solicitor appear because solicitors had no right of audience before the court in question.

The British Government also contended that certain features of the Scottish criminal appeal system worked in combination to eliminate any apparent unfairness. Since Scotland allowed criminal appeals as a matter of right, without any regard whatever to legal merit, the inevitable result was that unmeritorious appeals were pressed in some

[33] *Pakelli v. Germany.* 6 E.H.R.R. 1 (1983), paras. 35–40.
[34] *Granger v. United Kingdom,* 12 E.H.R.R. 469 (1990).
[35] Faculty of Advocates, *Guide to the Professional Conduct of Advocates* (1988), Guideline 4.3.9.

considerable numbers by desperate or unrealistic accused. It was unreasonable to expect that the state should be compelled to provide legal aid on an open-ended basis in such a situation. A decision requiring the blanket provision of legal aid for criminal appeals, the Government warned, might well have the effect of inducing—or virtually compelling—the Government to restrict the right of appeal itself, to the general detriment of accused persons.

Furthermore, there was what might be termed the general civil law style of the proceedings. In contrast to the English legal tradition, in which courts customarily take a passive, arbitral-style role, the Scottish High Court of Justiciary takes an active role in proceedings. Also, the appeals have an importantly non-adversarial character, in that the Crown is expected to play an impartial role. The Crown functions more in the nature of an adviser to the court than as a sworn foe of the appellant.

Cogent as these arguments were, they failed to persuade the European Court of Human Rights. Regarding the possibility that a decision adverse to the British Government could mean the end of open-ended rights of appeal in Scotland, the European Court of Human Rights merely stated that it could not be concerned with such matters. Its only function was to adjudicate upon the compatibility of the law as it then stood with the ECHR.

There were reasons for believing that the effect of the *Granger* case would not be serious because of a crucial special feature: the fact that, unusually for a "non-meritorious" appeal, an important legal issue did arise unexpectedly which called for extensive commentary by the Crown. It was not difficult to see that a defendant could be thought to be at a disadvantage, as the European Court of Human Rights pointed out, when the Crown was making an extended and detailed legal submission which an unaided appellant could not hope to match. The response to this decision took the form of a Practice Note issued by the Lord Justice General in December 1990, which permitted the appeal court *itself* to enter a legal aid request to the Legal Aid Committee on behalf of an unrepresented appellant before it, in the event that a legal issue of some difficulty arose in the course of an appeal.[36] The Government went no further than that; but there was no doubt that the Legal Aid Committee, upon the receipt of such a request, would invariably proceed to make a legal aid grant.

In due course, it became apparent that the consequences of the *Granger* case were not to be so easily dealt with. Two cases delivered together on October 28, 1994 saw to that: *Boner* and *Maxwell*.[37] In both of these cases, the distinctive feature of *Granger* was absent. No complex legal issue arose in the appeal, and the Crown remained resolutely silent throughout the proceedings. Otherwise, the position was essentially as in *Granger*. Both the Legal Aid Committee and the various advocates who were consulted concluded that the appeals had no reasonable prospect of success. The question was therefore presented

---

[36] *Parliament House Book*, p. E801.
[37] 19 E.H.R.R. 246 (1994), and 19 E.H.R.R. 97 (1994), respectively.

with some clarity: how essential was it to the *Granger* decision that a legal point had actually arisen?

The *Boner* and *Maxwell* cases established beyond any doubt that that feature of *Granger* was not decisive. Once again, the ruling was that legal aid was required. The features now emphasised were two. First was the fact that the court held extremely wide powers. Second was the fact that, in both cases, the appellants were facing significant deprivations of liberty (five years in the case of *Maxwell* and eight in the case of *Boner*). So Scotland was placed in the peculiar position that, according to the Convention, legal aid *must* be provided in criminal appeals, even in cases in which the legal profession is *forbidden* by its rules to provide it.

Since the handing down of the *Boner* and *Maxwell* cases, the British Government has dealt with the problem by enacting legislation to remove the automatic right of appeal in Scottish criminal cases. Under section 42 of the Criminal Justice (Scotland) Act 1995, leave to appeal in criminal cases will be required.[38] With the filtering-out of non-meritorious appeals that this process will introduce, there will presumably be no difficulty in then simply allowing legal aid for all appeals which survive the filtering.[39]

Children's hearings

Among the basic rights protected by the ECHR are the right of access to courts and to fair hearings upon arrival (found in Article 6). Also among the basic rights is the right—or rather, as will be seen, the complex of rights—to private and family life (found in Article 8). The two do not have an obvious connection with one another. But an interesting case in 1995 from Scotland, *McMichael v. United Kingdom*,[40] has shed some light on the interplay between them.

There were two applicants in this case, a male and female who had lived together in a non-marital relationship. The woman bore a child which she insisted for some considerable period of time had not been fathered by the man. The man was not registered on birth as the father. Later, he claimed to be the father, although the mother continued to deny this. Later still, the mother altered her position and contended that the man was indeed the father. His name was then duly added to the birth certificate as the father, and the two applicants proceeded to marry. The case arose from the attempt of the local authority to place the child in care and to deny access to it by either applicant. The two contested this decision on the local authority's part. And the issue came before, first, a children's hearing and then, on appeal, the sheriff court.

The principal human rights issue concerned the withholding, by both the children's hearing and the sheriff court, of social reports concerning the matter—although it should be noted that the hearing

---

[38] For the debate over this provision, including the question of its compatibility with the ECHR, see Hansard, January 16, 1995, at cols. 480–86.

[39] There is already authority, from a case originating in England, that the ECHR does not require the automatic granting of legal aid for the process of seeking leave to appeal. *Monnell and Morris v. United Kingdom*, 10 E.H.R.R. 205 (1987), para. 67.

[40] 20 E.H.R.R. 205 (1995).

informed the applicants of the basic contents of these reports.[41] The two applicants contended, *inter alia*, that this non-disclosure violated their rights, under Article 6(1) of the ECHR, which provides that, in "the determination of . . . civil rights and obligations", everyone has the right to "a fair . . . hearing . . . by an independent and impartial tribunal established by law."

Three issues potentially arose from this provision: whether "civil rights" of the two applicants were at stake in this case; whether a children's hearing is a "tribunal" within the meaning of the article; and whether the proceedings in the children's hearings were "fair." The easiest of the three proved to be the fairness question. The British Government conceded that the withholding of the reports from the applicants rendered the proceedings unfair.[42]

The issue of whether a children's hearing is a "tribunal" within the meaning of Article 6 of the ECHR was not resolved in the case. In Scots law itself, there would appear to be some ambivalence as to the nature of children's hearings. The 9th edition of Gloag and Henderson's *Introduction to the Law of Scotland* averred that children's hearings "are not in any proper sense courts."[43] They do not make determinations either of law or fact (in the sense of determining what actions occurred in the past). Rather, they are future-oriented bodies whose task is to determine whether, in their future lives, children ought to be subjected to various compulsory measures of care provided for by the legislation. The proceedings are also non-adversarial in character, oriented towards discerning where the best interests of children lie in particular situations.[44]

The European Commission on Human Rights, in its report on the case in 1993, concluded that children's hearings are not "tribunals" in the Article 6 sense.[45] The European Court of Human Rights, however, expressly declined to decide this point, contenting itself with the broader conclusion that the over-all proceedings amounted to a violation of Article 6(1).[46] Regarding the sheriff court specifically, which certainly is a "tribunal" in the Article 6 sense, the European Court of Human Rights found the proceedings to be unfair because "the requirement of an adversarial trial was not fulfilled."[47]

The question of whether "civil rights" were being determined in the proceedings was of the greatest interest. The European Court of Human Rights concluded that the male applicant had no civil right, properly speaking, at stake in the children's hearing because he had

---

[41] On the procedural aspects of children's hearings generally, see C. Godwin, "The Rules of Procedure", in F. M. Martin and Kathleen Murray (eds), *Children's Hearings* (1976) at pp. 118–23.

[42] 20 E.H.R.R. 205 (1995), paras. 79–80.

[43] Gloag and Henderson, *Introduction to the Law of Scotland*, (9th ed.) by A. B. Wilkinson and W. A. Wilson (eds), (1988) at p. 27.

[44] Interestingly, the new 10th edition of that same treatise omits this quoted language. Gloag and Henderson, *The Law of Scotland* (10th ed) by W. A. Wilson and Angelo Forte (eds), (1995), pp. 31–32.

[45] 20 E.H.R.R. 205 (1995), para. 114. The report was concluded by the Commission on August 31, 1993.

[46] *ibid.*, para 78.

[47] *ibid.*, para 83.

no parental rights at the relevant time (nor had he even applied for them). So there was no violation of Article 6 regarding him. But the male applicant was found to have another Convention right at stake: his right to private and family life, as protected by Article 8 of the ECHR. Article 8 contrasts with Article 6 in two important respects: it does not require that a "civil right" be at stake; and it does not explicitly include a fair-hearing guarantee. But it does include, by interpretation, a right of persons to be "involved in the decision-making process" in family matters "to a degree sufficient to provide them with the requisite protection of their interests."[48] The European Court of Human Rights held that this protection of family "interests" under Article 8 was relevant to the male applicant's position, even though the protection of "civil rights" under Article 6 was not. The non-disclosure of the social reports by the children's hearing was then held to constitute a violation of this legally protected interest.[49]

Changes are in prospect to the Scottish system of children's hearings pursuant to the enactment of the Children (Scotland) Act 1995. In due course, there will be new regulations on the subject, which presumably will take due account of the *McMichael* decision. But the case holds some more general lessons of possible relevance to other areas of law and other jurisdictions, That is, that issues of procedural fairness need not necessarily arise in the most obvious place: the Article 6(1) guarantees relating to determinations of "civil rights" by "independent tribunals." Important procedural protections can also arise in more subtle ways, as ancillary aspects of some substantive right, such as (in the *McMichael* case) the right to private and family life. In this respect, Scotland has (unwittingly) made an important contribution to general European human rights law.[50]

Conclusions

The failure thus far of Parliament to incorporate the European Convention on Human Rights into domestic law has resulted in the need to explore, through the courts, the extent to which it can play an indirect role in the domestic legal systems of the United Kingdom. As the first part of the discussion noted, some avenues do exist for utilising the Convention in Scots law. The most obvious one—utilisation as an aid to statutory interpretation—has been rejected by the Court of Session, meaning that Scots law has, so far, proved more impervious than its English counterpart to the influence of the European Convention. As noted above, however, a final determination by the

---

[48] *W. v. United Kingdom*, 10 E.H.R.R. 29 (1987), para. 64.

[49] In the *Weeks* case, *supra* n. 48, arising from England, there was held to be a violation of Art. 6(1), not of Art. 8, on the ground that no legal procedure existed for determining the specific question of access to children by parents whose parental rights had been suspended. In other words, there was held to be a denial of the "right to a court"; consequently no question of fairness of the proceedings arose, as they did in *McMichael*.

[50] Our thanks are due to Professor J. P. Grant for assistance with and information concerning this section.

House of Lords is still awaited. In addition, judicial review based on the principle of legitimate expectations remains, at present, an open possibility.

It may be, of course, that Scotland has less need than England for the oversight machinery which the Convention can provide because human rights are more consistently observed in Scotland than in England. This would, however, be a difficult proposition to establish on objective grounds. England, to be sure, has been the source of the vast majority of the adverse decisions which the European Court of Human Rights has handed down involving the United Kingdom. But that is only to be expected, as England is by far the larger jurisdiction. For the present, one can do little more than note, as the discussion above does, that in certain areas, such as criminal legal aid and the conduct of children's hearings, Scots law has been found to fall below the European norm.

PLEADINGS

Stephen Woolman

Most legal analysis and discussion focuses on issues of substantive law. Much less attention is paid to pleadings and procedure. For practitioners, however, the emphasis is different. Their concern is how to achieve a particular result for their clients. In deciding whether to raise proceedings, practitioners will often first study the Rules of Court. If a claim is novel or difficult, they will also consult a style to see how the case can be properly pled. The manner in which business comes before the court is a distinctive feature of the Scottish legal system. It drives the stage and circumstances at which decision are reached. Some of the key decisions in delict this century have been made without proof.[1] This is in marked contrast to the English approach. There, legal questions are normally decided only after the facts have been determined.

Recently, there has been something of a velvet revolution in our practice. It began with special rules being developed for particular types of actions. For example, a new form of petition was developed for judicial review. Similarly, a simplified summons was introduced for straightforward reparation cases brought under the "optional procedure". The Sheriff Court Ordinary Cause Rules were revised in 1993. They introduced option hearings and the requirement for written notice of the basis of preliminary pleas. The 1994 Rules of the Court of Session gave us notices to admit. Now Lord Cullen has issued his review of Outer House business in the Court of Session.[2] His comprehensive range of proposals is designed to reduce unnecessary delay and cost in civil litigation. One recommendation is that abbreviated pleadings be used in every case.[3] It is likely that such a move will further affect the practice of the court in a number of respects. This article considers the role of written pleadings within our system and what form abbreviated pleadings should take.

There are two schools of thought about written pleadings. Adherents of the first school believe in full pleadings. This is the traditional Scottish approach. It is based on the principle that the parties themselves should stake out the battlefield on which their dispute is to be fought. Each party begins by setting out his case in detail. Fair notice must be given of the facts on which he relies and the legal basis of the claim. There follows a period of adjustment. During that period each party is expected to answer the points raised by his opponent. A closed record is then made up. No final decision in the case is

---

[1] e.g., *Donoghue v. Stevenson*, 1932 S.C. (H.L.) 31; *Junior Books v. The Veitchi Co.*, 1982 S.C. (H.L.) 244.

[2] "Report on the Conduct of Outer House Business", January 1996.

[3] para. 4.8.

normally reached until that stage. Once closed, the record plays a key role in the litigation. It governs the evidence which can be led and the oral argument which can be presented. Underlying this approach is the theory that the fairest decision is reached "when two men argue, as unfairly as possible, on opposite sides" for then "it is certain that no important consideration will altogether escape notice".[4] The judge's task is to adjudicate upon the issues so raised.

The second school of thought attaches less importance to written pleadings. It is enough that each party gives a broad indication of its position. No detailed revision of the pleadings is required. Parties have more flexibility with regard to the evidence and the oral submissions. What can be said and done in court is not policed to the same degree by the averments. This pared down approach to pleadings is accompanied by greater involvement on the part of the court. Judges are no longer expected to be remote umpires. Instead they are involved in determining the procedure to be followed with a view to resolving the issues in the case. This approach has gained greater acceptance in recent years. In the Court of Session, it has been most fully developed in commercial causes. Lord Cullen's remit from the Lord President required him to consider what measures should be taken to "achieve a greater degree of judicial control and management of cases". He has recommended that after a shortened period of adjustment, there should be a case management hearing to consider the whole cause.[5]

Which approach is preferable? The answer requires one to consider first the function of written pleadings. Written pleadings are the nuts and bolts of litigation. No substantive question of fact or law can be resolved in any case until the matter is formally brought before the court by some form of writ. The writ often provides a key to the court's decision in a particular dispute.

For example, the court will only concern itself with the remedy sought by the party. Suppose a dispute arises in relation to a restrictive covenant in an employment contract. If the employer only seeks interdict, the court cannot award damages for breach of contract. Written pleadings are also important in another sense. The more cogent a party's case is on paper, the more likely it is that the court will find in his favour. In other words, the pleadings begin the process of persuasion on behalf of the client.

The traditional Scots system has many advantages. A well-pled record provides a convenient resumé of the case. The legal representatives and the court will be able to discern the main features of the case at a glance. It will be plain what remedy is sought and the legal basis which underlies the claim. The areas of agreed fact and disputed fact will be delineated. As Bill Wilson wrote, the record gives "fair notice of what each party wishes to prove."[6] Full written pleadings also tend to highlight any questions of relevancy which may arise in the particular case. Take an action of damages for personal injuries. Plead-

---

[4] Macaulay, quoted in I. D. Macphail, "The Path to the Summit", 1963 S.L.T. (News) 21.
[5] para. 6.15.
[6] *Introductory Essays on Scots Law* (2nd ed., 1984), p. 54.

ing such a case under the ordinary procedure requires precision. In particular, the fault article of condescendence must be carefully drawn in order to crystallise the exact duties of care which the defender has broken. That exercise often identifies any problems with the case at an early stage. In other words, the discipline of drafting full pleadings helps to isolate the problem areas in the case. By contrast, drafting a case under the optional procedure is a much easier task. However, it can conceal radical problems which only emerge at a later stage.

As well as strengths, the traditional Scots approach has a number of drawbacks. The first complaint is that it is too rigid. This particular criticism was voiced by Lord Diplock:

> "When I first became a member of your Lordships' House I was unacquainted with the niceties of the Scots system of pleading. Since then my acquaintance has grown; so has my disenchantment".[7]

His complaint was that the system led to excessively technical questions about the lines of evidence which each party could lead at the proof. He referred to Scottish litigation arising out of industrial accidents being "a game of skill and chance".[8] However, in the same case, Lord Kilbrandon provided a defence of the existing system:

> "The Scottish requirement of detailed pre-trial notice of the foundations of the parties' respective cases has been criticised in the past, and is not without its detractors in the present. But such defects as the system may exhibit can easily be matched by the unhappy consequences of more free-and-easy forms of procedure".[9]

He relied upon a quotation from Lord President Cooper's *Selected Papers*:

> "Lest it should be supposed that Scottish lawyers are unreasonably prejudiced in favour of their native methods, it is worth recording that, when the United States Government was engaged in 1912 in drafting what became the Federal Equity Rules, they applied for advice to Lord Chancellor Loreburn, who suggested that it would be worth their while to consider the Scottish method of pleading 'which in my opinion is the best'."[10]

A second criticism of the current Scots approach is that too much time is occupied by parties tinkering with their pleadings right up to the last minute. The final version of the written case, the product of perhaps more than one hand over a considerable period, can grow

---

[7] *Gibson v. BICC*, 1973 S.C. (H.L.) 15 at p. 27.
[8] *ibid.* at p. 30.
[9] *ibid., per* Lord Kilbrandon at p. 32.
[10] *ibid., per* Lord Kilbrandon at p. 32 quoting Lord President Cooper, *Selected Papers 1922–1954* (1957) at p. 193.

bulky and unreadable. Single articles of condescendence extend over several pages. What actually emerges is the antithesis of the candid, concise and lucid document which the system is designed to produce. Even worse, amendments are frequently moved late, sometimes on the morning of the proof itself. The parties and the court have legitimate cause for complaint if weeks or months are allocated to an adjustment period which is barely used and then a last minute attempt is made to cure the pleadings.

The third criticism is the language of pleadings. It must not be forgotten that the addressee of a summons is the defender. An individual defender who receives a summons by way of recorded delivery post or personal service by messenger at arms may suffer a degree of anxiety. It can only add to that stress when he or she is unable to understand the writ because it is written in terms more appropriate to the eighteenth than the twentieth century. Common terms still to be found include "condescendence" "quoad ultra", "brevitatis causa." "et separatim", "assoilzie", "hereinbefore", and "humbly sheweth that". Many pleaders' use of the term "said", which is almost always redundant, can only be described as promiscuous. In 1923, a commentator wrote:

> "it is in these days almost grotesque to find a writ like the Court of Session summons in existence when there are antiquarian libraries available for the repose of literary compositions of the kind".[11]

Time has been no healer. It does not need the Plain English Campaign to tell us to cease using such terms. Pleadings should be readily understood by laymen, as well as by practitioners.

How should a system of abbreviated pleadings work? The concepts of relevancy and specification must continue to discipline the approach which is adopted. Relevancy is the hallmark of the Scottish system. It is our pride and boast that we can isolate the law from the facts. In appropriate cases this allows us to argue the law without the need or expense of leading evidence. Bill Wilson described the test of relevancy as the "so what" test—"even if the facts are true they do not afford the remedy sought".[12] Perhaps the best example is *Donoghue v. Stevenson*.[13] That case went to the House of Lords on the basis of one factual article of condescendence and one fault article of condescendence, containing four alleged breaches of duty. Unfortunately, by the 1980s a general practice had developed in which the majority of cases were sent for debate. Often this was on the basis of "pleading points". In about three quarters of such cases, the debate was discharged. This caused substantial delay and prejudice, particularly to pursuers in personal injury cases. To counter this approach, parties were required to indicate the line of argument which they proposed to follow.[14] Since then the pendulum has swung in the opposite direc-

[11] (1923) 39 *Scottish Law Review* at p. 29.
[12] *Introductory Essays, op. cit.* at p. 66.
[13] 1932 S.C. (H.L.) 31.
[14] Practice Notes Nos. 3 and 5 of 1991.

tion. Today, there are relatively few debates. Counsel often recommend that they "keep their powder dry". They do not wish to
alert the opponent to some flaw in the case that might be cured if
warning was given. A legal point is then founded on at, or immediately before, the proof. This is also unsatisfactory.

It is at this point that relevancy connects with specification. Parties
are entitled to expect that they will not be taken by surprise either in
relation to the law or the facts. In essence, it is a question of fair notice.
Even with abbreviated pleadings, it will be necessary for the parties
to frame their respective cases with care. Lord Oliver has articulated
the duty of the claimant as follows[15]:

> "It is for the plaintiff in an action to formulate his claim in an
> intelligible form and it does not lie in his mouth to assert that it
> is impossible for him to formulate it and that it should, therefore,
> be allowed to continue unspecified in the hope that, when it
> comes to trial, he may be able to reconstitute his case and make
> good what he then feels able to plead and substantiate".[16]

That statement was made in the context of a large construction claim
which was appealed from Hong Kong to the Privy Council. Nonetheless, the same principle should continue to underpin Scottish
pleadings.

Suppose one could now devise a system using abbreviated pleadings. How could it best be achieved? Every pleader would nail their
own theses to the courtroom door. I would start by considering the
originating writ. The logic of the distinction between a petition and a
summons is clear.[17] A party proceeds by way of petition when he
seeks the authority of the court for a particular act. He proceeds by
way of summons when he raises an action against a particular person.
But the distinction is often blurred. Interdict proceedings can be raised
by way of petition, or by way of summons if some other remedy (such
as damages) is also claimed. A petition for judicial review bears more
resemblance to a summons than to a petition. Perhaps the most telling
argument against having two forms of process is that a contested petition proceeds like any other ordinary action. One can test the matter
in this way—what does the claimant seek when he comes to court? I
suggest that he seeks a remedy. It does not matter to him that there
are technical differences in the manner in which the remedy can be
granted. Accordingly, in my view there should be one writ.[18]

The model for that writ might usefully mix the best features of the
present styles for optional procedure reparation actions and petitions
for judicial review.[19] It would be in five parts:
(1) the parties;
(2) the orders sought;

---

[15] *Wharf Properties v. Eric Cumine Associates (No 2)* (1991) 52 B.L.R. 1 at pp. 20–21.
[16] *ibid.* at p. 23.
[17] *Tomkins v. Cohen*, 1951 S.C. 22 at p. 23 *per* Lord Keith.
[18] *cf.* Lord Cullen's review at para. 9.9.
[19] Rules of the Court of Session, Forms 43.18 and 58.6.

(3) the statement of facts;
(4) the grounds of action;
(5) the documents relied upon; and
(6) the backing sheet.
I propose to comment on each of these matters.

The parties

At present, there is often a substantial overlap between the instance and the first article of condescendence. It would be preferable if the name and address of each party was given at the beginning. A separate entry could be made if there was any special feature regarding the designation or the capacity in which that party was sued.

The orders sought

The terms "conclusion" and "crave" are unfamiliar to most laymen. It would be preferable to rename this part of the writ "orders sought", as in petitions for judicial review. It would also be useful to borrow the formula from such petitions that "The petitioners crave the court to pronounce such further order, decrees or orders (including an order for expenses) as may seem to the court to be just and reasonable in all the circumstances of the case". This should minimise the need for technical amendment.

The statement of facts

As a benign despot, I would issue the following rules about the statement of facts:
  (1) no statement of fact should exceed one A4 page (double spaced) in length;
  (2) companies should always be referred to in the singular and not the plural;
  (3) no Latin terms would be allowed (unless translated);
  (4) legalese would be frowned on;
  (5) all breaches of duties of care would be specified;
  (6) all claims for damages would itemise the head of damage and the sum claimed in respect of that head;
  (7) the pursuer would specify the date on which he made a formal demand for redress from the pursuer;
  (8) any adjustments should be shown by means of a different typeface or font.

The grounds of action

One of the most curious features of the present rules is that one is not entitled to plead law. The legal basis of the case is therefore to be found in the pleas-in-law. They themselves may make little sense to the lay reader. What does "due and resting owing" convey? I believe that any distinct authority founded upon by a party should be stated in the body of the writ. So far as the traditional preliminary plea directed toward relevancy and specification is concerned, in my view it must go. Nothing is more destructive of the Scottish system of pleading. It is itself lacking in specification. If a point is to be taken at debate, it should be reflected in a specific plea. For example, in an action for defamation relating to a statement in an employer's reference, the defender might plead "The action is irrelevant, in respect that malice is not pled".

The documents relied upon

An obvious rule should be that documents can be founded on at debate if they are in process and referred to in the pleadings, even if they are not formally incorporated documents.

The backing sheet

It would be most convenient if the writ listed the main stages in the litigation. This could be achieved by having a brief timetable on the backing sheet which listed the following dates: signetting, service, lodging of defences, case management hearing, debate, proof and judgment.

Pleadings and procedure are a means and not an end. The aim is to arrive at a fair result in the case with the minimum of expense and delay. Abbreviated pleadings could in my view work well with a system where the judge took a more active role. Together they should help to isolate the issues and maintain the procedural impetus of the case. This approach should also assist parties to assess the strengths and weaknesses of the case at an earlier stage. However, we must guard against a danger which may result from a move away from full pleadings. The risk is that excessive reliance will be placed on affidavits, notices to admit and written notes of argument. These are not adequate substitutes for good pleading. Some courts, notably the United States Supreme Court and the European Court of Justice, arrive at their decisions largely on the basis of the written case. In Scotland, "pleading" refers to both the written case and the oral submission. I hope that we continue to strive for excellence in both branches.

BIBLIOGRAPHY OF W. A. WILSON

Mora in Reparation Cases, 1955 S.L.T. (News) 169.
Some Limitations of Categories, 1957 S.L.T. (News) 65.
Foresight and Negligence, 1959 S.L.T. (News) 89.
The Analysis of Negligence, 1962 S.L.T. (News) 1.
Floating Charges, 1962 S.L.T. (News) 53.
Some Notes on Reasonable Care, 1962 S.L.T. (News) 57.
Companies (Floating Charges) (Scotland) Act 1961 (1962) 25 M.L.R. 445.
Common Market Regulations, 1962 S.L.T. (News) 181.
The Reform of Intestate Succession, 1963 S.L.T. (News) 141.
A Note on Fact and Law (1963) 26 M.L.R. 609.
Cleisham and Corroboration, 1964 S.L.T. (News) 57.
Dangerous Agencies, 1964 S.L.T. (News) 225.
Problems of the Cheques Act, 1965 S.L.T. (News) 218.
The Drunk Driver's Passenger (1965) 28 M.L.R. 235.
Doubts on Desertion, 1965 S.L.T. (News) 225.
The Valuation Process, 1966 S.L.T. (News) 85.
Scottish Commercial Law, 1966 J.B.L. 320.
999 for Rescission (1966) 29 M.L.R. 442.
The Betterment Levy, 1967 S.L.T. (News) 49.
In Modum Probationis, 1968 J.R. 193.
Questions of Degree (1969) 32 M.L.R. 361.
The Theory of the Case Stated (1969) B.T.R. 231.
A Note on the Hohfeld Analysis, 1972 J.R. 162.
Common Market Geography, 1973 S.L.T. (News) 73.
Community Law in Scotland, 1973 S.L.T. (News) 117.
Reading Community Cases, 1973 S.L.T. (News) 133.
Waiting for Measures, 1973 S.L.T. (News) 189.
The Complexity of Statutes (1974) 37 M.L.R. 497.
Trusts, Trustees and Executors (1st ed., 1975) with A. G. M. Duncan.
Battered Wives and Battered Law, 1976 S.L.T. (News) 11.
Divorce for Abracadabra, 1976 S.L.T. (News) 27.
A Note on Causation, 1976 S.L.T. (News) 193.
Seniors Without Juniors, 1976 S.L.T. (News) 297.
Introductory Essays on Scots Law (1st ed., 1978).
Case note on *Lord Advocate v. Royal Bank of Scotland*, 1978 J.R. 253.
Gloag and Henderson's Introduction to the Law of Scotland (8th ed., 1980) with A. B. Wilkinson.
The Product Liability Directive, 1980 S.L.T. (News) 1.
The Furthest Part of the Room, 1980 S.L.T. (News) 33.
The Report of the Royal Commission on Legal Services: an Academic View, 1980 S.L.T. (News) 165.
Recovery of Rates, 1981 S.L.T. (News) 245.
Consumer Protection in Eire, 1981 S.L.T. (News) 277.
Changes in French Law, 1981 S.L.T. (News) 304.
The Receiver and Book Debts, 1982 S.L.T. (News) 129.

Knowing the Law and Other Things, 1982 J.R. 259.
The Law of Scotland Relating to Debt (1st ed., 1982).
Romalpa and Trust, 1983 S.L.T. (News) 106.
The Legislation of 1982, 1983 S.L.T. (News) 116.
Introductory Essays on Scots Law (2nd ed., 1984).
The Nature of Receivership, 1984 S.L.T. (News) 105.
Tax Avoidance: Houdini, Magic and the Luncheon Party (1985) 30 J.L.S.S. 184.
Gloag and Henderson's Introduction to the Law of Scotland (9th ed., 1987) with A. B. Wilkinson.
Questions of Interpretation (1987) 8 Stat. L.R. 142.
Intellectual Property in Semi-conductors: the Pirates get their Chips (1988) 33 J.L.S.S. 322.
The Progress of the Law, 1888–1988, 1988 J.R. 207.
Unit Trusts Reformed, 1988 S.L.T. (News) 277.
Sir Thomas Smith, 1989 J.R. 1.
Photograph and Photofit, 1989 S.L.T. (News) 1.
Mapping Economic Loss, in A. J. Gamble (ed.), *Obligations in Context: Essays in Honour of D. M. Walker* (1990).
The Scottish Law of Debt (2nd ed., 1991).
The Bairns of Falkirk (Child Support Act 1991), 1991 S.L.T. (News) 417.
Trials and Try-ons: Modes of Interpretation (1992) 13 Stat. L.R. 1.
Studying Statutes, 1992 J.R. 213.
The Importance of Analysis, in D. L. Carey Miller and D. W. Meyers (eds.), *Comparative and Historical Essays in Scots Law* (1992).
Oblique Answers to Straight Questions: the Article 177 Procedure (1994) 15 Stat. L.R. 31.
Gloag and Henderson The Law of Scotland (10th ed., 1995) with A. D. M. Forte.
Trusts, Trustees and Executors (2nd ed. 1996) with A. G. M. Duncan.

INDEX